INTERIM SITE

Northern Protest

Northern Protest

Martin Luther King, Jr.,

Chicago, and the

Civil Rights Movement

JAMES R. RALPH, JR.

Harvard University Press
Cambridge, Massachusetts
London, England   1993

Library of Congress Cataloging-in-Publication Data

Ralph, James R., Jr.
   Northern protest : Martin Luther King, Jr., Chicago, and the civil rights movement /
James R. Ralph, Jr.
      p. cm.
   Includes bibliographical references and index.
   ISBN 0-674-62687-7 (acid-free paper)
   1. Afro-Americans—Civil rights—Illinois—Chicago—History—20th century. 2. Civil
rights movements—Illinois—Chicago—History—20th century. 3. Chicago (Ill.)—Race
relations. 4. King, Martin Luther, Jr., 1929–1968. 5. Afro-Americans—Housing—Illinois—Chicago—History—20th century. 6. Discrimination in housing—Illinois—Chicago—History—20th century. I. Title.
F548.9.N4R35 1993
323.1′196073077311—dc20

92-45231
   CIP

To my mother and father

Contents

Acknowledgments

This book could never have been completed without the generosity of many individuals and institutions. It gives me great pleasure to acknowledge their assistance here as partial, though far from sufficient, repayment for the many debts I have incurred. Grants from the Charles Warren Center for American History at Harvard University, the Harvard History Department, the Mark DeWolfe Howe Fund, and Middlebury College allowed me to travel to archives across the eastern half of the country and to spend many months researching in Chicago. Two Moody grants from the Lyndon Baines Johnson Foundation enabled me to visit Austin, Texas, to examine manuscript material at the Lyndon Baines Johnson Library.

Many archivists and librarians have answered my questions, retrieved boxes of documents for me, and suggested new avenues of exploration. I am particularly grateful to Jack Sutters of the Archives of the American Friends Service Committee; to Timothy Slavin of the Archives of the Archdiocese of Chicago; to Charlie Niels of the Special Collections Department of Boston University; to the staff of the Chicago Theological Seminary Library; to Janet Lange of the Everett Dirksen Center; to the staff of Harvard University's Widener Library, especially those of the microforms and interlibrary loan divisions; to Fred Bauman and his staff at the Library of Congress; to the staff of the Lyndon Baines Johnson Library, especially Linda Hanson and Nancy Smith; to D. Louise Cook, Diane Ware, Danny Bellinger, Bruce Keys, and Oladele Dare of the Martin Luther King, Jr., Library; to Elinor DesVerney Sinnette of the Moorland-Spingarn Research Center at Howard University; to the staff of the Illinois State Historical Library; to Philip Runkel and Tracey

Muench of the Marquette University Library; to the staff of the Middlebury College Library, especially Fleur Laslocky and Pamela McClain of the interlibrary loan department; to Claire Greenberg and the staff of the Municipal Reference Library of Chicago; to William Kevin Cawley of the Notre Dame Library; to Kevin Leonard of the Northwestern University Library; to Warner Pflug and the staff of the Walter Reuther Library at Wayne State University; to Mary Ann Bamberger, Alan Kovac, Zita Stukas, and Sandra Young of the Special Collections division of the University of Illinois at Chicago; to Stanley Mallach of the Wisconsin State Historical Society at Milwaukee; to George Talbot of the Wisconsin State Historical Society at Madison. Special thanks go to Clarence Clark, Claire Cass, Ralph Pugh, Corey Seeman, Bob Shaffren, and Archie Motley, who made the Chicago Historical Society seem like a second home.

This book is much richer because of the willingness of many individuals to share their recollections of the Chicago Freedom Movement, and I have acknowledged their assistance in the Note on Primary Sources. I have been helped in sundry ways by many others, especially Mathew Ahmann, Stuart Bruchey, Robert Dallek, Msgr. Edward Egan, Herbert Fisher, David Garrow, Barak Goodman, Richard Gutman, Mark Haller, Rick Halpern, Louis Harlan, Arnold Hirsch, the late Nathan Huggins, Archbishop Demetrios Iakovos, Gene Lewis, Horace G. Lunt, George McGivan, John McManus, August Meier, Leslie Orear, Gail Padgett, Mark Perlman, Joel Schwartz, and Stephan Thernstrom. Nicole Krieger and David Ralph performed timely research. Mary Lou Finley, Gilbert Corfield, Ed Marciniak, and Meyer Weinberg allowed me to examine their collections of documents on the Chicago Freedom Movement. I am grateful to Rob Nathan, Gary Orfield, Bruce Thomas, and Kale Williams for sharing the fruits of their oral history work; all of their interviews are part of the Chicago Freedom Movement Oral History Project, sponsored by the Leadership Council for Metropolitan Open Communities. This project was created and supervised by Jennifer Amdur-Spitz, Beth Campbell, Rob Nathan, Gary Orfield, Bruce Thomas, and especially Kale Williams, the former executive director of the LCMOC.

During my research trips many people were generous with their hospitality: the Carriera family, William DeSantis, James Fogarty, Martin Honigberg, David Iverson, the McIlvaine family, and Richard Present. I wrote the first draft of this book while serving as a resident tutor at

Winthrop House at Harvard University. There cannot be a finer place for intellectual endeavor. I owe much to the masters of Winthrop House, James and Martha Davis, to its tutors, and to its undergraduates. I completed this book at Middlebury College, where my departmental chairman, Travis Jacobs, my faculty colleagues, and my students have been most supportive.

I owe a special debt to those who read earlier versions of this study. Nicholas Clifford and Edward Marciniak reviewed a number of chapters, while Gil Troy offered incisive commentary on style and substance. Without the advice and encouragement of Professors Alan Brinkley and David Herbert Donald, this book would have far fewer virtues. This book also benefited greatly from the comments of two outside readers and from the advice and counsel of Elizabeth Suttell, Aida Donald, and Elizabeth Gretz of Harvard University Press.

Finally, words cannot adequately express my gratitude to my family and friends, who helped make an often solitary task more bearable.

Northern Protest

Introduction

In early April 1965 one of Martin Luther King's chief lieutenants, James Bevel, came to Chicago for a weekend of speeches, workshops on nonviolence, and fund raising. The triumphant march from Selma to Montgomery, Alabama, had occurred less than two weeks earlier, and as a key strategist of the Selma campaign, Bevel was greeted as a hero everywhere he went. By Sunday, as he awaited his turn to speak at a rally at Northwestern University, he was an exhausted conqueror. Yet he perked up when Studs Terkel, the event's emcee, introduced him. Known as one of the movement's most dynamic orators, Bevel rose to his reputation. In a piercing, tense voice, he transfixed the large crowd, surprising it by talking more about racism in the North than about racism in the South. He even predicted that "the nonviolent movement in a few days, in a few weeks, in a few years will call on Chicago to address itself on the racist attitude that is denying Negroes the right to live in adequate housing." "We're going to have a movement in Chicago," Bevel declared. "We plan to close [Chicago] down."[1]

It was a prophetic speech. In less than five months, Martin Luther King, Jr., and Andrew Young, encouraged by Bevel, announced that the Southern Christian Leadership Conference (SCLC) had selected Chicago as the target of its first northern campaign. From late 1965 to mid-1967, King and SCLC teamed up with Al Raby and the Coordinating Council of Community Organizations (CCCO), a federation of local civil rights groups, to form the Chicago Freedom Movement, an enterprise determined to root out racial injustice, particularly housing discrimination, in Chicago, to improve the quality of life for the city's black residents, and to prod the nation as a whole to combat urban ills.

In telling the story of their quest, this book chronicles the last of a series of major single-city campaigns directed by SCLC and revolving around the strategy of nonviolent direct action. From 1962 to 1966, SCLC annually targeted one city for an extended array of nonviolent demonstrations to dramatize the injustice of racial proscription. The most successful campaigns—Birmingham in 1963 and Selma in 1965—provoked national outrage and triggered legislative remedies that reshaped America's racial landscape. But until Chicago, SCLC had operated on familiar southern terrain. Now it would have to employ its principal tactic—nonviolent direct action—in a new setting. Much of the history of the Chicago campaign is the story of SCLC's difficult adjustment to northern realities.

The Chicago Freedom Movement also represented a decisive juncture in the civil rights revolution. As Bevel suggested to his Northwestern audience, the civil rights movement after the Selma crusade was about to enter a new phase, to shift its focus from the South to the North and from an attack on state-sanctioned denials of basic political and civil rights to an assault on social and economic inequities. The sweep of southern civil rights successes and the depth of despair in the northern ghettoes compelled Martin Luther King and SCLC to extend their civil rights ministry north of the Mason-Dixon line. Despite a deteriorating climate for reform after 1965—the war in Vietnam increasingly absorbed national energies, the rifts between civil rights organizations were fast becoming unbridgeable, and the Watts riot in August 1965 intensified pervasive feelings among whites that blacks were undeserving and ungrateful—SCLC and its Chicago allies nevertheless spoke sincerely of ending slums. That today many Americans would dismiss such a vision as hopelessly naive says as much about the diminished expectations and constricted imagination of our own age as it does about the lack of realism of the Chicago crusaders of the mid-1960s.

Now that more than twenty-five years have passed since Martin Luther King and SCLC went to Chicago, the available documentary record is full enough to permit a close study of their midwestern crusade. This book draws heavily upon newspaper accounts, magazine articles, government documents, oral history interviews, and a wealth of manuscript collections. It also profits from the recent outpouring of civil rights scholarship. Most of the newer studies focus on the civil rights revolution and the South and chronicle the heroic phase of the struggle for racial justice from 1954 to 1965. Two recent studies, however, comment extensively on the Chicago Freedom Movement. In his Pulitzer Prize–winning book, *Bearing the Cross,* David Garrow devotes more than 150 pages to the experience of King and SCLC in Chicago. In *Confronting the Color Line,* Alan Anderson and George Pickering examine in great detail the rise and fall of the Chicago civil rights movement.[2]

This book retraces some of the ground covered in *Bearing the Cross* and *Confronting the Color Line,* in particular the demonstrations against Chicago housing discrimination in the summer of 1966. Unlike Garrow's account, however, it does not examine the two-year Chicago campaign as one of the many episodes that composed the public career of King and SCLC. And unlike Anderson and Pickering's study, it does not devote as much attention to pre-1965 Chicago civil rights efforts as to the SCLC-CCCO alliance. Nevertheless, in its more exclusive focus on the Chicago Freedom Movement, this book also aims to extend our understanding of King and SCLC and the local antecedents of the movement.

Three distinct perspectives shape this study. The first is to acknowledge but then look beyond the roles of the most well known civil rights leaders of the Chicago campaign, in order to highlight the broader context out of which Chicago protest emerged. In so doing, I draw on the impressive array of monographs on black life and race relations in this midwestern city that once led Richard Wright to comment that "no other community in America [has] been so intensely studied, has had brought to bear upon it so blinding a scrutiny as" black Chicago. Allan Spear and William Tuttle have both contributed volumes on the consolidation of a black ghetto in Chicago. Thanks to the more recent work of James Grossman, the dramatic stories of black migrants from the South to Chicago during the first Great Migration no longer remain untold. With *Black Metropolis,* published in 1945, St. Clair Drake and Horace Cayton produced a highly nuanced portrait of black life in Chicago in the 1930s and early 1940s. All of this scholarship underscores one basic point: that black Chicago in the first half of the twentieth century was immensely complex and driven by intricate processes. Since then, black Chicago has become even more elaborate. During the 1950s, for example, a full-fledged ghetto emerged on the West Side that served as a port of entry for migrating southern blacks. At the same time, class stratification on the West Side and particularly on the South Side became more pronounced than ever before as more and more black Chicagoans entered the ranks of the middle class. This book pays as close attention as possible to the broad, underlying forces that shaped the contours of Chicago civil rights protest in the 1960s. Arnold Hirsch has analyzed the impulses at work maintaining and perpetuating a black ghetto after World War II and Nicholas Lemann has described the second Great Migration to Chicago after World War II. To date there is not, however, any rich portrayal of black life in the 1950s and 1960s comparable to *Black Metropolis*. Relatively little is known, for instance, about the nature of street and associational life, about the dynamics of the black church, and about the effect of the early stages of the decline of smokestack industries on the class structure, neighborhood vitality, and ultimately civil rights protest of black Chicago during these years.[3]

This book also examines the efforts of civil rights activists to kindle an insurgent consciousness among West Side blacks and to build a grass-roots movement in late 1965 and early 1966. Accounts of the Chicago Freedom Movement have often focused too exclusively on SCLC's top leaders or on local civil rights leaders and coalitions at the expense of what was happening (or not happening) in the neighborhoods. For much of the Chicago campaign, James Bevel, as captain of SCLC's Chicago advance team, was the pivot around which action revolved. It was often West Side activists, either SCLC field workers or their allies, who by their work determined the range of strategic choices available to King, Raby, and other leaders of the Chicago Freedom Movement. I seek to restore a better balance to the story of the Chicago Freedom Movement by stressing the importance of the interaction between civil rights field staffers and protest leaders and between civil rights field staffers and black communities.

The belief that a civil rights drama can only be understood from a race relations perspective also informs this study. By this I mean to do more than offer another version of the familiar tale of the clash between Martin Luther King and Richard Daley, the most famous big-city mayor of his age. Too often, the whites who appear in accounts of the struggle for black freedom are depicted without depth or texture. As Adam Fairclough has pointed out, "the tendency to segregate history by race" is "a major weakness of much civil rights historiography." The most penetrating studies of the civil rights era, such as William Chafe's *Civilities and Civil Rights,* have detailed the complex interplay between whites and blacks as the struggle unfolded. To be sure, this book is indisputably organized around the initiatives of civil rights forces, but other actors—

such as white politicians, conservative black clergymen, white religious leaders, Chicago business executives, and white homeowners—play significant roles as well. The critical encounter in the Chicago Freedom Movement was between civil rights activists and white ethnics during the season of open-housing marches in the summer of 1966. This clash generated a sense of crisis that in turn triggered an elaborate contest between city officials and civil rights forces to define the Chicago conflict as primarily an issue of either social order or social justice.[4]

The conviction that the full significance of the Chicago Freedom Movement can only be captured by reaching beyond the confines of the city of Chicago and placing the campaign within a national context is the third perspective influencing this analysis. The entrance of King and SCLC onto the Chicago scene instantly ensured that future civil rights developments in the city would have national implications. Although King and SCLC came to Chicago without a set plan for a direct action campaign, they were confident that they could devise an effective strategy on the run. In the end, after much frustration and deliberation, they fixed upon a scheme quite similar to those employed in their most famous southern campaigns. While the Chicago Freedom Movement initially seemed destined to turn on economic issues, it settled on a more traditional civil rights focus: the dual housing market that favored whites over blacks. The open-housing marches of the summer of 1966 proved that SCLC could engineer dramatic demonstrations in the North just as it had in the South. Moreover, much like SCLC's most renowned southern campaigns, the Chicago open-housing demonstrations stirred national debate about housing discrimination just as Congress was considering legislation to promote equal housing opportunity.

But here the parallels between northern and southern protest end. While the Birmingham, St. Augustine, and Selma campaigns all immediately boosted national civil rights legislation, the Chicago demonstrations did not promote the passage of the Civil Rights Bill of 1966. The Chicago Freedom Movement illuminated the difficulties faced by the nonviolent civil rights movement after the Selma campaign of 1965. It never energized black Americans, who were more divided over strategy and goals than in recent years, to embrace fair housing as enthusiastically as they had rallied behind the southern campaigns for equal access to public accommodations and voting rights. The Chicago experience, moreover, confirmed that the withering of white support for black demands resulted from more than the spread of the Black Power impulse and the explosion of ghetto riots. At the heart of the collapse of the civil rights consensus of the mid-1960s—that general outlook, shared by a majority of Americans outside the South, that decried legal barriers to full citizenship rights for blacks—was white resistance to the new quest to expand equality of opportunity into the more private realms of American life in the North as well as in the South. After Selma, a new fault line emerged, dividing white Americans on black demands and defined less by geography, as it largely had been before 1965, than by self-interest and ideological persuasion. Although eventually the principle of equality of results and its attendant remedies such as affirmative action and busing further defined and extended cleavages on racial issues, it was the dispute over fair housing that first dramatically exposed the limits of the civil rights consensus. As the bifurcated local and national response to the Chicago open-housing marches revealed, many Americans believed that housing discrimination was a violation of the American creed and demanded corrective legislation, which was finally realized with the Civil Rights Act of 1968. But others disagreed that the Chicago demonstrations exposed an American injustice. To them, the message of the demonstrations was ambiguous at best and, for not a few, reinforced their conviction that homeowners were entitled to determine the composition of their neighborhoods.

The Chicago Freedom Movement did not recast the American racial scene as had the Birmingham and Selma campaigns. It did, however, signal the coming of a new era of contentious debate over national policy to right racial wrongs. In particular, it revealed the broad belief that many whites—in the North and the South—shared regarding the extent of private domain in American life, a domain that in their view deserved protection from undue public efforts to integrate. This claim underpinned opposition not only to fair-housing measures but also later to busing, one of the most turbulent issues of the 1970s. Moreover, just as the Chicago Freedom Movement highlighted the decline of the civil rights consensus, it also shaped, and was shaped by, local and national political realignments that more squarely pitted blacks against whites, especially in regions outside of the racial battlegrounds of the South. Through protest in Chicago, Martin Luther King and his allies had hoped to usher in a more generous, more equitable era for both blacks and whites. But they could not overcome the powerful forces and impulses dividing the races. The story of the Chicago Freedom Movement is one that speaks directly to our own time.

Coming to Chicago

"Chicago is on fire with a nonviolent movement. They want us to come in September. We must not ignore their call," Martin Luther King, Jr., told his Southern Christian Leadership Conference colleagues in late August 1965. At King's command, SCLC geared up for a remarkable new departure, its first full-scale northern civil rights campaign. Until then SCLC had been a distinctly southern creation. Born in the South, it had spent the last eight years working almost exclusively in its native region. But times had rapidly changed. After the rioting in the Watts section of Los Angeles, the plight of urban northern blacks seemed at least as pressing as that of southern blacks. Only by doing something spectacular, by launching a northern nonviolent campaign, King and SCLC believed, could they offer hope to the "teeming millions of Negroes hovered in ghettoes" and steer them away from destructive violence.[1]

SCLC's decision to go to Chicago delighted Albert Raby, the leader of the Chicago civil rights movement. To Raby, the Chicago movement was not ablaze, but burning out. Convinced that Chicago could not be reformed from within, he had recently entered into talks with King and Andrew Young, trying to lure SCLC to Chicago. He thought that only a SCLC campaign could alter the segregative and discriminatory practices that plagued nearly one million black Chicagoans. With SCLC's impending arrival, Raby and his followers rejoiced. The civil rights spotlight, for the first time, would be focused on northern racial problems and, more specifically, on their city.[2]

* * *

For Al Raby the summer of 1965 was a season of both exhilaration and disappointment. Early in the summer the Chicago civil rights movement reached a new peak of intensity. At the movement's height in June, Raby regularly led over two hundred black and white protesters in marches against the reappointment of Chicago's superintendent of schools, Benjamin C. Willis. These were more than polite protests. Hundreds of demonstrators were arrested, and for many protesters the trip to a police station was a seminal experience, intensifying (at least for a time) their willingness to sacrifice for civil rights success. Raby himself was stirred by the new militancy. "I got my catharsis; I was free," he later remarked about his decision to escalate the protests. Yet the Chicago activists' early zeal proved unsustainable. As September neared and more than two months of almost daily marches produced no concrete achievements, the ranks of demonstrators thinned. Raby now found himself marching with, as he later joked, "nine people and a dog."[3]

That the Chicago civil rights movement was dissipating stung Raby, for his life had become completely fused with Chicago's struggle for racial justice. A soft-spoken yet determined man with a thin face and thin mustache, Raby had climbed swiftly into the Chicago civil rights vanguard. Born in Chicago in 1933, he knew poverty firsthand. His father, a postal clerk, died when he was two, and his mother's health faded trying to raise her children on Chicago's South Side. Raby floated in and out of Chicago's public schools until the eighth grade, when he dropped out, presumably for good. In a sense, however, Raby's education had just begun. Carroll Maynard, a black photographer, took Raby under his wing as an assistant and became a strong father figure for him. Maynard, "a proud man" according to Raby, broadened the youngster's awareness of the enduring black struggle for freedom. "It was," Raby later remembered, "a tremendous learning experience." Raby found a job at a label-printing plant and quickly learned more about the inequities facing blacks in the workplace. His outrage over the unequal employment opportunities there propelled him into union activity. These formative teenage experiences, Raby later recalled, "laid the foundation" for his activism in the 1960s.[4]

Like so many young men in the postwar era, Raby soon found himself serving in the armed forces. His stint in the army opened his eyes to his limited formal academic skills, and when he left the service he doggedly earned his high school diploma. That same determination drove him to a junior college and then to Chicago Teachers College, where he garnered academic honors.[5]

Raby was teaching junior high students at a nearly all-black school on Chicago's West Side when in 1961 he was pulled into organized civil rights activity. The triggering event was the firing of a black Chicago teacher, Doris Baker, because she had joined a picket line protesting discriminatory school policies. Outraged by Baker's treatment and alerted to the extent of public school segregation in Chicago by a white junior college professor, Meyer Weinberg, Raby—who already recognized the importance of organization from his labor union involvement as a teenager—helped found Teachers for Integrated Schools (TFIS). In 1963 TFIS selected him to be one of its delegates to the newly formed Coordinating Council of Community Organizations. In January 1964 Raby became the convenor of CCCO, by then a broad interracial coalition of Chicago civil rights, religious, professional, labor, and community groups. As the protests heated up in the summer of 1965, Raby quit teaching to become a full-time activist.[6]

Raby took his role as a civil rights leader seriously, recognizing that he was the caretaker of something remarkable in Chicago public life: independent citizens' insurgency. Only a few years earlier, it had been impossible to speak of a Chicago civil rights movement. Indeed, in the 1950s it was fashionable (and accurate) to lament the lack of a "vigorous civic life" in the black community.[7]

There were, to be sure, organizations that toiled to improve race relations in the city and to better the lot of black Chicagoans. During World War II, prominent black and white Chicagoans formed what would commonly be known as the Council Against Discrimination, whose goal was to remove the sources of racial violence. In its customarily self-effacing manner, the Chicago chapter of the American Friends Service Committee (AFSC) strove for interracial harmony and equity by developing an effective fair employment program and by responding to white outbursts over black neighbors, particularly after the highly publicized assault in 1951 on a black couple who moved to Cicero, an all-white industrial city bordering Chicago's West Side. Out of Chicago's labor movement, the packinghouse workers' union emerged as a strong force for racial justice. With blacks dominating the work force at Chicago's famed, though rapidly declining, stockyards, the local United Packinghouse Workers affiliate stressed racial equality both within the packinghouses and throughout the city of Chicago. In the late 1940s Packinghouse crusaders spearheaded a campaign against segregated eateries and over the course of the next decade advanced a host of civil rights causes.[8]

The most important traditional race advancement organizations, which were deeply rooted in the black community, were not silent either. Especially in the mid-1950s, the Chicago branch of the National Association for the Advancement of Colored People (NAACP), with over fifteen thousand members, condemned discriminatory practices in the city. After struggling during the first half of the decade, the Chicago Urban League rebounded under the leadership of Edwin "Bill" Berry to become one of the most dynamic Urban League chapters in the country.[9]

Nor was Chicago without some notable examples of collective action in the 1950s. Thousands of black Chicagoans attended Emmett Till's funeral after the fourteen-year-old had been lynched while visiting relatives in Mississippi. In 1955 blacks picketed Chicago's City Hall to protest official inaction on the Trumbull Homes riots, in which angry whites attacked blacks who had just moved into a public housing complex located in an all-white South Side neighborhood. In the summer of 1960 thousands of marchers, led by Martin Luther King and A. Philip Randolph, descended upon the Republican National Convention in Chicago to demand a strong civil rights platform. Nevertheless, these were individual, isolated episodes that did not add up to coordinated, sustained civil rights protest.[10]

The absence of a Chicago civil rights movement in the 1950s defies a simple explanation, for there was no dearth of grating issues. In the immediate postwar era, blacks were often the target of vicious white violence, and structural injustices—including housing discrimination, school segregation, employment inequities—defined city life as well. Despite the hopes for a new progressive racial order held by reformers like Elizabeth Wood, director of the Chicago Housing Authority, white Chicagoans from working-class and white-collar regions, the University of Chicago, the city's business leaders and realtors, and, ultimately, Chicago politicians and city agencies combined in the postwar years to ensure not the dispersal of the city's black population but, rather, its concentration in a more expansive and hardened ghetto. There had, however, been marked progress in curbing the daily blatant indignities that southern blacks protested against in the 1950s. State laws, though often honored only in the breach, had long outlawed segregation in schools and other public arenas. During the early 1940s the Committee on Racial Equality, later to be known as the Congress of Racial Equality (CORE), had sprung to life in Chicago by exposing many of the double standards that hobbled blacks. It staged sit-ins and turned to other direct action tactics against discriminatory practices at Chicago restaurants and roller rinks. As the 1950s wore on, fewer establishments refused black patrons. In the early 1960s the chairman of the Chicago Commission on Human Relations seemed almost startled that in 1946 his organization had bestowed an award for good citizenship on a restaurant for serving all of its customers without distinction to race. In the 1940s this restaurant was a pioneer; by 1963 so much progress had been made that such a nondiscriminatory policy seemed "commonplace."[11]

On other fronts there were signs of progress as well. After 1940 blacks broke into occupations hitherto reserved for whites only. In the early 1950s, major Chicago department stores such as Weiboldt's and Carson Pirie Scott devised merit employment programs to open up white-collar positions to blacks. In 1953 the giant retailer Marshall Field finally parted with its policy of not hiring blacks. During the 1950s, Chicago's major banks, one by one and with some reluctance, began employing blacks to fill skilled positions. The advances impressed Bill Berry, who noted in the late 1950s: "Racial discrimination in job opportunity is being reduced every day." In 1961 Berry had even more to praise on the employment front. After years of effort, the Illinois legislature finally passed a fair employment practices law. While still formidable, the color line in economic life—which had long served to protect and profit white Chicagoans—had eroded.[12]

Tumbling barriers to black opportunity did not alone dampen Chicago's protest impulse. The great flood of migrants that swelled black Chicago after 1940—topping twenty thousand a year, according to some estimates—threatened the vitality of the community networks so crucial to popular protest and thus stymied mass insurgency. So too did a general lack of conspicuous models of sustained, successful mass protest. No northern city could claim a strong civil rights movement in the 1950s, an era in which popular dissidence in general was stifled by anti-Communist anxieties. Moreover, as Drake and Cayton observed in 1961, "full-time fighting against discrimination and segregation" was "considered a specialist activity—the job for Race Leaders and Race Heroes, for a certain kind of white person, for job holders in the newer race relations organizations, and for college kids who go Freedom Riding in the South or take part in sit-ins and swim-ins in Midwest Metropolis." Chicagoans viewed the resolution of civil rights questions not as the mission of a "mass movement" but, rather, as one civil rights professional put it, "as the civic work of the people of good will, some from religious motivations, some from civic motivations, to try to heal the number one problem in the community."[13]

Black Chicago's political leadership welcomed the stress on a steady yet calm resolution of black grievances. Unlike their southern counterparts, black Chicagoans had not been disfranchised after Reconstruction, and by World War II they constituted a large bloc of Democratic votes, carefully managed by Congressman William L. Dawson. In 1939 the ambitious Dawson had jumped from the Republican party and had quickly built a formidable political submachine. Dawson and his minions practiced the politics of organization. They were wary of tackling controversial race issues that might convulse the Democratic party apparatus in Chicago. They downplayed the value of controversial demands such as open occupancy or integrated education and stressed the tangible benefits they could bring to their constituents—low-paying jobs, general services, and political favors. They pressed for black advancement but disdained unsettling and unpredictable mass action. Dawson perhaps stated his position on civil rights work most bluntly when he faintly praised the Urban League as "all right . . . I guess, as long as they stick to their knitting, and [do] not get into politics."[14]

The politicos' desire for calm even led to the muzzling of potentially disruptive organizations. In the mid-1950s labor activists infused new life into the listless Chicago branch of the NAACP. This progressive surge led to the election of Willoughby Abner, a United Automobile Workers representative, as the branch's president. As the head of an invigorated NAACP, Abner immediately began to spotlight racial injustices and criticize black politicians, in particular Congressman Dawson, for their silence on important racial issues of the day. This aggressive style alarmed Chicago's white and black politicians, and in 1957 Dawson, with the support of Mayor Richard J. Daley, maneuvered to depose the militant Abner from the Chicago NAACP's presidency. This episode soon became part of city lore attesting to the power of Chicago's Democratic party organization, and it ensured enduring suspicions about the commitment of the local NAACP to black advancement.[15]

The Cook County Democratic organization operating through

Dawson's black submachine could hinder yet, as the 1960s proved, not halt black protest. It lacked the resources to curb the explosions unleashed by festering black grievances and by black alienation from traditional sources of authority. But that was to come. In the 1950s the image of the city as a promised land, cultivated in the early years of the twentieth century, still retained some of its lustre among blacks. In 1957, a leading black entrepreneur could still write a booklet of a hundred pages entitled "Chicago: City of Progress and Opportunity." By 1960 the median black family income approached $5,000, far higher than the national black average, and though the black unemployment rate tended to run roughly three times as high as the fluctuating figure for whites during the 1950s, most blacks could secure jobs. No wonder Drake and Cayton could conclude in 1961 that by 1950 "the lean years had gone" for black Chicago. More than anything else, the evident prosperity, the ebbing discrimination, the general optimism of the 1950s blunted black activism. One NAACP member provided perhaps the best explanation for the general apathy toward race advancement work when she noted that with the hardships of the South so vivid to so many black Chicagoans, the Windy City, by comparison, seemed "near heaven."[16]

 But then in the early 1960s, black Chicagoans (assisted by some whites), like blacks across the North, broke the relative calm by raising their voices and taking to the streets to protest racial inequities in their own neighborhoods. The new militancy sprang in part from the erupting southern civil rights movement. Chicago blacks, many of whom were born in the South, closely followed the unfolding drama of black rejection of the Jim Crow South. During the Montgomery bus boycott, they held supportive rallies and collected money to send to Alabama. Inspired by the southern student lunch counter sit-ins, a resurgent Chicago chapter of CORE and the NAACP Youth Council picketed local Woolworth stores in 1960. The next summer black youths and progressive whites staged "wade-ins" at a South Side beach to protest the customary exclusion of blacks from the public recreation site. Despite beatings and ugly threats, the white and black activists flouted established custom at the beach for over two weeks. "The example of southern Negroes who have successfully used direct action techniques to combat segregation in environments much more hostile than Chicago cannot but have some effects," one observer noted.[17]

As the southern struggle legitimized insurgency, a wave of civil rights activities struck Chicago in the early 1960s. The Chicago Urban League sought to use the Illinois fair employment practices law to boost black employment, while other organizations employed more dramatic tactics. The University of Chicago branch of CORE, for instance, staged demonstrations against the university's housing policies, and Chicago CORE tackled problems of unequal employment opportunities and housing discrimination in Chicago neighborhoods.[18]

Anger over Chicago public school policy, however, was the principal source of black unrest. Black Chicago already had a long history of fighting for good education when the 1954 *Brown v. Board of Education* decision spurred further questions regarding the racial basis of unequal education in the Chicago public schools.[19] But it was distress over a concrete change—a ballooning student population that caused severe overcrowding in many schools, particularly those in black residential regions—that triggered local civil rights insurgency. Even though Superintendent Willis had supervised a massive school building program since 1953, the soaring student enrollment outpaced the building expansion. From 1953 to 1963 the number of Chicago public school pupils skyrocketed from 375,000 to more than 520,000, an increase roughly equal to the total enrollment of the entire Baltimore school system. To ease the overcrowding, Willis was forced to step up a double-shift program: two sets of students attended school each day, one early in the morning, the other later in the day.[20]

This maneuver pleased no one, but it especially distressed black Chicagoans. The double-shift burden, while citywide, was heaviest for predominantly black schools, which accounted for more than ninety percent of double-shift students. Black students, who made up over forty percent of the total enrollment, went to public schools that were overflowing, while white students often attended schools with underutilized classrooms. In the late 1950s blacks had publicly demanded a redress of this imbalance, but the Chicago Board of Education and the school administration had shrugged off any responsibility, calling for patience until the building program ended overcrowding.[21]

By 1961 the patience of many blacks had been exhausted. Nowhere was exasperation more pronounced than on the southern fringes of the Black Belt, the traditional home of most Chicago blacks, which was rapidly expanding as the old South Side boundaries that whites had zealously guarded since the 1920s proved too limited for the swelling black population. Seeking a better life, middle-class blacks by the 1950s had breached the traditional Black Belt borders for nearby communities with comfortable apartments, cozy homes, and better schools. Upon the arrival of blacks into these neighborhoods, however, most whites fled, fearing encroaching slums. The white exodus baffled the black newcomers. "[T]hat's what I'm running from myself," explained a black lawyer who had recently moved to Chatham, a community deep on Chicago's South Side and popular with aspiring blacks.[22]

The whites generally left peacefully, thus sparing Chatham and other desirable South Side communities much of the ugly violence that often accompanied changing Chicago neighborhoods. But the region's public schools now overflowed with students, most of whom were black. Like middle-class parents everywhere, Chatham-area parents placed a high priority on good education for their children and were willing to battle for it. On the whole they felt secure enough to act on their own, despite the antipathy toward public protest of many black and white politicians, businessmen, and clergy.[23]

At the same time, the Chicago NAACP reentered the schools dispute. Before the ouster of Willoughby Abner in late 1957, the local NAACP education committee, inspired by the *Brown* decision, had attacked discriminatory school policy, as described in a report by Faith Rich, "De Facto Segregation in the Chicago's Public Schools." After a few years of relative quiescence, in the summer of 1961 the Chicago NAACP, led by the Reverend Carl Fuqua and spurred by cries for action from the *Chicago Defender,* the city's leading black newspaper, called for black parents to register their children in less crowded, all-white schools.[24] Chatham-area parents, along with parents from other black communities, enthusiastically participated in "Operation Transfer." After school officials refused to grant the requested transfers, aggrieved parents, supported by the Chatham–Avalon Park Community Council (CAPCC), filed a class-action suit, subsequently known as the *Webb* case, to correct racial imbalance in the Chicago public schools. By 1961 Chatham-area residents, like increasing numbers of other black Chicagoans, directly linked the intolerable overcrowding of black schools to intentional segregation.[25]

Directly to the south of Chatham, school overcrowding sparked even more militant action. For months black parents in Vernon Park, another black middle-class enclave, had requested relief from congested schools without success. When the Board of Education transferred students from the severely crowded Burnside School to a more distant school, while an uncrowded all-white school stood nearby, black parents exploded. In early January 1962 an outraged group of local women staged at the Burnside School the first "sit-in" of the emerging Chicago civil rights drama. And they kept coming back. "We weren't looking for any notoriety or anything like that. We just wanted our school situation straightened out. We didn't like the fact that they were going to school on double shift," Alma Coggs, mother of two students and one of the sit-in leaders, recalled. "We were just protesting the fact that they [the school officials] had ignored us."[26]

Like a number of Burnside demonstrators, Coggs was also associated with the *Webb* suit and had turned to direct action out of frustration. The Burnside protests were inspirational, and ministers from across the expanding South Side Black Belt, including the Reverend James Webb, joined the sit-ins at the school. Black citizens were now ahead of established civil rights organizations like the NAACP in their assertiveness, and the gap widened when roughly two weeks after the protests began, police arrested the sit-in participants, bringing more exposure to the unjust treatment of black students. Alma Coggs and the Burnside protesters had popularized a new form of communication, a dramatic language based on action and outside of traditional political channels that would be employed by many other black Chicagoans over the next few years to voice their anger over unequal education. Their bold stroke also upset broadly held assumptions about Chicago race relations. The judge who heard their case claimed that while he was in sympathy with the southern sit-ins for civil rights, he never thought he would "see the day that in an enlightened community such as Chicago I would be hearing a similar case." So great was the uproar over the Burnside issue that it prompted Mayor Daley and five black aldermen to hold an unprecedented meeting with Superintendent Willis to discuss the state of the public schools.[27]

Middle-class blacks were not the only ones leading community protests against Chicago public schools. In North Lawndale on Chicago's West Side, for instance, black residents, along with Chicago CORE and local ministers, turned to demonstrations against school overcrowding in the early 1960s. Yet the North Lawndale protests—like those in many other poorer communities—never reached the intensity of the Burnside sit-ins even though school conditions were deplorable on the West Side. Lacking strong and independent local organizations, North Lawndale, like most less affluent communities, remained a secondary player in the schools controversy.[28]

Nevertheless, it was the working-class Woodlawn community, just south of the University of Chicago, that gave birth to the strongest local protest movement. Woodlawn was unusual not because it was poor but because it had been seeded for protest by Saul Alinsky, the famed neighborhood organizer. With the assistance of Alinsky organizers, a host of local groups had coalesced into an expansive community organization, the Temporary Woodlawn Organization (subsequently known as The Woodlawn Organization, or TWO). From the start, TWO was feisty, aggressive, and resistant to pressure from local politicians and businessmen. Led by the Reverend Arthur M. Brazier, a hard-nosed black Pentecostal minister, TWO quickly focused its attention on the jam-packed local public schools. In late September 1961, TWO backed the *Webb* suit. Two months later, it began a "death watch" of the Chicago Board of Education. At each school board meeting, two or three TWO members, dressed in black, sat silently through the proceedings. Then in February 1962, after Superintendent Willis refused to release an inventory of Chicago classrooms, Woodlawn parents formed a "truth squad" in order to compile their own. While searching for unused classrooms in nearby all-white schools, the parent investigators, to TWO's outrage, were arrested. Three months later Woodlawn residents flocked to TWO protests, including school boycotts, against the use of mobile classrooms at a local elementary school. "The whole Negro community is positively opposed to mobile classrooms, because we believe this is a means of maintaining segregation," Brazier declared.[29]

In 1962 efforts to harness and coordinate the mounting local disaffection began. That February the Chatham–Avalon Park Community Council held a public conference on segregation in the Chicago public schools. A month later PTA leaders and the Chicago Urban League cosponsored a well-attended seminar on promoting quality education. Most important, a new organization emerged, the Coordinating Council of Community Organizations, founded by the Chicago Urban League, TWO, the Chicago branch of the NAACP, and the CAPCC, among others.[30]

Bill Berry of the Urban League was especially influential in the formation of CCCO. Ambitious and gifted, Berry harnessed these two qualities in his lifelong pursuit of black advancement. Raised in Oberlin, Ohio, in a well-to-do home and educated at Oberlin College, Berry nevertheless went through a bleak ordeal as a young black college graduate unable to find suitable employment in Pittsburgh during the 1930s. "I was one of the Depression's children," he later recalled. He worked as a chauffeur before landing a job with the Works Progress Administration as a liaison to the Pittsburgh Urban League. He soon joined the Urban League as a full-time staffer and later won praise for building a strong Portland, Oregon, affiliate. Berry endorsed the league's traditional emphasis on promoting the social welfare of blacks, but he disdained its conservative approach. "We have played it so safe," Berry claimed, "that we [are] well behind the safety zone." The league, he insisted, would have to "accept the risk of irritating some people[,] both black and white[,] who cling stubbornly to the status quo while declaring they believe in equality—but not now." The "new" Chicago Urban League quickly shed its stodgy image, and Berry developed a reputation as an aggressive leader. Yet the urbane and persuasive Berry remained an avid coalition builder who glided through corporate and political circles spreading the message of the need for action on questions of racial justice. CCCO, he hoped, would further black advancement by coordinating Chicago civil rights activity.[31]

Civil rights agitation reached new heights in Chicago, as it did elsewhere across the North, in 1963. Reviewing the rising assertiveness of black Chicagoans, the *Chicago Daily News* declared that the "militant crusade by Negroes who seek the full rights of citizenship" represented "a social revolution in our midst" and a "story without parallel in the history of our city." During 1963 groups as varied as the Chicago chapter of the Negro American Labor Council (NALC), an organization founded by the trade unionist A. Philip Randolph, and the Clergy Alliance of Chicago, a group of black ministers, mounted campaigns to prod companies like Motorola to open more jobs to blacks, while more and more whites took aggressive stands for racial justice. White nuns and priests, for instance, broke traditional taboos by mounting protests against discriminatory practices in Catholic institutions. The reverberations of national civil rights activity seemed to energize local efforts. That over two thousand black and white Chicagoans, guided by Timuel Black of NALC, traveled east in August to join the March on Washington illustrated the galvanizing power of the national black freedom struggle.[32]

Chicago protests were often far more pointed and barbed than the elevating call for racial brotherhood in Washington that summer. In early July a group of black and white hecklers jeered Richard Daley when he tried to deliver a speech during a large rally at the NAACP national convention not long after he had declared that there were no ghettoes in Chicago. Stunned by the hostile reception, a perturbed Daley scoffed that "this must be a contingent of Republicans." Next to suffer was the prominent conservative black clergyman the Reverend Joseph H. Jackson. When Jackson tried to address the rally, the crowd chanted, "Uncle Tom must go!"[33]

An intensifying sense of outrage also sparked a new round of school protests. On July 10 the interracial Chicago chapter of CORE staged its boldest action to date: a sit-in at the Board of Education that lasted more than a week. A couple of weeks later neighborhood protests, which had flickered with varying intensity since the Burnside sit-ins, reached their zenith. In Englewood on Chicago's South Side, irate parents, led by Rosie Simpson of the 71st and Stewart Parents Council and aided by Chicago CORE, launched a campaign against the installation of mobile classrooms at a lot on 73rd Street and Lowe Avenue. Their boldness signaled that the center of school agitation had shifted from middle-class to less affluent black communities. Their zeal also attracted the support of Chicago Area Friends of SNCC (a new group that had recently been founded to support SNCC's work in the South, but which quickly developed its own action program), the NAACP Youth Council, stalwart activists such as the comedian Dick Gregory, and eventually even distinguished southern civil rights crusaders like the Reverend Fred Shuttlesworth. The "shadows of Mississippi," in the words of one reporter, seemed to fall over Chicago when the police arrested demonstrators as they resorted to "lay-downs" and other stratagems to stop the construction of portable schoolrooms. The mass arrests only strengthened the will of the demonstrators, and the protests turned into "a movement." Local residents, bolstered by Chicago sympathizers, refused to yield until the Board of Education canceled the mobile school project. Furthermore, the 73rd and Lowe demonstrations were infectious; later that summer other neighborhoods rose up against the use of mobile classrooms.[34]

It was, however, the imperiousness of Superintendent Benjamin Willis that fully galvanized the Chicago civil rights movement. In many ways it is ironic that Willis generated so much controversy and bitterness. Although his predecessor, Herold Hunt, had earned more praise as a progressive reformer, Willis was a tireless supervisor whose professionalism had won the admiration of Chicago's business community and whose commitment to expanding the school system made him a generous source of jobs and of service and building contracts. As the 1960s began, he was one of the most admired men in American public education. Harvard University had awarded Willis an honorary degree, calling him "a determined defender of the proposition that American cities deserve good schools." But the gruff Willis was not the right man to lead the Chicago public schools in an era of black assertiveness. He seemed incapable of adapting to changing times. He obstinately defended the integrity of the neighborhood school when even many whites urged more flexibility, and he rejected the notion that integration should be a goal of school policy. Schools should not "disperse" their energies on broad social reforms, thus "deflecting them from the main business of education," he told his critics. His inflexibility on the question of integration led many to the conclusion that he had never outgrown prejudices fashioned early in his career while teaching and serving as a principal in segregated rural Maryland. Willis's detractors transformed Willis into the symbol of Chicago segregation. When in 1962 mobile classrooms were placed near predominantly all-black schools to relieve overcrowding, Willis's critics labeled these temporary additions "Willis wagons," employed simply to avoid integration. By 1963 Willis had become, according to the *Chicago Defender*, "the Gov. Wallace of Chicago standing in the doorway of an equal education for all Negro kids in this city—a one-man educational John Birch Society, incarnate and inviolate."[35]

In the fall of 1963 Willis triggered more controversy by removing a number of all-white high schools from the list of schools designated to receive transfers in a new Board of Education student transfer plan. When the board demanded that Willis carry out its original program, the superintendent refused. He even resisted a court order to implement the board's plan. When authorities tried to serve him the decree at his office, he slipped away. On October 4, rather than obey the court order, Willis resigned. The black community hailed the end of the Willis era. Even Chicago's dailies agreed that Willis had become too controversial to continue as superintendent. But the drama had not yet ended. Three days later the Board of Education, which with its nearly all-white and generally conservative membership had not forcefully endorsed the principle of integration, rejected Willis's resignation and appointed a committee to bring back the wayward superintendent. In mid-October Willis finally announced that he would indeed continue to supervise

Chicago's public schools and strive to provide the "best education for each and every child."[36]

The wildly divergent reaction to Willis's return illustrates how tightly racial issues were woven into this controversy, which on the surface was a question of authority over school policy. Many whites, particularly those on Chicago's Northwest and Southwest sides, cheered the return of the staunch neighborhood school defender. Willis had become their great protector, a man who would not permit the fast-expanding black student population to attend traditionally all-white public schools. "Probably no large city has seen such a groundswell of support for one man as Chicago has seen for Dr. Benjamin Willis," gushed a Southwest Side paper.[37]

Chicago civil rights forces, however, were outraged. Inspired by a plan devised by Lawrence Landry, a young black graduate student and the fiery leader of the Chicago Friends of SNCC, CCCO immediately called for a school boycott to protest Willis's return, and for the next two weeks it labored mightily to stage the event. When the boycott took place on October 22, 1963, it surpassed the organizers' headiest expectations. Many classrooms in predominantly black schools were empty, as nearly 225,000 students stayed home. The boycott promoters, to ensure that they did not encourage a day of glorified "hookey," established "freedom schools" in churches and neighborhood clubs. There students sang freedom songs and discussed pressing civil rights issues. It was a grand day for Chicago civil rights activists. "Freedom Day has stamped the word 'lie,' on the claim of professional educators, social workers, newspaper publishers, that Negroes do not care about the type of education they are receiving, or that they would not take whatever just action they deemed necessary to achieve their rights," Landry asserted.[38]

The spectacular school boycott, Chicago activists claimed, signaled that a mass movement was erupting in Chicago. Black Chicagoans had turned to school boycotts in the past—in the 1930s and in individual communities in the early 1960s—but these earlier boycotts were never as sweeping as the 1963 extravaganza. Moreover, the October boycott leaders had capitalized on the surge in local groups such as the 71st and Stewart Parents Council, devoted to transforming school policy. "This demonstration," Landry insisted, "was not a middle class movement for suburban housing or the right to eat in a restaurant; it was a movement of people from all social classes. People who ignore such a movement are ignoring history itself." Not only did the 1963 boycott attract national attention, it also helped inspire an epidemic of school boycotts across the country in early 1964.[39]

The October boycott marked a transformation in CCCO as well. The Coordinating Council was now much more than a citywide consultative body on civil rights matters. It had become the foremost organizing vehicle for mass protest in Chicago. And yet even as delegates to CCCO basked in their success, the pattern of race relations remained remarkably resilient. In spite of broad participation, the October boycott hardly altered school policy.[40]

After weeks of futile negotiations with school officials, CCCO—though deeply divided over the wisdom of such a course of action—returned to the boycott tactic, despite firm opposition from many black politicians and clergymen. On February 25, 1964, roughly 175,000 students stayed home from school. The second boycott, though smaller than the first, nevertheless underscored the potential for grass-roots support for Chicago civil rights protests: lower-class blacks were less likely to refrain from boycotting than were their well-to-do counterparts. In the end, however, the outcome of the second boycott matched that of the first: it failed to persuade the Chicago public school administration to adopt an aggressive integrationist stance. Nonetheless, both boycotts reflected an elemental shift in attitudes among black Chicagoans: they were now more likely to focus on the obstacles, rather than the opportunities, that Chicago presented than ever before. They were also now more likely to question white authority, to suspect dark and devious motives.[41]

Just as mass action yielded little change in policy, the civil rights legal thrust stalled as well. The Chicago branch of the NAACP had responded coldly to the *Webb* suit filed in 1961 after its "Operation Transfer" initiative. While the Chicago branch defended its slowness as prudence, its critics offered far less generous interpretations. The conservative leanings of the Chicago NAACP and its ties to centers of power, including the Democratic party, continued to limit its assertiveness. The plaintiffs, as a result, rested their hopes for redress on Paul Zuber, whose direction of a New Rochelle, New York, school case had led in 1961 to the first judicial attack on de facto segregation. By the early 1960s, Chicago civil rights forces had rejected the notion of de facto segregation as purely the product of natural residential patterns. When they used the phrase "de facto segregation" they meant segregation buttressed by deliberate, though sometimes subtle, public policies. Chicago segregation, in the words of Meyer Weinberg, was an "artifact," not a "fact." Yet even with Zuber's leadership, the *Webb* suit did not yield many benefits, and in the summer of 1963 it was suspended after the Board of Education agreed to sponsor a thorough study of school practices, which was quickly completed under the direction of Philip M. Hauser, a well-known sociologist.[42]

Chicago civil rights forces had reached a strategic impasse. Their legal thrust had yielded little thus far, and school boycotts could not be launched every day without undermining the education of black students and without eventually losing community support. No group felt the pressure to devise a successful program more intensely than CCCO, which by the spring of 1964 had expanded to include delegates from more than twenty organizations. Among these were several religiously oriented groups with largely white constituencies, including the Catholic Interracial Council of Chicago, the Episcopal Society for Cultural and Racial Unity (ESCRU), and the Presbyterian Interracial Council.[43]

CCCO was undergoing a change in leadership as well. Arthur Brazier had resigned as convenor in late 1963, and Lawrence Landry, dissatisfied with CCCO's lack of militancy, had joined other militant leaders throughout the country to found a new organization, ACT. In this time of transition Al Raby, hitherto CCCO's secretary, assumed the post of convenor. He would later call the appointment "accidental," because he was neither a dynamic speaker nor a particularly charismatic leader. But Raby was patient, a good listener, and a skilled reconciler—three essential qualities for a successful CCCO convenor.[44]

Raby presided over a dedicated, talented, and opinionated group of delegates. CCCO delegates were generally, though not exclusively, well-educated men, often professionals, and now as likely to be white as black, though a black male, never over forty-five years old, always held the top leadership post. Although it possessed a middle-class flavor—which was a target of criticism—CCCO was not without internal tensions. A diverse collection of organizations with distinct interests—labor organizations, religious groups, professional societies, and mainline civil rights organizations, among others—sent delegates to CCCO meetings, and the convenor had to fashion consensus delicately and diligently so that decisions would be made and programs undertaken. Raby had to contend with three major divisions within CCCO, none of which was primarily shaped by the racial background of its delegates. There was a conservative wing led by the Chicago Urban League (which, according to its charter, could not be a protest organization and thus contributed to civil rights activity in many other ways, particularly through its first-rate research department), a fluctuating group of moderates who were largely from religious and community groups, and a militant wing paced by Chicago CORE and Chicago Area Friends of SNCC that wanted to propel CCCO to new levels of aggressiveness. Not surprisingly, CCCO delegates endured seemingly interminable meetings and heated debates about strategy.[45]

For most of his first sixteen months as convenor, Raby sought to keep the CCCO forces focused on challenges against Chicago school policy, but these efforts never rivaled the intensity of the 1963 sit-ins or achieved the mass backing that the two school boycotts had attracted. In the fall of 1964, CCCO adhered to the moratorium on marches called for by leading national civil rights figures and concentrated on a voter registration project. The centerpiece of this effort, designed primarily to undercut Barry Goldwater's presidential ambitions, were Freedom Democratic Clubs, but CCCO delegates also hoped that Chicago authorities would recognize that a rise in black voting rolls represented a potential political challenge. "CCCO has tried direct action and sitting around the table. We must now add action in the political arena," a CCCO program committee stated. The voter registration effort, with much assistance from the Urban League, was successful, but CCCO—constrained by the nonpartisan leanings of important affiliates like the Urban League and the Catholic Interracial Council—never directly entered the political fray.[46]

The creation of Freedom Democratic Clubs was an achievement, but these associations did not threaten the regime of Benjamin Willis, an "old codger," in the words of one civil rights advocate at the time, who was "more clever than ever." Willis's building program had eliminated the double shift by 1963. Willis seemed impregnable, deftly dodging the proposals from two highly regarded studies of Chicago's school system by Professors Philip Hauser and Robert Havighurst, respectively, both of the University of Chicago, and civil rights morale fell. No new energizing issue emerged as a unifying point of action, even though black and white activists throughout the early 1960s had protested against unfair employment practices, housing discrimination, inadequate welfare programs, and unresponsive political leadership.[47] To make matters worse, neighborhood protests had peaked in 1963, and by 1964 the two most aggressive organizations a year earlier, Chicago CORE and Chicago Area Friends of SNCC, were foundering. The spectacular sit-ins in the summer of 1963 had ironically led to a crippling division over Chicago CORE's leadership, and Chicago SNCC was still coping with the fallout after Landry's shift to ACT. (Chicago SNCC eventually expelled Landry from its organization.)[48]

As the months passed without civil rights success, some Chicago observers thought they heard the death rattle of CCCO. Surveying the lull in nonviolent direct action since early 1964 and sensing a change in the tenor of the black freedom struggle away from protest and toward community organizing, one Chicago reporter, Georgie Ann Geyer, claimed that CCCO belonged to a bygone era and "for all effective purposes . . . [had] expired."[49]

Geyer's assertion might have proved correct had not in late May 1965 the Board of Education injected new life into the civil rights movement by renewing Willis's contract, despite the opposition to any extension of the superintendent's tenure not only by CCCO but also by the authors of the two school reports, Professors Hauser and Havighurst. Shortly after the school board's decision, the local NAACP—whose more energetic impulses had temporarily surfaced—announced plans for an extended school boycott. Though suspicious of the NAACP's motives, CCCO nevertheless agreed to participate.[50]

On Tuesday, June 8, the Board of Education threw a wrench into the boycott plans when it secured an injunction restraining the NAACP and CCCO leadership from directing the boycott. But the protest impulse was not so easily stifled. Even without visible leadership, over a hundred thousand black students stayed home from school on June 10 and 11. Raby, prevented from guiding a school boycott, turned to another expression of discontent, even as the Chicago NAACP again slumped into paralysis. On Thursday, June 10, he and several hundred black and white demonstrators sat down in the broad avenue next to Chicago's City Hall. The next day, more Raby-led marchers, en route to City Hall and angered by police commands, stopped in the middle of one of Chicago's major thoroughfares crossing Grant Park on the edge of Lake Michigan. This time Chicago police arrested over two hundred protesters for disorderly conduct, including Raby, Dick Gregory, the national director of CORE James Farmer, and several clergymen. The confrontation, claimed the *Chicago Tribune*, was the "largest mass arrest in any civil rights disorder in the city's recent history." The following day, Saturday, June 12, this scene was virtually replayed as nearly two hundred demonstrators, including nuns, sat down between State Street and Madison Street, the "world's busiest intersection," and were carted away by police.[51]

That Chicago activists marched on City Hall signified an important shift in their assessment of where responsibility lay for Chicago's school crisis. Until now Chicago insurgents had accepted, halfheartedly at least, Mayor Daley's plea that resolution of the crisis was beyond his control. In one sense Daley was correct. By statute the Chicago mayor had little control over school affairs. Civil rights activists had long believed, however, that Daley, like Willis, opposed aggressive policies to promote school integration and favored Willis, if only because the controversial superintendent conveniently deflected criticism away from City Hall. That the Daley-appointed school board still supported Willis reaffirmed their suspicions that Daley wanted him to remain for at least two more years.[52]

In retrospect, the civil rights assessment seems accurate. Although at least one president of the school board in the early 1960s later stated that Daley never interfered with school matters and though Daley had little contact with Willis, the mayor did exercise important, if subtle and indirect, influence on public school policy. Clair Roddewig, the school board president from 1962 to 1964, once told Warren Bacon, a black school board member during the 1960s, that he spoke "to the mayor almost daily about school matters." Cyrus Hall Adams, another school board member and a Daley supporter, also believed that the mayor occasionally intervened to guide school policy, in particular when Willis was rehired in the spring of 1965. That spring Adams had initially informed Daley that the board was not going to renew Willis's contract. "Neither he [Daley] nor Willis knew this," Adams later noted in a summary of the whole affair, "and the Mayor was shocked and pulled Virgil Martin [president of Carson Pirie Scott and a well-connected Chicago civic leader] into the act." Adams believed that some sort of deal was arranged. Martin talked to Willis, Adams conjectured, and "Ben gave his assurances" that "if given a four-year term by the board he would guarantee to retire early." Because Martin had taped the conversation, he knew "he had him if Willis tried to renege."[53]

For the rest of June and into July the downtown marches continued almost daily, leading to the most sustained civil rights protest in Chicago's history. Dissidents with differing motives could readily rally together—as they had in the past—on the issue of Willis's tenure and public school policy. The demonstrations simultaneously served as expressions of frustration with city leaders, outrage against the injustice of segregation, the yearning for better schools for black communities, and, finally, the need for integration. "[T]he state has the right to demand," Raby asserted, "that all children be sent to school, not only to learn to read and write but to learn how to live in society . . . Children must be prepared to live with others of differing backgrounds." Despite challenges to the strategy of nonviolent direct action across the country during the summer of 1965, the Chicago demonstrators remained committed to this tactic and on occasion turned to civil disobedience. Some of the momentum of the first protests of the summer had been lost and these interracial marches—smaller in size than the first demonstrations—suffered, one observer noted, from a "lack of planning and clarity of purpose." These shortcomings were in part compensated, however, by the "strength and courage" of a "hard core of civil rights people who consistently present[ed] themselves untiringly."[54]

On the whole, Raby estimated that roughly six thousand people marched during the summer of 1965. For a city of three million this number might not seem impressive (and it led some to conclude that there was not a broadly based civil rights movement in Chicago), but Raby also pointed out that not every sympathetic person felt able or eager to march. Many offered other forms of support. Raby accepted a Chicago newspaper columnist's assertion that 990,000 out of Chicago's one million blacks supported the insurgency. This claim was no doubt an exaggeration, given the criticism Raby and his followers endured from some black circles, but there was little evidence of widespread black opposition to the protests.[55]

The 1965 anti-Willis demonstrations, like those during the previous four years, were ultimately cries of disappointment over stubbornly misguided public policy. And while many Chicagoans, as in the past, criticized the protests as unconstructive and damaging to civic order, the response to the 1965 marches revealed that persistent local agitation, along with progressive national trends, had slowly but steadily sharpened public sensitivity, in at least some quarters, on the schools question. At the start of the decade, few influential white Chicagoans believed that Chicago schools were faltering on the issue of race. In mid-July 1965, a host of prominent Chicagoans—including Joseph L. Block, chairman of Inland Steel; Peter G. Peterson, president of Bell and

Howell; and Ben W. Heineman, head of the Chicago and North Western Railway—underscored a new set of assumptions when they issued a public letter calling for "equal access to our schools by all races, with a positive policy and program to eliminate segregation."[56]

The widely publicized and frequent marches intensified the pressure on City Hall. Mayor Daley agreed to meet with Raby and other protest leaders, but such gestures of openness did not lead to substantial school reforms, particularly the dismissal of Superintendent Willis. The Daley administration retaliated against civil rights forces with a public relations offensive that included an old tactic that had undercut popular dissidence in the 1950s and was still effective in the 1960s—accusations of Communist infiltration of civil rights groups. Daley also openly wondered who had elected Raby and other civil rights leaders to speak for black Chicago. "Who is this man, Raby?" the mayor asked reporters. "He doesn't represent the people of Chicago. I've received almost a thousand phone calls from Negro mothers saying he doesn't represent them." Moreover, Daley blamed the press for instigating the disturbances. "If we didn't give [the protesters] all that publicity," he asserted, "they might get on a bus and go back home."[57]

Chicago activists had provoked a reaction from City Hall, but not the commitment to school integration that they had hoped for. Given their already strenuous efforts, they began to despair of their capacity to force constructive change. Their next step was to seek outside help.[58]

CCCO reached as far as it could. It sent a detailed complaint to the U.S. Office of Education requesting the suspension of funds earmarked for Chicago public schools because local segregative policies violated Title VI of the Civil Rights Act of 1964. It encouraged the maverick Adam Clayton Powell, Jr., chairman of the House of Representatives subcommittee on education, to hold hearings on the Chicago school crisis. Above all, it urged Martin Luther King and SCLC to swing through Chicago on an upcoming northern exploratory tour.[59]

"I want to join . . . what I consider a very significant struggle," Martin Luther King declared on July 7, 1965, after announcing that he and SCLC staffers would spend three days in Chicago later in the month. The news thrilled Chicago civil rights advocates, who looked to King and SCLC to electrify their cause. "Chicago needs all the help you can possibly give to us to rid ourselves of a system of segregation which throttles the life and growth of the city," one Chicagoan wrote to King. "[T]he people in Chicago," another insisted, "are elated over the fact that you are coming to help us in our struggle."[60]

King's decision to bring his civil rights workers to Chicago for a short visit was not surprising. The civil rights movement was in a state of flux. Even amid its greatest triumphs—the passage of the Civil Rights Act of 1964 and the Voting Rights Act of 1965—the venerable crusader for black freedom, A. Philip Randolph, warned of the dangers of a "crisis of victory." As the Jim Crow South crumbled, questions followed. Where should the movement go next? What should be its targets? What tactics should be employed? Bayard Rustin, coordinator for the March on Washington and longtime adviser to Martin Luther King, contended that the age of protest was ending and that civil rights forces should focus on building an expanded coalition of blacks, liberals, trade unionists, and religious groups to enact a sweeping agenda of social democratic legislation. "What began as a protest movement is being challenged to translate itself into a political movement," Rustin wrote in an influential essay in early 1965. Yet even as Rustin issued his appeal, SNCC and CORE were turning inward, away from interracialism and nonviolent direct action and toward developing power within black communities. Community organizing had become the watchword among young black activists. Nonetheless, out of this confusion and debate in movement circles a consensus was emerging that more attention had to be paid to the North. By 1965 SNCC staffers were moving north to begin urban programs, and early the next year CORE targeted Baltimore as the site for a major project to assist inner-city blacks.[61]

Only a few years earlier the notion of southern blacks traveling across the Mason-Dixon line to help northern blacks would have been dismissed as preposterous. Southern blacks had long considered the North something of a sanctuary, a region where black men and women could at least carve out a decent life. Before the Civil War, runaway slaves escaped to the North for freedom. In the twentieth century, hundreds of thousands of blacks migrated north in search of a brighter future. The South—the home of slavery, lynchings, and legalized segregation—had always been the great oppressor of blacks.[62]

Though a son of the South, King, even early in his career, recognized that the North was not a racial paradise. As a student in Pennsylvania and Boston, he had encountered the sting of northern prejudice firsthand. In one of his earliest speeches during the Montgomery bus boycott of 1955 and 1956, King warned against rosy views on the status of blacks throughout the country: "Let's not fool ourselves, we are far from the promised land, both north and south," he told his listeners.[63]

Yet however injurious discriminatory northern racial practices were, in the 1950s and early 1960s they seemed less oppressive than the southern caste system that denied blacks even the basic rights of citizenship. In its first years SCLC, founded in 1957 by King and fellow southern ministers, diagnosed the race problem in regional terms: the South was the target, and the North, though no interracial utopia, offered abundant resources that could be tapped to fuel the southern crusade against racial injustice. SCLC could cultivate financial assistance from northern liberals, encourage the federal judiciary to step up its assault on Jim Crow practices, and entice the federal government to intervene on behalf of southern blacks.[64]

King's diagnosis also highlighted the daily indignities that southern blacks endured under the Jim Crow regime. He sought to end the reign of violence designed to intimidate blacks and to abolish offensive practices such as public segregation on buses, at lunch counters, and in school systems. This was a natural, almost instinctive response. The career of nonviolent direct action after World War II correlates closely with blatant discrimination in public arenas. The first wave of protests struck against segregated northern lunch counters, restaurants, and other public accommodations. As glaring discrimination in public places receded in the North, segregated public facilities in the border states and then in the South became the target of nonviolent direct action.[65]

To King and his followers in the 1950s and early 1960s, the enemy was clear—legalized segregation and discrimination. With the Jim Crow system so palpable and so seemingly intractable and with the assault upon it so consuming, there was little pressure for a more extensive examination of racism in America in civil rights circles. Yet as southern barriers fell and northern unrest mounted, civil rights advocates felt compelled to develop a more sophisticated analysis of America's race problems, an analysis that doubted whether de facto segregation was generally a natural, rather than a contrived, phenomenon and that detected the blight of institutional racism—inequities grounded into the fabric of American life—everywhere. Charles Silberman, a respected commentator on American race relations, wrote in 1964: "What we are discovering, in short, is that the United States—all of it, North as well as South, West as well as East—is a racist society in a sense and to a degree that we have refused so far to admit, much less face."[66]

King was particularly vulnerable to the mounting pressure for a more searching analysis of American racism. The Montgomery bus boycott had catapulted him into the national limelight, and despite his focus on the South, he had become a spokesperson for all black Americans. Moreover, the underlying principles behind his civil rights ministry ensured that his social vision was not fixed, but eminently expandable. The Southern Christian Leadership Conference might have been a regional organization, but from the beginning its aims reflected its Christian, universalistic spirit. It hoped not just to redeem the soul of the South but, in the words of its founding slogan, "to redeem the soul of America." King and SCLC were moral voices whose domain could reach far beyond the Mason-Dixon line.[67]

By 1963, King's public remarks reflected his growing concern over the state of race relations in the North.[68] Like many civil rights activists, he had anticipated that northern blacks "would benefit derivatively" from southern victories. But now, with the tide turning decisively against the Jim Crow South and with the outpouring of northern support for the southern black freedom struggle, he stressed that sympathetic northerners should neither be content with helping southern blacks nor be quietly reaping benefits from the southern struggle. In a series of speeches delivered across the country in the aftermath of SCLC's Birmingham campaign, King called upon northerners to boost the freedom struggle directly by "getting rid of segregation and discrimination—such as de facto segregation"—in their own communities.[69]

A surge of northern school boycotts in 1964 prompted King to assess further the damage produced by northern racial inequities. With hundreds of thousands of black students in Boston, New York, and Chicago refusing to go to school because of alleged unequal education, the depth of northern black alienation could not be denied. King extended his "moral support and deepest sympathy" to the boycotters, commending black parents for "fighting for the deepest needs of grossly deprived children" and "trying to loosen the manacles of the ghetto from the hands of their children." Inspired by the northern insurgency, he told an interviewer in May that "while I have been working mainly in the South and my organization is a southern-based organization, more and more I feel that the problem is so national in its scope that I will have to do more work in the North than I have in the past."[70]

The explosion of urban riots in the summer of 1964 served as the catalyst that drove King and SCLC to work in the North. The violent uprisings struck at the heart of King's and SCLC's vision of social change. Nonviolence was more than just a tactic for King—it was a way of life—and SCLC was more committed to nonviolence than any other civil rights organization. King and his SCLC lieutenants felt compelled to offer northern blacks an alternative to violence, and after receiving an emergency call from local ministers, Andrew Young and James Bevel led a team of seven organizers to riot-torn Rochester, New York. Drawing on their celebrity status and wearing overalls, the civil rights veterans reached out to disgruntled and disaffected blacks, stressing that violence would not solve their problems. Young thought the "group had amazing and almost immediate success."[71]

In the summer of 1964, King even found himself trying to heal northern racial wounds. When a New York City riot—the first major black uprising since 1943—threatened to spiral out of control, Mayor Robert Wagner pleaded for King to use his influence to help calm the city. Even though the rioting had already subsided, King acceded to Wagner's request and traveled to the city, where he quickly found himself embroiled in controversy. As King headed to Gracie Mansion to see Wagner, Harlem leaders lambasted him for neglecting them and for allowing himself to be used by the "white power structure." It would not be the last chilly welcome King would receive as he became more active in the North. King consulted with Wagner, but he also cooled the tempers of local black leaders by meeting with them and touring New York's black communities. Although to gauge King's effect on easing tensions is difficult, the episode broadened the Baptist minister's awareness of ghetto conditions and the depth of inner-city inhabitants' rage. King warned of future "social disruption" until "the Harlem and racial ghettoes of our nation are destroyed and the Negro is brought into the mainstream of American life."[72]

The upsurge of northern civil rights protest and the summer rioting prompted King to stress SCLC's obligations to northern blacks at the organization's annual convention in the fall of 1964. He did not propose a northern project, but it was clear that northern racial problems would become more prominent in SCLC's agenda. The bestowal in October 1964 of the Nobel Peace Prize pressed King to widen his social mission even more. "[The prize] was a great tribute, but an even more awesome burden," Coretta Scott King remarked. King could no longer focus so exclusively on the problems of southern blacks; his arena of reform had to expand. In his Nobel address King dwelled on the three issues that were to shape the rest of his public career. Before an enthusiastic crowd jammed into a University of Oslo auditorium, King spoke of the necessity of eliminating war and poverty as well as racial injustice from the world.[73]

For the moment, however, King remained focused on southern racism. In February and March 1965, King and SCLC executed their brilliant Selma campaign. Aided by the country's shock at southern white brutality, they ignited a national demand for voting rights legislation. The Selma campaign would, however, be the last great, heroic episode of the southern civil rights drama. Across the rest of the South, the tide of nonviolent direct action had already passed. A time of debate, confusion, and decision was at hand.[74]

At a Baltimore strategy session in early April 1965, shortly after the conclusion of the Selma project, King and SCLC hinted that they too would soon embark on a new departure. Though King's proposed boycott of Alabama dominated press coverage of the proceedings, the SCLC executive board took an important institutional step toward broadening the scope of SCLC's activities by announcing that SCLC would extend its operations into the North. "You can expect us in Baltimore, you can expect us in New York and in Philadelphia and Chicago and Detroit and Los Angeles," King pledged.[75]

Eight weeks later, after trips to Boston, New York, and other cities, King solidified his northern plans. At a meeting in Warrenton, Virginia, in late May, King and his top advisers debated whether SCLC should go north. There was not yet a formal proposal for a specific northern campaign, but some of King's colleagues, questioning the wisdom of any extended northern thrust, argued that there was still much to be done in the South, that SCLC would find the North unreceptive to its efforts, and that heading north would harm SCLC's fund raising, which relied heavily on northern contributors. But King thought otherwise, and he rejected this counsel just as he would subsequent warnings. He felt a duty to go north. He had to reach out to northern blacks. Norman Hill of the Industrial Union Department of the AFL-CIO recalled that after one session in which he and Rustin tried to dissuade King from heading north, King responded less with well-honed arguments for his next move than with the almost unassailable assertion that "this is where our mission is, we have received a calling to come north."[76]

There was another important but unstated reason that King argued for a northern initiative: in the spring of 1965, SCLC had never been stronger, healthier, or richer. The Selma success had triggered a financial windfall. From September 1964 to June 1965, more than $1.5 million had poured into SCLC's coffers, a sum more than one and half times as much as SCLC had received during any other year. Gone were the days when SCLC had to restrict its operations because of scanty funding. In 1960 SCLC operated on $60,000 and had only 3 full-time employees. After the Selma bonanza, SCLC added over 125 new workers, giving it a staff of about 200. Free from the great worry about organizational constraints, King could contemplate heading north with a large staff and not fear painful retrenchment of SCLC's existing southern programs, which included its massive, recently launched voter registration effort led by Hosea Williams.[77]

CCCO's insistent invitation to SCLC helped King and his colleagues formulate their northern plans. SCLC now had the first stop on its exploratory, fact-finding swing through the North, which it christened a "People to People" tour. In addition to Chicago, SCLC selected four other cities to visit—Cleveland, New York, Philadelphia, and Washington, D.C.—which together housed roughly fifteen percent of the nation's blacks. By going north, SCLC was in one sense simply reacting to a major shift in the epicenter of black America. It was following the great demographic flow of black Americans from the rural South to the urban North.[78]

After an evening of briefings by Chicago civil rights leaders and a night's rest at the downtown Conrad Hilton Hotel, King kicked off the People to People tour early Saturday morning, July 24, by addressing an overflow crowd of ministers. Accompanied by SCLC associates, Raby, and other Chicago protest leaders, King then crisscrossed the city, appearing at rallies in several different black neighborhoods. Though often late, he received warm greetings from crowds averaging over five hundred admirers. Chicago activists had made sure that not a moment of King's stay would be wasted.[79]

The next morning King conducted Sunday services at the Quinn African Methodist Episcopal Church, the oldest black church in Chicago, and at a local Baptist church, while other SCLC leaders, Young, Ralph Abernathy, and Walter Fauntroy, joined services at other churches. A weary King later spoke briefly at six neighborhood stops, encouraging Chicagoans to join the large protest march scheduled for Monday. That evening the King entourage traveled up the north shore to Winnetka, an affluent Chicago suburb. There, on the village green, King delivered a forty-five-minute speech to nearly ten thousand people. The largely white crowd cheered as King denounced the perpetuation of Chicago's slums and urged his listeners to dedicate themselves to social reform.[80]

On Monday morning, July 26, King awoke suffering from bronchitis and the hectic pace of the past two days. A visit to a doctor forced him to miss a breakfast sponsored by labor representatives, but he managed to speak to more than two hundred friends of the Chicago Catholic Interracial Council. King then joined business leaders at a luncheon in his honor. That afternoon he addressed a huge crowd at the Buckingham Fountain next to Lake Michigan. "Negroes have continued to flee from behind the Cotton Curtain, but now they find that after years of indifference and exploitation, Chicago has not turned out to be the new Jerusalem," the SCLC leader declared to a roaring crowd. Locking arms with Abernathy, King then led fifteen thousand marchers through Chicago's downtown, slowing traffic to a standstill "in the greatest civil rights demonstration Chicago ever has seen." "We march here today," King told his followers, "because we believe that Chicago, her citizens, and her social structure are in dire need of redemption and reform."[81]

Cleveland was the next stop. On Tuesday a "visibly fatigued" King spoke briefly at appearances on Cleveland's East Side, presided at a breakfast meeting with local clergy at a downtown hotel, and concluded the day with an evening address. King's Cleveland speeches repeated the themes of his Chicago addresses. "[T]he Negro is not free in the North. He is at the bottom of the economic ladder[,] often without a job and with inadequate educational opportunities for his children," he asserted. The next day he explained to a crowd of over three thousand the pressing need for a "grand alliance" of "intellectuals, liberals, labor, management, churches" to combat existing inequities.[82]

But then the tour ran into obstacles. Soon after King's Chicago visit, Adam Clayton Powell, one of black New York's power brokers, informed reporters that he had recently told King not to visit New York City. Powell had been among those who had sharply criticized King for his role in the aftermath of the 1964 riots, and he did not want an outsider meddling in his city again. "I told him [King] to go to cities where they had no real Negro leadership—like Chicago, Cleveland, and Washington," Powell explained.[83]

SCLC's problems only multiplied after the cancellation of the New

York visit. From Philadelphia, too, came the cry "not wanted." Even though a coalition of blacks and whites had invited SCLC to visit, Cecil B. Moore, the outspoken president of the local NAACP chapter who was often at odds with the association's national office, decried King's upcoming stopover. By coming to Philadelphia, the temperamental Moore snapped, King would be "an unwitting tool" in the "egghead white power structure's" plans to diminish "my stature in the Negro community" and to divide the black community. Not wanting "to create dissension," King asked his lieutenant Fauntroy to call off the impending visit. But Moore's imperiousness enraged King's Philadelphia supporters. Hoping to energize the local civil rights movement, they desperately wanted the renowned leader to visit. Moore, fearful of a public rebuke, later met with King's supporters and agreed to endorse another invitation.[84]

King accepted the new appeal. Flanked by his SCLC entourage, he arrived in Philadelphia late on August 1 for two days of whirlwind activity. He visited black neighborhoods; attended dinners; spoke to a group of ministers; assisted the local effort to open Girard College, a school for white male orphans, to blacks; and led a large protest march through the city's downtown. He even patched up differences with the unpredictable Moore. He did not wince when at a joint press conference Moore declared that "we can ill afford division among Negroes." At the end of the press session, King and Moore even raised their locked hands in a gesture of unity. Despite the internal tensions, publicly King termed the visit "an overwhelming success."[85]

King and his staff next headed for Washington, D.C., for the final leg of the People to People tour. The three-day visit followed the now familiar pattern: a round of speeches, banquets, and neighborhood stops, all to cheering crowds. On the second day, King met with President Lyndon Johnson at the White House to deliver a summary of his findings on his northern tour. He urged the President to take further action on the behalf of northern blacks. The next morning King and his associates proudly watched the signing of the Voting Rights Act, which SCLC's Selma campaign had done so much to produce. The SCLC contingent then returned to Atlanta.[86]

Meanwhile, back in Chicago, civil rights leaders tried to harness the surge of enthusiasm prompted by King's visit. Chicagoans were still buzzing about King's impact on the city. One Chicago activist called the big march through the Loop "the most invigorating experience of my life." Another labeled it "beautiful," even comparing it to the "millen-nium." "Chicago will never be the same again as a result of Dr. King's visit," Philip Hauser claimed. CCCO leaders also lauded the pilgrimage through the Loop, but they were especially pleased with the neighbor-hood rallies. "It was a careful decision we made," Raby acknowledged, "bringing Dr. King to the people, instead of duplicating another one-shot affair where we asked the people to come out for King." The King tour had reached into the neighborhoods and spurred the development of a "grass-roots movement," Raby believed.[87]

After King's visit Chicago dissidents staged more marches and, as CCCO's coordination of the insurgency continued to lessen, escalated their tactics to heighten the social disruption. In early August, a group of activists, led by Dick Gregory, even though he lacked official ties to CCCO, ventured into Bridgeport, a white working-class community on Chicago's South Side, to demonstrate in front of Mayor Daley's home. Now the protesters sought more than to remove Superintendent Willis. They went to Bridgeport to expose the "systematic exclusion" of blacks from white communities, Raby stated. Bridgeport residents did not greet their visitors warmly. On the night of August 2, thousands of white hecklers bombarded protesters with eggs, stones, and tomatoes as they walked through Daley's neighborhood. Chicago police arrested the peaceful marchers.[88]

Though daring, the Bridgeport visits, like every thrust of the summer of 1965, neither removed Superintendent Willis nor significantly changed school policy. The Bridgeport demonstrators found themselves the target of criticism from both city officials and civil rights sympathiz-ers, who thought such evening forays into white working-class commu-nities to be counterproductive. Cecil Partee, a black state representative, feared that "night marches" could lead to "a riot." Joseph Block, an Inland Steel executive and head of the Business Advisory Council to the Chicago Urban League, wrote to Bill Berry "that night marches in a residential district could lead to violence and escalate into troubles of a most serious nature for our city and all its people." Then in mid-August the West Side erupted with anger when a swerving fire truck, manned by an all-white crew, struck and killed a black woman. Although in comparison with subsequent ghetto upheavals the riot was rather lim-ited, it further diminished the confidence of Chicago civil rights forces. "We had pretty much thrown every shot we had. We had done every-thing . . . on schools, and made as much concentration as could be reasonably expected," Raby later recalled. Nonviolent direct action, as practiced by CCCO and its allies in the summer of 1965, had not even brought the Daley administration to the negotiating table; CCCO had failed, in short, to reap tangible success. As their movement sagged, Chicago activists hoped for SCLC's return.[89]

Chicago activists had reason to be hopeful. SCLC was indeed sending signals that it might return to Chicago, perhaps on a more permanent basis. Yet the SCLC leadership seemed in no great rush to devise a formal northern program. Even though King spoke on the severity of northern racial problems at an August 9 meeting of the SCLC board of directors, Andrew Young told the board members that the best course for SCLC would be to hold a retreat that fall to devise "a plan for building a movement over the next year or two."[90]

A new crisis—the Watts riots of mid-August 1965—dramatically accelerated SCLC's decision making. When word of the Los Angeles uprising reached King en route to Puerto Rico for a much-needed vacation, he hesitated about what to do. Rustin advised him to stay away from the exploding ghetto. Reluctantly King agreed and continued traveling. But when the rioting escalated, King felt compelled to go to Los Angeles. Surveying the devastation wrought by the rioting depressed him, as did the spreading criticism that the Watts uprising exposed the civil rights movement's failure to help disaffected urban blacks. Something must be done, he insisted. Yet he was still uncertain whether SCLC should concentrate on the North. "You know, you're damned if you do, damned if you don't. If we don't go north, we're damned, but if you go you've got some problems," King confided to a close adviser, Stanley Levison. But at the very least King thought it essential for SCLC to reevaluate its "whole programmatic thrust for the next few months, particularly re[garding its] . . . work in the North." Troubled, King called for an emergency meeting of the SCLC executive staff.[91]

Gathering in Atlanta from August 26 to 28, the SCLC leadership debated its next move. But it was now a resolute King who dominated discussion. SCLC had not yet committed itself to any new venture for the fall of 1965, and the SCLC chief had decided that the cause of northern blacks could no longer be ignored. For too long they had remained invisible and only now, through violence, were they being heard. Their lawlessness was understandable—it was the cry of the dispossessed—but it also represented the ultimate threat to King, "a challenge to the nonviolent movement." SCLC had to prove that non-violence could work in the North. Otherwise, not only would King and SCLC forfeit moral leadership, but they could fade into irrelevancy. "The present mood dictates that we cannot wait," he argued. The future was clear: SCLC would launch its first full-scale northern civil rights campaign.[92]

Selecting Chicago as the target was not difficult. Adam Clayton Powell's warnings and Cecil Moore's unpredictability ruled out New York and Philadelphia. It would have been imprudent to risk destroying working relationships with the Johnson administration and Congress by mounting a campaign in the national capital. Cleveland, the other stop on the People to People tour, did not seem a big enough target, and no other northern city was particularly inviting.[93]

Yet SCLC's decision represented more than a process of elimination. For many reasons, King was particularly attracted to Chicago. He had always been well received there. The July 1965 stop had been triumphant. King was, according to one of the Chicago coordinators of his visit, "quite impressed" by the public response as well as the planning and execution of the three-day series of events. King could also recall his speech to seventy-five thousand cheering admirers at the 1964 Illinois Rally for Civil Rights held in Soldier Field, after which he had told the sponsors that "very seldom, if ever, have I had a more inspiring afternoon." King recognized the potential resources which his new allies commanded, for CCCO represented the strongest indigenous civil rights movement in the North. He had good friends in Chicago, too. He loved to listen to the beautiful voice of Mahalia Jackson, and he had benefited from the counsel and friendship of the Chicago attorney Chauncey Eskridge. Moreover, Chicago had two other appealing inter-related attributes. Unlike most mayors, Chicago's Richard Daley possessed the power—if properly channeled—to change social conditions in the city. And from King's perspective, Daley's power needed to be fully tapped, for he regarded Chicago as America's most segregated big city. The enormity of Chicago's race problems only further whetted his desire to work there. Attacking the northern capital of segregation would make for better drama, a quality whose importance King never underestimated. Furthermore, King was enticed by CCCO's urgent invitation. Throughout the month of August Raby had conferred with the SCLC hierarchy about SCLC's return to Chicago, and in late August he had traveled to Atlanta for negotiations. It had always been SCLC's policy to work only in communities where the local protest leadership invited it. This had been the case with SCLC's campaigns in Albany, Georgia, in 1962, Birmingham, Alabama, in 1963, St. Augustine, Florida, in 1964, and now it would be the case with SCLC's Chicago initiative in 1965.[94]

That James Bevel, SCLC's director of direct action, had moved on his own to Chicago was another factor—the critical factor, according to some civil rights insiders—propelling SCLC to the Windy City. Regarded as an eccentric but indisputable civil rights genius, Bevel had always been in the vanguard of the black freedom struggle. Born in Itta Bena, Mississippi, in 1936, Bevel had grown up shuttling between rural Mississippi and Cleveland, Ohio. Aspiring to the ministry, he went to the American Baptist Seminary in Nashville, Tennessee, where he emerged as a campus leader and then a protest leader in the city's burgeoning civil rights movement. A devout disciple of nonviolence, Bevel became a charter member of SNCC before joining SCLC in 1962. He soon fashioned an impressive reputation as an inspiring orator, a brilliant civil rights strategist (playing leading roles in SCLC's Birmingham and Selma campaigns), and one of the few people who could sway King's decisions.[95]

After the Selma drive, Bevel advocated a national boycott of Alabama, but his interests soon turned elsewhere. Like King—indeed, even earlier—Bevel believed that the movement had to "come up with a way by which nonviolence can be applied to this situation in these northern cities, because if people don't have adequate tools to solve a problem, they are going to get off on disorder." Bevel had helped quell the Rochester and Philadelphia riots of 1964, but he did not relish the fireman role. "Revolutionaries," he stated, "do not go around putting down riots." And so he began discussions regarding a position with the West Side Christian Parish (WSCP), a Chicago inner-city outreach ministry with a largely white staff. As a teenager in Cleveland, Bevel had been impressed with the work of a sister ministry of the WSCP. The Cleveland parish, Bevel remembered, "had done some innovative work in trying to find out how to motivate inner-city people to real Christianity in light of the fact that the Europeans who built the inner city were moving out."[96]

Bevel liked what he knew about the work of the West Side Christian Parish as well. Since the early 1960s, the WSCP, thanks largely to the efforts of its young white youth organizer, David Jehnsen, had developed close links to the southern movement and had gradually become part of the civil rights network. In 1962 it had sent three of its members to Albany, Georgia, in response to King's call for northern witnesses in that civil rights campaign. In 1965 it had dispatched workers to Alabama to assist with various movement projects.[97]

The West Side Christian Parish desperately sought Bevel. For some time, the parish had been troubled by uncertainty about its role and efficacy. The prospect of Bevel joining its ranks dazzled the WSCP staff, particularly its executive director, Robert Mueller. The dynamic Bevel seemed the perfect prescription to cure its ills. No one in America seemed better equipped to galvanize a southern-style movement in a northern city.[98]

In addition, Bevel's wife, Diane Nash Bevel, also a leading civil rights activist, was a native Chicagoan, and Bevel's close friend Bernard La-Fayette had been working on the West Side for over a year. These personal connections helped make the WSCP's overtures virtually irresistible. LaFayette, also a graduate of the American Baptist Seminary in Nashville, a former SNCC activist, and already a legendary figure in civil rights circles, had come to Chicago at the urging of the American Friends Service Committee, to bring the principles of nonviolent social change to the northern ghetto. (Bevel himself had directed a Chicago workshop on nonviolence in 1964 and had made rounds as a speaker in the area for the AFSC, which had a long but unheralded history of civil rights work throughout the North and the South.) In the past LaFayette and Bevel had been close collaborators. They had helped direct the Nashville movement, had been fellow freedom riders, had served time in Mississippi's Parchman Penitentiary together, and when Bevel had been in the midst of directing the Selma protests, he had summoned his friend from Chicago to assist him. LaFayette, Bevel later commented, was "the only other person I knew who really knew nonviolence as a science." To entice LaFayette to come south, Bevel agreed that once the Selma campaign was over, he would "come to Chicago" and help "mount a nonviolent movement." LaFayette looked forward to his friend's entrance onto the Chicago scene, because Bevel was already a guiding influence for a cadre of organizers committed to nonviolence, some of whom, like David Jehnsen, worked for the West Side Christian Parish. This informal group operated largely independently of CCCO as it cultivated a West Side movement.[99]

The impact of Bevel's presence in Chicago on SCLC's northern decisions cannot be underestimated. At the SCLC emergency session in Atlanta, Bevel was a most vocal advocate of an SCLC northern thrust. To an extent, his verbal advocacy was unnecessary; in his eyes SCLC's decision had been determined the minute he had accepted a post with the WSCP. "If I'm working in Chicago, it means that SCLC is working in Chicago," he later remarked.[100]

On September 1, 1965, Andrew Young announced to reporters that SCLC had selected Chicago as its first northern target. The fates of SCLC and Chicago had now become linked. The task ahead was daunting. "The only solution to breaking down the infamous wall of segregation in Chicago rests in our being able to mobilize the white and black communities into a massive nonviolent movement," King insisted. With their newly fashioned alliance, SCLC and Chicago activists were optimistic about the future. SCLC brought charisma, talent, and an impressive record of success to a Chicago movement that had struggled valiantly, if not triumphantly, for racial justice. It now remained to be seen if SCLC's magic would work in the North.[101]

Mobilizing the City

2

In early January 1966, Martin Luther King alerted Chicagoans that the new year would be extraordinary. After a month's absence King returned to the midwestern city for three days packed with activity. He huddled with advisers to refine a battle plan for the Chicago civil rights campaign, briefed Coordinating Council of Community Organizations delegates on the plan, and then presented it to an eager press. On January 8 King left Chicago, but eleven days later he was back to reiterate his pledge to intensify the SCLC-CCCO civil rights drive. "I am here to get things started," he declared.[1]

Though not a precise program, the "Chicago Plan" did broadly suggest how King and his colleagues would guide the Chicago campaign.[2] Their mission was to end the city's sprawling slums, a far more ambitious endeavor than CCCO's long campaign to remove Benjamin Willis and to desegregate the city's public schools. Nevertheless they believed their goal attainable. If the Chicago movement could mobilize the black community and forge a "coalition of conscience" backed by Chicagoans of good will, it could spur the city to eliminate its ghettoes. Their work would, then, like the Birmingham and Selma campaigns, have national implications and reverberate across the country. "If we can break the backbone of discrimination in Chicago, we can do it in all the cities in the country," King noted.[3]

King and his advisers envisioned a three-phase battle plan. Until February the movement would concentrate on educating and organizing potential recruits for a nonviolent army. Then specific, highly focused demonstrations designed to "reveal the agents of exploitation and paint the portrait" of ghetto evils would begin. In May, with the warming weather, the movement would embark on "massive" protests. Neither King nor his advisers were embarrassed that they could not yet pinpoint the exact form direct action would take. Others might find such imprecision maddening, but veterans of the southern movement valued flexibility and had great faith that effective tactics would emerge naturally. About one thing they were certain: Chicago was on the verge of a year of civil rights insurgency unlike any other it had yet witnessed.[4]

King stretched the truth when he declared that he had returned to start the Chicago movement, for his staff had been laying the groundwork for the campaign for the past few months. Under the direction of James Bevel, a small interracial SCLC team had opened its headquarters in September in the heart of Chicago's West Side ghetto at the Warren Avenue Congregational Church.[5] As so often happened in the civil rights movement, organizational lines blended. Bevel, recently appointed program director for the West Side Christian Parish, was now also the head of SCLC's Chicago project. Consequently much of the parish's staff merged with SCLC's staff under Bevel's leadership. Bernard LaFayette's AFSC Urban Affairs contingent also became part of this combined effort. That LaFayette's wife, Colia Liddel LaFayette, herself a southern civil rights veteran, served as a staff member of the West Side Christian Parish exemplified the extensive cooperation among SCLC, WSCP, and AFSC.[6]

For some of Bevel's SCLC team the Chicago crusade was a homecoming. Jimmy Wilson and Suzi Hill were young Chicago natives who had joined SCLC for the Selma campaign. Hill had been so stirred by events in Selma that she had left "right in the middle of a class" at her junior college to join the Selma to Montgomery march. Wilson had been sent to Selma by the West Side Christian Parish and now returned to familiar organizing turf. Another member of the SCLC vanguard, Jimmy Collier, had Chicago ties as well. Southern-born, Collier had come to Chicago for college and was soon working with West Side organizers. He too was drawn south by the Selma crisis. There this inspiring singer and guitar player joined SCLC's field staff, and he too became a logical selection for SCLC's Chicago advance team.[7]

Not everyone in SCLC's vanguard found the transition from south to north so easy. When Dorothy Wright came to Chicago from Alabama, she was a "movement baby," only eighteen years old. SCLC's reception in Chicago unnerved her. Too many prominent black Chicagoans, she later noted sadly, "told us to go back down south where we came from." SCLC's Chicago campaign also vaulted James Orange, at twenty-two a senior member of the advance team, into an unfamiliar world. A hulking, charismatic man who had almost played professional football, Orange—born and raised in Birmingham, Alabama, where he became a valued staffer during SCLC's 1963 campaign—had spent little time outside the South. He found Chicago far different from the southern cities and towns that he had helped SCLC organize.[8]

Chicago was gargantuan; it dwarfed the South's largest cities in virtually every way. Its buildings were taller, its pace of life faster, and, above all, its inhabitants more numerous. With over three million people packed into an area five miles wide and stretching more than twenty miles from north to south, Chicago had ten times as many residents as Birmingham and one hundred times as many as Selma. Another three and a half million people lived in suburbs ringing the central city. No southern city, moreover, possessed such a diverse population. Throngs of blacks, Poles, Czechs, Irish, Italians—indeed, representatives from almost every ethnic group—had flocked to Chicago in search of a better life. For most migrants the search was fruitful. They found well-paying jobs in this financial, marketing, and manufacturing dynamo, which in the 1960s accounted for an extraordinary five percent of the nation's gross national product.[9]

More blacks had poured into Chicago than any other ethnic group. In 1900 only thirty thousand blacks lived in Chicago. But with the coming of World War I, tens of thousands of blacks, in pursuit of work and freedom, journeyed up the Mississippi River Valley to the midwestern city. This migration tapered off during the Depression, but World War II triggered another immense influx. By 1965, as Chicago's black population approached one million and accounted for almost a third of the city's residents, more blacks lived there than in the entire state of Mississippi.[10]

The sweeping migration transformed black Chicago, making it a capital of black America. The city became a wellspring for cultural innovations and a center for great black business enterprises and institutions, including Johnson Products (manufacturers of grooming accessories), Johnson publications (publisher of *Ebony* magazine), Provident hospital, and the *Chicago Defender*, the city's black daily newspaper. Good jobs propelled many blacks into the rapidly growing category of black homeowners. According to one report, by 1960 over thirty percent of black Chicagoans had climbed into the middle class.[11]

Most blacks, however, did not find Chicago a land of milk and honey. Although Chicago lacked, as one historian has noted, a full-fledged "public ideology of racial dominance" and offered far more opportunities to blacks than were available in the South, black Chicagoans nevertheless had to compete against whites for jobs, housing, and other valued but limited resources. This fierce contest ensured that race relations in Chicago were volatile and, as its 1919 race riot, one of the country's worst, attested, potentially explosive. While blacks could advance through this competition, it was a contest stacked in favor of whites. Though white manufacturers and entrepreneurs in the early 1900s tried to promote their own interests by pitting black workers against white workers, white solidarity on race issues was the more enduring trend through the 1960s. The result was the unofficial but effective containment of black Chicagoans. A job ceiling, which persisted despite fair employment legislation and postwar prosperity, limited occupational possibilities for blacks, thus generating a distinct class structure tilted heavily toward semi-skilled laborers and correspondingly shaping a distinct social outlook for black Chicago. Along with economic discrimination came unequal housing opportunities. Unlike European immigrants, blacks were forced to live among themselves. So severe was the residential separation between blacks and whites that Bill Berry of the Chicago Urban League did not exaggerate when in the late 1950s he condemned Chicago as America's most segregated large city.[12]

By 1965, roughly seven hundred thousand black Chicagoans, hemmed in by housing and job barriers, lived in two expanding slum ghettoes, one on the South Side holding more than four hundred thousand blacks and another on the West Side housing a quarter of a million more. Within these ghettoes were some of America's poorest neighborhoods, communities where unemployment and underemployment marked the lives of most adults. Many lived in crowded, dilapidated apartments or equally dismal, impersonal public housing projects like the two-mile stretch on the South Side of the sixteen-story Robert Taylor homes. James Orange, for one, "had never seen those types of conditions."[13]

SCLC staffers concentrated their efforts on the West Side ghetto.

With their headquarters in East Garfield Park, such a focus made good sense. In addition, by targeting the West Side, SCLC's staff could profit from the experience of Bernard LaFayette, who not long after coming to Chicago had been working out of the American Friends Service Committee's Project House in East Garfield Park. Resourceful, insightful, and serene—so much so that James Farmer had dubbed him "Little Gandhi" when they were jailed together during the Freedom Rides of 1961—LaFayette had been a groundbreaker for more than one important civil rights campaign. As a SNCC organizer in 1963 LaFayette, along with his wife, had planted the seeds for the Selma movement. When he moved to Chicago, he represented the vanguard of the southern movement heading north.[14]

LaFayette was a careful, deliberate organizer. Although he possessed northern urban roots—and had even joined a gang in Philadelphia for a time—he wanted a deep understanding of the dynamics of Chicago's West Side before jumping into action. In 1965 he came upon a potentially promising cause. Alerted to the pervasiveness of lead paint in the old and declining West Side buildings, LaFayette encouraged high school students to begin a testing program so that they could eventually convince the Chicago city government of the magnitude of the lead poisoning problem. Though hardly a headline-attracting initiative, this innovative campaign nonetheless won LaFayette and his colleagues much respect. Equally important was its impact on the local residents. "[W]e helped people," LaFayette later recalled, "to recognize their own resources and begin to use these resources effectively to bring about some changes, and therefore they began to have a greater appreciation for themselves and some hope that things [could] be done." Bevel and his staff benefited from such groundwork.[15]

Strategic factors also dictated a West Side emphasis. Unlike the older South Side Black Belt, the extensive West Side ghetto was a recent development. There had been small clusters of blacks on the West Side for years, but until the 1950s the West Side communities of North Lawndale and East Garfield Park had been filled with whites typically living in modest but comfortable apartments. Many of North Lawndale's residents were Jewish, while East Garfield Park's population was more ethnically diverse. As thousands of blacks, many of them recent migrants, poured into the region, the whites—relatively few of whom were homeowners—rapidly left without, interestingly, putting up the fight that marked racial transition on the South Side. Some of the new residents lived in "neat, well-kept homes on shaded streets" and were homeowners, but poverty followed most blacks to the West Side. In the past, black migrants had often secured a decent living with modest-paying, semi-skilled industrial jobs, but by the mid-1950s Chicago's manufacturing base was eroding. This trend exacerbated hardship in lower-class communities, and on the West Side nearly a quarter of the men were out of work and over twenty percent of the households earned incomes that placed them below the poverty line. The black influx also prompted a decline in the quality of housing stock in North Lawndale and East Garfield Park, as landlords subdivided larger accommodations and often suspended routine maintenance on their properties. City services to changing neighborhoods declined as well. "Strewn glass crunches underfoot. The curbs are piled with broken-down autos. In the old buildings, the rats grow so vicious they run the cats out of business," was how one reporter described the worst of the West Side. On top of this, North Lawndale and East Garfield Park lacked the established voluntary associations, responsive political representation (many ward officials were absentee whites), and strong sense of community so essential to easing the crushing effects of deprivation.[16]

By focusing on the West Side SCLC could thus meet an important social need and not have to worry about encroaching on the turf of too many entrenched race advancement groups. The South Side had been the traditional preserve of the Chicago NAACP and Urban League. When CCCO opened up a regular headquarters, it was located on 47th Street on the South Side. Moreover, the West Side Federation, a new group with much promise, guided by a black Baptist minister, the Reverend Shelvin Hall, a Jewish community organizer, Lew Kreinberg, and a white Catholic priest, Father Daniel Mallette, welcomed a West Side movement; indeed, the West Side Federation, in principle a coordinating body for West Side organizations, was born out of the efforts to transport West Side blacks to the 1964 Soldier Field civil rights rally featuring Martin Luther King. Closer to home, the East Garfield Park Community Organization, one of the few truly activist local groups, also desired a larger movement. William Briggs, the young white pastor of the Warren Avenue Congregational Church, was one of its leading spirits.[17]

The strong southern orientation of these communities also appealed to movement veterans. "We had a lot of experience dealing with black Mississippians," Bernard LaFayette would later point out, "and here they were transported north." And while the direct flow of southern migrants to Chicago had tapered off by the 1960s, James Bevel still felt "right at home" on the West Side: it was "very much Mississippi in terms of the ethos of the black people—church and life." This southern background would likely make West Side residents more receptive to the entreaties of Christian-inspired civil rights crusaders.[18]

A West Side thrust also fixed SCLC squarely within the general tide toward community organizing. Bevel concurred with the complaints of Lawrence Landry and other activists that the established Chicago civil rights movement had not reached out enough to the common people. Bevel criticized CCCO, which included only a few community organizations, for being "controlled . . . by middle class people" and thus alienating "those poor people who do come in contact with it." In Bevel's view, a West Side mobilized for racial justice would go a long way toward overcoming the Chicago civil rights movement's greatest weakness: its lack of ties to ghetto dwellers.[19]

Though he had no master plan for the Chicago campaign, Bevel remained unruffled. "[W]e'll get good education and housing here in Chicago . . . I don't know how just yet. I don't get hung up on application," he told reporters. Bevel and SCLC had conquered Birmingham and Selma, and they were confident they could conquer Chicago. Bevel envisioned a nonviolent army of at least forty thousand. "It'll make a brand new city out of Chicago," he predicted.[20]

In late September Bevel took the first steps toward devising a formal program of action by holding a five-day retreat for nearly a hundred civil rights sympathizers at Pleasant Valley Farm in rural Aurora, Illinois. "We sang together, prayed together, but mostly we talked," Bevel noted. "We talked about who we are, what we are doing." Bevel next sponsored open, twice-weekly Wider Community Staff meetings, designed to promote greater understanding of the problems afflicting black Chicago and, most important for the moment, staff cooperation and togetherness. "Only if we are willing," Bevel insisted, "to accept truth and love as the basis upon which we as a staff will function can we hope to create a loving community within the city."[21]

The Wider Community Staff meetings attracted a potpourri of activists, ranging from young SCLC field organizers to Students for a Democratic Society (SDS) leaders like Rennie Davis to veteran Chicago civil rights insurgents, including Al Raby. To at least one observer, the incipient coalition emerging from these sessions constituted "the most important political force for social change developing in the country." The activists often listened to talks by experts on Chicago politics and social conditions and then exchanged opinions in exciting free-for-alls about how the Chicago movement should proceed.[22]

Bevel, however, remained the dominant figure. A spellbinding speaker, a religious radical, a man dedicated to ushering in a new age (he once described himself as having been "called out of the Isaiah mold"), he was an elemental charismatic leader. In Chicago he exchanged his customary denim overalls for corduroy suits, but the perpetually idiosyncratic black activist still differentiated himself by wearing his trademark yarmulke atop his shaven head and by carrying Leo Tolstoy's *What Then Must We Do?* "Bevel had enormous influence and prestige over other people in these meetings," one activist recalled. "We thought he was a genius," an SCLC staffer said. "[I]t always seemed that Bevel was the one who got up and drew the diagrams on the blackboard and had all these new insights and ideas," remembered another civil rights worker. "He was a real philosopher."[23]

Bevel's ascendancy also well characterized SCLC's style of leadership. While SCLC leaders encouraged group involvement, they did not endorse the concept of participatory democracy so central, for a time, to SNCC and SDS. SCLC shunned the notion that natural leaders such as Bevel or, for that matter, Martin Luther King should subsume themselves into the larger pack. There was no doubt that the West Side initiative was Bevel's operation and that Bevel was the preeminent spokesperson for West Side activists.[24]

As the fall of 1965 rolled on, some activists, despairing of too much "wheelspinning," became frustrated that these loose, unstructured staff sessions did not produce a comprehensive, tidy plan of action for the Chicago movement. These meetings, moreover, never effected a truly unified alliance of all the participating organizations. Too many groups were reluctant to forsake their individual programs for a larger mission.[25] Nonetheless, the meetings presented welcome free space for creative discussion in which problems were freshly diagnosed and hidden relationships exposed. For one activist, the intellectual effervescence was so inspiring that she claimed she would never miss a meeting. With time, civil rights staffers increasingly recognized that there "were strong relationships between what previously seemed like dozens of separate problems." They now glimpsed a "systematic institutionalized system which created and perpetrates slums and poverty."[26]

Not surprisingly, this consensus dovetailed with Bevel's thinking. Over the previous few months Bevel had irked many Chicago civil rights leaders by belittling their focus on Superintendent Willis. In August, Al Raby and CCCO leaders had consulted with SCLC's Walter Fauntroy about using King and SCLC to spearhead a new campaign against Willis and segregated education. But Bevel, like other West Side activists, hardly considered Willis the issue around which a mass movement should be built. "Concentrating too much on Willis is like knocking off the chiefs instead of educating the Indians," Bevel asserted. "Down South we didn't say, 'Get rid of Jim Clark.' We said, 'Let's us vote.'" Bevel, moreover, seemed less concerned about the direct pursuit of integration than many CCCO representatives had been. The energetic SCLC lieutenant envisioned a sweeping movement to end slums, to dismantle the totality of segregation and inequality that shackled black Chicago.[27]

While Chicago activists searched for an effective strategy to "end slums," which became their rallying cry, they had no doubt that it would be rooted in nonviolence. King and his lieutenants passionately professed the tactic's universal efficacy. "Nonviolence is potent, it is a science," Bevel declared. "And if you are going to get anything done it is because you used nonviolence." Bevel made sure that his staff was committed to nonviolence (though few would ever develop Bevel's intense devotion to this way of life), and that wider staff meetings grounded other Chicago activists in nonviolent principles. Bevel did not see himself guiding a civil rights movement; he was a leader of something much broader, even more universal, "a nonviolent movement."[28]

Bevel and his followers also embarked on preliminary steps to organize black Chicago. They conducted workshops to educate local residents. They staged rallies in the Near North Side, Near West Side, Oakland, and East Garfield Park communities. Bevel, as usual, pumped up the crowds with provocative speeches. "The people of this community have to decide: are they going to make this community or is [it] going to make them?" he thundered.[29]

Bevel's staff also started long-term projects. Some activists sought to forge links beyond the black community. Eric Kindberg, an experienced white SCLC organizer, reached out to poor white Chicagoans. Lynn Adler, a white woman staffer, teamed with Louis Andrades and Felix Valluena to garner support from Chicago's large Spanish-speaking community. Still, the focus remained on Chicago's blacks. Mindful of how important young blacks had been during SCLC's Birmingham and Selma campaigns, Jimmy Wilson and Dorothy Wright organized students in Chicago schools. James Orange, meanwhile, approached the city's powerful gangs to persuade them to back the nonviolent crusade. Charles Love worked with community groups on the Near North Side so that residents in that smaller black enclave were not neglected. At the same time, West Side activists began the tiring and underappreciated work of door-to-door canvassing, which was essential for the realization of Bevel's dream of a huge nonviolent army. The movement, one staffer declared optimistically, was "developing a stronghold at the grass roots level. People are responding with tremendous enthusiasm. And they are learning about their rights and responsibilities." SCLC's initiative also grabbed the attention of activists across the country. "We in other cities," James Farmer of CORE declared, "have our eyes on Chicago, watching your experiment."[30]

While the Bevel-supervised organizing efforts whipped up enthusiasm, they also rankled some veteran Chicago civil rights activists. To a striking degree Bevel proceeded as if no one else had ever agitated for racial justice in Chicago before. As Al Pitcher, an influential CCCO coordinator, later remarked, to Bevel, CCCO "did not exist, it was nothing, it would become nothing, and therefore it was not worth making into something." Bevel's disregard for existing civil rights efforts triggered the rise of tension between himself and CCCO's head, Al Raby. By nature a conciliator, a coalition builder, Raby—whom Ralph Abernathy later called "perhaps the best local leader [SCLC] worked with during those years"—sought to unite Chicago's civil rights forces around a concrete plan of action. In the fall, he tried to reach out to Bevel's West Side efforts by attending Wider Community Staff meetings, but Bevel favored a more amorphous battle plan and remained focused on cultivating a West Side movement. "In your training program, once people get information, they will develop strategy," Bevel insisted. "In the process of developing people, a strategy will evolve and tell you what to do."[31]

This tension might have been reduced had Martin Luther King or Andrew Young been in Chicago more often in the fall. King especially was a unifying force. He left an indelible imprint on many of the Chicago activists, who were struck by his natural reasonableness, genuine humility, and deep spirituality. King, however, still had a spate of previously scheduled commitments to fulfill, including a European trip. He was in Chicago for only three days during the last three months of 1965. Young—the well-educated son of an affluent New Orleans dentist—whose task was often to smooth over potential strains within civil rights coalitions in which SCLC worked, came to Chicago more often, but he never stayed for long stretches of time.[32]

Only on one weekend in early October did SCLC activists, CCCO leaders, and Chicago civil rights advocates meet en masse to cement their alliance and discuss future plans. Gathered for a retreat outside Lake Geneva in Wisconsin, they learned from workshops, sang movement songs led by Jimmy Collier, and listened to speeches, including a riveting talk by King himself. King stressed the need for a black and white alliance and the importance of victory in Chicago. "If we can break the system in Chicago, it can be broken any place in the country," he declared. He also warned that a successful movement in the North would require much hard work and skill. "There will be fewer overt acts to aid us here; naive targets such as the Jim Clarks and George Wallaces will be harder to find and use as symbols." Yet King was fundamentally optimistic. "There are giants in the land, but we can possess the land of freedom . . . Let us be dissatisfied with things as they are. Then, in some bright future, we will say with a cosmic past tense, 'Deep in my heart, I *did* believe, we *would* overcome.'"[33]

The SCLC spirit—with its deep faith in the power of nonviolence and its grand vision of a new age of mutual respect and understanding—stirred many Chicago activists. The Chicago civil rights movement had relied on nonviolent direct action, but it was certainly not committed to nonviolence as a way of life and as a broad strategy of social change to the extent that King, Bevel, and other SCLC leaders were. SCLC, said John McDermott of the Chicago Catholic Interracial Council, was offering "a theology and philosophy which is new to us. This will require a great deal of training on our part." "We must rely on SCLC to give us a new understanding for organization to create a new society," declared Herbert Fisher, a veteran CCCO delegate from the Chatham–Avalon Park Community Council. While McDermott, Fisher, and others anticipated valuable results from their association with SCLC, they still knew that in spite of all the enthusiasm, the retreat was fundamentally more a get-together and a revival than a planning session for a full-scale civil rights campaign. CCCO representatives now could not even hope that

SCLC had a secret "blueprint to liberate Chicago." Without an overall plan of action to set goals and delegate responsibilities, internal troubles hampered the Chicago initiative throughout November and December.[34]

After a whirl of activity in September and October, the SCLC staff, which one activist described as having earlier responded "to each other much like the French respond to people in their own family," had become dispirited and "frustrated with" their "formidable task." "[M]orale" had "hit a new low," according to Mary Lou Finley, Bevel's assistant at the West Side Christian Parish, and intra-staff tensions had mushroomed. A "series of personal problems" had surfaced that "nearly rent the staff asunder." Three or four were even "talking about going back to the tranquility of being a civil rights worker in Alabama." Bevel seemed strangely ineffectual in soothing his troubled troops. Though a brilliant strategist and an inspiring speaker, Bevel was not a "nurturer," a skilled trustee of his troops' personal and psychological needs.[35]

Longtime Chicago civil rights activists were anxious as well. They agreed on the importance of bringing the West Side into the movement and they tried to relate their programs to the new force in the civil rights arena. The Chicago chapter of ESCRU, for instance, recognized that it had to determine "how to 'act' with CCCO and SCLC." Some civil rights sympathizers were not, however, satisfied with SCLC's outreach or its fluid, unsystematic modus operandi. Bevel spoke at many gatherings during the fall of 1965, but he did not always attend sessions that needed his presence. Bevel's unexpected absence at a gathering of church-based, inner-city development staff in mid-November, for example, provoked an outpouring of questions and concern. Disappointed by SCLC's seeming nonchalance regarding this meeting with experienced urban workers, one of the participants in the session frankly asked how SCLC was gaining "technical know-how and especially political know-how." A perturbed William Robinson, a staff member for the Church Federation of Greater Chicago, CCCO's treasurer, and a former Republican state legislator, flatly stated, "The Movement must make up its mind if Chicago is really to be one of the demonstration centers for the urban North." CCCO members, SCLC's erstwhile partners, also grew increasingly alarmed at Bevel's neglect of and, at times, disdain for them. At the November CCCO meeting, one delegate remarked that the West Side activists "seem to bypass CCCO and make unilateral decisions which could lead to dissension."[36]

Partly to allay fears that the Chicago SCLC field staff had mounted its own independent venture, movement leaders in early January formalized the SCLC-CCCO alliance. Ever since CCCO's first steering committee meeting in September after SCLC announced it was heading north, Chicago activists had mulled over, as Bernard LaFayette put it, "what decision-making body will be formed, who will give direction to the movement, and who will be the spokesman for the movement." The Chicago Freedom Movement, it was now agreed, would be the name of the combined project. King and Raby were appointed co-chairmen and a Chicago Freedom Movement advisory committee was established, though its structure remained murky. Despite this stride toward coordination, some Chicago civil rights advocates had found the fall of 1965 unsettling. They had welcomed SCLC as a savior, but now they began to share the doubts of one civil rights sympathizer who questioned whether SCLC knew "how to operate in the urban north." He had become tired, he grumbled, of "singing evangelistic songs."[37]

Like surges of adrenaline, King's frequent 1966 visits energized the Chicago Freedom Movement. Shortly after presenting the Chicago Plan, King directed his lieutenants to find him suitable living quarters in the city. After some difficulty, they leased an apartment at 1550 South Hamlin Avenue in North Lawndale, nearly two miles to the southwest of the Warren Avenue Congregational Church, to widen and to bolster SCLC's West Side organizing efforts.[38] Upon learning the identity of his new tenant, the apartment's owner spruced up the shabby place. Still, the ninety-dollar-a-month flat was hardly a couple's dream when, in late January, King and his wife moved in. Coretta King was startled by the unlocked front door, the ground-level dirt floor, and the "overpowering" smell of urine as she made her way to their new third-floor apartment. Though not accustomed to squalor, Martin Luther King nevertheless believed his ghetto witness essential to maintain. "I have to be right here with the people," King said. "I can learn more about the situation by being here with those who live and suffer here."[39]

Though King only stayed at his new home part time (he generally spent from Wednesday to Saturday in Chicago before flying back to Atlanta to conduct Sunday services at the Ebenezer Baptist Church), it became a "sort of a revolutionary headquarters," according to one observer: "People swarm in and out. [King] has to hide because so many people come in. Little kids come in just to look at him." Even one of the West Side's most notorious gangs, the Vice Lords, paid him a visit. King's willingness to live in North Lawndale inspired many of Chicago's downtrodden and socially concerned. "I am happy that you are here in Chicago, you are really doing a wonderful job, Rev. King," declared one admirer. "Everyone in the Lawndale Dist. that I've talk[ed] to are still thanking the day you came to our aid," a West Side resident wrote to King. The SCLC chief was pleased by his reception. "It meant so much to the area where I am living. It gave them a big lift," he confided to his advisers. The dramatic move, King knew, also meant much to the Chicago campaign. It heartened many activists who desired action and it focused the attention of the local and national media on the Chicago movement.[40]

King did not simply receive guests at his new flat. When he could, he took to the streets to inspect conditions on the West Side. On one occasion, accompanied by Raby and the Reverend Joseph Lowery, an SCLC officer, King toured a crowded, decrepit apartment building, then visited Marshall High School, where students cheered his arrival, and later slipped into a local billiard hall to shoot pool and to talk with the regulars. This final outing might have offended the truly righteous, but, as Don Rose, an activist with expertise in public relations, commented, it would "humanize him" in a northern urban, lower-class community. King, Rose noted, thoroughly "understood" the importance of projecting an appropriate image. King's reception on Chicago's West Side proved what public opinion surveys indicated: that King was a national black leader whose popularity surmounted regional and class boundaries.[41]

In late February King garnered even more publicity for the Chicago movement. After learning about the plight of a sick baby in a run-down apartment building lacking heat, King and his advisers decided to assume "trusteeship" of the structure. On February 23, SCLC, CCCO, and the West Side Federation seized the building at 1321 South Homan Avenue, not far from King's Lawndale apartment. Cameras flashed as King, Raby, and other activists, dressed in work clothes, grabbed shovels and brooms and began cleaning the decrepit building. When asked about the legality of the takeover, King expanded upon the distinction between moral and immoral law that he had made so famous with his "Letter from a Birmingham Jail." "I won't say that this is illegal, but I would call it supralegal," he argued. "The moral question is far more important than the legal one."[42]

With the takeover, King and his advisers hoped to corner a greedy slumlord. They were disappointed to learn that the owner of the building, John Bender, was an ailing, financially strapped white octogenarian. After hearing about King's action, Bender was initially contrite. "I think King is right. I think his intentions are right, and in his place, I'd do the same thing," he told the press. Later, however, Bender took the "trustees" to court for an illegal seizure. Many Chicagoans rallied behind the old man. Yet in the controversy King and his associates never lost sight of the essential fact that no matter how much Bender deviated from the conventional image of a slumlord, the residents of 1321 South Homan still suffered.[43]

The Townes family, residents of the disputed building, exemplified how the ghetto entrapped even diligent, striving blacks. Following a well-worn path, R. V. Townes had migrated to Chicago from Mississippi in 1954. Two years later he married Rosie, another Mississippi native. In their quest for decent housing, R.V., Rosie, and their growing family—by 1966 there were seven children—moved from one apartment to another before settling at 1321 South Homan. A good home seemed the least that they deserved. R.V. had held the same job in a printing plant for eleven straight years and brought home $100 a week, and Rosie, a hard worker, kept the apartment as clean as she could. But they soon discovered that their new residence was hardly an improvement. In the dead of a cold Chicago winter and with their youngest child very sick, their rat-infested apartment lacked heat. The Towneses applauded the Chicago Freedom Movement's takeover of their building. "How can people continue to care and make their children care about the property when they get no cooperation from the landlord or from people who are paid to see that buildings like this don't happen?" Mr. Townes asked. "A bad system makes good people bad."[44]

King and his fellow activists recognized that a single dramatic episode would not improve the lives of tens of thousands of people like the Towneses. Yet the well-publicized takeover catapulted slum conditions into wider discussion, just as King's move to Lawndale had. King, as West Side activists soon came to recognize, was the equivalent of a powerful "camera"; his very presence could serve to spotlight an injustice. The "trusteeship" also furthered the Chicago movement's foremost aim: organizing the disenchanted. The initiative underscored King's and the movement's desire to help. "I am so glad you came to Chicago to make a social revolution because—it was absolutely necessary to be done where city authorities talk and talk—but do not do nothing right," exclaimed one Chicagoan soon after the 1321 South Homan takeover. A Lawndale black thanked King "for bringing our condition to those, who are our civic officials" and for "helping to improve our lot." An enthusiastic, hopeful community would make the difficult task of organizing much easier.[45]

While King attracted headlines through his actions in Lawndale, Bevel and his expanding staff targeted East Garfield Park for the Chicago Freedom Movement's most vigorous organizing blitz. They had decided to create a union to end slums. The precise origin of the concept is unclear. "It grew out of the workshops" held that fall, Bevel later recalled, and thus it reflected a variety of influences: SDS's inner-city program; CORE's and SNCC's expanding commitment to organizing in black neighborhoods; the rapid rise of tenant organizations in the early 1960s, especially those in New York City; labor's intensified commitment to organizing impoverished urban areas; and the Alinsky tradition of strong community organizations. But even more fundamentally, it reflected Bevel's and King's conviction that the Chicago movement needed to mobilize ghetto dwellers and to create institutions that would endure after SCLC had left the city.[46]

While inspired by many sources, SCLC's organizing thrust had its own flavor. It certainly differed in spirit from the most important tradition of community organizing in Chicago. In the 1930s the shrewd and irrepressible Saul Alinsky had founded the Industrial Areas Foundation and had set out to organize the white ethnic, working-class population of the Back of the Yards community, which abutted Chicago's vast stockyards. In the late 1950s he embarked on his most famous initiative, The Woodlawn Organization, which Charles Silberman praised as "the most important and the most impressive experiment affecting Negroes anywhere in the United States." Highly pragmatic, the Alinsky method appealed, according to Silberman, to "the self-interest of the local residents and to their resentment and distrust of the outside world." Alinsky organizers sought to exploit grievances among residents within well-defined communities in order to build independent, indigenous organizations, empowered by a vibrant sense of community self-help and strong enough to effect meaningful social change.[47]

In the mid-1960s, Alinsky expressed interest in building a West Side counterpart to TWO, provided hundreds of thousands of dollars were committed to fund the project. Yet after months of internal debate, the

West Side Christian Parish elected not to turn to Alinsky and instead chose James Bevel as its program director. Bevel, according to the parish's director, Robert Mueller, represented a "prophetic" tradition of organizing. As an exponent of nonviolence and Christian redemption, Bevel, Mueller was convinced, would bring something much more majestic than a West Side TWO to Chicago. Bevel was not simply a community organizer but a manufacturer of movements infused with Christian brotherhood and a nonviolent spirit.[48]

Mueller had gauged Bevel accurately. "I was aware of Alinsky," Bevel observed later. In Bevel's eyes, Alinsky "simply taught how to, within the context of power, grab and struggle to get your share." Bevel desired to ground community organizing, which he did not associate with geographical divisions to the extent that Alinsky adherents did, in a nonviolent, holistic ethos. He believed that once people are taught "to be nonviolent, they become totally resourceful and intelligent and creative."[49]

An important slice of Chicago activists shared Bevel's perspective on the difference between Alinsky's approach and that of the nonviolent movement. "Alinsky was trying to organize people on the basis of their hate. And SCLC and the rest of us were trying to organize people on the basis of love," noted William Moyer, an AFSC field director. "Our idea of change is not rearranging the furniture and just mobilizing people around feeling," asserted David Jehnsen of the WSCP. "We were really loyal to traditional nonviolent strategy and use of nonviolent strategy to obtain our goals," Jimmy Collier of SCLC recalled. A nonviolent approach, for Collier and others, meant "leading by example," whereas with the Alinsky approach often "the ends could justify the means." "From the outside, the Southern Christian Leadership Conference and the Industrial Areas Foundation must seem like very similar organizations doing very similar things," another West Side activist remarked. "Unlike traditional Social Work approaches to the ghetto, both refuse to accept the dependency of the poor. Both seek to involve the poor in the struggle to solve their problems. Both use a highly organized door to door contact and block organization structure." But as Kale Williams, the executive secretary of the Chicago Regional Office of AFSC, asserted, the Alinsky approach lacked a larger vision. To be sure, he noted, it won victories, but it largely aimed to redistribute, to grab a bigger share for one group or a segment of a community. The southern civil rights movement, Williams believed, had developed a more desirable organizing philosophy, based on nonviolence and Christian love and with universal redemption as its fundamental goal.[50]

In late January 1966, more than seven hundred people, including Martin Luther King and James Bevel, streamed into the Church of the Brethren in East Garfield Park for a mass meeting to discuss a plan of action to attack community problems. What followed resembled the mass meetings of Montgomery, Birmingham, and Selma. Rousing singing led to calypso clapping before local residents began pinpointing ghetto problems. The crumbling of the black family was bemoaned, and overcrowded schools were denounced. A pregnant woman passionately recounted how she had been refused admission at a local hospital, one man scored banks for their failure to make loans to blacks, and many more complaints followed. Just when the time for airing grievances seemed to have passed, a woman jumped up, removed her coat, and declared that she was so "fed up" with slum life that she had decided to "pay no more rent" for miserable housing. The audience roared with approval. When King rose to offer a few concluding remarks, the crowd greeted him with a thunderous ovation. "An atmosphere of hope and defiance filled the air," reported a fascinated observer. King thanked the throng for coming out on a cold night and then pledged SCLC's assistance in their efforts to overcome slum conditions. He promised to help the community organize a union to end slums. "We must find ways to bargain for freedom."[51]

This mass meeting paved the way for an all-day People's Conference in early February at the Mozart Baptist Church, whose minister, Arthur D. Griffin, had earlier demonstrated against school segregation and was active in the West Side Federation. Hundreds of East Garfield Park residents participated in discussions and workshops which spotlighted the need for the community to gain control of its resources. "To get 450 neighborhood people to stay through an all-day meeting was an achievement," one rally organizer remarked. King himself capped the conference with a short address to an even larger audience.[52]

Yet however inspiring the revivalistic mass meeting was and however consciousness-raising the workshops were, West Side activists knew that a permanent structure was necessary if East Garfield Park residents were to seize their community's destiny from exploitative outsiders. From the People's Conference emerged the East Garfield Park Steering Committee, composed of full-time activists, local pastors, and community residents. The steering committee, spurred by its own subcommittees, in turn founded the East Garfield Park Union to End Slums (EGPUES), a federation consisting of SCLC and over twenty East Garfield Park organizations, including the East Garfield Park Community Organization.[53]

Chicago Freedom Movement activists envisioned great things for the EGPUES. It would be not simply a focused, large-scale tenant union but, rather, the backbone of a multidimensional attack on the forces perpetuating slums. In the first half of 1966, West Side organizers also sought, for instance, to establish a welfare union and to channel high school students into a student union.[54] Given its grand mission, that West Side activists devised an elaborate structure for the EGPUES, to be anchored by scores of block councils, is not surprising. Each multiple family building would elect a building steward and delegates to a block council. Each block would have its own council, headed by a chief steward. The steering committee divided East Garfield Park into eleven locals, with the intention that each local would have its own council (composed of the chief stewards) and elect its own officials. Such a structure was designed to ensure mass participation (West Side organizers stressed the power of numbers), community accountability (even homeowners were incorporated), and the development of indigenous leaders (a pressing theme in the West Side activists' strategy). Thus, while each building was capable of tackling immediate and localized problems, the entire union promoted a "large mass of informed and involved people who will be needed in those future actions which will be designed to lift up before the whole society the nature of the problem to be faced."[55]

Some local residents, particularly those who had staffed the East Garfield Park Community Organization, immediately embraced the union. "I started working for the union because I was so mad at my landlord," explained one resident, Minnie Dunlap. "The doorbell didn't work. The rooms hadn't been painted in three years. The mailboxes had no locks, and anyone coming in off the street could tamper with the mail." A. L. Collier, another early member of the East Garfield Park Community Organization, recognized the importance of community commitment to clean up the "junk" that neglect allowed to flourish in his neighborhood. If West Side blacks elected not to follow Martin Luther King, insisted one new member of the union, they would "wind up like a ball in tall grass. Lost."[56]

Aware, however, that joining the union would not be a natural response for many East Garfield Park residents, Bevel and his assistants launched a recruitment campaign based on the theme of exploitation. Flyers with the headline "We Are Being Robbed!" were passed out, and handouts detailing the extraction of community resources by outsiders were distributed. But the purpose of this message was not to incite anger; dramatizing the causes of slums was the goal. The leaders of the West Side movement insisted on the higher aims of their education efforts. They wanted to enlighten the people. They wanted, one West Side Christian Parish report said, to help local residents "to understand that the slum is not the result of the planned vindictiveness of a man or a class, but the logical product of a social order which places a higher value on economic power than it does on the development of human beings." They sought to teach West Side blacks "that the struggle to which they are being called is not merely the besting of an enemy, but the renewal and re-democratization of the social order itself."[57]

Charting a structure for the EGPUES proved to be much easier than implementing it. Most East Garfield Park residents did not rush to join the new union. West Side organizers found it particularly difficult to recruit men, especially those in the prime of their lives. "Very few men were willing to get involved," remembered Herman Jenkins, a resident of East Garfield Park who, inspired by Bernard LaFayette, devoted himself to organizing his community. "Most people who lived there perceived themselves as taking some type of risk [if they joined,] irregardless of how bad their circumstances may have been." Efforts to develop a sister union in Lawndale moved even more slowly. King's presence in North Lawndale was an asset, but the Lawndale staff was small, consisting of only four SCLC organizers and three unpaid volunteers.[58]

The slow progress disheartened many civil rights workers. It was so much easier to mobilize residents to attend a mass rally to listen to Bevel or King than to recruit members for the unions to end slums. Bevel's SCLC team now included over twenty field staffers. As had been true of those in the vanguard, many of the newcomers were Chicagoans who had joined SCLC after service in the local civil rights struggle. Earless Ross had marched as a member of Chicago CORE against Willis in the summer of 1965. Billy Hollins had landed with SCLC after tours of duty as a foot soldier in Dick Gregory–led demonstrations in Chicago.[59] Yet enthusiasm and optimism—and not experience—still constituted the animating power of the SCLC staff. The staff was embarked on an unfamiliar project for SCLC: developing urban community organizations. In the South, the church had often served as a focal point for organizing efforts. In impersonal Chicago, it was much harder to reach the people. "We were struggling and competing against a lot more distractions in the city," one SCLC field worker remembered. "We had to create our own communications network, so to speak." The occasional tips from professional organizers were helpful, but by and large civil rights workers had to learn how to organize by trial and error. "It is difficult to picture how laboriously day after day we knocked on doors, talked to people," Jimmy Collier of SCLC later recalled. "Months went by with nothing seemingly happening." Community organizing was a slow, halting process, certain to breed discouragement that was only intensified by the field workers' youthful impatience, their yearning for quick success, their lack of discipline (in some cases), and, ultimately, their unrealistic expectations. "I doubt if even top-notch professional organizers could have organized this community of 70,000 in just a few months," commented another SCLC staffer.[60]

In late March, West Side activists began to see at least a partial return on their investment of so much time and energy. Pressured by disgruntled tenants, the managers of more than thirty apartment buildings in the community, John Condor and Louis Costalis, agreed to answer their critics publicly. Six hundred residents packed a local church to "testify" against the landlords, with Martin Luther King looking on as if in final judgment. (King had earlier toured a rundown Condor and Costalis building, and the East Garfield Park Community Organization had been protesting Condor and Costalis practices for some time.) When Condor responded with "We're with you, believe it or not," the crowd shouted, "No, you ain't." The landlords then skillfully redirected some of the crowd's hostility toward the big bankers and mortgage lenders, as both pledged to cooperate with the tenants to make East Garfield Park a better place. King closed the session, reminding everyone that the larger system of slum exploitation and not two men, Condor and Costalis, had been on trial. Only by working together, King told his listeners, could they build a better world. "We have a power that nobody in Chicago can stop," King declared. "All you have to do is organize. By the thousands, we will get together. The people in City Hall will see a throng that no man can number and say, 'Where are they coming from?'"[61]

When Condor and Costalis failed to follow through on their pledges, complaints evolved into militant protests. With the backing of the EGPUES, local residents, sometimes nearly a hundred of them, picketed the landlords' office. Gaining no satisfaction, the tenants then staged a rent strike, a tactic that TWO, Chicago CORE, and other Chicago groups had employed in recent years and that the Harlem activist Jesse Gray had popularized in New York only a couple of years earlier. Finally the landlords agreed to negotiate. But as one of the EGPUES lawyers, Gilbert Cornfield, a specialist in labor law with close ties to labor progressives, noted, "the struggle had been so hard fought and the momentum of tenant involvement [was] so high that simply presenting a statement of grievances and protests no longer seemed appropriate." With the help of Cornfield and other labor attorneys, EGPUES decided to extend the "union" theme and secure a collective bargaining agreement. At first Condor and Costalis's lawyers balked. But after an unsuccessful attempt to procure a court injunction restraining the striking tenants, the landlords' lawyers surrendered.[62]

The signing of the collective bargaining agreement between Condor and Costalis and the East Garfield Park Union on July 13 helped write a new chapter in the history of tenant-landlord relations in America. In exchange for prompt and thorough maintenance of their apartments, the tenants agreed to follow a set of specific rules on tenant behavior. But if the landlords reneged on their promises, then the tenants had the right to withhold their rent. The contract thus restricted the hitherto virtually unlimited rights of landlords over tenants, signaling an important shift in the conception of private property.[63]

The Condor and Costalis agreement—a genuine victory for community organizing—boosted the Chicago movement's reputation on the West Side. The collective bargaining accord had another feature that pleased civil rights activists as well. The pact was not just a concrete accomplishment. It also promised to be a mechanism to promote ongoing community involvement in the union and, correspondingly, to develop local leadership. The agreement required monitoring. Tenants needed to fulfill their half of the pact, and the performance of Condor and Costalis needed to be closely watched. The potential of the developing unions seemed unlimited to some West Side organizers. Unions promised, according to Herman Jenkins, to become the "locomotive that could drive the efforts to end slums not only in Chicago but in other cities across the nation."[64]

* * *

Despite their commitment to ghetto organizing, King and his followers recognized that they could not just rely on the support of committed West Siders. They needed more allies, black and white. Unlike the leaders of SNCC and CORE in 1966, King still believed in the potential of a diverse coalition, not so much Bayard Rustin's dream of a powerful, progressive political coalition as a broad movement devoted to nonviolent social change. The Selma campaign had reaffirmed King's coalitionist tendencies, and these were shared by SCLC leaders like Andrew Young and James Bevel (even though he disparaged CCCO) and Chicago activists like Al Raby and Bill Berry. From the beginning of the Chicago campaign, King dreamed of a "convergence" of religious, labor, academic, and liberal supporters "under a nonviolent umbrella" to "demand a solution to Chicago's problems." Chicago civil rights forces, especially after January 1966, intensified efforts to build as broadly based a movement as possible.[65]

The Coordinating Council of Community Organizations, itself a diverse federation with now roughly forty affiliates, would be a central anchor in any broader movement. To be sure, the momentum behind civil rights insurgency in Chicago had shifted from CCCO and the South Side to SCLC and the West Side. But Raby and other CCCO leaders were determined to preserve the Coordinating Council as a vital force. Over the past year, CCCO had become much more than the framework for holding together diverse organizations. As its operating budget grew, it had hired more full-time staffers to advance CCCO's work. Raby now believed that more coordination among its constituent groups was essential. The "casual ad hoc cooperation born of crisis and desperation" that had often marked the alliance of CCCO affiliates in the past had to be replaced by "long-run, deepening relationships," Raby asserted. Moreover, in response to the persistent criticism of its lack of grass-roots ties, he argued that CCCO must not be content with its traditional role as an association of already established groups. CCCO members, he added, "must enlarge their community support, as well as shape new forms of community mobilization and organization that can be joined to CCCO."[66]

Not surprisingly, from late 1965 into the first half of 1966 CCCO continued to express dissatisfaction with the public schools. In the fall of 1965, it focused on the resolution of its complaint filed with the U.S. Office of Education detailing Title VI violations of the Civil Rights Act of 1964. Then in the late winter and spring of 1966, it championed the cause of parents and teachers unhappy with the white principal, Mildred Chuchut, of the nearly all-black Jenner Elementary School on the Near North Side. Accusing her of maladministration and prejudice, Chuchut's critics had long demanded her removal. Their frustration led to student boycotts, teacher walkouts, and support from individuals and organizations across the city. In late February, King, along with Raby, addressed disgruntled North Siders at a rally. In mid-March, roughly 150 demonstrators, including local parents and clergy as well as members of CORE, SCLC, and CCCO, followed Raby and the president of the Concerned Parents of Jenner School as they marched on the Board of Education offices. CCCO's assertiveness in the Jenner School dispute had even larger ramifications than simply the removal of a controversial principal. Since SCLC's arrival, CCCO had mounted few new initiatives; it seemed to be waiting for King and SCLC to call the shots. The well-reported Jenner protests, one activist said, eased fears that CCCO was being "dwarfed by SCLC in the public mind."[67]

The Jenner protests also highlighted the determination of civil rights leaders that the Chicago Freedom Movement be more than the sum of SCLC, its Chicago spin-offs, and CCCO affiliates. It should welcome all Chicagoans who desired social change. In late May King, for instance, pressed this point by addressing a rally on Chicago's Near West Side sponsored by the West Side Organization (WSO), a black grass-roots community group interested in bread-and-butter issues such as welfare reform and jobs for the community. WSO had remained unaffiliated with CCCO largely because of its disappointment with the outcome of the anti-Willis campaign. Many of WSO's staffers, including its tough and determined executive director, Chester Robinson, had found their pilgrimage to Selma in 1965 exhilarating. They desired to work with King and the freedom movement and gladly shared their knowledge about how to organize on welfare issues, even though they did not always find SCLC field workers to be the most reliable collaborators.[68]

While CCCO bolstered protests on the Near North Side and King and SCLC recruited on the Near West Side, Jesse Jackson was at work on the South Side. Tall, athletic, charismatic, and ambitious, Jackson had come to Chicago in 1964 to study at the Chicago Theological Seminary. A native of South Carolina, Jackson had emerged as a student protest leader during the Greensboro, North Carolina, antisegregation demonstrations of 1963. Once in Chicago, he did not simply immerse himself in his studies. Even while a student, he spent some of his time working for the West Side Christian Parish, and in early 1965 he went south to Selma to fight for voting rights. When the nonviolent movement came to Chicago, Jackson committed himself to it.[69]

Chicago activists, well aware that the West Side held no monopoly on slums, encouraged Jackson to cultivate black grass-roots support on the South Side. Jackson targeted the depressed North Kenwood–Oakland region and prodded local ministers to establish an effective local community organization. At a rally in early February 1966 King and Raby both helped christen the Kenwood-Oakland Community Organization (KOCO), a group which they also hoped would be the vehicle to ensure that when "Bevel got ready to move, we had the troops" from the South Side ready to march.[70]

Jackson's most important initiative went beyond community organizing, however. During the fall of 1965, Jackson, along with Al Pitcher of the University of Chicago Divinity School, began meeting with Clay Evans, pastor of Fellowship Baptist Church and the president of the Baptist Ministers Conference of Chicago and Vicinity, and a few other clergymen to plot a strategy for clergy participation in the Chicago movement. Though the black church did not shape the lives of northern urban blacks to the extent that it did those of southern blacks, it was still influential in black Chicago. Chicago activists knew that the support of the local black clergy would provide an important link to black Chicagoans and ultimately to thousands of additional followers. Yet many black ministers were cool to the freedom movement. Some saw no point in a civil rights campaign in Chicago; others worried that charismatic southern outsiders might diminish their own prestige; and still others feared reprisals if they worked too closely with Chicago activists. Jackson, Evans, and their small group soon realized that while many ministers wanted to help the Chicago movement, most desired a separate program related to the projected direct action campaign.[71]

A Chicago version of SCLC's Atlanta-based Operation Breadbasket program, which was designed to bring better jobs and more income into the black community, especially appealed to the Jackson-Evans cadre. Although the Reverend Leon Sullivan of Philadelphia, not King and SCLC, had popularized the selective buying campaign in the 1960s, this strategy had deep roots in Chicago. In 1929 the *Chicago Whip*, a militant black newspaper, had called for a "spend your money where you can work" campaign, and blacks regularly turned to this weapon during the

Depression years. In the early 1960s black Chicagoans—like their counterparts across the North—staged selective buying campaigns. In the summer of 1963 a group of black ministers formed the Clergy Alliance of Chicago and targeted the Bowman Dairy Company for a consumer boycott. By late fall, however, the Clergy Alliance seemed to vanish. Nonetheless the selective buying concept—a variant of black self-help—carried a great deal of weight in black Chicago.[72]

Martin Luther King himself assumed a leading role in cultivating ministerial support for a Chicago version of Operation Breadbasket. The southern movement, King knew, relied heavily on the leadership of black ministers. By contrast, even though black (and white) clergy and denominational-based organizations had contributed immensely to the Chicago struggle for justice, the leading figures on the local civil rights scene were not men of the cloth. Al Raby, for instance, was a teacher; Bill Berry was a race relations professional. That King's only major address in Chicago in the fall of 1965 was delivered at a gathering of Baptist ministers (hosted by Clay Evans) attested to his desire for support from the black church. To reach out further to the black religious leadership, King met with a core group of clergy, including William L. Lambert of the Greater Mount Hope Baptist Church, Frank Sims of the Ebenezer Baptist Church, and John Porter of the Christ Methodist Church, and then on February 11, 1966, delivered a recruiting pitch to a large, interracial gathering of priests and ministers at a South Side Church.[73]

Shortly after King's appeal, over forty members of the clergy, mostly black but some white and affiliated with a variety of denominations, joined committees charged with investigating the employment practices in four industries—bread, milk, soft drink, and soup companies. The work of these committees marked the emergence of Chicago's Operation Breadbasket. Although formally an overall steering committee composed of ministers active in the program governed Operation Breadbasket, Jesse Jackson, by this time an associate pastor at Clay Evans's church, coordinated the group's efforts. In effect, he became the director of Operation Breadbasket and its spokesperson. Caretaker of an important source of institutional power, Jackson now joined the front rank of Chicago civil rights leaders.[74]

The Breadbasket clergy first sought employment information from companies active in the black community. When an official of Country's Delight Dairy insulted a group of information-gathering ministers, Operation Breadbasket called for a consumer boycott of the dairy's products. Alarmed by the potential consequences of the boycott, Country's Delight Dairy soon consented to hire additional black workers. Later in the spring and early summer, Operation Breadbasket staged successful selective buying campaigns against several other dairies. Less than five months after its founding, Operation Breadbasket had gained more than two hundred new jobs for black Chicagoans.[75]

Yet Martin Luther King recognized that "[t]o free [the northern black] we can't just rely on the support of Negroes to win, we must have the support of the other 90 percent who are white." When King had sought white assistance on earlier occasions, he had looked to the North—often to Chicago organizations, institutions, and individuals. In 1962, for instance, over forty Chicagoans, white and black, had answered SCLC's call and journeyed to Albany, Georgia, to bear witness to that local freedom struggle. Three years later, in response to a similar appeal, a much larger delegation of Chicagoans had traveled south to boost SCLC's Selma campaign. Now that the southern crusade had come to Chicago, King and his colleagues had their first opportunity to build a truly interracial local movement. They hoped that whites and Chicago's growing Hispanic community would rise up against racial injustice in their own backyard.[76]

Chicago activists instinctively turned to colleges and universities for support. Bevel, always a college favorite, spoke at the University of Chicago and other schools; King addressed faculty and students at the University of Chicago and the University of Illinois at Chicago. West Side organizers entertained ambitious hopes of drawing hundreds of college students to Chicago. Under the auspices of the National Christian Student Federation (whose Chicago field staffer, Patti Miller, had become part of SCLC's West Side effort), they plotted for a northern version of the Mississippi project by sending flyers to colleges and universities across the country to recruit volunteers for a "Chicago! Summer '66." They hoped, said Candy Dawson, one of the college coordinators, that the role of students in the movement would be "similar to that played by students in the South, where they served as a main focal point of activity."[77]

Civil rights leaders also expected the backing of Chicago-area progressives. Their hopes had been heightened when nearly ten thousand people, mostly whites, gathered on the Winnetka village green in July 1965 for a King speech. In search of liberal assistance, King attended a mid-February fund raiser in Northbrook, a plush Chicago suburb. Lucy Montgomery, the millionaire wife of one of Chicago's most notable corporation lawyers, hosted the affair. One of SNCC's most generous contributors, Montgomery now desired to help King's Chicago campaign. Two weeks later King was the special guest for a dinner at a Hyde Park home. Among other influential Chicagoans, Robert Merriam, renowned Chicago reformer and one-time mayoral candidate, was in attendance.[78]

King expected generous assistance from organized labor as well. For years King had tried to fashion a civil rights–labor alliance with only modest results. He often lamented that a "missing ingredient in the civil rights struggle as a whole has been the power of the labor movement." In 1963 the powerful AFL-CIO had even refused to endorse the March on Washington. But since then there had been some encouraging signs. The AFL-CIO had backed both the Civil Rights Act of 1964 and the Voting Rights Act of 1965. King now thought the Chicago campaign offered a special opportunity for a civil rights–labor partnership. With its economic thrust, the Chicago campaign shared many of organized labor's goals. The civil rights and labor movements, King believed, needed to join forces "for the needs of a society as a whole."[79]

King was forced, however, to lower his expectations for labor cooperation. In Chicago, the most powerful workers' body, the Chicago Federation of Labor and the Industrial Union Council (CFL-IUC), had close ties to the city's political structure. The CFL had a venerable history of assisting workers, and in the post–World War II era, particularly since Richard Daley had been elected Chicago's mayor in 1955, it had decided that it could secure the most benefits for its constituents with its own version of a bread-and-butter strategy. In exchange for its political support and a disinclination toward labor militancy, the CFL gained an extremely competitive wage scale from the Daley administration on municipal contracts. The CFL almost blended into the Daley political apparatus.[80] Its longtime president, William Lee, was a close friend of Daley. So too was the federation's vice president, William McFetridge, head of the building service employees' union. To be sure, the CFL backed the liberal legislative agenda of the 1960s, including civil rights measures, and it endorsed the southern black stride toward freedom. McFetridge served as an honorary chairman of the 1964 Illinois Rally for Civil Rights in Soldier Field, at which King delivered the keynote address. Moreover, the CFL's own newspaper, the *Federation*

News, warmly covered SCLC's Selma crusade, highlighting the participation of union representatives. But on race issues at home, the CFL was not in the progressive vanguard. Competition over jobs had long generated friction between blacks and whites in Chicago. Labor tension had been one of the underlying causes of the 1919 race riot. Traditionally, the most powerful labor unions in Chicago were the preserve of whites, though with the labor activism of the 1930s and the rise of the CIO direct conflict between black and white workers in the economic arena diminished. By the 1960s there were, according to one estimate, over a hundred thousand black trade unionists in Chicago, and a few blacks held important posts in the local union hierarchy, including James Kemp, who was a member of CFL's executive board. Nevertheless, into the 1960s some of the CFL's affiliates, particularly the building trades, only grudgingly accepted a few token trainees or refused black apprentices altogether.[81]

Not all of Chicago's unions were so closely tied to the city. The United Packinghouse Workers (UPWA) took the lead in bringing organized labor behind the Chicago Freedom Movement. Under the stewardship of Ralph Helstein, the UPWA had a long history of independence and progressive politics. Helstein was part of a small contingent whom King and SCLC leaders regularly consulted for advice. Moreover, Packinghouse activists such as Charles Fischer had been active in CCCO and the Chicago civil rights movement. In the summer of 1965, the District 1 branch of the UPWA joined CCCO. It was Charles Hayes, the black chief of District 1 and one of the protesters who had opened Goldblatt's lunch counter to blacks in the late 1940s, who invited labor leaders to a mid-February luncheon in 1966 to discuss how organized labor could contribute to the civil rights struggle. At the luncheon King delivered a formal appeal for support to a wide assortment of labor leaders, including William Lee.[82]

Although Lee heard King's call, he did little to bring the power of the CFL behind the Chicago Freedom Movement. The *Federation News* chose not to report on any Chicago movement developments. There were, however, other more favorably disposed labor union leaders. In late March, local and national labor leaders, including Helstein and Hayes, Jack Conway and Norman Hill of the Industrial Union Department (IUD) of the AFL-CIO, and Brendan Sexton of the United Automobile Workers, huddled with King, Bevel, Young, Raby, Rustin, and Richard Boone of the Citizens Crusade Against Poverty to fashion a framework for civil rights–labor cooperation. The centerpiece of the program, the conferees decided, would be the infusion of labor organizers into the ghettoes, an initiative that the IUD had endorsed at its 1965 annual convention.[83]

Charles Chiakulas, a UAW representative and now an IUD organizer who had worked behind the scenes to arrange the mid-March civil rights–labor summit, became the chief administrator of the new program. After holding planning sessions and securing funding from the IUD and the UAW, Chiakulas oversaw the opening in July of a labor-backed community union in North Lawndale. Headed by Ted Black of the IUD via the United Automobile Workers with assistance from other professional union organizers, the Lawndale Community Union (not to be confused with the Lawndale Union to End the Slums) brought "the whole concept of trade unionism to the community level." It offered job referrals, job training, and encouraged worker solidarity. Labor organizers also trained residents to become tenant union stewards in their apartment buildings. To James Bevel, the Lawndale Community Union exemplified the "meshing" of the labor and civil rights movements.[84]

Not long afterward, labor activists and civil rights leaders designed another pilot program to link issues of labor and race as they sought to unionize one of the most unorganized sectors of Chicago's labor force: hospital employees. Historically underpaid, many of the hospital staff workers lived on Chicago's South and West sides. By sending organizers into the hospitals, civil rights–labor forces hoped to cultivate yet another progressive phalanx. Though some of the organizers, such as Heather Tobis (who worked in Provident Hospital, serving the South Side) successfully recruited workers, the whole effort, never well coordinated, died when it became entangled in sectarian and turf battles with the Teamsters Local 743 and the Building Service Employees Local 73. Nevertheless this was an early initiative in SCLC's evolving immersion in labor matters, which would eventually lead Martin Luther King to Memphis, Tennessee, and the sanitation workers' strike in 1968.[85]

Just as with organized labor, King and the Chicago Freedom Movement expected support from Chicago's established religious community. To build a bridge between the Chicago Freedom Movement and Chicago's white religious forces, King met in late January with representatives of the Chicago Conference on Religion and Race (CCRR), a confederation of religious and lay leaders of the major faiths. On this occasion King must have felt like a patriarch. Three years earlier during a keynote address at the historic National Conference on Religion and Race, the first ecumenical gathering of Jewish, Catholic, and Protestant leaders in American history, he had challenged the assembled religious leaders by asking, "Will this conference end with a high blood pressure of words and an anemia of action?" Shortly thereafter, Chicago's largest predominantly white religious denominations responded to King's challenge by establishing a local ecumenical body concerned with racial issues. With an executive director and its own staff, the CCRR was more than a blue-ribbon gathering of Chicago religious figures. In its first few years, it endorsed open-occupancy laws, helped quell an interracial housing riot, and began a fair-employment agency. Now Dr. Edgar Chandler, the white executive director of the Church Federation of Greater Chicago, the social service arm of white Protestantism in Chicago, Rabbi Samuel Karff, and other prominent Chicago clergy, along with the business leaders John Baird and Erwin A. Salk, who served on the CCRR executive board, listened attentively as King, Raby, and Young outlined the "Chicago Plan." King stressed that northern blacks had not benefited from the dramatic gains of the South. They possessed basic human rights but had been "imprisoned in the urban ghetto." The CCRR contingent pledged its assistance, though some members warned King that "all the support he had in Selma was not also committed to support of the CCCO's operations in Chicago." Despite this warning and despite King's and Young's self-acknowledged lack of a concrete plan, the presentation prompted one CCRR representative to predict that SCLC's determination to gain broad support and to organize the ghetto would give the impending "Chicago demonstrations a wholly new strength and character."[86]

Two weeks later, King visited Chicago's most important religious leader, Archbishop John Cody, at his sprawling mansion on Chicago's North Shore. Overseer of the largest Catholic archdiocese in America and the largest denomination in Chicago, the prelate had arrived in Chicago in August 1965 touted as an effective advocate of racial justice. As the coadjutor archbishop and then archbishop of New Orleans, Cody had directed the desegregation of New Orleans's parochial schools. Cody's actions had generated fierce opposition, but he had not flinched under pressure.[87]

With this visit King hoped not only to become better acquainted with Cody but also to ensure the continuation of Catholic contributions to improving race relations. Unlike other primarily white denominations, the Chicago Catholic Church had not abandoned the inner city. Even though their traditional congregations had fled, many Catholic churches and schools continued to operate in black neighborhoods and, as a result, boosted the number of black Catholics. Some white Catholic priests, such as Daniel Mallette of St. Agatha's Church in Lawndale, became virtual folk heroes in the black community. Determined to ease hardships among blacks, the Catholic Church, encouraged by Monsignor John Egan, had largely bankrolled Saul Alinsky's experiment in organizing Woodlawn. Moreover, the head of the Chicago archdiocese from the late 1950s until his death in 1965, Albert Meyer, had not hesitated to speak for racial equality. In his seven years as leader of the archdiocese, Meyer testified before the United States Civil Rights Commission on the urgent need for better race relations in Chicago, ordered parish priests to deliver at least three sermons a year on racial justice and brotherhood, and played a pivotal role in the National Conference on Religion and Race.[88]

Since the early 1960s Chicago Catholics had been in the front lines of the local civil rights struggle.[89] When in 1963 a priest and, even more striking, a contingent of nuns picketed the Illinois Club of Catholic Women for discriminatory practices, they sent a signal across the nation that Catholics were taking a stand for racial equality. The principal conduit for Catholic activism in Chicago was the Catholic Interracial Council (CIC). Founded in 1945 to promote interracial understanding, the Chicago CIC, which was headed largely by laypeople and not under diocesan control, underwent a resurgence when in 1960 Sargent Shriver and other board members tapped John McDermott as its new executive director. Raised in Philadelphia during the 1930s, McDermott benefited from a strong Catholic education and, after a stint as a graduate student in philosophy at Georgetown, embarked on a long career in public service. Before taking charge of the Chicago CIC, he gained a wealth of experience on racial questions in the 1950s as a housing inspector for the city of Philadelphia, as a race relations specialist with the National Conference of Christians and Jews, and then as a fairhousing expert for the federal government. Energetic and bright, a good administrator and talented writer, McDermott led the CIC to new levels of assertiveness. Under his direction, the Catholic Interracial Council became one of CCCO's most important affiliates.[90]

McDermott also cultivated Catholic ties with the southern civil rights movement. He helped coordinate Chicago participation in SCLC's Albany and Selma campaigns, and he invited Martin Luther King to Chicago in late 1964 to receive the CIC's John F. Kennedy award. McDermott recognized the "profound impact" King—"a deep Christian without hate"—had on Chicago Catholics. King himself valued support from Chicago Catholics and even took the opportunity during his July 1965 whirlwind tour of Chicago to single out their assistance for praise. Reflecting on the surge of Catholic witnesses during the Selma campaign, King claimed that "the new dimension of nuns and priests in the struggle gave the movement unstoppability."[91]

It was with this understanding of the potential power of Catholics in Chicago that King conferred with the new Chicago archbishop. The two men talked for more than a hour as King briefed Cody on the Chicago movement. After leaving the archbishop's residence, King told waiting reporters that it was "a very friendly and I might say fruitful discussion."[92]

The Chicago Freedom Movement's efforts to recruit support climaxed on a Saturday night in mid-March when twelve thousand people, roughly ten percent of whom were white, filled Chicago's International Amphitheater (while hundreds of others waited outside) to watch performances by Harry Belafonte, Mahalia Jackson, and Dick Gregory and to listen to Martin Luther King. The Freedom Festival, as the affair was called, grossed more than $100,000 from the contributions of whites and blacks, both rich and poor. The prefestival pledges confirmed that a wide-ranging coalition was emerging. Black ministers such as Clay Evans and Stroy Freeman of the New Friendship Baptist Church had promised substantial contributions. So too had Rabbi Jacob J. Weinstein of the KAM Temple, Lucy Montgomery, and James Wright of the UAW.[93]

After an introduction by Raby, King in his keynote address went to the heart of the preeminent problem in Chicago: the plight of urban blacks, men and women who had not found "a land of plenty but a lot replete with poverty," who had not "experienced the buoyancy of hope but the fatigue of despair," and who had not discovered "a promised land but rather another Egypt-land of denial, discrimination, and dismay." In short, he asserted, urban blacks were "exploited by the community at large," by realtors, business owners, and politicians. The solution to ghetto ills required more than just patience. King urged blacks to rally behind a program of direct action, "the time-honored tactics and strategies that have served us so well in the past ten years."

He also appealed to whites: "There can be no lasting escape for those of you who have fled behind the suburban curtain, for your black brother yet languishes in the slums, crying out to you. Your lot is inextricably interwoven with his, since he retains the capability of ringing down the curtain on the American dream." Once more, King called for a "grand alliance of the forces of good will with the underprivileged to end the dark days of powerless existence."[94]

The Freedom Festival was a glorious occasion for the Chicago movement. "They've really got a movement going there," commented King's adviser Stanley Levison. "When they start mass action in the spring that is when everybody will start paying attention."[95]

Not all Chicagoans greeted the Chicago Freedom Movement enthusiastically. While Martin Luther King was the most respected black leader in the country and his philosophy of universal brotherhood and nonviolence was widely admired, many blacks balked at his northern crusade. The hostility of the Black Muslims was expected, as was the antipathy of the most radical black activists. The most formidable opposition, however, flowed from conservative forces within the black community, just as it had in southern cities in which SCLC had operated. Some blacks were temperamentally averse to a protest strategy, not a few were ideologically hostile, and still others were disinclined for reasons of self-interest. These blacks preferred a more gradual approach to social change and often extolled the beneficence of the existing political process. The coolness and, at times, outright opposition of important segments of black Chicago prompted some SCLC activists to long for southern hospitality.[96]

In late February King sought to neutralize a potentially powerful bloc of black opponents by dining with Elijah Muhammad at the Black Muslim leader's palatial home in North Kenwood. Though the statistics are fuzzy, nationwide the Nation of Islam had thousands of members, many of whom were young males. A substantial share of its members no doubt resided in Chicago, the headquarters of the sect. A racial separatist, the aging Muhammad was a sharp critic of King's interracial vision. After the meeting King reported that Muhammad insisted that "all of his followers would be in sympathy" with the Chicago Freedom Movement. No one really believed this. Indeed, only a few days later Muhammad blasted King at the Nation of Islam's annual convention.

"King does not understand the Negro problem," he declared. "The white people want to buy King. He loves the white folks and the white people know it."[97]

Some black militants looked skeptically upon the Chicago Freedom Movement as well. ACT, the group that Lawrence Landry had helped found after leaving CCCO, preferred a more revolutionary program. "King has been talking in general terms about slums, but he'll have to get more definite or he'll just be leading the people down a blind alley," asserted one ACT leader. Yet ACT elected not to challenge the Chicago movement. It recognized that even an aggressive civil rights group like Chicago CORE had decided that this broad coalition had the potential to bring about far-reaching change, while Chicago SNCC, which was suffering from "severe financial problems," had virtually disappeared from the local scene. "Chicago has bought the nonviolent movement," Nahaz Rogers, an ACT leader, said ruefully.[98]

The chief critics of the Chicago Freedom Movement, however, were not those who thought it too moderate but those who worried that it would be too disruptive. Perhaps nowhere were these fears more graphically articulated than in the pages of a small weekly black newspaper, the *New Crusader*. While the more established and more influential *Chicago Defender* covered the SCLC-CCCO campaign favorably, the *New Crusader* ran columns and articles assailing it. In late May, its columnist "Da Brien" boasted that black Chicagoans were "far better off than [their counterparts in] many large cities" and that they were improving their lots "on a larger scale in Chicago than any other city." The editorialist then lamented that the Chicago Freedom Movement threatened "to destroy what husbands and wives have worked years to pay for." Finally, the pseudonymous columnist delivered a stinging wish: "Dr. King, will you take your 'Firebugs' and 'Outdated plans' away from our city, if you cannot provide better leadership."[99]

Pointed barbs from a small weekly like the *New Crusader* would have been almost meaningless if its opinions did not echo those of important leaders in the black community. "We were rejected by most of the black leadership," one SCLC staffer, with slight exaggeration, later stated. Though proud of southern black assertiveness, not all black Chicagoans favored civil rights insurgency in their city, where basic rights had already been secured, where blacks already had a political voice, where a good living could be earned, and where members of their community served as high-ranking police officers, as school principals, as judges, as labor leaders, and in a host of other prominent positions. In particular, well-to-do, older, more established members of the black community with ties to the city's civic, business, and political elite tended to view the Chicago Freedom Movement skeptically, just as they had earlier local civil rights initiatives. Some worried that another season of protests and demonstrations might do more harm than good. They believed that there were city programs addressing virtually every problem King raised when he came to Chicago. Other blacks complained that the Chicago Freedom Movement's pursuit of social justice threatened their own interests. Many blacks praised King's attacks on slumlords, but not a few glimpsed a terribly misguided assault. "I have since come to wonder if you are for or against us," one black wrote. "Your current stand on the slum property owners initiated this doubt in my mind. I wonder if you can . . . see that the majority of the slum land owners are Negroes—the very people you owe your allegiance." Still other blacks questioned a strategy that criticized outside forces for the problems of the black community. King should concentrate, one black advised, on "exhorting our people to help themselves instead of insisting that the government (national and local) do everything for them."[100]

Much of the skepticism about the Chicago Freedom Movement translated into private decisions by many Chicagoans not to commit themselves fully to the SCLC-CCCO campaign. Some well-known black Chicagoans, however, expressed their reservations much more publicly. James Parsons, a prominent federal judge and a chairman of the National Conference on Religion and Race, openly denounced seizure of 1321 South Homan Avenue. It was "theft" and "a revolutionary tactic," Parsons declaimed. Like many black Chicagoans, Parsons believed that legal redress and private pressure on decision makers were the best remedies where inequities still existed. Ernest Rather, a black entrepreneur who became a regular critic of the freedom movement, wondered what King and his followers hoped to accomplish in a city where "much has been done, is being done, and is planned by city officials and private organizations." Like Parsons, Rather questioned any approach which advocated disobedience toward laws. "Dr. King," Rather asserted, "has advocated—that bad laws should be disobeyed. Perhaps in those parts of the South where the law has two faces, one black and one white, this may be appropriate. But in Chicago, the law has just one and is applicable to all. No one is above the law here."[101]

The spectrum of responses by prominent blacks to the Chicago Freedom Movement illustrated the stark limits of King's desire for an unstoppable coalition. This bundle of fears and anxieties underlay the refusal of the city's most senior and largest civil rights organization, the Chicago branch of the NAACP, to join the Chicago Freedom Movement. The widespread skepticism, moreover, only strengthened the position of the Chicago campaign's most ardent critics, and no critic was more insistent and more defiant than the Reverend Joseph H. Jackson.[102]

Pastor to one of Chicago's largest congregations and president of the National Baptist Convention, Jackson was a man of wide influence, a man whose voice carried. Son of a Rudyard, Mississippi, minister, Jackson knew well the scourge of southern poverty and racism. Early in life he decided to dedicate himself to God. He pursued a formal education, eventually earning a bachelor of divinity degree. After a couple of stints as a pastor in southern towns, Jackson followed the path of many black southerners to Chicago. In 1941 he became the pastor of the prestigious Olivet Baptist Church, where he quickly established himself as one of the city's most inspirational preachers. "Nobody sleeps through a Jackson sermon," was a common saying on the South Side. In 1953 Jackson was elected to the presidency of the National Baptist Convention (NBC), the most powerful institutional post in black America's largest denomination. From this post, he oversaw huge financial investments and wielded substantial influence in black America.[103]

In the mid-1950s it seemed that Jackson might become a strong ally of the rising black protest movement. His church—which reportedly had one of the largest congregations in the nation—sent $1,000 to the Montgomery Improvement Association, and National Baptist Convention affiliates raised even more. In a tribute to Martin Luther King, he introduced the young minister from Montgomery to the cheers of the 1956 National Baptist Convention in Colorado.[104]

Yet Jackson's embrace of black assertiveness was limited. He was philosophically and temperamentally opposed to civil disobedience and protest. "There are two distinct philosophies on civil rights," he noted. "One group emphasizes protest and employs the techniques of the 'sit-ins,' 'wade-ins,' 'freedom riders.'" The other philosophy, which Jackson favored, stressed the capacity of the due process of law to solve America's race problems. That Jackson lobbied Congress to make May 17—the date of the *Brown* decision—a national holiday exemplified his broad commitment to racial equality but also his preference for conservative methods.[105]

It was only a matter of time before Jackson's conservatism (and his willingness to bend NBC's election rules in order to remain in charge) would spark challenges to his leadership. King and fellow black clergymen began to plot ways to gain control of the National Baptist Convention so that it could become a powerful agent of reform. Their efforts failed, however, and their frustration and disappointment was so great that in 1961 more reformist ministers bolted from the NBC to found an alternative national Baptist organization, the Progressive National Baptist Convention.[106]

Now in 1966, much to Jackson's dismay, King was again invading the older man's turf. Jackson thought Chicago race relations were progressing nicely. He could not understand why King would hitch himself to CCCO, a group that had made life miserable for "one of the best trained and most dedicated educators in the United States of America," Benjamin Willis. As King's troops prepared for a summer of action, Jackson assailed civil disobedience as a method that "relies on the emotions of fear, and seeks through harassment, threats, and intimidations, to force an official or an unwilling person to surrender to the demands made by the group upon him."[107] Jackson's voice carried weight beyond his own church in Chicago. His stance on SCLC and its strategy constituted part of the mix of factors that ensured that the local black church only partially backed the Chicago Freedom Movement. Operation Breadbasket, for instance, would never win the loyalty of all of Chicago's black clergy because of, in the words of one SCLC administrator, "the fragmented Negro ministry in Chicago." Some of this fragmentation, this SCLC official continued, was "due to the influence of Reverend J. H. Jackson."[108]

Chicago's entrenched black political leadership also bemoaned the intrusion of King and SCLC into their city's affairs. The first half of the 1960s had been trying enough as civil rights protest, particularly over the schools issue, had catapulted a new generation of black leaders— Raby, Landry, and Brazier, among others—unconnected with the Democratic party apparatus into prominence and had fueled citizens' unrest. In 1963, blacks in the Seventeenth Ward on the South Side, which only in the past decade had turned from white to black, registered their disfavor with the current political establishment by electing Charles Chew, a black independent Democrat, as their alderman. In 1966, nevertheless, traditional black politicians like William Dawson still controlled most political offices and proclaimed that as the duly elected representatives of black Chicagoans they served the interests of black residents. "We have competent leadership in Chicago and all things necessary to work out our city's own destiny," Alderman Ralph Metcalfe, a former Olympic sprinter, retorted after learning that SCLC had selected Chicago for its first northern venture. To underscore black Chicago's self-reliance, he, with Bishop Louis Henry Ford of the Church of God in Christ, announced the formation of their own civil rights organization, the Chicago Committee to Fulfill These Rights.[109]

Mayor Richard Daley, of course, looms large in any explanation of Metcalfe's and other black leaders' hostility toward the Chicago Freedom Movement. "Daley wanted King out of town," one city official insisted. He was tired of civil rights insurgency. The 1965 summer marches, some in front of his own home, had so exercised the mayor that his friends had become alarmed. In August 1965 the Illinois congressman Dan Rostenkowski had told one of the President's aides that he was "most concerned" about Daley's current race relations problems and their effect "on the Mayor personally." Rostenkowski even had suggested that the White House give Daley an assignment "to take him out of the country for a week or two." Now in early 1966, with a full-scale King campaign impending, Daley seemed on the verge of yet a more trying year.[110]

It riled Daley that outsiders threatened to cause him so much trouble. Like most mayors, Daley chafed at intruders—whether they were probing federal officials from Washington or civil rights leaders from the South—in his domain, the domain he, not they, had been elected to govern. "Daley was very dogmatic," said Charles Swibel, one of Daley's close associates. "He felt that no one was going to come into his city . . . and disrupt it." In this massive city, composed of a mosaic of tightly knit neighborhoods, where so many citizens treasured territory and turf, crusading outsiders—who were certain, Daley believed, to have an inadequate appreciation of Chicago's dynamics—spelled trouble. Chicago's leaders needed a sensitivity to neighborhood rhythms and to interlocking relationships that could come only from intimate knowledge of the city.[111]

Daley knew Chicago. Son of an immigrant Irish sheet-metal worker, he had lived his entire life in Chicago and since 1955 had been its mayor. He loved his city and felt he understood what was best for it. Reared in the hothouse of Chicago politics, Daley instinctively connected the fortunes of Chicago with the fortunes of the Cook County

Democratic organization, a great umbrella of an organization under which blacks and whites, natives and immigrants could all find shelter. He had been a loyal soldier as a state legislator, as director of the Illinois Department of Finance, and as Cook County Clerk before he assumed the chairmanship of the Democratic organization in 1953. From this post he captured the mayor's office when the incumbent Democratic mayor, Martin Kennelly, antagonized the party bosses. Yet unlike many machine mayors, Daley did not consider governing the city a mere hobby, to be indulged in between party raids on the public treasury. The Cook County Democratic organization prospered under Daley's reign, but Daley strove to be a good mayor. Although he harbored no grand, elaborate vision, he did desire a city with a strong economy, good jobs, and quality neighborhoods—in short, a fine place to raise a family. He selected capable public officials, labored to keep the city fiscally sound, and demanded efficient delivery of important city services. That the Chicago business community, which had eyed Daley suspiciously in 1955, enthusiastically endorsed his reelection in 1959 and 1963 attested to the mayor's strong performance. As Daley liked to say, "Good government is good politics, and good politics is good government."[112]

Daley's electoral success also flowed from a remarkable (though fundamentally fragile) coalition of blacks and white ethnics. A heavy black vote brought Daley victory in 1955, and he never took black support completely for granted. The Chicago congressional delegation unanimously supported national civil rights legislation. At the height of the Selma crisis, the Daley-dominated Chicago City Council passed a resolution commending the southern voting rights drive. The next year it praised Lyndon Johnson's decision to seek a federal fair-housing act. Daley on occasion even linked himself with the national civil rights movement. He spoke at a 1963 Chicago rally featuring Martin Luther King in the aftermath of the Birmingham campaign. Closer to home, the mayor lobbied for an Illinois fair-employment practices law until its passage, and he annually urged the state legislature to pass a fair-housing law. In 1963, he backed the passage of the Chicago Fair Housing Ordinance. "I believe it is the right of all people to be treated with respect and dignity," he stated. The next year he encouraged top Chicago business leaders to form the Chicago Merit Employment Committee to widen job opportunities for black Chicagoans. During the mid-1960s, Daley embraced the War on Poverty. Even before congressional passage of antipoverty legislation in 1964, Chicago had developed a local apparatus, the Chicago Committee on Urban Opportunity, to dispense the anticipated millions. While the Chicago program, headed by a black director, endured sharp criticism—it showed little concern for maximizing the participation of the poor in the administration of the program—Daley did secure massive sums of federal antipoverty money.[113]

But Daley never sought to become the champion of black Chicago. As one Daley observer put it, the mayor "leaned against" the civil rights movement. He never took a public stand for school integration or against Superintendent Benjamin Willis. He never battled for a strong local fair-housing law. He never considered awarding blacks a share of patronage jobs equal to their percentage of the Democratic vote. He never sought to use public housing to promote integration and thus reverse the legacy, particularly pronounced since the end of World War II, of governmental cooperation with private interests to contain Chicago's black population within specified regions.[114]

Daley's diffidence toward black demands did not spring from fundamental antipathy toward blacks. A devout Catholic, Daley treated blacks who worked for the city or who visited him with respect. He flinched when racist remarks were uttered in his presence, and he shunned the racial humor still commonplace in the 1960s. Moreover, he could appreciate the plight of blacks at least to some extent, particularly those in hardworking families.[115]

Yet Daley would only reach so far for black Chicagoans. Despite bursts of empathy, Daley's background made it difficult for him to understand the special predicament of black Chicagoans, to recognize that they were not simply another immigrant group. He never stepped forward as a moral leader on the important question of race. This stance dovetailed perfectly with Daley's political instincts, for in the world of political calculation in which Daley thrived, black Chicago as a voting force simply demanded less from Daley. The mayor recognized that he presided over an unstable coalition—in which black and ethnic white interests often collided—but he also knew that blacks lacked political options. Few blacks looked to the Republican party, particularly in the aftermath of Barry Goldwater's run for the presidency, for a helping hand. In the end, Daley did what he could to satisfy black demands without incurring the wrath of the white ethnics and risking driving them into the Republican party.[116]

Daley had made this difficult task more manageable by making shrewd decisions in the first years of his mayoralty. When elected mayor in 1955, Daley set out to make the entire Democratic party dependent on him. First he refused to relinquish the party chairmanship, a post that held vast patronage and endorsement powers. Then he eliminated any existing independent bases of power. Congressman William Dawson watched helplessly as black aldermen and ward committeemen he had formerly controlled became dependent on Daley. By 1960 the chieftains of black politics, including every black alderman, were loyal to Daley. As a result, the mayor was buffered politically from the growing black discontent of the 1960s. Daley could rely on surrogates, the elected black leadership, to neutralize activists and to bear the brunt of insurgents' criticism.[117]

"Clout," more than his respectable record, brought many blacks into Daley's corner. Wilbur Daniel, a prominent Baptist minister, learned how compelling this mix could be. In 1964 Daniel, who had served a term as president of the Chicago NAACP, challenged the aging Dawson for his congressional seat. Even though Dawson did not deliver a single campaign speech, Daniel, running as a Republican, lost by a large margin. Shortly after his defeat, Daniel scheduled an appointment with Mayor Daley. "I went into his office and won him over," Daniel later remembered. "I realized that I lived in a city that Daley was running, and I wanted to be with him. I wanted to be with him because he could help me with what I wanted to do." The powerful Pentecostal bishop Louis Ford admitted that he too became "deeply indebted to the Democratic machine." In Chicago, he explained, when a pastor's congregation needed jobs, day care facilities, or educational centers, "you talk to Mayor Daley." And if the pressure to conform seemed great to established black ministers like Daniel and Ford, it was even greater for the many storefront preachers or, for that matter, for any black Chicagoan, in any endeavor from law to business, who wanted to get ahead.[118]

Insurgents characterized the vast network of black ministers, civic leaders, and politicians linked to the Daley regime as "plantation politics." Civil rights critics reserved special barbs for the six black aldermen—Metcalfe, Claude Holman, William Harvey, Kenneth Campbell, Robert Miller, and George Collins—who sided with the Daley machine. Their general silence on race issues brought them the appellation "the silent six." Pulled by the competing pressures of constituent demands and the needs of the Democratic machine, the black aldermen behaved erratically on civil rights issues in the first half of the 1960s. At one

moment they might attend a rally against segregated schools, thus identifying with local civil rights aspirations, and then shortly thereafter they
might condemn a schools protest as destructive. In the end, their ties to
the Democratic machine prevailed: they denounced measures designed
to aid black Chicagoans if such denunciations would help the party (and
help keep themselves in office). Like thousands of other blacks, the
black aldermen had a treasured stake in the perpetuation of the status
quo.[119]

Civil rights activists hoped that Martin Luther King's arrival in Chicago would shake the Daley-backed black political establishment's
influence in the black community. Some even anticipated that it would
ultimately unravel Daley's carefully cultivated coalition of black and
white supporters. King was a hero to many blacks and whites, and in
the South he and his SCLC colleagues had upended other entrenched
political establishments. Little wonder, then, that the Daley administration sought to minimize the political damage King could cause. Daley,
according to one city official, feared that "King would bungle it, that he
didn't understand the dynamics of the city—that this wasn't Birmingham. And he might bungle it in the sense that he would create a
political maelstrom beyond his control." To contain the civil rights crusade, Daley and his supporters relied on a combination of strategies:
naked pressure, deflection, and accommodation.[120]

Strong-arm tactics were hardly innovations specific to Daley's Chicago, but Daley loyalists used them with great effect. The Reverend Clay
Evans, for example, felt the sting of Daley's powerful political arsenal.
Instrumental in organizing Operation Breadbasket, Evans was one of
the few influential black Baptist ministers to support King enthusiastically. At the same time he was building a new church for his expanding
congregation. One day, however, he was told that if he wanted a loan
approved by a local bank that he would be wise to cut his ties with the
Chicago Freedom Movement. Evans refused to buckle, and for the next
seven years his congregation worshiped without a new church. An
uncompleted foundation stood as a testament to both the Daley camp's
immense clout and Evans's enormous willpower. Such muscle—and,
more important, the growing reputation of the Daley administration's
power—was likely to intimidate other less determined blacks who
thought about crossing the Daley machine.[121]

Though intimidation was always a weapon in his arsenal, Daley
preferred to undercut the King crusade in more subtle ways, in keeping

with his general strategy toward the local civil rights movement since the early 1960s. Daley did not want to become a northern Jim Clark or Bull Connor. "We weren't looking for . . . confrontation, and we would not do things to create a confrontation," remembered Ed Marciniak, the Daley-appointed executive director of the city's Commission on Human Relations and one of Daley's closest advisers on racial issues. When King arrived at O'Hare Airport for the Chicago stop of the People to People tour in late July 1965, Marciniak—with Daley's consent—made sure that he, as an official representative of the city of Chicago, was the first person to greet the distinguished civil rights leader.[122]

Marciniak's greeting set the tone for the Daley administration's response to SCLC's presence in Chicago. The administration sought to shorten the distance between civil rights demands and city policy. Thus in the winter and spring of 1966 Daley trumpeted his own campaign to end slums in Chicago by the end of 1967, and in early 1966 city officials stepped up their efforts to eliminate dilapidated housing and punish slumlords. The city's slum drive clearly had multiple purposes. Tighter inspections would spur slum landlords to maintain their properties and thus improve the lot of ghetto residents, but it was certainly no coincidence that soon after Bernard Lee had secured an apartment for King, city building inspectors combed the Lawndale area. It was also no coincidence that the city's war on slums was fought most fiercely on the West Side, where SCLC had concentrated its forces. "If Daley makes a mistake, it will not be for a lack of interest in the slums," one observer noted. "He has always beaten his enemies by taking their programs and running with them. Before he's through, his crusade will make King's look minor league."[123]

The Daley antislum campaign was indeed impressive. In a well-publicized progress report issued in July, Daley proudly announced that in the past eighteen months the city had demolished 1,409 abandoned buildings and had brought 9,226 other buildings containing 102,847 dwelling units into compliance with city housing codes. The mayor hailed the "most massive and comprehensive rodent-eradication program ever undertaken in this country," which had sealed 140,000 rodent holes since December 1965. He also stressed that since March more than 16,000 buildings in North Lawndale and East and West Garfield Park had been inspected and reinspected.[124]

Chicago's version of the War on Poverty ensured that federal beneficence reached into the ghettoes. A Head Start program, Upward Bound clubs, and job training initiatives sought to expand opportunities to Chicago's less privileged. Seven Urban Progress centers were founded to coordinate programs in Chicago's most depressed regions, including two in Lawndale and East Garfield Park, and program stations were located in a number of black churches. The Chicago Committee on Urban Opportunity boasted that in the first sixteen months of operation, the Urban Progress centers had made over one million "personal contacts" with Chicagoans. Here, Daley loyalists claimed, was evidence that City Hall cared about the future of the disadvantaged. Pumped up with federal funds, the centers, recalled one West Side activist, "hired a whole lot of people out of all the community organizations" to serve as their "staff people." These centers were, in a sense, competition for the Chicago Freedom Movement. They were designed to "curb any organizing activity that would break loose, that would be too independent of the powers to be."[125]

The Daley regime—continuing the pattern of Marciniak's July 1965 trip to O'Hare Airport—also went out of its way to welcome King to Chicago. Though the Chicago police, along with the FBI, spied on civil rights activists, Chicago's renowned police superintendent, Orlando W. Wilson, invited King for discussions about the Chicago campaign in late January. A leading law enforcement expert, author of the standard textbooks in his field, and tapped by Daley to clean up the police department after the Summerdale scandal broke in 1960, Wilson certainly styled himself as a progressive police chief. And leading voices in the black community agreed. "O. W. Wilson strikes us as very much the brightest star in Chicago's galaxy of government," the *Chicago Defender* asserted in 1966. When first appointed, the silver-haired, distinguished-looking Wilson had issued an antidiscrimination order for police personnel decisions and had sought—by deploying his police force to protect black rights—to prove to "the entire Negro community that the Chicago Police Department belonged to them just as much as it belonged to white people." Not surprisingly, King's session with the police chief and sixty high-ranking officers was amicable and not adversarial. Although King warned that civil disobedience was likely (noting that it is sometimes necessary to break "a particular law to reach the higher law of brotherhood and justice"), he expressed his faith that the Chicago movement would have good relations with the city's police. After the meeting King, who had come to expect cold receptions from law-men, remarked that it was "refreshing to engage in a dialogue [with police] in good faith." He then added, "this was a first for me."[126]

Daley himself invited King to City Hall. A White House conference kept King from accepting the mayor's first invitation, but near the end of March, King, along with forty ministers, met with Daley and other top city officials for nearly four hours. Afterward King called the meeting "very meaningful, frank and exhaustive." Such an exchange was unlikely in a southern city.[127]

The Daley administration, black politicians, and black conservatives, Chicago activists recognized, were not the only impediments to a successful campaign. The indifference of many of the city's one million blacks was the most serious obstacle. Chicago insurgents knew that the movement's power for producing social change would be formidable if they could galvanize even a modest percentage of the city's black residents. Yet civil rights workers quickly realized that mobilizing a huge nonviolent army was not easy. It seemed that those who had the most to gain from a successful movement were the most difficult to recruit.

Influenced not only by new perspectives on urban problems circulating through the country and by analyses worked out during staff sessions and private discussions in the fall but also by the history of Gandhi's campaign for India's independence from Great Britain, Bevel had come to conceive of Chicago's ghettoes as "internal colonies." The larger society ruthlessly extracted resources from ghettoes without providing the means for their development. "The northern slum is no different from the African colonies," Bevel noted. "Both are exploited—that is, outsiders take things out and don't put anything back in."[128]

King, who since the Watts riot had been searching for a deeper understanding of the urban predicament, found Bevel's ideas timely and persuasive. In his speeches he demanded the end of ghettoes, "maintained because of powerful forces operating to keep them intact." He lambasted public school officials for providing blacks an inferior and unequal education. He indicted the "selfish profiteering real estate interest and white residents with their restrictive covenants and (un)gentlemen(ly) agreements, abetted by the prejudicial practices of mortgage-money lending institutions" that confined blacks to the city's worst housing. Accordingly, King and the Chicago Freedom Movement concentrated on spotlighting the exploiters, whether they were inept school administrators or negligent landlords.[129]

Yet the ghetto, King and his colleagues recognized, was also anchored from within. The Daley administration's campaign against slums diminished the likelihood of collective, independent black activism. The explosion of official city activity dampened the insurgent spirit. Moreover, many ghetto dwellers shied away from the Chicago Freedom Movement because they feared reprisals from politicos and government officials. "It's amazing how the people on relief believe that if they vote against the Democratic ticket they will get pushed out on the street," a Catholic nun mourned.[130]

But there was another reason, King and his associates argued, why many inner-city blacks did not flock to the crusade to end slums. King often pointed out that the travails of ghetto life were too much for some residents. Too many blacks had "given up every hope" and were "the ill-starred and deeply wounded veterans of what can be called 'slum shock.'" King hoped that the campaign to end slums would instill in disaffected black Chicagoans "new dignity, new self respect and new power." A surge of self-reliance and self-esteem would accompany participation in a crusade. Involvement in a mass movement would not only further social change but would trigger individual regeneration and self-actualization. To be a complete person, a full citizen, King believed, meant more than simply possessing a set of rights; it required active pursuit of those rights and of a better society. Collective and personal freedom could be achieved in the same enterprise. "Do not stand by and be a conscientious objector in this war to end slums," King urged Chicago's deprived blacks.[131]

James Bevel took this appraisal of northern blacks to even more critical lengths. "[T]here was greater crisis facing people in the North," Bevel said. "There was greater despair, less community spirit, more crime, violence and drug addiction here than in the South." Perhaps, above all, "there was more apathy." Bevel thus turned to an old theme in black history: self-reliance and self-assertion. "Tyranny exists because people will bow to a tyrant," Bevel argued in the fall of 1965. The movement's goal was "to so move people that they will not bow, that they will stand up and say to the whole city that they refuse to live in such houses, that they refuse to go to such schools—to say that they have been treated indecently and in inhuman ways—and that they will no longer stand for it." Bevel stated this theme more concisely on

another occasion, in words that were echoed by other West Side workers: "We have to work to restore people to humanity, and once this is
done in the black ghetto, that is the movement."[132]

In these exhortations King and Bevel focused on the most dispossessed ghetto dwellers, the hard core of what sociologists now term the
underclass, men and women either on relief or unemployed, socially
isolated from more successful blacks, suffering from broken dreams, and
often leading dismal lives. "I remember going down this one hallway
with no paint and plaster on the walls. It was almost like a dungeon
and into this room where a woman was sort of crouched on the floor
with a young child and nothing, nothing, on the walls, and no furniture," recalled one civil rights worker. This activist found it difficult to
reach this woman, to persuade her to join the nonviolent crusade. Like
many West Side blacks, this young mother had no reserve of energy to
offer the movement. Survival was her preoccupation. "Some of the
conditions," remembered another SCLC field staffer, "seemed worse
than anything I had seen in the South—large, rat-infested, dark, crime-
ridden buildings that were cold in the winter time and just blistering,
miserably hot in the summer." Some ghetto dwellers were so helpless,
so destitute, so removed from networks of support and affection that "it
was difficult," he noted, to imagine that they could ever be mobilized,
that "you could get people in some of these buildings to actually organize, to withhold their rent, to put it into an escrow account, and try
and force meaningful changes and the relationship between the tenant
and the landlords."[133]

Chicago movement organizers even found it difficult to reach West
Side blacks who could not be categorized as part of the underclass. To
be sure, as the Towneses demonstrated, there were West Side blacks
who had faith that collective action could improve their lives. But most
ghetto dwellers, confined to an impersonal urban environment with a
diminished community spirit, responded to a world of scarcity and
blocked opportunities in less political, collective ways. They sought to
make a hard life a little softer by gathering with their families, however
much they departed from the middle-class ideal, by consorting with
friends and associates at a local hangout, or by engaging in hundreds of
other little yet comforting activities. Ironically, then, despite all the
deprivation, the ghetto was not a place teeming with eager recruits for
a nonviolent crusade.[134]

* * *

As the months rolled by, tensions within the Chicago movement mounted. One of the leaders of the SCLC staff, James Orange, was (according to the FBI) tired of the endless organizing and longed to return south, where "the action was." Clashes between SCLC leaders flared up. Bevel criticized Andrew Young for not consulting him on the seizure of the 1321 South Homan apartment building. The Chicago movement still lacked a well-formulated program to end the slums and even a precise plan for the promised season of direct action. "We haven't gotten things under control. The strategy hasn't emerged yet," Young admitted in late March.[135]

The absence of a well-focused strategy began to wear on King. SCLC's financial state had eroded severely since Selma, and now SCLC's principal project, lacking direction, was an easy target for criticism. The *New York Times* quoted a Chicago black woman who asked, "Is this [Chicago movement] something to read about or is it something to help us?" In early June a Chicago daily generally sympathetic to liberal causes featured one Chicagoan's dismissal of SCLC activists as "romantic, disorganized tin gods who don't know the city." Such criticism hurt, for the stakes were high. "The whole future of SCLC depends on whether we are successful here. We'll just have to fold up if we fail in Chicago," Andrew Young had stated. The Chicago movement could not afford to give the impression that it had stalled.[136]

The Open-Housing Marches

"There is a good nonviolent fight in Chicago now and I challenge you to get in it," boomed Martin Luther King at a mass meeting on Chicago's South Side in early August 1966. The events of the previous week had invigorated King and his followers. In five of the past seven days, angry whites had terrorized peaceful civil rights demonstrators as they marched through white neighborhoods to dramatize the depth of housing discrimination. Drawn by the tumult, the press rushed to file reports on Chicago civil rights developments. To many observers and participants, it must have seemed as if the scripts of the Birmingham and Selma campaigns had been recycled.[1]

The surge of the Chicago movement could not have been more propitious. For weeks the standard line on the Chicago enterprise had been discouraging. "I think King is finished," Saul Alinsky snapped to a *Washington Post* reporter in mid-July. "He's trapped. He can't get out of [Chicago] in less than ten months to a year and he doesn't know what to do if he stays." Worse, King's leadership of the black freedom struggle was in jeopardy. A rising black militancy challenged King's vision of a better America. Then in mid-July, to his horror, a riot erupted on Chicago's West Side, in the very region that his movement had tried to mobilize for a nonviolent campaign. Not since the Montgomery bus boycott, the reporter Nicholas Von Hoffman observed, had the position of King and the nonviolent movement been so insecure.[2]

Then, almost miraculously, the beleaguered campaign was transformed into a confident crusade. The marches through all-white neighborhoods dramatized that Chicago was a divided city and that northern prejudice rivaled southern prejudice in intensity. Just as Bull Connor's police dogs had ignited the Birmingham campaign and just as the flailing nightsticks of Sheriff Jim Clark's men had energized the Selma campaign, white violence, especially on the Southwest Side, galvanized the Chicago campaign. One marcher wrote in early August to a southern friend, "I'm sure the news has spread to Atlanta by now that at last WE GOT US A MOVEMENT in Chicago. And, oh, a glorious feeling it is to finally start sitting straight and standing tall."[3]

In May and June of 1966, as the summer neared, few Chicagoans expected a season of exceptional racial strife. The economy was robust; the unemployment rate was well below three and a half percent. The head of the city's human relations commission circulated a hopeful, confidential forecast. Even fewer Chicagoans foresaw that the freedom movement would dramatically alter traditional summer routines. During these months the Chicago crusade rarely made the headlines. Community organizing continued but went virtually unnoticed. So, too, did Operation Breadbasket's program. And some initiatives fizzled. By late June the organizers of the Chicago student summer project had drastically lowered their expectations. After initial predictions of a thousand student volunteers, the project administrators admitted that the movement could not comfortably handle more "than fifty." In the end even that estimate exceeded the actual number of recruits.[4]

Only the Chicago Freedom Movement's work with black gangs attracted much attention—little of which was favorable. It was inevitable that King and SCLC staffers would search for support among the city's gangs. They possessed no illusions that young blacks in the North would be as receptive as young blacks in the South to their appeal. As King himself told representatives from a variety of Chicago social service agencies, southern youth were more "church-oriented" and less torn by "conflicting ideologies." Yet like the early Christians, SCLC workers were convinced that their message—the message of nonviolence—could win over even the most cynical, the most hardened. The workers were also pragmatists who recognized that the gangs represented some of the strongest grass-roots organizations in the ghetto. If the gangs could be persuaded to channel their power constructively, they would become much-needed allies in the quest to end slums.[5]

Rebellious youths have always been a ghetto fixture, but in 1966 many Chicagoans believed that their city was suffering from a gang crisis that was particularly acute. In the mid-1960s Chicago gangs had grown in size, organization, and ferocity. No one had yet offered a convincing explanation for the explosion, but one of its consequences was regularly reported: rampant violence. Though gangs roamed both the South and the West sides, their impact was felt most in the Wood-lawn region. There two gangs, the Blackstone Rangers and the East Side Disciples, battled for dominance.[6]

Into this troubled scene stepped Albert Sampson and James Orange, two experienced SCLC organizers. Sampson, a young black minister who originally hailed from Massachusetts, was committed to introducing gangs to the "mystery of the nonviolent movement." Orange, a massive man whose size was physically intimidating, developed an un-usually strong rapport with gang members and earned the respect of even the toughest Chicago youths. Once, at a meeting, when Blackstone Rangers jeered the suggestion that everyone sing freedom songs, Or-ange bellowed: "You think you're too bad to sing? Well I'm badder than all of you, so we're going to sing." He then strode into the crowd of gang members and quieted the unruly. "It looked as though he might really *be* badder than all of them," wrote a dazzled reporter.[7]

Sampson, Orange, and SCLC turned to hard-hitting workshops in their effort to reorient Chicago gangs. On May 9, at one of the largest workshops, the SCLC staff showed the roughly four hundred Blackstone Rangers in attendance a documentary on the Watts riot that depicted the senselessness of violence. James Bevel delivered a fiery speech, denouncing racial inequality but also assailing the gangs for playing Mayor Daley's game, for "fighting each other while he gets free." "The moment the people come together and look at the problem," Bevel predicted, "what you're going to discover is that the boys who live across the freeway ain't your problem. They aren't your problem be-cause you're raggedy . . . and they [are] raggedy."[8]

Two days later, on May 11, King met with a large contingent of South Side gang members. He encouraged them, most immediately, to assist with an upcoming SCLC-CCCO voter registration campaign, but his larger hope was to halt gang warfare and to draw more youths into the Chicago movement's orbit. But the gangs were not ready to grab the olive branch. On May 13 a melee broke out at an SCLC-sponsored peace conference that King planned to attend. When the Blackstone Rangers, led by Jeff Fort, walked into a South Side YMCA, a contingent of East Side Disciples, who were already there and were not expecting their archrivals, thought they were under attack. Punches were thrown, guns were fired, and the meeting was promptly canceled. The incident intensified criticism of SCLC's recruitment of gang members and the group's general performance. YMCA youth workers—who had tried to cooperate with the Chicago Freedom Movement—assailed SCLC's maneuvering. One Chicago police commander claimed that the gangs had been "stirred up" by SCLC's activity. A city youth official criticized SCLC for urging the gangs to unite against the white establishment. "This," she said, "is negative. To me, this is inciting."[9]

With the Chicago movement sputtering, internal divisions within the civil rights coalition continued. There was, for instance, increasing alarm about the direction of the Chicago drive among some board members of the Chicago Catholic Interracial Council, an important CCCO affiliate. Civil rights leaders in Chicago, one director charged, were "spreading hate" by their "attacks on the city administration, the school system and the police department." Conflicts rocked CCCO, too. Although the money raised from Freedom Festival cheered activists, it also provoked disagreement about how the funds should be spent. Some individual members of CCCO, including Chicago CORE and the West Chatham Community Improvement Association (WCCIA), wanted to draw on the festival receipts to fund their own projects. The CCCO steering committee, however, wanted to use the money to expand the CCCO staff. The steering committee's proposal passed, but only narrowly, and criticism about the CCCO leadership mounted. Later that spring differences within the Chicago movement became more obvious to the general public over a June referendum on a $195 million city bond issue covering a wide range of municipal improvements. CCCO and SCLC denounced Mayor Daley's proposal because it contained no guarantee that the additional funds would not be channeled into programs that would perpetuate segregation. But powerful CCCO affiliates such as the Chicago Urban League, the Chicago Catholic Interracial Council, and TWO publicly endorsed the bond issue as necessary and good for the city. In the end, this dispute did little damage to the Chicago Freedom Movement; it did, however, remind everyone that the movement remained a coalition comprising independent groups and organizations whose agendas were not identical.[10]

The Chicago Freedom Movement had long given up its original goal of beginning "massive action" by May 1. In late May it settled on June 26 as the date for a rally, to be held in Soldier Field, designed to kick off direct action. Although this was "rather late in the summer to begin action," Bill Berry and other strategists insisted that the movement was simply not prepared to hold a rally any earlier. "[A]nything less than spectacular success in turning people out for any rally will be a severe blow to the entire movement and its leaders," Berry warned King and Raby.[11]

The decision to delay proved wise. On June 6, only two weeks later, a new crisis forced a rescheduling of the rally. James Meredith, in 1962 the first black to attend the University of Mississippi and now on the second day of his "march against fear" in Mississippi, was gunned down by a white sniper. When news of the shooting reached King in Atlanta, he set out with his staff for Memphis, where the injured Meredith had been taken for medical treatment. King hoped that Meredith would allow SCLC and other civil rights groups to continue his trek. A massive march, he believed, would highlight the persistence of southern lawlessness and the need for federal protection of civil rights workers.[12]

The march, however, turned out to be one of the great trials of King's life. Rather than promoting unity, the Mississippi march showcased "Black Power," the new rallying slogan of a movement that was destined to divide civil rights groups and alienate many whites sympathetic to the black freedom struggle.[13] The Black Power rhetoric rattled King. Believing that Black Power was at heart an understandable "cry of disappointment," King never became an outspoken critic as some, including Roy Wilkins of the NAACP, did. Nevertheless he shunned the slogan for tactical and philosophical reasons: philosophically, because no amount of rationalizing could mask the fact that Black Power rhetoric (at least as expressed by Stokely Carmichael of SNCC and other militants) represented a turn away from interracialism, from nonviolence, and, ultimately, from SCLC's overarching goal of a "beloved community"; and tactically, because no matter what the virtues of Black Power—its emphasis on black pride, black assertiveness, and black autonomy—the slogan imperiled the black and white coalition that King believed essential for black advancement.[14]

The Mississippi march slowed the progress of the Chicago movement. Soon after the Meredith shooting, Chicago activists formed a local Meredith Mississippi March Committee to raise money and to mobilize marchers for the Mississippi protest. Scores of Chicagoans went south, including gang members and key Chicago Freedom Movement activists such as Bernard LaFayette and James Orange. With their energies diverted, King and Chicago civil rights leaders postponed the big Soldier Field rally until July 10.[15]

The Mississippi march also heightened the importance of the Chicago movement to King and SCLC. Confronted by fierce white resistance and by challengers from within the black protest movement, King more than ever seemed an embattled, perhaps even declining, leader. To regain his ascendancy in the civil rights struggle, he needed to rebound in Chicago. Black Power rhetoric, observers predicted, would appeal to angry and militant ghetto blacks. A big victory in Chicago would help silence critics who claimed that nonviolent direct action was no longer an effective or even a relevant strategy.[16]

As the Chicago activists prepared for a season of direct action, they did so with a keener grasp of Chicago's racial woes than they had possessed ten months earlier. The pressure of mounting a civil rights campaign had sparked intense inquiry into the dynamics of racial injustice in Chicago. As even the dullest observer of the ghetto could recognize, the limited prospects of black Chicagoans resulted directly from their lowly position on the American economic ladder. To free ghetto blacks from the snare of poverty, Chicago activists called for a domestic Marshall Plan, dwarfing the Johnson administration's War on Poverty, which would channel millions of dollars into the ghettoes.[17]

Chicago activists, however, did not view blacks simply as victims of their socioeconomic status. Race, they argued, still preceded class as the ultimate determinant of prospects for blacks. Racial discrimination had been so institutionalized, so woven into the fabric of Chicago society, that blacks suffered from differential treatment in almost every realm of Chicago life. Some discriminatory practices were overt, such as the refusal of certain trade unions to accept blacks into their ranks; others, such as the city's willingness to extend contracts to firms that discriminated against blacks, were more subtle. Taken together, these practices, Chicago insurgents concluded, had led to the systematic "subjugation" of black Chicagoans.[18]

Yet discovering the thread to undo Chicago's "system" of racial injustice proved difficult. The Chicago movement's West Side ghetto organizing had not yet turned up a compelling issue on which to base a direct action campaign. The seizure of the 1321 South Homan building highlighted slum conditions, but it had become so entangled in legal questions that an expanded assault on slumlords was unpromising. By spring, despite countless strategy sessions, the Chicago movement, in the words of one activist, still "did not have a real handle on a direct action strategy."[19]

The imposing, almost bewildering, complexity of Chicago racial injustice was at the heart of the freedom movement's troubles. The planning sessions of the past fall and winter had provided "a tremendous education on how things worked," one SCLC field staffer remembered. But "even after looking at all the different pieces and how they fit, we still had difficulty finding the right issue." In contrast to the South, there was no de jure discrimination in Chicago, and thus there was no critical, obvious target symbolizing injustice in the way that a southern courthouse did. How did one root out injustice when it was built into the very structure of society, when virtually every Chicago institution bore a measure of responsibility for it? A lack of quality jobs, King and Bevel recognized, was perhaps the fundamental ghetto problem. But who was at fault? Should the movement indict the school system for failing to prepare students adequately for future employment? Or were businesses the villains for failing to hire lower-class blacks, despite the claims of the head of the Chicago Merit Employment Committee and president of Illinois Bell, John Debutts, that the Chicago business community had "faced up to the need for equal employment opportunities" and was "way ahead of other cities"? Or were government agencies at fault for ineffectual programs that failed to boost minority employment? Moreover, the Chicago Freedom Movement already had a program— Operation Breadbasket—that was addressing the jobs problem, somewhat autonomously and on a small scale, but successfully nonetheless. It was debatable whether a full diversion of movement resources to Operation Breadbasket would result in a proportional expansion in its effectiveness.[20]

Compounding the Chicago movement's troubles was Superintendent Benjamin Willis's announcement in late May of his intention to retire early. Willis's impending exit removed the symbol of Chicago racial injustice, the man who had for so long rallied Chicago civil rights forces. Now, even as a last resort, a campaign against school segregation made little sense. It seemed only decent to give Willis's successor a chance to enact reforms.[21]

Nor was the Chicago movement ready to enter the political arena— the only way, argued the television commentator Len O'Connor and the white opposition alderman Leon Despres, to effect great changes in a city as political as Chicago. "[A]ll of the things that Dr. King decries—poor education, poor housing, poor job opportunities, 'economic exploitation': trace back to the Plantation Politics of City Hall," O'Connor contended. But to protect its tax status and its reputation, SCLC had always avoided outright partisanship. King, Raby, and other civil rights leaders hoped that their movement might trigger a reorientation of the consciousness of the electorate and the stance of politicians, but they did not propose constructing an alternative political vehicle. "I'm not leading any campaign against Mayor Daley," King asserted in late March. "I'm leading a campaign against the slums."[22]

In the desperate search for a focus, one target finally emerged as a favorite: housing discrimination. Chicago activists were not the first to discover this form of discrimination, of course. Throughout the first half of the 1960s, blacks across the North had protested against housing barriers. Moreover, civil rights forces had lobbied for President John Kennedy's 1962 executive order banning discriminatory practices in federally assisted housing, and even after the order they pressed for further equalization of housing opportunities. On one of his first visits to Chicago, in early 1965, James Bevel had blasted Chicago's real estate industry for exploiting blacks for "personal gain." In the Chicago Plan King himself had sharply criticized realtors for restricting "the supply of housing available" to blacks, and a month later Al Raby assailed the policies of the Chicago Real Estate Board. Yet it was not until late spring of 1966 that any SCLC leader spoke of fair housing as the Chicago movement's top priority.[23]

That the Chicago movement did ultimately turn to fair housing resulted largely from the work of William Moyer, the white housing expert for the Chicago chapter of the American Friends Service Committee. Reared in Philadelphia, Moyer had come to Chicago in 1962 to help with the AFSC's fair-housing program, which had been developed shortly after the Cicero housing riots of 1951. He soon decided that AFSC's quiet educational effort to disarm white fears about black neighbors was inadequate to the task of changing housing patterns in a city where almost every neighborhood was completely segregated by race and in a metropolis where most Chicago suburbs either had no black residents or just a handful. "Chicago's system of separation of the races differs from Mississippi's only in degree," Moyer explained. "In Mississippi, the Ku Klux Klan burns churches. [In 1964,] in Chicago, three houses were burned to the ground because they were purchased by black citizens." Inspired by his participation in the Mississippi Freedom Summer Project of 1964, Moyer developed a northern counterpart designed to end discriminatory real estate practices in the affluent suburbs to the north of Chicago. Staffed by more than a hundred students, the North Shore Summer Project of 1965 surveyed nearly fifteen hundred homeowners about fair housing, staged rallies, and invited Martin Luther King to speak at Winnetka.[24]

With SCLC's arrival in Chicago, the calm yet persuasive Moyer, already close to Bernard LaFayette, befriended James Bevel. Moyer participated in many movement staff sessions that fall. He told Bevel and other leaders that he "was as lost as" they were on how to end slums. But he did know that housing discrimination was a critical factor in creating and maintaining slums, and he pressed this point with Bevel and other Chicago activists. By mid-February 1966, Moyer, at the request of Bevel and Andrew Young, prepared a report documenting what everyone intuitively knew: that white prejudice and discriminatory real estate practices greatly restricted the housing stock available to Chicago blacks. Moyer's report—which followed a long and important local tradition of applicable research fueling civil rights endeavors that stretched back to Faith Rich's and Meyer Weinberg's studies on school segregation and to Hal Baron's productive research wing of the Chicago Urban League—also demonstrated that Chicago's dual housing market, one for blacks and another for whites, harmed not just middle-class blacks who could afford to live in white neighborhoods but all black Chicagoans. Limited in their housing choices, black Chicagoans, both the well-to-do and the poor, paid more for lesser housing confined to specific regions. They suffered from a "color tax" on housing, which was doubly burdensome because blacks on average earned far less than whites.[25]

Moyer had little desire to turn out more reports exposing the plague of housing discrimination. In March he and his AFSC staff began a campaign even more militant than the North Shore project. Project Open Communities attacked housing discrimination in Oak Park, a comfortable suburb bordering Chicago, well known as Ernest Hemingway's birthplace and as the site of many Frank Lloyd Wright homes. Oak Park residents characterized themselves as enlightened on race issues, especially after the communitywide embarrassment over the harassment Dr. Percy Julian, one of America's most prominent black scientists, and his family endured when in the early 1950s they purchased a home in the village. Project Open Communities, however, proved that equal housing opportunities were still lacking there. After two months of real estate testing, civil rights sympathizers marched through downtown Oak Park on every Saturday from mid-May to July. Usually ranging from fifty to one hundred in number, the marchers stopped at local real estate offices to protest discriminatory service and then continued to the village hall to demand a local fair housing ordinance. To boost the Oak Park campaign, Moyer recruited Bernard La-Fayette, Jesse Jackson, and James Bevel for these Saturday marches.[26]

Moyer knew that Bevel and other West Side activists had hoped to no avail for an action plan "coming right out of the inner city and taking on inner city issues directly." But here, Moyer told Chicago protest leaders, was at least a model for a northern direct action campaign. Real estate discrimination was neither as subtle nor as elusive as most forms of northern discrimination. It was very much like the lunch counter discrimination that had been so triumphantly eliminated by the southern black protest movement. Specific culprits could easily be fingered. To Moyer, Chicago realtors were the northern George Wallaces, standing "in the doorway of thousands of homes being offered for sale or rent" and preventing "Negroes and other minorities from choosing freely where they may live." In 1917 the Chicago Real Estate Board had passed a well-known resolution condemning the sale or rental of housing to blacks beyond blocks contiguous to the ghetto. Though the courts subsequently struck down measures such as racial zoning ordinances and restrictive covenants to ensure block-by-block segregation, real estate practices remained virtually unchanged. The real estate industry, Moyer contended, was a "ghetto-maker and ghetto-keeper."[27]

But the industry, Moyer insisted, could be reformed. Persistent discrimination by realtors could be readily detected through the use of black and white testers. By then marching on offending realty firms, protesters could transform these publicly licensed institutions into symbols not only of housing discrimination but, by extension, of northern racial injustice. Once the problem was clearly dramatized, men and women of good will would demand that every American be treated fairly and equitably.[28]

As summer approached, more and more leading Chicago activists lined up behind the open-housing strategy. The plan was appealing at least in part by default: it was the only feasible proposal advanced. The housing focus, Kale Williams, the executive secretary of the AFSC Chicago Regional Office, remembered, seemed to be "a practical decision because there [were] staff who had worked on this, who were prepared to work on it, who had made an analysis, who had things they could suggest doing right away." But the open-housing thrust possessed positive appeal as well. For one thing, it attacked a central problem of the ghetto: too many blacks squeezed into too little territory. For another, insurgents agreed with Moyer that such a thrust made good tactical sense. "[I]n demonstrations you can't have some obscure issue that is cloudy in the minds of people," Bevel insisted. "Should a man have a right to rent and buy a house in the city if he works or lives in that city and he is a citizen of that city? It is closed." Raby stressed the advantages of an open-housing focus over other targets. "It is not clear to me," Raby later noted, "how we might have taken the issue of unemployment, for example, . . . or doing a variety of other kinds of things." Furthermore, exposing discrimination in housing choice also exposed direct violation of the law. The 1963 Chicago Fair Housing Ordinance, after all, prohibited discrimination "against any person because of his race, color, religion, national origin or ancestry in the terms, conditions, or privileges of the sale, rental or lease of any housing accommodation or in the furnishing of facilities or services in connection therewith."[29]

But Bevel and his followers were attracted to the open-housing initiative for more than tactical reasons. More fundamentally, this strategy exposed a moral transgression, an offense against the dignity of human beings and the American creed of equal opportunity. In a real sense an attack on housing discrimination could be seen as a crusade, not just a campaign, whose mission was to root out an intolerable injustice. Jesse Jackson likened the breaching of the walls of segregation to an "exodus west." To men and women committed to racial justice, a crusade to rectify a "clear violation of basic principles" was, as Moyer had anticipated, compelling.[30]

When in late June King met with other Chicago movement leaders at a steering committee meeting, he too was ready for action. He endorsed the idea that the overarching goal of the movement should be to transform Chicago into a city with equal opportunity and equal benefits for all residents in all realms of city life. He thus sanctioned the shift in the Chicago campaign from an "end the slums" theme to an "open city" focus, even though it implied a change in emphasis from the daily, immediate concerns of black Chicagoans to dismantling barriers to black participation in the larger community. Equally important, he backed the decision to make housing discrimination the movement's first direct action target.[31]

In reaching this decision, King recognized that the movement's goal of organizing the ghettoes had not been fully realized. Yet as a leader of a national movement, a movement that had not won a major victory since Selma a year earlier, King was under pressure to turn to protests. King understood, as did his lieutenants, that movements, unlike institutions, are not self-perpetuating. To flourish, movements need sequential, even escalating successes. To allow the summer to evaporate without dramatic action was unthinkable, especially in light of recent events in Mississippi. Yet unfocused, unrequited activity, even on a mass scale, was not enough. It was King's genius—but also his dilemma—that he intuitively understood the essential link between direct action, substantive reform, and movement morale. Without a tangible response by America's centers of power—or "power structure," as King often said— the nonviolent movement would inevitably falter; many supporters would turn to other strategies for advancement. King believed that a successful Chicago campaign against housing discrimination would recharge the nonviolent civil rights movement and shape debate on fair housing, which he knew would be a prominent issue on the national agenda when Congress considered President Johnson's newest civil rights bill. So once again King prepared to lead a nonviolent battle. As he later told reporters, "I've been all over and I've found there is nothing more effective than the tramp, tramp, tramp of marching feet."[32]

Many Chicago protest leaders agreed with this last assessment. The power of the civil rights movement, as John McDermott saw it, "was not money; it was not organized bodies of workers; it was volunteers. It was people pouring in out of their conscience to help." The participation of these supporters, who usually had to be galvanized through dramatic, compelling action, was crucial; as McDermott put it, "If they didn't come, you closed down." An open-housing strategy seemed likely to generate that participation for the Chicago civil rights forces.[33]

The stride toward direct action excited many Chicago activists, who, while recognizing the importance of grass-roots organizing, preferred the drama of demonstrating. What was more exciting, more exhilarating, more noble than risking injury or arrest in a defiant protest for social justice? One Chicago civil rights leader joked, "We probably ended up on housing marches because we had a lot of people who liked to march." Aggressive protests were all the more appealing because of SCLC's track record. History's message seemed clear: if Chicago activists wanted a triumph on the scale of Selma, they needed to march.[34]

A direct action campaign would certainly enable many CCCO affiliates to play more central roles in the Chicago Freedom Movement, which had thus far been dominated by West Side initiatives. That in late May CCCO delegates met with King and SCLC representatives in an official setting for only the first time since early January illustrated the relative decline in importance of traditional CCCO groups to Chicago civil rights activity in the first half of 1966. Yet like the anti-Willis marches in the summer of 1965, open-housing marches needed hundreds of participants to be successful. Established Chicago civil rights organizations, most notably those not rooted in the inner city, would now be highly valued for their capacity to recruit volunteers. Spreading responsibility in a collective initiative would also likely improve intra-movement relations. One well-connected Chicago activist had reported earlier in the spring of 1966 that he often found "tensions between CCCO and SCLC . . . openly abrasive."[35]

The decision to demonstrate excited far from all within the civil rights ranks, however. Some activists did not think fair housing a critical issue. "Not a lot of black folks wanted to move to Cicero," one West Sider stated. "I did not think that open housing was a fundamental issue," Jimmy Collier of SCLC remembered. "It was more of a middle-class issue, even though there were people who wanted to live in better housing." Perhaps the strongest community organization in black Chicago, TWO—which with its Alinsky orientation had been somewhat cool to the notion of a sweeping, crusading citywide movement—virtually ignored the broad open-housing campaign, because it feared that such an effort would impair its work in the Woodlawn region and was bound to fail. Other activists, particularly those with social democratic leanings, flinched at a strategy destined to pit blacks against whites with limited financial resources. The SDS-backed JOIN saw no benefits for its poor white constituency emerging from an open-housing crusade. Many civil rights workers also worried that the thrust toward direct action was, as David Jehnsen put it, "premature." Thus far their community organizing efforts had not generated spectacular successes, but such work generally yielded long-term change, not immediate results. "Organizing is a tedious, day-to-day kind of thing," Herman Jenkins noted. "You have to settle in. There is no glamour to it." Yet, as Jenkins recalled, civil rights leaders seemed unprepared to commit themselves to such an extended endeavor. SCLC leaders, he felt, "had gotten trapped by their mode of operation"—direct action. Despite the movement's stress on community organizing since the fall of 1965, the coming of mass marches confirmed the suspicions of Jenkins and others that SCLC was ultimately more interested in "mobilizing" than in "organizing." Some of the West Side activists felt, Jehnsen added, "a need to dig deeper to do more leadership work, to build a broad and ever-expanding base before launching a direct action phase." "We weren't really ready for marches," Robert Mueller wrote later that year. "[N]ot enough people unified, not enough people understanding, not enough people even hoping." Yet, like many activists, Mueller conceded, "something very active and very visible had to happen."[36]

By the early summer national pressures, even more than local imperatives, were defining strategy. King valued community organizing, but that was not SCLC's preeminent role. Although he had long hoped that SCLC's organizing efforts would lead to enduring community groups, he had always expected that they would underpin a season of demonstrations. And now King and SCLC needed dramatic action to serve as a counterpoint to Black Power impulses and to the ever-present threat of riots, a threat that was heightened when a Chicago Puerto Rican neighborhood erupted in mid-June. Financial realities also shaped the decision of King and his lieutenants. In the first half of 1966 SCLC expenses were far outstripping revenue. Al Pitcher, a leading CCCO staffer, noted shortly after the summer of 1966 that King and SCLC had "need for a public image and for a national victory. They are very scattered and unless they have action going and unless they have a public image, it is very difficult to raise the money needed to keep the organization going."[37]

On Sunday, July 10, the Chicago Freedom Movement finally kicked off a direct action campaign by staging its long-awaited rally. Over thirty thousand people streamed into Soldier Field, the giant stadium set on the shore of Lake Michigan, for the summer extravaganza. Rally organizers had predicted a crowd of a hundred thousand, so the press immediately began to speculate on the significance of the smaller turnout. Did the modest attendance diminish the threat the Chicago Freedom Movement posed to Mayor Daley and other city decision makers? Perhaps it did, for even civil rights activists admitted that the Chicago movement had not yet electrified the city. Yet more immediate, concrete reasons better explain the undersized crowd. Surely the intense heat—thermometers registered more than ninety degrees—dampened enthusiasm for the rally. So too did inadequate recruiting efforts by the Chicago movement. "Martin's staff," one Chicago civil rights leader lamented, "always had this problem of thinking that Chicago was Selma, and anything could happen by just saying, 'you all come.'"[38]

Despite its shortcomings, the rally was still the largest civil rights gathering in the country during 1966. Blacks and whites (the latter forming roughly ten percent of the crowd), adults and families turned out for the rally, many to catch a glimpse of Martin Luther King. "We came to hear Dr. King and we want to hear what he says about Chicago" was how one middle-aged man explained his and his wife's attendance. "I came to hear Dr. King. It's a good cause and I believe in it," said a married woman who came alone. Andrew Young was impressed by the audience's willingness to brave the stifling heat. The crowd gave him "the feeling that they would go all the way to jail, if necessary, in a nonviolent program."[39]

The civil rights enthusiasts were treated to a long program, which included a rendition of the National Anthem by Coretta Scott King, performances by Dick Gregory, Oscar Brown, Jr., and other entertainers, and addresses by an emissary of Archbishop Cody and a diverse group of speakers appropriately reflecting the broad coalition that the freedom movement was fashioning.[40] Two speakers in particular drew great attention. One was Floyd McKissick, the executive director of CORE, who had recently presided over a CORE convention that had endorsed a Black Power program. No one knew what a professed militant would say about the Chicago movement, and his words took on added import when a hundred black youths waving a "Black Power" banner assembled on the stadium field. Yet, on this day, McKissick's remarks were soothing. Wearing a straw hat, the North Carolina lawyer denied that Black Power implied violence and hatred; rather, it meant political and economic power and a new self-image for blacks. "It is a means to bring the black American into the covenant of brotherhood," McKissick asserted. His conciliatory speech suggested that the old civil rights coalition had not permanently fractured. "If Dr. King calls me for help, no matter what our ideological differences are, I will come," he insisted.[41]

King was, of course, the headline speaker. Shielded by a single umbrella from the fierce afternoon sun (so fierce that it caused the collapse of over twenty members of the audience), King began by declaring, "We are here today because we are tired." It was a refrain echoing one he had employed eleven years earlier in his first public protest speech, when he was known only as the minister of the Dexter Avenue Baptist Church in Montgomery, Alabama. But he was not simply recycling stale rhetoric. His words had not changed because whether he was in Montgomery or Chicago, whether the year was 1955 or 1966, the cause remained the same: "We are tired of being seared in the flames of withering injustice." He made it clear that despite new stirrings, nonviolent direct action, the strategy forged in Montgomery and refined in the field of action over the years was still freedom's best instrument. "Our power does not reside in Molotov cocktails, rifles, knives and bricks," he proclaimed. "I am still convinced that nonviolence is a powerful and just weapon. It cuts without wounding. It is a sword that heals." Finally, King challenged racial separatists. It made no sense, logistically or morally, for blacks to go it alone. "So, let us all, white and black alike," he urged, "see that we are tied in a single garment of destiny. We need each other."[42]

After the rally a weary King, riding in an automobile (air-conditioned, his critics carped), led over five thousand followers on a mile-long trek to City Hall. "Like a huge tidal wave," the march traveled from Soldier Field, through Grant Park and into the Loop. As the demonstrators paraded up State Street, they filled the wide avenue from curb to curb while singing "We Shall Overcome" and "Freedom." "The numbers swelled, the spirit was buoyant, cheerful, with a sense of movement and purpose," was one activist's description. In the fashion of his namesake, King taped the movement's comprehensive demands on a City Hall door while the crowd witnessed the symbolic act. Open housing was but the most prominent of the many items, which ranged from aggressive steps by Chicago businesses "to integrate all departments" to measures ensuring a quality education for all Chicago youths to political reforms.[43]

The next day, Monday, July 11, King, Daley, Raby, and their aides met at City Hall to discuss the demands. King and Daley were cordial, but the meeting was not as friendly as their first one had been. King opened the session, characteristically, by refraining from accusations. He spoke of the injustices and disadvantages that urban blacks faced, yet he insisted that none of those present had created this deleterious situation. "It was," he noted, "left to us by a prior generation." Still, he continued, we "must deal with it in a massive way." He then listed the Chicago Freedom Movement's grievances, stressing the importance of the housing question but also calling for "a police-civilian review board," much like the one recently introduced in New York City. At Mayor Daley's request, Superintendent Wilson politely but firmly explained that such a board would hamper Chicago's renewed efforts to curb police misbehavior. A solemn Raby, no stranger to unproductive meetings in the mayor's office, quickly countered that from his experience the previous summer he knew of "at least fifteen men who contribute to the bad image of the department." Wilson coolly replied, "I am sure there are more than fifteen and I am trying to rid the department of these men."[44]

Daley then entered the fray, noting that he was pleased to hear that King did not think that his administration was to blame for the plight of Chicago's blacks. Under his tenure, he stated, the city of Chicago had embarked on a host of programs to improve urban life. He and his city government had little control over the destructive behavior of Chicago's poor, but "were dedicated" to ending slums. Daley seemed almost to invite King and his followers to join his crusade against urban decay. "We have the desire and we are trying, and we need your help," Daley declared.[45]

Daley would not, however, respond concretely or specifically to the movement's demands. He was "in agreement" with their spirit but would venture no further in offering any promises. King, however, suggested that this was not enough. There was a need for bold action and fundamental change. Blacks, King noted in his closing statement, were losing faith in the capacity of traditional processes to effect improvements. "We cannot wait. Young people are not going to wait," he warned.[46]

The two-hour session failed to satisfy either protagonist. When he met the press afterward, Daley was "scarlet faced," upset because he suspected that the King forces had sought the session not because they desired a fruitful meeting but because they wanted to justify an upcoming shift to direct action. No doubt Daley burned over King's recent threats of massive civil disobedience, which included the possibility of staging sit-ins on the Dan Ryan Expressway, one of the busiest highways in America. At first Daley's "words tumbled over each other in indignation," but Daley was too smart to lose control and allow himself to be portrayed as a northern version of a coarse southern official. As the press conference progressed, the mayor became more subdued, adeptly playing the politics of reasonableness. Ending ghettoes and poverty was no simple task, he reminded reporters. "Problems the city face[s] cannot be resolved overnight," he insisted. "No reasonable person can expect that." Moreover, Daley painted himself and his administration as undeserving targets of civil rights criticism. "We have the best record of any city in the country and we are committed to having the best city for all people," the mayor declared. He told reporters that he had listened to the complaints of King and his followers, but, he shrugged, "they have no solutions."[47]

King emerged from the session calmer than Daley, but no less dissatisfied. The mayor, he announced, had made "no commitments that will meet the specific demands of the time." Daley's reaction did not surprise King (a few days earlier he had told a television audience that "privileged groups seldom if ever give up their privileges"), and he did, as Daley expected, capitalize on the unfulfilling meeting to build support for impending demonstrations. Daley, King remarked, did not understand the "depth and dimension" of racial injustice in Chicago. In light of official recalcitrance, he stated, the members of the Chicago Freedom Movement would be forced to "escalate" their confrontation.[48]

On Tuesday, July 12, the temperature soared above ninety degrees for the fifth consecutive day and the ninth time in the young month. Seeking relief from the terrific heat, black youths on the Near West Side, a poor community full of public housing projects, played in the cool water flowing from opened fire hydrants. By law the hydrants should have been closed, but opened hydrants were a Chicago tradition. Even Mayor Daley admitted that as a boy in Bridgeport he too had frolicked in their spray on hot summer days.[49]

On this evening, however, the innocent tradition triggered an uprising. The episode began when an ice cream truck got stuck in a hole near the intersection of Roosevelt and Throop streets on the Near West Side. As the driver sought help, black youths slipped into the vehicle and took a few ice creams. The police then arrived. Noticing a flowing fire hydrant, they promptly closed it. The youths would not be denied their fun, and they again turned on the water. The police countered this move, but they were soon encircled by unfriendly local residents. Pushing and shoving began, followed by flying bricks and bottles. A score of police cars, blue lights flashing, raced to the scene to confront a swelling, boisterous crowd.[50]

In no time, the whole neighborhood plunged into disorder. A mob attacked passing cars and smashed store windows. Chester Robinson and two of his WSO staff members, alarmed by the spreading unrest, tried to direct the crowd to the West Side Organization's nearby headquarters. Shortly thereafter, James Bevel and James Orange joined WSO's peacekeeping force.[51]

King too rushed to the scene. He knew Chester Robinson, for earlier in the spring the WSO had invited him to speak at a community rally, and now Robinson and the WSO worked to bring King to the people once again. Late that evening King presided over a mass meeting at the Shiloah Baptist Church, two blocks west of WSO's headquarters. There he called for an end to the disorder and issued a plea for nonviolence. But his appeal went unheeded; many members of the restless audience walked out of the church while he spoke. For one of the few times in his life, King felt the pain of being unable to hold an audience. Out on the streets tumult triumphed. Large groups of blacks, mostly teenagers, roamed the neighborhood, occasionally throwing Molotov cocktails. Powerless to quell the disturbance, SCLC and WSO staffers abandoned their street patrols and returned to WSO's headquarters.[52]

On Wednesday activists scrambled to prevent a recurrence of Tuesday's explosion. They held meetings and toured the community, urging peace. Despite another blast of sizzling heat, calm reigned for most of the day—until city officials fixed fire hydrants throughout the Near West Side so that youths could no longer open them. By doing so, they ensured another evening of upheaval in the streets. The renewed disturbance confirmed a shift, first indicated by the 1965 West Side rioting, in the pattern of racial violence in the city. It was now clear that the borders dividing black and white neighborhoods held no monopoly on racial tension.[53]

Thursday night the Near West Side, though still tense, escaped rioting. But new outbreaks erupted in Lawndale (and, to a lesser extent, in East and West Garfield Park), two miles to the west, not far from King's Hamlin Avenue apartment. Though King and Chicago activists tried to contain the fury, the Lawndale violence surpassed that on the Near West Side. Thousands of blacks, mostly young men, many of whom were reportedly affiliated with gangs—precisely the group that West Side activists had had difficulty drawing into the unions to end the slums—took to the streets, looting stores, setting fires, and confronting the police. The police, according to some observers, displayed little reluctance in swinging their nightsticks or firing their weapons. The shooting "sounded like that in a movie," reported one witness.[54]

On Friday morning, July 15, an unsettled Mayor Daley requested that Governor Otto Kerner mobilize the National Guard to restore order. It had been a tough week for the mayor. Certain that he knew who was to blame for the city's racial woes, Daley lashed out at suspected provocateurs at a Friday press conference. Though not blaming King personally for the spreading riots, he singled out King's staff. Bevel and his lieutenants, the mayor charged, had "been talking for the last year of violence, and showing pictures and instructing people in how to conduct violence."[55]

This accusation stung King. His staff had been working the streets continuously, trying to contain the West Side fury, and King himself had just that morning met with prominent Chicago leaders, including Archbishop Cody, to discuss ways to restore peace to the city. "If we [had not been] on the scene," King told one reporter, "it would have been worse than Watts."[56] Later that day, after the SCLC leader and his advisers had been unable to arrange an appointment with Mayor Daley, they headed over to City Hall. It was a virtual "sit-in," remembered one member of the civil rights delegation. Soon King's party was joined by the city's religious leaders, including Archbishop Cody. He came from the West Side, where he and others had made a plea for peace; the day before he had met with the mayor to seek solutions to the rioting. Despite his earlier criticism of King and his colleagues, Daley received his unexpected visitors, though not without a delay. "Everybody was frustrated" at Friday's meeting, Ed Marciniak later recalled. Daley, however, was receptive to the demands of the civil rights delegation. Having already scored points with those Chicagoans who instinctively linked the disturbances to civil rights agitation, Daley could now become a conciliator, not an accuser, a mayor who wanted to restore peace and tranquillity to his city. With King seated to his immediate right, the mayor said, "Doctor, you know you are not responsible for these unfortunate happenings." He then listened to the advice of the civil rights and religious leaders. He consented to provide sprinklers to attach to fire hydrants, to construct more swimming pools, and to appoint a civilian committee (not, however, a more substantial review board) to improve police-community relations, long a subject of inner-city blacks' complaints. These measures fell far short of the sweeping change that the movement envisioned, but King stressed that they were something, a concrete achievement and a first step.[57]

New swimming pools, however, could not compensate for the damage wrought by the rioting. When the thousands of National Guardsmen finally left after several days of patrolling West Side streets with rifles ready and bayonets fixed, the extent of the devastation—though mild compared with the outbursts in Watts in 1965, in Detroit in 1967, and on the West Side in 1968—became clearer. Two people had been killed, over eighty injured, and more than four hundred arrested. Property damage topped two million dollars. It seemed doubtful that the ravaged neighborhoods would recover quickly. Roosevelt Road, according to one surveyor of the wreckage, "looked like a tornado had churned through."[58]

King had no difficulty explaining why the West Side had exploded. Ghetto misery, which white America tolerated, was the ultimate cause of the rioting. "A lot of people have lost faith in the establishment," King asserted. "They've lost faith in the democratic process." Although no adequate study of the 1966 disturbances exists, there is enough evidence to dismiss the claim that the riots were entirely "aimless." Much of the black rage was directed toward outsiders who were thought to exploit their communities: the police and white-owned businesses.[59]

Yet the directed, purposeful side of the rioting did not cushion the blow it delivered to the Chicago movement. Only a small part of the black community took to the streets, but more blacks had expressed themselves there, in the spontaneous, more immediately gratifying act of rioting, than in the movement's West Side organizing efforts. "No more marching. It don't accomplish nothing. From now on we're using black power, muscle. We're going to tear Chicago up," warned one West Side black, expressing the sentiments of many others. The atmosphere was so explosive that white activists and clergy, on the whole, were relegated to very restricted roles on the West Side, a disturbing omen for the nonviolent, interracial civil rights coalition. Even black leaders like King, Young, and Dick Gregory met with rebuffs when they sought to calm the West Side. This response suggested a conclusion painful for them to face—their irrelevance to large segments of ghetto dwellers.

Young, for instance, tried in vain to redirect West Side blacks to the goal that the Chicago Freedom Movement was currently addressing. "I'm [as] ready to die as any man," Young told a group of West Siders. "But get yourself something worth dying for. In Watts a lot of people got hurt because they weren't organized. Sure the kids need swimming pools here. But the main problem is that there are too many of us packed in here. We need living space." Young's listeners seemed unimpressed with this logic, and as he continued a group of youths started chanting, "hate . . . hate . . . hate." Bernard LaFayette and other activists now discussed whether they should replace "nonviolence" with a more vigorous term, because it carried connotations of weakness among inner-city youth. The Chicago movement was clearly in trouble in the ghetto neighborhoods. "Dr. King," one journalist noted, "very quickly discovered he had little influence in the West Side community."[60]

The West Side rioting prompted the *Chicago Defender* to question, though not to repudiate, the direction of the Chicago Freedom Movement. "[I]t is regrettable that Dr. King did not avail himself of the counsel and influence of the whole local leadership, some of which he assumes to be a bulwark of the status quo," the *Defender* editorialized on July 18. "In his perfectly legitimate quest for a cure of ills that beset Negroes, he could have used help that was available. Had he done this, his crusade would have yielded greater rewards." And while King could dismiss the Reverend J. H. Jackson's charges that "civil disobedience" was at the heart of the disturbances, he did not completely exculpate himself or the movement for the violence. "We neglected Chicago at a time when it needed our greatest resources," King conceded. "The rioting could have been avoided if we had . . . got[ten] our action program started a little earlier." Young agreed. The SCLC staff, he noted, felt responsible in part for the riots. They had warned, he added, "that unless the nonviolent movement got a good start there would be trouble before the 4th of July." King and his lieutenants could counter advocates of rebellion with sermons on the immorality and impracticality of violence, but they could hardly extol the accomplishments of nonviolence in the North, for the Chicago movement had little to show thus far. Rather than projecting confident leadership, King seemed almost a supplicant, imploring powerful whites for help. "I need some victories. I need some concessions," he said. The nonviolent direct action movement, he confessed, was "in deep trouble."[61]

* * *

King nevertheless retained hope that the Chicago movement would prevail. He knew that, lost among the headlines reporting the West Side riots and Richard Speck's brutal July 13 slaying of eight Chicago nurses, were the opening acts of the Chicago movement's direct action campaign. Even before the rioting, Chicago activists had unsuccessfully sought to persuade the Chicago Real Estate Board to fight housing discrimination and then had started testing real estate offices for discriminatory practices in the Gage Park area on Chicago's Southwest Side.[62]

Gage Park was not a random choice. This Southwest Side community was exactly what Chicago activists were looking for. Only whites lived in Gage Park, yet its modest homes—well-kept but closely packed brick bungalows—and comfortable apartments on peaceful and well-groomed streets were not beyond the financial means of most blacks. Moreover, the Gage Park region did not yet border the line of black settlement. Aware of the historic and often explosive pattern of block-by-block expansion of black Chicago, protest leaders had no desire to accelerate the severe racial transition in which neighborhoods rapidly changed from all white to all black. Instead, they hoped to open more housing to blacks. "That's why," Bernard LaFayette later explained, "we had to skip over the color line and move further on into" the white residential regions.[63]

The initial testers generated little commotion, but on Monday, July 11, the day after the Soldier Field rally, LaFayette and Bevel outlined the movement's open-housing "battle plan" to over five hundred enthusiasts at a mass meeting at the New Friendship Baptist Church on the South Side. Over the next few days, scores of white couples and black couples visited real estate offices seeking service. Nearly all of the black couples were discriminated against, receiving either no service or worse service than their white counterparts. By Thursday, Chicago activists claimed to have documented seventy-eight cases of discrimination.[64]

The civil rights probes alarmed Southwest Side leaders.[65] "Gage Park's Big Test," declared the *Southwest News-Herald,* an influential local newspaper, after learning that Chicago Freedom Movement workers had begun testing Gage Park area realtors. Local leaders recognized that the community response to the intruders would likely determine the length of their stay. The president of the Gage Park Civic Association called for a "sensible reaction" on the part of Gage Park natives. The *Southwest News-Herald* seconded his advice, urging area residents "to exercise calmness, courage, and conviction."[66]

Yet community leaders had reason to fear that residents would not take the civil rights probes lightly. They could not ignore the long heritage of white conflict and competition against blacks that had fueled the race riot of 1919 and the skirmishes over housing and recreational spaces since World War II. Until the early 1960s the Southwest Side had been largely insulated from the racial hysteria that gripped other Chicago neighborhoods as blacks poured into previously all-white communities (with the notable exception of a white riot in 1946 to prevent blacks from moving into the Airport Homes public housing project at 60th and Karlov streets). From the late 1950s until 1962 Southwest Siders had focused more on policies to quiet the jet noise from Midway Airport and the route that the proposed Crosstown Expressway would take than on racial issues. Nevertheless, local leaders knew that for the past three years Gage Park and much of the Southwest Side had been greatly disturbed by racial fears.[67] In 1963 Southwest Side natives became alarmed when blacks entered the eastern edge of West Englewood, less than twenty-five blocks from Gage Park and its neighboring community, Chicago Lawn. That same year a race riot in a changing section of nearby Englewood served as a grim reminder of the seriousness of racial transition in Chicago. Gage Park and Chicago Lawn now seemed in the path of an expanding black Chicago—from which many current Southwest Siders had already fled at least once before—that week after week engulfed blocks of hitherto white apartments and homes. In 1963 as well, white protests erupted against plans for limited integration of the Southwest Side's all-white schools, plans enacted to satisfy black demands. Southwest Siders also thundered against Chicago's weak fair-housing ordinance, which was a city response to civil rights pressure. After guiding the open-occupancy measure through a divided Chicago City Council in September 1963, the Southwest Side alderman James J. Murray became an outcast in his own community. Angry Southwest Siders chased him out of an auditorium during a meeting, pestered him with nasty phone calls, and even picketed his house for nearly a week. "My family's going through hell," Murray told reporters.[68]

During the next two years emotions on the Southwest Side rarely reached the high pitch of the fall of 1963, but open occupancy and school integration were still volatile issues. Southwest Siders remained Superintendent Willis's strongest supporters, and new community organizations denounced Chicago's fair-housing ordinance and the state's proposed fair-housing legislation as "forced housing," violating property rights and individual freedoms. Beneath the rhetoric of rights lay the knowledge that housing discrimination fulfilled a much-desired function: it excluded blacks from Southwest Side neighborhoods. At the polls, Southwest Siders also voiced their discontent over fair-housing proposals. In the 1964 race for state senator from the Twenty-Seventh District on the Southwest Side, John Lanigan, a young arch-conservative Republican, defeated the Democratic organization's candidate, also endorsed by Alderman Murray, largely because of Lanigan's militant opposition to fair housing.[69]

In selecting open-housing targets, Chicago civil rights strategists did not systematically explore the history of prejudice in each Chicago neighborhood. Above all, they searched for communities with housing costs equal to or below those found in the ghetto. But many recognized the importance of staging dramatic demonstrations. The initial selector of targets, Richard Murray, a white sociologist affiliated with the American Friends Service Committee, relied on what he called a "brickthrowing index" to carry out his job. Drawing on census data, Murray looked for middle-income communities whose residents still valued their ethnic identity and were not highly educated. In other words, he sought communities drastically different from the more affluent and sophisticated Oak Park and his own cosmopolitan Hyde Park, home of the University of Chicago. Instead, he found middle-income, heavily blue-collar, and ethnic communities such as Gage Park, Chicago Lawn, and Belmont-Cragin, a Northwest Side neighborhood.[70]

Murray's expectation that the open-housing demonstrations would be something other than peaceful walks through white neighborhoods was not unique. At the July 11 mass meeting, protest leaders warned potential marchers to expect a hostile response. Indeed, some leaders believed that, just as with SCLC's Birmingham and Selma protests, the key to successful demonstrations in Chicago rested on a rowdy white response. The Chicago movement, advised Bernard LaFayette in a well-circulated memo, should "demonstrate in one area at a time, evaluating the response of the demonstrators, the reaction of the residents in the area, the results and effectiveness of the demonstration, and the amount of publicity received."[71]

On Thursday, July 14, civil rights forces expanded their Southwest Side excursions beyond regular real estate testing and shopping visits to local businesses. Nearly one hundred civil rights sympathizers marched on real estate offices in the Gage Park–Chicago Lawn region. James Bevel mischievously told local reporters that the group was on a tour of the neighborhood "to see if we like it here." The visitors then headed for Marquette Park, a spacious, heavily used park on the Southwest Side, where they demonstrated their goodwill by joining local residents in a basketball game.[72]

That evening Martin Luther King, though tired from trying to calm the West Side, spoke at a civil rights rally at the New Friendship Baptist Church and, according to one observer, "brought the clapping, cheering, stomping crowd to its feet time and again." During these dark days, the movement, King reported, had already secured one small victory—Governor Otto Kerner's recent executive order, in the absence of state fair-housing legislation, banning discrimination in the sale or rental of housing. Now, King declared, "we want that thin paper to turn into thick action." In so doing, King would not be intimidated by his critics. "I have to do what God tells me to do," he asserted. Reflecting his dismay over the continuing civil disturbances, King insisted that success would not come "with bricks and Molotov cocktails"; rather, "we will make [Chicago] an open city through non-violence." Nor would King suspend his faith in an interracial coalition. "We welcome our white brothers in the movement. Together we will build a new Chicago where every child will be able to walk in dignity," he declared.[73]

On Saturday, July 16, an integrated group of a hundred civil rights workers picnicked in Marquette Park. On Sunday two hundred demonstrators strolled through the Gage Park community and held a prayer vigil outside St. Gall's Catholic Church. Though most Southwest Siders ignored the vigil, a group of teenagers heckled the protesters as they sang and prayed.[74]

King returned to Chicago later the next week and on Thursday, July 21, announced that "we shall step up our plans for nonviolent direct action to make Chicago an open and just city." At the same time he conferred with movement leaders over a new, more formal command structure.[75] King and Raby would remain the two heads of the Chicago Freedom Movement, while a Chicago Freedom Movement Assembly, consisting of representatives from all participating organizations, would, in theory, set general policy. Two other bodies, however, would guide the Chicago movement through the summer of direct action. The Agenda Committee plotted strategy. This group included, in addition to King and Raby, executives of the most influential constituent groups, such as Bill Berry of the Urban League, who had been raising funds and lining up support for the movement among businessmen professionals; Charles Hayes of the Packinghouse Workers; John McDermott of the CIC; and Kale Williams of the AFSC. The Action Committee, a much larger and less well defined body to which virtually any supporting organization could send a representative, made day-to-day tactical decisions. Some membership lists of this committee included over thirty individuals. The committee was dominated by SCLC, CCCO, and AFSC staffers but also included representatives from the West Side Federation, the West Side Organization, the Kenwood-Oakland Community Organization, the East Garfield Park Community Organization, and similar groups, though they rarely all met together. The Action Committee was led by Bevel, LaFayette, and Jesse Jackson, youthful but experienced veterans of southern campaigns who had been preparing for the upcoming demonstrations for weeks and who were not closely tied to CCCO. Although this new arrangement offered more structure than the ad hoc decision-making process that had been relied on thus far, it nevertheless left much room for disagreement over what constituted strategy, what constituted tactics, and whether the composition of these two committees was truly representative.[76]

While civil rights leaders worried about the decision-making structure, they also sought to calm local organizations concerned that the open-housing campaign might sap the strength of their own programs. Bernard LaFayette developed a strategy that he and other civil rights leaders hoped would dispel such fears. LaFayette saw no fundamental clash between the needs of the citywide movement and local interests. He proposed that local groups "agree to spend five days a week working in their community and any two days a week demonstrating or helping the city-wide movement in some way." Everyone could benefit from the "enthusiasm" generated by the open-housing demonstrations. Local organizations could, for instance, host mass meetings with prominent civil rights figures. These gatherings not only would recruit troops for the larger movement but would provide a "platform" so that the local organization could "reach a large number of people." This bold plan to develop a "platoon" system was never fully enacted, however. Local groups never became the real backbone of the open-housing initiative.

Such a goal may not have been realistic, given the territorial instincts of community organizations and given the logistical difficulties of effective coordination of a "2–5" plan. Yet, as Al Pitcher later remarked, the stillbirth of LaFayette's plan also reflected the decision to escalate the direct action campaign quickly, a decision which ensured that "there was not enough staff or time to develop these community organizations." The open-housing effort thus drew its troops through less formal channels.[77]

In the meantime real estate testing continued, though the number of testers on the South Side had "dropped off" since the first week of activity. The Southwest Side forays were complemented by intensified visits to Belmont-Cragin realtors on the Northwest Side, which had begun in mid-July. But the focus remained to the south, and on Sunday, July 24, another prayer vigil was held at St. Gall's Church. This time the demonstrators attracted more attention; "young toughs" tossed eggs and jeered the intruders.[78]

As the end of July neared, protest leaders were distressed that the open-housing campaign had not yet jelled. The real estate testing program had documented pervasive discrimination in the Gage Park area, which was essential for a legitimate protest thrust, but the program had been virtually ignored by the press. The media was still preoccupied with the aftermath of the West Side rioting and with the capture of Speck; small, peaceful, civil rights excursions did not constitute front-page news. Simply continuing the present program was not the dramatic direct action that King and other leaders had long promised. Something big was needed to focus the public spotlight on housing discrimination. Andrew Young may have summarized movement wishes best when he bluntly complained that "the trouble here is that there has been no confrontation . . . the kind where they interrupt the network TV programs to say that Negroes in such and such a white area are doing something."[79]

Civil rights leaders pressed forward. On Thursday, July 28—just as Stokely Carmichael was in town extolling the virtues of Black Power—King announced plans at a South Side rally for an all-night vigil on Friday on the Southwest Side. "Seething" was how the *Southwest News-Herald* described the Gage Park area when James Bevel and Jesse Jackson led demonstrators from the New Friendship Baptist Church, which had been designated as the action center for Southwest Side demonstrations, to F. H. Halvorsen Realty at 63rd Street and Kedzie Avenue for an all-night vigil. At first the protesters attracted little attention, but as the day wore on more and more whites surrounded the civil rights group. By late evening a large hostile crowd was heckling and taunting the demonstrators. Concluding that the protest had made its point, Bevel and Jackson accepted a police escort to the safety of the New Friendship Baptist Church.[80]

The suspension of the vigil disturbed some protest leaders, who worried that it would be interpreted as a sign of weakness. Gathered in the church's basement, leading insurgents decided that the movement must return to the Southwest Side the next day. On Saturday, therefore, Raby and Bevel led roughly 250 marchers through the Southwest Side back to Halvorsen Realty. Along the way hostile white onlookers cursed the demonstrators and pelted them with rocks, bottles, and pieces of coal.[81]

The next day Raby and Bevel headed an even larger march. The protesters, blacks and whites, parked their cars in Marquette Park, which was bordered by a tight-knit Lithuanian enclave, and proceeded two by two up Kedzie Avenue toward a Methodist church. There they planned to pray "that the real estate brokers . . . might be moved to open their doors to serve Negro families in the same way that others are served." But now the hostility they encountered surpassed their worst expectations. From the start, local whites, whose eyes "were glazed with hate," hounded the five hundred marchers. They hurled cherry bombs, rocks, and bottles as well as insults and invectives. "I'd love to be an Alabama trooper / That is what I'd really like to be / For if I were an Alabama trooper / Then I could hang a nigger legally," chanted a group of young boys carrying an oversized noose.[82]

The white outburst was more than the product of troublemakers who came "from other parts of town" or of youthful hooligans, as some Southwest Siders asserted. What made the rioting so fierce and so disturbing was its communal quality. Young men dominated the angry crowd, but fathers and mothers taunted the demonstrators as well and, more important, sanctioned the unruly behavior of the youths, many of whom styled themselves the community's protectors. One marcher sadly noted that many of the "residents of the neat bungalows" gathered to "enjoy the spectacle, as did their counterparts in the ancient Roman arena."[83]

Besieged, the marchers closed ranks; each gripped a partner's hand until, according to an insurgent, "the six hundred were One." But the fury of the white crowd was so great that march leaders called off the prayer vigil and ordered their troops to return to their cars. Back in Marquette Park, they discovered further evidence of the white rage. More than ten cars had been set on fire, two had been pushed into a lagoon, and dozens of others had had their tires slashed and windows smashed. By this time one marcher believed that the "feeling of the crowd had definitely changed from hating us—but mainly just wanting us to go away—to wanting to kill us." The demonstrators marched toward the black ghetto and safety. As they crossed Ashland Avenue, the edge of black settlement, they were greeted by the "soft smiles on black faces, children waving and shyly singing 'We Shall Overcome.'" Relieved, the marchers began to sing too.[84]

At the New Friendship Baptist Church the march finally ended. It had been an exhausting day. More than fifty protesters had been injured during the ordeal. Many demonstrators were almost numb from the shock of the day's events. Few had ever been "in the midst of such anger and hostility" before. But the marchers were not just stunned by the white hatred; many were also angered by the performance of the police. Why hadn't the police controlled the white mobs? Why hadn't they protected the demonstrators' automobiles? Why did the marchers have so many stories of police who failed to apprehend violent offenders or who arrested them and then let them go? The next day Raby and King, who was in Atlanta for services at the Ebenezer Baptist Church, issued a statement condemning the lack of police protection. Yet despite the events of this disturbing Sunday, the demonstrators remained committed to the open-housing thrust. "We will march for two weeks or two years if necessary," Raby proclaimed. "We will not be diverted by turning our anger against the police or the misguided people who attacked us."[85]

For the next few days, however, civil rights forces shifted their attention away from the Southwest Side. The open-housing campaign had never been intended to single out one Chicago community. "Our project is not against the people of Gage Park," stated Elbert Ransom, one of the march coordinators. The Chicago movement sought to expose the city's pervasive system of housing discrimination, which sprang from more than the racism of a few middle-income communities or the unjust practices of the real estate industry. Ultimately it was a system sanctioned by Chicago's most powerful leaders and institutions.[86]

The Chicago movement now targeted the Northwest Side, where

blacks were as unwelcome as on the Southwest Side. After nearly two weeks of testing real estate offices in the Belmont-Cragin community, activists had exposed an almost universal pattern of discrimination against prospective black clients. Local hostility toward integration was not confined to realtors. On Friday, July 29, whites heckled Bernard LaFayette as he spoke on racial justice at a Northwest Side Catholic Church. The following Tuesday and Wednesday, the Chicago movement staged marches in Belmont-Cragin. Although these two protests seemed like peaceful strolls compared with Sunday's explosion on the Southwest Side, hundreds of white onlookers, restrained by scores of police officers, cursed and jeered civil rights demonstrators.[87]

On Thursday, August 4, King was back in Chicago to address an energetic crowd of two thousand at the New Friendship Baptist Church. "The air" inside the church, said one activist, "was electric with the spirit and conviction of the Movement." First Raby, Bevel, and the independent black alderman Charles Chew addressed the congregation, and then Mahalia Jackson led everyone in song. Next King strode to the pulpit. King was energized by recent events, and his speech was one of his most inspiring of the Chicago campaign. "Stay in your place in the North means stay on the reservation," he proclaimed. "Stay in your place in the North means to be content with the low paying job . . . Stay in your place means that you must be content with overcrowded, inadequate schools." King refused to be subservient. "I have a place," he said. "My place is in the sunlight of opportunity. My place is in the dignity of a good job and livable wages. My place is in the security of an adequate quality education." The audience moved to King's rhythm. "My place," it shouted with King, as he began his next line: "My place is in comfort and in the convenience and in the nobility of good, solitary living conditions and in a good house." And when King finally exploded, "My place is in Gage Park," the crowd roared in agreement.[88]

The open-housing protests had now become the city's hottest story. Reports on unruly white crowds and speculation on the Chicago crusade's next move dominated newspaper headlines. More important, as one Chicago civil rights leader later recalled, "the reaction of the white community was so virulent and so fearful, it made a terrific story on television."[89]

The marches and the accompanying white violence jarred the conscience of many Chicagoans, and no example better illustrates this than Rabbi Robert Marx's reaction to the open-housing protests. Before the

July 31 Southwest Side eruption, Marx, a distinguished rabbi and Selma veteran, had been asked by the Chicago Conference on Religion and Race to do what he could to bring peace and order to the Gage Park area. On Sunday he joined local clergy in helping to disperse the crowds. He found himself "standing guard like a policeman, over a pile of rocks," to prevent local residents from throwing them at the protesters. "What I saw in Gage Park seared my soul in a way that my participation in no other civil rights event had done." He soon realized that he "should have been with the marchers."[90]

On Friday, August 5, Marx joined King and over five hundred marchers, the largest group thus far, as they set out on a trek through Marquette Park and Chicago Lawn. The march had barely begun when a rock "as big as [a] fist" struck King in the head and dropped him to his knees. Suffering only a slight wound, he kept on marching, as his aides and bodyguards doubled their efforts to protect him from further injury. The demonstrators headed north up California Avenue for Halvorsen Realty on 63rd Street. As the column advanced, white hecklers continued to taunt and assault the marchers. Someone hurled a knife at King. It missed its target, but struck a nearby white demonstrator in the left shoulder. One block from the real estate company, nearly three hundred whites sat in the middle of the street to stop the march, only to be chased away by a contingent of the twelve hundred police. A half a block to the north, whites again clogged the street, only to be foiled by the police once more. At Halvorsen's, the demonstrators knelt in prayer before embarking on their return march. The homeward trek was uneventful until they reached Marquette Park, where an estimated four thousand hostile whites had gathered to assail them. Thirty demonstrators were injured, but casualties would have been far more numerous had not the police intervened with great vigor. Father George Clements, a black Catholic priest, had to be rescued by the police from an angry white mob. Even veterans of southern marches were rattled by what they had seen. "Now, in the South," Andrew Young later remarked, "we faced mobs, but it would be a couple of hundred or even fifty or seventy-five. The violence in the South always came from a rabble element. But these were women and children and husbands and wives coming out of their homes [and] becoming a mob—and in some ways it was far more frightening." After the march, a tired King, speaking slowly, told reporters that he had "never seen as much hatred and hostility on the part of so many people."[91]

* * *

To many observers, the white violence was easy to explain. Southwest Side whites were so hostile and so hateful because they were bigots. A writer for *Ramparts,* for instance, concluded that there was no virtue on the Southwest Side. "There isn't any white backlash in Chicago," he stated. "There was never any forward point to lash back from."[92]

Ample evidence existed to support this contention. "Men, women, and children," wrote one reporter of the August 5 march, "sat on their front steps yelling 'Cannibals' and 'Savages' and 'Go home, niggers.'" One sign displayed that day read: "The only way to stop niggers is to exterminate them." Some whites randomly attacked black passersby who were not part of the marches.[93]

Yet racism alone did not trigger the white explosion. Most Southwest Siders were not raw, hard racists. Edward Vondrak, the publisher of the *Southwest News-Herald,* claimed that local residents had accepted the southern civil rights movement "as a normal effort by people seeking a better way of life." While Vondrak failed to point out that many Southwest Siders harbored racist attitudes (attributing to blacks a host of undesirable qualities such as laziness, slovenliness, and ingratitude), he did pinpoint the root cause of the Southwest eruption over the open-housing marches. The typical Southwest Sider, Vondrak explained, viewed the "civil rights movement as a threat to the security of his own community and his own home."[94]

White violence sprang from fear and resentment as well as from racism. Thinking of themselves as "just ordinary people," Southwest Siders feared Chicago Freedom Movement activists, whom they saw as hard-nosed, successful professionals. "They are veterans in civil rights activities," the *Southwest News-Herald* commented. "Many of them have previously participated in the movement elsewhere. They have been carefully trained in nonviolence and their actions Sunday night proved it." Unlike the small, almost spontaneous, and rather unfocused marches into Bridgeport in August 1965, which were aimed in part at residential exclusion, the current open-housing campaign was impressive. Southwest Siders took Jesse Jackson at his word when he declared: "We will have 40 to 50 families move into the Gage Park area by September."[95]

No prophecy could have more alarmed Southwest Side natives. Open occupancy legislation was bad enough; black neighbors represented the ultimate calamity. Southwest Siders were typically not doctors, lawyers, and professors, but men and women "who had scrimped, and saved and sacrificed" to buy homes in desirable neighborhoods. They trembled at the consequences of opening up the Southwest Side to black residents. They knew of no examples of Chicago neighborhoods—except for the Hyde Park area, in which the powerful University of Chicago had intervened—that had integrated successfully. To them, integration—the time between the entrance of the first blacks into a community and the departure of the last whites—inevitably meant the loss of their homes, their principal investment.[96]

The predominance of modestly middle-class whites helps explain the intensity of Southwest Siders' reaction to the open-housing protests. In contrast, the Saturday marches through Oak Park never elicited such a violent response. One reason was that Oak Park civic and police officials made it clear that they would not tolerate lawlessness. Another was the participation of a good number of Oak Park residents in the demonstrations. But the relatively high social class of Oak Park residents, which meant not only that they subscribed to a certain standard of public decorum but also that they had sufficient resources to be confident about meeting future exigencies, was at least an equally crucial factor. Many Southwest Siders did not feel they could afford to uproot and join the great migration of whites to the suburbs. "These people here have invested all their hard-earned savings in their homes, their churches and their hospitals," said one local realtor.[97]

But integration threatened more than Southwest Siders' financial security. It endangered their turf, their community, the place they called home. It jeopardized networks of associations centered on clubs, churches, schools, and neighborhoods—which in this quite diverse region were not in general based as squarely on ethnic identity as they had been in earlier inner-city communities—that give purpose and pleasure to life. If Southwest Siders were dislodged, all this would disappear, never to be reconstituted elsewhere.[98]

The possibility of black neighbors also imperiled Southwest Siders' own sense of their identity. Residence in a safe and stable all-white community, particularly for the many first- and second-generation Americans, was a principal badge of their social achievement, of their much coveted middle-class status. Their position in society, one local resident asserted, was "measured by how far they stand above the Negro."[99]

Fear alone, however, did not fuel hostility to the open-housing marches. Resentment gave it an even fiercer edge. Blacks, Southwest Siders complained, wanted to be given everything that whites had earned. Southwest Side natives and their immediate ancestors, many of whom had immigrated to America, had overcome, they reminded one another, mighty obstacles on their road to respectability. "We had eleven dollars when we landed in New York in 1949," declared one Lithuanian immigrant. "We've worked hard for what we have here." Blacks needed to do the same; but, above all, they needed to improve their own neighborhoods instead of threatening the stability of the Southwest Side through integration. "[T]he Southeast side of Chgo. had many beautiful areas that have become slums because of dirty & sloopy [sic] people. Why don't Dr. King, Al Raby & his fellow followers work at educating these people on *fundamental* cleanliness & moral obligations," one enraged white wrote in a letter to Illinois Senator Paul Douglas.[100]

Confronted by the civil rights challenge, Southwest Siders united. The region had a few racial liberals, who condemned the white violence and praised the civil rights demonstrations. Moderates like the *Southwest News Herald* criticized the excessive militancy of the white counterprotests. But the progressive voice was completely overmatched, and too much was at stake for moderates to excoriate, rather than just criticize, local residents who assailed civil rights activists. Moderates and militants treasured their turf and their traditional way of life. The Southwest Side, they agreed, needed to defend itself.[101]

The Southwest Side explosion constituted more than retaliation against blacks and the threat of integration. It also represented the cry of a community under siege. Southwest Siders had acted in a time-honored Chicago tradition toward potential black neighbors, but in the mid-1960s, because of heightened public disapproval of bigotry and because of Martin Luther King's presence, their response had engendered metropolitan, even national, scrutiny and harsh censure from influential quarters. Southwest Side residents now felt abused and abandoned by the world beyond their borders, a world seemingly full of social engineers bent on interfering with their communities. It was this broader expression of grievance that most alarmed city elites and that spurred frantic efforts to defuse the crisis.[102]

White liberals were a special target of Southwest Side anger. While Southwest Siders themselves had voted for Lyndon Johnson over Barry Goldwater in the 1964 presidential election, most now thought that Great Society liberals had endorsed too many preposterous positions on too many issues, particularly racial issues. They swamped Senator Douglas, a prominent liberal and an aggressive advocate of civil rights legislation, with hostile letters accusing Congress of mistreatment and of subversion of the Constitution. One Chicago Lawn man informed Douglas shortly after a Marquette Park open-housing march that "since the Civil Rights Act was passed all we have seen is violence, riots and general defiance of the laws of the land by the Negroe [*sic*] population, under the guise of this nebulous term, civil rights." This man found it inexplicable that Congress was currently considering federal fair-housing legislation. "We work hard, pay our taxes, improve ourselves, only to find the more we improve ourselves and our property the more we are taxed and told what we can and cannot do with it."[103]

Class resentment also crept into Southwest Siders' complaints. Liberals, they claimed, had scores of different proposals to promote integration, but all the plans were similar in that each required great sacrifices on the part of the common people and none or practically none from the liberals. A Southwest Side man accused two of the nation's most prominent liberals of such hypocrisy. "Just because people like you and President Johnson have large esstates [*sic*]," he wrote to Governor Otto Kerner during the open-housing marches, "you don't need to worry who lives next door or whether your child or daughter will be raped or stabbed when they leave their home." A West Lawn couple extended this man's accusation. "We notice some of our elected representatives, and some other people who get their names in the papers, scream for Civil Rights for the Negro," they observed. "Yet they happen to be just the people least affected. They have expensive homes on 2 to 5 acre estates, far from the common man, and that is the way they like it and want it to remain." They concluded, "IT IS EASY TO TELL SOMEONE ELSE WHAT TO DO, WHEN YOU DON'T HAVE TO DO IT YOURSELF."[104]

Southwest Siders were particularly surprised by the many clerics who joined their critics. Southwest natives considered themselves good Christians, and in turn expected ministers and priests to back their defense of their territory. Many local clerics did, most notably Vernon Lyons, a conservative Baptist minister. An outspoken defender of an all-white Southwest Side, Lyons insisted that the Bible supported his stand. "There is no open occupancy in heaven," Lyons informed Southwest Siders at the height of the open-housing crisis.[105]

But many Chicago spiritual leaders took a much different stand on fair housing. Chicago Freedom Movement activists distributed flyers throughout the Southwest Side, a heavily Catholic region, on which were emblazoned statements by Archbishop Cody endorsing open occupancy. Many priests, nuns, ministers, and rabbis participated in the marches. Nothing infuriated Southwest Siders more than these religious activists. On the Sunday, July 31, march Sister Mary Angelica, a nun, was struck in the head by a rock. When her wound began to bleed, the gathered crowd cheered. Even local clergy who did not march were endangered. During the same march, Monsignor James Hardiman, a respected Southwest Side pastor, tried to pacify the crowd, urging restraint. Not only did his pleas go unheeded, but Hardiman himself was abused. "After last Sunday," Hardiman later remarked, "I can honestly say I wouldn't go near the mob again unless I was armed . . . We learned that the sight of a Roman collar incited them to greater violence and nastier epithets."[106]

"There is a general anti-Church reaction to the clergy," commented a Presbyterian minister. "It's the same kind of reaction as to the marchers." The church, especially the Catholic Church, had lost the respect of many local residents. It had moved, many Southwest Siders felt, beyond its traditional sphere and was now unwisely meddling in social questions. Even at St. Rita's Catholic Church in Chicago Lawn, whose pastor opposed integration, parishioners placed notes in the Sunday collection addressed to "that fat guy, Cody, the pig."[107]

The Southwest Side had become a bunker community. Stung by criticism of the clergy, liberals, civil rights activists, and the press, Southwest Side natives turned inward, indignant that their position on residential integration had been so easily dismissed. The aggressive assaults on civil rights demonstrators represented only the most public manifestation of the popular mood. A wave of mass meetings swept across the Southwest Side that well illustrated the extent of white mobilization and insurgency. More than six hundred people attended one rally in Marquette Hall. They listened to some of the most vehement critics of the Chicago Freedom Movement: Vernon Lyons, who believed that civil rights leaders were professional agitators with "documented communist sympathies," and Ted Moleski, who had organized the White Hat Brigade, an anti–civil rights youth group. Many residents said that they no longer cared what the outside world thought and that only they knew what was in the best interest of their community. In early August 1966, the Thirteenth Ward's Republican committeeman voiced the prevailing Southwest Side view. "I . . . am fed up with sociologists and bearded weirdies telling me that I am incapable of brotherly love," he said. "I am tired of metropolitan newspapers, out of state marchers, and Martin Luther King telling me how I must live and who I must live with."[108]

It was with great disappointment, then, that Southwest Side residents realized they could not rely on Mayor Daley and City Hall as allies in this crisis. Though they had not always voted for Daley—in 1963 the Republican Benjamin Adamowski, a former Democrat with white ethnic appeal, had outpolled Daley on the Southwest Side—many had assumed that the mayor, a native son of the Irish working class from nearby Bridgeport, understood their predicament. But on the open-housing question it seemed that the Daley administration was at best neutral and at worst had sided with the Chicago Freedom Movement. Though Daley never marched, many Southwest Siders believed that the mayor was represented too well by the Chicago police, especially after the July 31 protest. To clear the path for the marchers, the police shoved white onlookers—with glee, some residents thought—and they arrested young men who residents believed were defending their community. The police protection of the marchers was especially galling because Southwest Siders were good taxpayers (and many were good Daley voters). "The peace and serenity of our neighborhoods has been taken from us," mourned a member of the Chicago Lawn Civic Association. Her community, she complained, had been "invaded by throngs of troublemakers—riot inciters" who were "given protection by the police whose salaries are provided out of taxes which we pay. We are, in effect, paying for the destruction of our way of life."[109]

Daley himself offered few hints that he sympathized with the Southwest Side's plight. On Tuesday, August 2, he met with Southwest Side aldermen, clergy, and civic leaders, but his public statement was simply a call for law and order. "Violence never led to anything constructive, and disorder leads to disorder," the statement declared. Moreover, Daley was unresponsive to the pleas of Southwest Side representatives at another City Hall meeting after the August 5 march. Some of the Southwest Side delegates called for an investigation of "communist influence" in the civil rights ranks. Others begged Daley to stop the marches. "It was a plea, not a demand," said one petitioner, "and the Mayor's only answer was 'They have a right to march.'"[110]

But Daley indeed recognized that Chicago was caught in an explosive situation. A year earlier, when relatively small groups of civil rights demonstrators paraded outside of his Bridgeport home, his ward and precinct captains had been able to contain his neighbors' fury. Now Daley's political team seemed unable to reassure Southwest Siders, who were not as thoroughly connected to the Daley political machine as Bridgeport residents were and who had good reason to believe that this time the civil rights movement had the power to produce unwanted change. On August 9 the mayor in a strained voice announced: "I am asking for calm. I will meet with anyone and do anything to prevent what is happening to our city. I will meet with Dr. Martin Luther King or anyone else at any time. We cannot get anywhere through violence."[111]

Yet the city seemed destined for more conflict. Whites on Chicago's Southwest and Northwest sides had dug in to defend their turf. The Chicago Freedom Movement had no intention of backing down. After the August 5 march King had declared: "We shall have to keep coming back until we are safe from harassment. Until Negroes can move into the neighborhood the tenets of freedom will continue to decay."[112]

The City in Crisis

"Never has this city been so consumed with hatred," a Chicago columnist concluded in early August 1966. Chicago tottered on the edge of a "race riot," the superintendent of police warned. The foundations of civic order, many Chicagoans believed, were rapidly crumbling.[1]

Cries of impending disaster hardly ruffled civil rights activists. They knew that crisis was often the father of reform. They would continue marching, for they believed that the city needed an even more vigorous jolt. "We haven't been able to put on enough pressure yet," Andrew Young explained. "In Birmingham and Selma we almost needed martial law before we got anywhere."[2]

Yet for many Chicagoans, including influential supporters of the Chicago Freedom Movement, there had already been too many marches and too much pressure. No clear-headed person could now deny that racial intolerance infected the city. Further disorder, many citizens contended, would set back racial justice rather than speed its arrival. It was time for the civil rights crusaders to settle their grievances in the conference rooms and not in the streets.

The Daley administration seconded such exhortations. But it did not simply rely on pleas to realize its wishes; it maneuvered to regain the upper hand. The Chicago police beefed up their protection of the marchers so that there would be no recurrence of the terrible Southwest Side violence. More important, Daley and his lieutenants challenged the civil rights leaders' contention that at the heart of the open-housing crisis was the question of social justice. At stake, the Daley forces argued instead, was the city's civic order.

Over the next month the Chicago Freedom Movement and the

Daley administration squared off in an elaborate duel of thrusts and counterthrusts. There were limits to the tactics each side was willing to employ. To promote social justice, King and the Chicago Freedom Movement would not recklessly flout civic decrees and topple Chicago into true chaos. To secure social order, Daley and his supporters would not forfeit their claim to benevolence by nonchalantly spurning calls for equal rights. Within these boundaries, however, two competing visions of social progress clashed. The Daley camp believed that working through the established machinery was the best hope for advancement in a complex and uncertain world. King and his fellow insurgents, in contrast, feared that such a view too often emphasized, in King's words, "the progress that has been made." They believed that "we must always look at progress not in terms of the distance from which we have come, but in terms of how far we have gone toward the democratic dream and the democratic promise." By carefully directing their power—generated through demonstrations and marches—they could prod reluctant political leaders and other prominent Chicagoans to embrace innovation. It was a delicate mission, fraught with potential pitfalls and countered by skillful rivals. The success of each side in advancing its vision—one stressing social justice, the other, social order—would ultimately determine the outcome of Chicago's civil rights ordeal.[3]

Al Raby and his fellow insurgents would have been hard pressed to devise a better recruiting pitch than the stoning of Martin Luther King, Jr. On Sunday, August 7, two days after that shocking event, nearly one thousand people marched for open housing in Belmont-Cragin on Chicago's Northwest Side. At the front of this large contingent were the three men whose names had become virtually synonymous with open-housing demonstrations. No one was surprised that Raby, the co-chairman of the Chicago Freedom Movement and CCCO's convenor, and James Bevel, SCLC's master of direct action, were in the vanguard. The rising newcomer—who seemed on this day to broadcast his ascendancy with his flashy clothes, a red hat and a red tie set against a dark suit—was Jesse Jackson, now regularly referred to as a Chicago civil rights leader. As usual, white hecklers lined the route of the protest and shouted invectives. Some of the angry whites, it seemed, desired another violent showdown. Early in the march they launched a "volley of missiles" at the demonstrators. For a moment, one officer reported, it "looked like there was a danger of riot." But the police restrained the crowd, and the rest of the march, including prayer vigils at two churches and a real estate office, was remarkably peaceful.[4]

The relative absence of violence mystified few insurgents. "[T]he difference," Jesse Jackson claimed, "was the police." He was right, to an extent. Since the first Southwest Side eruption Chicago had stiffened its protection of the marchers. On this march more than five hundred police dressed in riot gear encircled the demonstrators by forming lines to either side of the protesters. The aggressive protection dampened the crowd's desire for a confrontation. At the same time the skillful police-work subtly altered the dynamics of the open-housing demonstrations. With "[t]he police literally a wall between the march and the people in the community," the later protests became less dramatic and, in turn, less effective.[5]

James Bevel and other protest veterans believed that little attention should be given to the role of the police, because to do so would direct focus from the ultimate goal of the demonstrations—open housing. A few activists, however, came to lament the early demand by the movement for more police protection. This was not because they relished violence. Although the open-housing campaign was intended to expose white hostility toward blacks, the structure of the protests—public processions covered by a phalanx of reporters—was designed to limit, and not simply to foster, acts of intense violence. Nonetheless, some activists believed, as Kale Williams of the AFSC later suggested, that "a wiser and more consistent response within the nonviolent philosophy" would have been "to take more of the violence upon ourselves rather than to seek to be protected from it." Such a response, Williams argued, would have more faithfully captured the "redemptive quality of unearned suffering" and thus heightened the moral power of the movement. But neither this voice nor Bevel's carried the day. Raby spoke for most demonstrators when he called upon the city to fulfill its civic obligation by protecting peaceful marchers exercising their constitutional right to public assembly.[6]

Better police protection alone, however, did not soften the Northwest Siders' reception of civil rights visitors. Determined to avert an eruption like the one that had occurred on the Southwest Side, Northwest Side precinct captains had urged residents throughout the area to ignore the upcoming march. From the local pulpits came a similar message. "All we have left is our respect for one another. So let's go out and act like Christians," one Northwest Side priest implored. The demonstrators "are very peaceful people. Let them come and go," exhorted another.[7]

The ultimate source of Belmont-Cragin's restraint was even deeper. After all, calls for calm had hardly checked Southwest Siders, and Belmont-Cragin, full of white ethnic homeowners, was very much like Chicago Lawn and Gage Park. But Belmont-Cragin residents differed from their Gage Park and Chicago Lawn counterparts in a crucial respect. Because the black ghetto was more than thirty blocks away and expanding to the west (not to the north), they lacked a sharp and palpable community-wide fear of racial transition.[8]

The Belmont-Cragin pilgrimage was not as dramatic as the Southwest Side protests, but civil rights leaders were nevertheless delighted that so many had marched. The Southwest Side mobs had sent a strong message to future demonstrators that marching was hazardous to their automobiles and to their health. But Sunday's big protest proved, Bevel declared, that the Chicago activists would "not be intimidated by crowds and violence." One demonstrator noted, "We march, we return home emotionally drained, from some inner reservoirs replenish our strength and go back."[9]

This fearless civil rights army, though marked by youth, was remarkably diverse, comprising men and women, the young and the old, blacks and whites, and a broad spectrum of social classes. Some, like Jessie "Ma" Houston, an elderly black missionary to the Cook County House of Corrections, had become local legends because of their commitment to direct action. "I used to be an invalid unable to work and then I started marching," Houston declared. "Every day I got stronger and stronger and now, this year, I am working. The Movement made me strong and will make others strong, too." A few, like Jim Letherer, a one-legged white Northerner who had traveled on crutches from Selma to Montgomery in 1965, were professional marchers. Still others, like Vivian Campbell and Wendy Sandifer, black high school students, had never demonstrated before. "I just thought it was time," Campbell explained, "and I called Wendy and said 'let's go.'"[10]

It is difficult to determine precisely the motivations of the marchers. Some demonstrators saw a direct connection between the goals of the marches and their own futures. "If we could get a house in Bogan with some fresh air and some grass," noted one Lawndale woman, "we'd move out of the ghetto tomorrow." Most, however, did not expect to reap any direct material advantages from their participation and were propelled by moral imperatives. One white woman remarked, "A Negro can't buy a home in [a white neighborhood] but Richard Speck [the infamous mass murderer] could." A black marcher from Englewood, echoing a dominant outlook, later commented: "It wasn't about our wanting to live [in all white communities]. It was about our right to live there." Others cared little about the specific goal of fair housing. Chicago CORE, stated its chairman, Robert Lucas, "didn't really believe in open housing," but it sent a sizable contingent on the marches because it wanted to show "the rest of the world how racist Chicago was." Still others relished the power that was generated through defiant collective action. "You had people involved in the movement for various reasons," Billy Hollins, a SCLC Chicago staffer, noted. "Some people were involved because it was a lifestyle, it was a way to get attention. There are always ulterior motives."[11]

One generalization is incontestable, however. The demonstrators did not represent a simple extension of the West Side organizing effort. Middle-class blacks and whites were well represented in the marches. Some West Side residents, particularly those affiliated with the unions to end slums, threw themselves, like most West Side organizers, into the open-housing campaigns. But not all considered fair housing an imperative goal or marches into white neighborhoods the best tactic. Many West Siders, recalled one local organizer, were primarily "concerned about their own building or their unemployment or something of that nature. They were not concerned about moving out to the suburbs. They did not have enough money to pay the rent where they were." Some activists later regretted that the movement did not do more to broaden this perspective by better publicizing the connection between housing discrimination and ghetto conditions.[12]

Many of the marchers shared a history of earlier involvement in protests against schools, fair-housing efforts in suburban Chicago, or human relations gatherings. In other words, they were already connected to civil rights networks before the open-housing drive. Through the established channels of the Chicago Catholic Interracial Council, John McDermott, for instance, recruited scores of Catholics, often from comfortable white neighborhoods, whom he "could count on to do about anything." Taking part in civil rights demonstrations was, according to McDermott, "one of the highpoint experiences of their lives." The CIC contingent was not alone in such feelings.[13]

A remarkable feature of this army, especially in a time of intensifying racial polarization, was its strong interracial character. Its leading figures, to be sure, were black—King, Raby, Young, Bevel, and Jackson—but there were high-ranking whites as well. The tall, older Al Pitcher, who had taken a year's leave of absence from his teaching at the University of Chicago Divinity School, served as Raby's chief of staff. In addition to McDermott, Kale Williams participated in the movement's top planning councils. Williams, a Quaker, exemplified the strong religious orientation of many committed whites. Raised in Kansas, Williams attended the University of Chicago in the 1940s and was drawn into civil rights work there because of his distress over white hostility to black neighbors. In 1958 he took over the Chicago Regional Office of the American Friends Service Committee. By 1966, with its resourceful urban affairs program under Bernard LaFayette and its strong housing opportunities program under Bill Moyer, no group was more valuable to the Chicago Freedom Movement.[14]

Even more significantly, whites generally made up nearly half of the protesters on most marches. SCLC had never before spearheaded such a diverse coalition in a sustained campaign. In the southern initiatives, whites constituted a small part of the nonviolent army and were more important for the symbolic power their presence generated than for their numerical force. Though growing numbers of blacks nationwide questioned whether whites could play an effective role in the civil rights struggle, the Chicago movement styled itself as an exemplar for the better America that it sought. In the quest for equal housing opportunities, blacks and whites crusaded together.[15]

In addition to a belief in racial brotherhood, the demonstrators shared a commitment to nonviolence. Despite all the taunts, slurs, and rocks, marchers resisted the impulse of retaliation. No doubt for many this restraint derived in part from their predisposition to nonviolence. But not all activists were unshakably committed to the philosophy. CORE's Robert Lucas stated after the July 31 march: "We can't continue the passive reaction to all hatred." To maintain a nonviolent demeanor, the Chicago movement insisted upon tactical discipline, which was reinforced by proper training. When activists gathered before a protest at one of the two Action Centers, either a South Side or a West Side church, veteran demonstrators like Jesse Jackson would guide them through a nonviolent training session. We used to "pretend we were being attacked," one regular marcher recalled. "And we would roll up in a ball to get the least amount of harm done. We used to play games where we would call each other real terrible names, 'niggers,' and all kinds of obscenities."[16]

Even gang members, who often served as march marshals—directing the column of demonstrators and shielding it from the worst of the angry whites' fury—toed the nonviolent line. Although King knew it was unlikely that gang members would accept nonviolence as a creed, their behavior on the marches proved that even the most intractable could productively use it as a tactic. "I remember walking with the Blackstone Rangers while bottles were flying from the sidelines, and I saw their noses being broken and blood flowing from their wounds; and I saw them continue and not retaliate, not one of them, with violence," King later marveled.[17]

On Monday, August 8, protest leaders decided to take a break from marching, and an evening rally at the Warren Avenue Congregational Church became the high point of the day. Protest leaders used the mass meetings—which had been so central to success in southern campaigns—to spread news about strategy that had already been set and, more important, to whip up enthusiasm. Usually staged in churches serving as Action Centers—appropriately so, as one black minister put it, for the church "should be the meeting house"—at least twice a week during the open-housing protests, the rallies brought together all kinds of people from a sprawling, impersonal city and reinforced their commitment with defiant songs and buoyant speeches. Because WVON, a black radio station, sometimes broadcast the meetings, they also reached out beyond the confines of the church. The rallies were, in the words of one activist, "the great spiritual engines of the movement."[18]

Yet though the mass meetings dramatized the spiritual strength of the movement, they also, strangely enough, exposed its limits. Despite the upsurge of moral fervor sparked by the rallies, few black churches desired to host them. Many ministers, one pastor supportive of the civil rights movement commented, "were afraid of inviting Dr. King to their churches because they were afraid they would alienate the feelings of Mayor Daley." "A number of them," he continued, "were eating at the mayor's table." Nor would an old-line conservative like the Reverend J. H. Jackson have ever opened his church to the movement.[19]

Those ministers who considered inviting in the Chicago Freedom Movement knew that they would have to endure fierce pressure. The physical danger was great enough that protest leaders were forced at least once during the summer to switch command sites. In July and early August, the New Friendship Baptist Church was the staging ground for the Southwest Side protests. Its pastor, the Reverend Stroy Freeman, an Arkansas native, had begun his ministry in 1946 and in 1961 brought his swelling congregation to a large church on 71st Street in Englewood. Freeman never forgot his roots. When Martin Luther King issued a call for help during SCLC's Albany, Georgia, campaign in 1962, Freeman—a member of the Progressive National Baptist Convention—answered. He traveled with a large Chicago delegation and eventually landed in jail. His time behind bars did not dampen his civil rights enthusiasm; in 1966 he openly endorsed Operation Breadbasket and readily turned over his church to King and his followers. Such commitment exacted a price, however. Freeman and his family soon became the target of threats and his church the target of bombings.[20]

To relieve the pressure on Freeman, whom one parishioner described as "fearless," the Chicago Freedom Movement shifted its base of operations a few blocks north, to the Greater Mount Hope Baptist Church. Though smaller than New Friendship, the new site of the South Side Action Center was the domain of a pastor with credentials quite similar to Freeman's. Like Freeman, the Reverend W. L. Lambert had migrated from the South, had joined the Progressive National Baptist Convention, and had been arrested in Albany in 1962 as part of the Chicago delegation. The next year Lambert spearheaded the Clergy Alliance of Chicago, the short-lived minister-backed effort to boost the black economy through selective buying campaigns, and then later backed Operation Breadbasket. Lambert was many years Freeman's senior, but he was, as a fellow minister remarked, "an older man" with "young ideas."[21]

The West Side Action Center also struggled to find a permanent home. For a few weeks in July, the Stone Temple Baptist Church in Lawndale served as a base, but by late July the Warren Avenue Congregational Church had become the center's site. This location was of course familiar to Chicago activists, but the shift also meant that protest leaders could not use the Action Center as a recruiting station within a large black Baptist congregation.[22]

No matter where they were held, each mass meeting had its share of drama. Few, however, were as memorable as the August 8 rally at the Warren Avenue Congregational Church. With a crowd of nearly five hundred before him, Jesse Jackson reminded his listeners of the overriding importance of the larger struggle in which they were engaged. Even the threat of death, Jackson insisted, should not dampen commitment. With his right hand thrusting downward on each word, he emphasized: "I've counted the costs." At that, he turned his head to the right, pointed in the same direction, and declared: "I'm going to Cicero." This was stunning news, for Cicero—the site of a vicious race riot in 1951—was the preeminent symbol of northern bigotry.[23]

James Bevel, the next speaker, tantalized the crowd further. "If the people of Cicero are going to buy guns because Negroes are coming out there, it won't make any difference," he told a cheering congregation. "They can buy tanks and they can arm every child, but we're going to Cicero."[24]

Besides generating an unusual amount of commotion, Jackson's surprising and unauthorized Cicero pledge also underscored the "guerrilla army" quality of the Chicago movement. No protest leader ever boasted about its tight, well-defined command structure. Strategy was often forged in the field of action. Even as civil rights representatives in Chicago told reporters that Jackson's announcement was unauthorized, King, now down south preparing for SCLC's annual convention, informed the press that he himself would go to Cicero if Chicago did not combat housing bias.[25]

A trek through Cicero, however, was still in the future, and Chicago civil rights leaders focused on more immediate concerns. At a lengthy Tuesday night strategy session they debated whether to stage, as planned, another Southwest Side march. Distressed that the press had become preoccupied with white violence rather than with housing discrimination, the target of the protests, many insurgents now argued for postponement of the Southwest Side excursion. Swayed by this logic, the strategists tentatively decided that a march on the Chicago Real Estate Board, the city's powerful association of realtors, would be wiser.[26]

The decision was controversial within the movement. The next morning, August 10, Bevel became livid when he learned that the press was quoting Raby on the cancellation of the Southwest Side protest. Who had made a final decision? Bevel stormed. Incensed by what he considered a breach of trust, Bevel wanted to venture into the Southwest Side as originally planned. Only spirited afternoon conferences prevented the leadership rift from becoming public. To conceal their differences, both Raby and Bevel agreed to lead a demonstration in front of the Chicago Real Estate Board.[27]

More than just another clash in the ongoing Raby-Bevel struggle, this incident also reflected flaws in the Chicago movement's command structure. Since the creation in mid-July of the Agenda and Action committees, Bevel and the Action Committee—more militant than the Agenda Committee because of the age, temperament, and background of its members—had held a virtual monopoly on movement directives. Unlike many of the members of the Agenda Committee, who as heads of large, established civil rights and human relations organizations had to worry about day-to-day managerial responsibilities, the staff of the Action Committee could fully devote themselves to the orchestration of protests. They believed that once the Agenda Committee had singled out open housing as the movement's goal, all other decisions "fell into the category of tactics"—a conviction that inevitably catapulted them into conflict with the makers of movement strategy.[28]

The consequences of this tension were not overly destructive, however. Members of the Agenda and Action committees each complained about the personnel on the other committee. Yet lines of communication between the two groups remained open. Representatives of the Action Committee, particularly Bevel, Jackson, LaFayette, and Pitcher, attended meetings of the Agenda Committee, and Raby, Young, and even King himself joined sessions of the Action Committee. In the end, internal squabbling—which plagues every social movement—did not cripple the Chicago campaign. Decisions were reached, mass meetings held, and protests staged.[29]

The white violence prompted many whites and blacks in the city to rally for civil rights. Chicagoans expressed their solidarity with the movement in many ways. Some marched, while others attended mass meetings, contributed hard-earned dollars to the cause, offered their legal talents, or prepared sandwiches for those who did demonstrate. There were also those who, though on the sidelines, joined the protesters in spirit. Wanting "to stand up with the marchers," one seventy-year-old woman, for example, wrote to Senator Douglas, hoping that "Doctor King's marches will continue, and be protected, until our white citizens recognise that we must unite, to change the pattern of conditions, that reminds one of the 'Warsaw Ghetto.'"[30]

Women especially seemed to be swept into Chicago's racial crisis. Alarmed over the West Side riots, a group of black and white women met with Coretta Scott King in mid-July to discuss ways that women could mobilize for racial justice. A few days later they met again to form a new organization, Women Mobilized for Change (WMC). Two weeks later WMC staged its first protest, a women's "witness" outside City Hall designed to force Mayor Richard Daley to crusade for black rights. The spectacle of dignified, well-dressed (and in many cases, well-connected) women marching around City Hall so distressed Daley that on the day of the witness he met with a delegation of the female demonstrators.[31]

The significance of Women Mobilized for Change extended far beyond its lobbying. Though not a feminist organization—that is, women bonding together to advance a female agenda—it nevertheless was emblematic of the fresh currents stirring women in the 1960s. In troubled times, explained one WMC founder, women could not remain "like a beautiful painting that hangs in a closet and never is seen." They had a special duty to act and special powers on which to draw.[32]

Yet however many Chicagoans the civil rights crisis spurred to fight for racial justice, even more were provoked to condemn the open-housing protests as the source of needless unrest.[33] Attacks on civil rights marchers were only the most extreme expressions of this outlook. Most critics relied on the more peaceful weapon of denunciations instead, and few were more outspoken than Chicago's white aldermen. The Southwest Side alderman David Healy warned that further marches would create "a clear and present danger of riots and civil disorder"; his Northwest Side counterparts, Edward Scholl and John Hoellen, demanded city measures to stop the open-housing protests. On August 8, Hoellen met with Daley in the mayor's office to urge him to halt the marches because, according to Hoellen, they could "serve no purpose except to foment armed insurrection in Chicago."[34]

Daley, guided by Raymond Simon, the city's top legal adviser and a close associate of the mayor's, responded that he had no authority to do such a thing. "All we can do is talk with the people and plead for reason," Daley contended. But that Daley received Hoellen without an appointment dramatized how mightily the Chicago Freedom Movement had rocked city politics. A Republican and vocal Daley critic, Hoellen had not been in the mayor's office in over a decade. Yet in these difficult days, Daley patiently listened to Hoellen's condemnation of the open-housing demonstrations.[35]

For Daley, the open-housing protests were a nightmare.[36] They tarnished Chicago's image as a first-class city, threatened its civic order, and, worst of all, imperiled his political dominance. Daley and his lieutenants recognized that the Chicago Freedom Movement's power flowed as much from a political source as from a moral source. Chicago activists knew that the Daley machine faced state and congressional elections in the fall of 1966 and that it was priming for aldermanic and mayoral elections in the spring of 1967. They also knew—though protest leaders would not openly state this strategy—that they had constructed a "box for Daley . . . if he didn't protect us he was in serious trouble with blacks . . . He could become the [next] Bull Connor. If he did protect us it would hurt him in his white constituency." The Chicago Freedom Movement was seeking not only to persuade Chicagoans of the justness of their cause but also to force reforms through, in the words of one activist, "coercive nonviolence." And just as in the South, the role of law enforcement was a key dynamic—albeit in a different fashion. Here the issue was not overt police defense of current racial patterns but, rather, the extent to which police protection was given to advocates of racial change. Faced with a political dilemma, Daley had elected to protect the marchers, thus weakening the moral claims of the Chicago Freedom Movement but at the same time exacerbating his political problems in white communities. "We lose white votes every time there's an outburst like this," groaned a Daley precinct captain after one open-housing protest. Daley could not afford to allow the marches to continue. Somehow he would have to control events that had previously escaped his command.[37]

By the second week in August the Daley forces were rallying to minimize the Chicago movement's moral advantage with greater force than they had during the summer of 1965, when prominent business, labor, and civic leaders had called for an end to the anti-Willis marches. In Washington, D.C., Congressman Roman Pucinski released a letter he had sent to President Johnson claiming that Chicago protesters were "not interested in furthering the cause of social justice and human dignity but instead are bent upon a policy of turmoil to tear down democratic processes in our republic." In Chicago, Ed Marciniak of the Commission on Human Relations repeatedly expressed his exasperation that Chicago activists staged protests without having tried to remedy individual complaints of housing discrimination through the existing machinery established by the Chicago Fair Housing Ordinance of 1963. Most important, Chicago's renowned police chief, O. W. Wilson, undercut the Chicago movement by constantly complaining that the police were not being given sufficient warning of the time and place of demonstrations.[38]

Even as it orchestrated a public relations offensive, the Daley administration also sought a settlement with civil rights forces. On Thursday morning, August 4, a group of elected officials, mostly black, accepted the invitation of the freedom movement and met with King and Raby at the Washington Park YMCA. Until this three-hour meeting the city's black aldermen—the elected voices of Chicago's black community—had been conspicuously silent in the open-housing drama. At one point the session seemed destined to inflame, rather than to resolve, differences. Charles Chew, the self-proclaimed black independent alderman, charged Raby and the civil rights hierarchy with freezing out politicians who endorsed civil rights demands. King helped refocus the meeting when he urged everyone to "forget about the past and start from here now." From that point consensus was the order of the day. It was clear that the six Daley-aligned black aldermen sought a rapprochement. Led by Ralph Metcalfe, the highest-ranking black councilman in the Daley camp, the black politicians endorsed a wide range of civil rights demands, including forceful open-housing proposals and a nondiscriminatory mortgage policy for banks and savings institutions. Only on Raby's proposal that political precinct captains be required to live in the precincts they represented did the politicians firmly balk.[39]

That the open-housing campaign was not simply a reckless effort to divide Chicago was the underlying message of King's and Raby's presentation. To close the session, King reinforced this theme in a short address. He was, he intimated, a reasonable man who knew that the demonstrations would succeed only if they prompted discussion with the leaders of Chicago. But he was exasperated. He had met with Mayor Daley on July 11 without results; then came the West Side riots, and Daley responded to black demands. "That action signified to others," King said, "that not peacefulness but violence will bring the granting of demands." It was now the obligation of politicians to respond to the nonviolent civil rights movement, for—and here King repeated one of his favorite themes of the past few weeks—"nonviolence needs some victories." After this short plea for cooperation, the mild-mannered Metcalfe put his arm around King's shoulder, signaling his empathy for the civil rights leader's stance. This meeting, however, was only the first step in what would have to be an elaborate dialogue between the

movement and the city administration. Without Daley's direct participation no differences could be formally settled. Moreover, when the
politicians decided not to reconvene until August 25, three weeks later,
it became obvious that the current Chicago crisis would have to be
resolved in another forum.[40]

Other Chicago leaders and opinion makers shared the Daley administration's desire for a halt to the marching. Once the shock of the white
violence had lessened, the Chicago press began assailing the open-housing protests. The arch-conservative *Chicago Tribune* now detected a plot
to "sabotage" Chicago. *Chicago's American* called the marches "a deliberate attempt to perpetuate violence." The more liberal *Chicago Daily News*
was also critical. "We question the sense of Sunday's march," the paper
stated on August 9. "[W]e doubt that many whites in the Belmont-
Cragin neighborhood were brought to a more tolerant point of view."
The next day it took an even firmer position. Insisting that "Dr. Martin
Luther King has made his point in Chicago," the *Daily News* asserted that
"the most rational course would be to call off the marches entirely and
turn to more constructive pursuits."[41]

Chicago's influential television stations called for calm as well. "As
strongly as we believe in . . . and support . . . the civil rights movement," WBKB-TV, ABC's Chicago affiliate, declared in an editorial aired
seven times in mid-August, "we would like to hope that the marchers
and their leaders would realize that they have made their point and
would therefore cease these demonstrations. They can only lead to
more bloodshed." The drama of neighborhood marches and their potential for disorder also rekindled debate about a 1955 Chicago policy—
a set of restrictions on the timing and specificity of news bulletins—designed to prevent radio and television broadcasts from inadvertently
inflaming racial tensions. At the height of the marches, city officials and
broadcasters huddled to discuss possible revisions in the restrictive
guidelines (with which not all parties were currently complying), but in
the end the radio and television executives and editors elected against
fundamental change in policy when the "heat is on."[42]

From the academy, too, came anxious voices. Morris Janowitz, a
University of Chicago sociologist, endorsed the goal of fair housing, but
he told the *Chicago Sun-Times* that it was a "human tragedy" that "integration at the moment is being promoted among lower-middle-class
people, those least equipped in terms of education and social control to
absorb it." Another University of Chicago sociologist, Philip Hauser, who

had been a leading critic of Superintendent Willis, also publicly questioned the Chicago movement's targets. "The areas in which the white population has rioted are still in the process of culturalization and Americanization," Hauser explained.[43]

Even some allies of the Chicago movement issued calls for an end to the marches. On Tuesday, August 9, Robert Johnston, midwestern regional director of the United Auto Workers, conferred with Raby about possible ways to begin negotiations. Johnston then spoke with Walter Reuther, the UAW president. Reuther later phoned King (who was in Jackson, Mississippi, where he had taken ill and where he would soon be joined by Raby and Berry for the annual SCLC convention) to discuss the Chicago situation.[44]

Reuther's and Johnston's concerns could not be lightly brushed aside. Reuther, almost alone among major union leaders, identified closely with the civil rights movement. One of the few whites to speak at the March on Washington, he had also joined the controversial Meredith march through Mississippi. Johnston, a Reuther protégé from Iowa, had gone to Mississippi, too. The Chicago Federation of Labor ignored the Chicago civil rights movement, but in the spring of 1966 the Midwest UAW had affiliated with CCCO and had dispatched its organizers to help build tenant unions in the ghetto. "The UAW is in this thing all the way," Johnston had declared at that point. "We are not giving lip service to the civil rights movement here." That Raby wore a UAW jacket during one open-housing protest and that one of Johnston's lieutenants, James Wright, served on the freedom movement's Agenda Committee illustrated the ties between the Chicago movement and the union.[45]

On Thursday, August 11, Johnston, whose union would soon endorse Daley for a fourth term as mayor, arranged for a meeting between Chicago labor leaders and Daley that boosted the mayor's efforts to halt the marching. After conferring for two and a half hours with Chicago's labor czars, a happy Daley emerged with "the unanimous support" of labor leaders—including William Lee and William McFetridge of the Chicago Federation of Labor; Joseph Germano, regional director of the United Steelworkers; and Johnston—to bring the open-housing conflict to the conference table. "We must," Johnston insisted, "try to resolve the problem without more violence."[46]

The most important appeal for a moratorium on marches came, however, from Archbishop Cody. The new archbishop had lived up to his reputation as a civil rights sympathizer with his message of un-equivocal endorsement for the Chicago movement read at the July 10 Soldier Field rally. "Your struggles and your sufferings will be mine until the last vestige of discrimination and injustice is blotted out here in Chicago and throughout America," Cody had declared. He had also decreed that a letter condemning prejudice be read at all masses that Sunday. "A crusade for freedom and equality is well under way," he had noted in his letter, "and you and I, as Catholics and Americans, must be part of it."[47]

Cody failed, however, to anticipate the path that the crusade would follow. Never a believer in street demonstrations, he favored education, discussion, and negotiations as the instruments of social change.[48] In late July he had become very disturbed that the Chicago Freedom Movement had seemingly singled out a Southwest Side Catholic church, St. Gall's, whose pastor had been working to promote interracial understanding among his congregation, as a target on its early Gage Park forays. Now a vexed ally, he relayed, through his assistant Father Edward Egan, his indignation over this unwarranted attack. When white violence erupted over the open-housing protests, Cody was shocked and distressed by the open hatred and "mass emotionalism." By mid-August he worried that more marches could very likely result in "serious injury to many persons and perhaps even the loss of lives." Thus it was "with a heavy heart" that he urged civil rights leaders to suspend demonstrations. Instead he called for negotiations between realtors and civil rights advocates to "achieve a just and lasting resolu-tion of the present crisis."[49]

Civil rights leaders did not welcome Cody's plea. "When there's trouble, Daley sticks up his liberal bishop to say, 'You've gone far enough,'" James Bevel snapped. "He should not abandon us now," but "stand with us." Raby and Young were also disappointed, though they expressed their displeasure more diplomatically. They shared the Chi-cago Catholic Interracial Council's complaint that a moratorium on marches before "there is any real evidence of a more effective good faith program . . . is unfair and unrealistic. It is like asking a labor union to call off a just strike before a single grievance has been righted."[50]

Cody's call for restraint did not spring only from antipathy to direct action. Leader of 450 parishes, 13,000 priests and nuns, and more than two million parishioners, Cody worried about the divisiveness of the current conflict. The Catholic Church in Chicago was a complex institution composed of people who differed in cultural background, social class, and political persuasion and who were united only by their common faith. Few issues, Cody knew, divided his flock as sharply as open housing.[51]

Some Chicago Catholic clergy and laity, Cody recognized, were among the country's staunchest Catholic civil rights crusaders.[52] Aggressive Chicago Catholic activism, which had first stirred in the early 1960s, increased in 1965 when scores of Chicago Catholics traveled to Selma. A few months later, Chicago Catholics joined the anti-Willis marches in great numbers, which resulted, reputedly, in the first arrests of nuns for social activism in American history.[53]

But most Catholics, Cody knew, hardly applauded the new militancy. Even some who had gone to Selma in 1965 challenged whether it was appropriate for clergy to engage in civil disobedience during the Willis protests. Demonstrating against a school superintendent who struggled with the enormous problems of a big city school system hardly compared with traveling to Selma, where the police unhesitatingly bludgeoned peaceful demonstrators seeking the right to vote. "The issue of how to get quality education and school integration in Chicago," argued one priest who had led a delegation of Chicagoans to Selma, "is not clear—even among the educational experts and civil-rights leaders."[54]

To many Chicago Catholics, the rise of an activist clergy—on the heels of sweeping changes emerging from Vatican II—was more than distressing; it was anathema. In the summer of 1965, scores of Catholics bombarded Chicago rectories and the offices of the *New World*, the archdiocese's newspaper, with complaints about the participation of clergy, especially nuns, in "the foolish, sickening" anti-Willis marches. The crusading clergy who joined the open-housing protests in 1966 convinced even more white Chicagoans that the Church had turned its back on their needs. With his empire divided, Cody—still a newcomer to the Chicago scene and a man who needed to be in control—wanted the civil rights dispute resolved.[55]

The pleas for a moratorium went unheeded. On Friday, August 12, James Bevel led six hundred demonstrators on an open-housing march in the Bogan High School area on the Southwest Side. Many observers feared that the Bogan march would spark "even more violence" than the others had, because the Bogan region had been peopled by many residents who had "fled . . . changing communities to the east" and because Bogan natives had already aggressively resisted integration of their high school in recent years. But the march did not live up to its billing, largely because local leaders had labored mightily to keep local residents away from the protest. Members of civic groups and over seventy precinct captains, mobilized by Alderman James Murray at Mayor Daley's request, had gone from house to house, distributing thousands of leaflets urging the residents to ignore the civil rights marchers. Protected by eight hundred helmeted policemen with a surveillance helicopter whirling overhead, the demonstrators, walking two and three abreast, proceeded unscathed. Hundreds of hecklers, some holding banners with the inscriptions "Join the White Rebellion" and "We Worked Hard for What We Got," lined the route of the march, but few threw rocks or attempted to injure the civil rights demonstrators.[56]

Two days later, Sunday, August 14, the Chicago movement staged its most ambitious series of demonstrations. Bevel led one contingent of marchers through Jefferson Park, another Northwest Side neighborhood whose realtors refused to service blacks. To the south, Raby took 300 protesters to Gage Park for the first major demonstration in that Southwest Side community in nearly four weeks. Meanwhile, three miles to the southwest, Jesse Jackson led 350 activists on another march through Bogan. This time local reaction was so fierce that police advised Jackson to change the route of the pilgrimage. Instead of striding up Pulaski Avenue, a main business strip, the demonstrators paraded along smaller residential streets. "We took an educational tour," Jackson explained. "We wanted some of our people to see the homes they will be living in soon."[57]

Although Sunday's violence hardly equaled that which had marred earlier Southwest Side marches, a disturbing new specter now haunted the Chicago scene. Like vultures in search of carrion, white extremists—the American Nazi Party, the National States Rights Party, and the Ku Klux Klan—flocked to America's second city in August 1966. They sensed a large pool of potential converts. They also knew that they would command wide attention. Experience told them that cameras followed Martin Luther King, and, lacking numerous supporters, the white extremists maneuvered for easy publicity.[58]

Of all the extremist groups in Chicago, the Nazis attracted the most attention. Founded in the late 1950s by George Lincoln Rockwell, the

American Nazi Party had labored for years in vain to establish a Chicago beachhead. But finally the uproar over the open-housing marches raised Nazi hopes. On August 14, in Marquette Park, the editor of the Nazi party's magazine, *The Stormtrooper,* took advantage of a last-minute change in the Chicago Freedom Movement's plans. When the civil rights demonstrators who had been expected did not appear, the editor delivered an inflammatory speech to the more than one thousand white counterdemonstrators who had gathered. Afterward, the crowd poured out of the park into the adjacent streets, taunting the police and attacking passing black motorists. One black woman suffered a broken jaw when her car was hit by bricks and bottles. Only a quick rescue by an off-duty cadet policeman and his friends saved her and her child from further injury.[59]

Each new report of violence confirmed the worst fears of Chicago's rapidly multiplying doomsayers. "I'm afraid that Chicago is girding itself for an all-out race battle," said one worried Southwest Sider. "Chicago today," J. H. Jackson declared, "is caught in grim conflict that has already done untold injury to the cause of civil rights, human rights, good will and to the American way of life." The marches, in the opinion of Ed Marciniak, "had set back peaceful integration in these neighborhoods many years." Chicago, many believed, had tumbled into a disaster, a crisis of a magnitude unrivaled in the postwar years.[60]

Ending the crisis had become the preoccupation of the Chicago Conference on Religion and Race (CCRR). On Friday, August 12, after securing support from other prominent Chicagoans, the Episcopal bishop James Montgomery, chairman of the CCRR, and Eugene Callahan, its executive director, announced that the group would sponsor a negotiating session scheduled for the middle of the following week. "[T]he current marches," they said, were "achieving their stated goal in focusing public attention on the artificial and immoral restraints placed upon the freedom to seek and secure residences for Negroes in Chicago." But now frank discussion at the conference table was necessary to redress grievances and restore civic harmony.[61]

That the CCRR found itself playing the role of peacemaker sprang directly from its close connections to Chicago's power elite. The CCRR did not originate the idea of a meeting with Mayor Daley, civil rights leaders, the Chicago Real Estate Board, and other interested parties to resolve the city's racial crisis; such a gathering was first proposed on Tuesday, August 9, at a special noon meeting of the Commission on Human Relations, the city agency which was most directly charged with promoting racial harmony and which had tried to arrange a settlement of the 1965 schools dispute, albeit unsuccessfully. Later that afternoon, the commission broached its proposal to a sympathetic Mayor Daley. He knew that the current civil rights crisis far outstripped last summer's in seriousness. In the summer of 1965, Daley had attended a Board of Education meeting for the first time in ten years in order to speed resolution of the schools controversy, but he never consented to full-fledged negotiations with protest leaders and eventually the demonstrations stopped. A year later Daley felt he could not respond the same way. During the summer of 1965 he had tried to sidestep the Willis matter by claiming that official jurisdiction rested with the Board of Education and not the mayor, a contention he could not make about the open-housing crisis. Even more important, the bolder demonstrations of 1966, under the auspices of not just Raby and CCCO but the nationally renowned Martin Luther King, were exerting far greater pressure on the mayor than any civil rights protest of the 1960s. A peace conference should be held, but the caucus at City Hall decided that neither the mayor nor the city should serve as the sponsors. Instead Daley phoned Ross Beatty, president of the Chicago Real Estate Board, and persuaded him to call a negotiating session.[62]

Not everyone on the Commission of Human Relations was convinced that this plan for starting negotiations would work. Worried that the real estate board could not properly host such an event because it would be partisan in any negotiations, two commissioners, Hale Nelson and William Caples, both influential businessmen, called upon Paul Lund, a mutual friend, executive with Illinois Bell, and CCRR board member. The next day Caples and Lund visited Eugene Callahan, hoping to convince him that the CCRR, as a well-respected independent body, should convene a settlement session. Callahan then conferred with Bishop Montgomery, who agreed with the proposal. At the same time Caples and Lund persuaded a reluctant Beatty, who had yet to arrange a summit meeting, to follow the new plan of action, which ensured that the realtors would participate as protagonists in the struggle.[63]

The request from Lund and Caples brought relief to the CCRR, which had thus far found itself on the sidelines during the crisis, struggling to find a meaningful role. The group had never fully aligned itself with the Chicago Freedom Movement. Although in late August 1965 it had expressed its desire "to participate in the planning of [SCLC's] programs for Chicago," the CCRR had never felt comfortable with the movement. Civil rights insurgents were too quick to abandon established channels for reform. And they seemed reluctant to work closely with the CCRR. As Archbishop Cody had complained at a July CCRR meeting shortly after the disturbing West Side explosions, if the group was to back King then he "must cue us in on his plans." Yet now as mediators, the CCRR could be a constructive force as it had been in the past. During the summer of 1965 CCRR member Dr. Edgar Chandler and others had sought to find common ground between the demonstrators and Daley and the Board of Education. A year later, during the West Side riots, the CCRR had worked to bring the Daley administration and civil rights leaders together and thus, according to one of its members, was able to "draw comfort" from a productive "intervention." By sponsoring a session to resolve the current crisis, the CCRR was again interceding for the welfare of Chicago.[64]

The CCRR's call for a peace conference with scores of participants also brought relief to the Daley administration. Such a negotiating session, as Marciniak put it, "took the focus off" of city officials and "spread the responsibility" for ending the crisis. It diminished the possibility of a direct confrontation between the Daley administration and the Chicago Freedom Movement. Daley, Marciniak later recalled, was "delighted" by the turn of events. "Once the Conference on Religion and Race decided to move ahead, we saw light at the end of the tunnel."[65]

Civil rights leaders also accepted the CCRR's invitation to attend a peace conference. They were reluctant to reject a call from a religious source and, perhaps, they thought, negotiations would be the first step toward an open city. They were pleased with their success so far. They were following SCLC's traditional formula, in Andrew Young's words, of "challenge, conflict, crisis, confrontation, communication, compromise, and change." The marches had precipitated a crisis for the "established power structure." Indeed, on the eve of the conference, Young saw great potential for the Chicago marches. "If we can bust the closed-housing market here for Negroes, it will be the first time anywhere in the nation," he said. "If we're successful here, then we can expect the same results in Philadelphia, Cleveland, and other cities."[66]

Confident that their strategy was working, Chicago insurgents did not want to relieve the "creative tension." They decided to stage more demonstrations than ever before on Tuesday, August 16, the day before the "Summit conference," as the press now called it. Civil rights activists held real estate vigils into the evening in Jefferson Park and mounted small downtown demonstrations designed to spotlight those who bore responsibility for the current crisis. For four hours picketers circled not just City Hall and the offices of the Chicago Real Estate Board but also the First Federal Savings and Loan Association, a mortgage lender, and the Cook County Department of Public Aid and the Chicago Housing Authority, two public agencies that shaped local housing patterns.[67]

The Chicago police once more complained that this multiple effort only stretched their ranks even thinner at the expense of protection for the rest of the community. Protest leaders, however, shrugged at these complaints. While they might not have provided the police with detailed specifics about the demonstrations, they had notified them—as promised—of their intention to march. "We have never depended on police protection," one civil rights activist noted. "They have had the manpower to protect us adequately under most circumstances though."[68]

The next day, Wednesday, August 17, in a meeting room cooled by a single floor fan at the parish house of the St. James Episcopal Church, civil rights leaders gathered with some of the most powerful members of Chicago's elite to discuss the open-housing crisis. In Chicago it had become a tradition to convene "blue-ribbon committees" whenever "there was a problem," but this group, according to Charles Swibel, a Daley confidante, was especially distinguished and represented "a cross section of" the power centers in Chicago. The conferees sat at long tables arranged in a U configuration, with civil rights representatives, including Martin Luther King, who had just returned from the South, sitting across from city officials, including Mayor Daley. Not one of the city's black aldermen—the elected representatives of much of black Chicago—was present, however. At the head table and presiding over the conference was Ben Heineman, the head of the Chicago and North Western Railway, who at Daley's request had interrupted his vacation. Bishop Montgomery had told the group that no one from the CCRR wanted to serve as chairman. The CCRR members, he explained, did not "feel that they were neutral," but that they "agreed with the demands of the Chicago Freedom Movement." The CCRR had, after all, endorsed the principle of fair housing many times in the past. Now its members did not want to be constrained as impartial convenors from speaking freely. Heineman had the right credentials for this new assignment. A Democrat and one of Chicago's top industrialists, he was a leader in a business community that was dominated by Republicans but was nevertheless on close terms with Mayor Daley. Heineman had also been chosen by Lyndon Johnson to serve as the chairman of the recently held White House Conference on Civil Rights.[69]

Though Heineman opened the session, Ely Aaron, chairman of the Chicago Commission on Human Relations, kicked off the hard negotiating with an eleven-point plan to end the crisis. The city's wide-ranging proposals included a moratorium on "marches into neighborhoods" and pledges by various bodies—the Chicago Real Estate Board, the Chicago Mortgage Bankers, the Chicago Conference on Religion and Race, and the Chicago Commission on Human Relations—to work for equal opportunity in housing. While hardly innovative and certainly not sweeping enough to placate the Chicago Freedom Movement, the proposals suggested that the Daley administration was neither indifferent nor inflexible. The city's strategy, Marciniak remembered, was "not to be defensive. We had our own program that ought to be recognized."[70]

After Aaron's presentation, Al Raby countered with the movement's demands, which went well beyond the city's proposals. Raby made no mention, of course, of a moratorium on marches, and he called upon the Daley administration and the Chicago Real Estate Board to take specific steps. And unlike Aaron, Raby stressed that other public agencies—including the Chicago Housing Authority, the Cook County Department of Public Aid, and the overseers of Chicago's urban renewal projects—had to commit themselves to a policy of open housing.[71]

Almost instantly Clarke Stayman, president of the Chicago Mortgage Bankers Association, revealed the business community's desire for an end to the crisis by stressing his industry's commitment to making mortgages available regardless of race, which was one of Raby's demands. "[T]his was a good first break-through," noted John McKnight, a U.S. Civil Rights Commission observer. Mayor Daley then read the two-page list of civil rights proposals, the first five of which were directed at his administration. Yes, the city would enforce its fair-housing ordinance more vigorously, he promised. Daley's pledge was encouraging, but Raby wanted to hear whether the other conferees were ready to act as well. At that, Charles Swibel, head of the Chicago Housing Authority, stated that his agency would build as much "non-ghetto low-rise" public housing "as is feasible." Swibel's promises hardly reassured the civil rights camp, however. A refugee from Poland, Swibel had amassed a fortune first as an owner of slum properties and then as the developer of Marina City, one of the early landmarks of the renaissance of Chicago's skyscrapers in the 1960s. Daley had appointed the ambitious businessman to the CHA Board of Commissioners in 1956, when Swibel was not yet thirty years old, and seven years later he became its chairman. Over the past decade, the CHA had not spread public housing across the city, but rather had concentrated its new projects—many of which were dreary high-rise buildings—in poor black communities. Myriad connections with politicians, the business community, and labor unions had earned Swibel the reputation of a power broker. Engaging and energetic, Swibel had already sought to resolve the open-housing crisis on his own by meeting with Chicago protest leaders and trying to arrange a token settlement to get King out of town.[72]

Of the prime participants only the realtors had yet to respond to the movement's demands, and it was now clear that their position would decide the fate of the negotiations. There was little reason to expect a remarkable breakthrough. White realtors were, by and large, convinced that fair-housing measures violated fundamental property rights, certain that exclusionary racial practices were essential to the health of white communities, and, of course, worried that broad change in the dynamics of the housing market would lead to financial disaster for their industry. The Chicago Real Estate Board (CREB) had contested the legality of the Chicago Fair Housing Ordinance. It had also offered logistical and strategic support to the Property Owners Coordinating Committee, a statewide federation of local property owner, improvement, and taxpayer associations, with strong roots in Chicago's Southwest Side, in its 1964 campaign for an ill-fated referendum designed to prohibit fair-housing measures. Little wonder, then, that Arthur Mohl, a past president of the CREB, immediately revealed his group's intransigence. Realtors, Mohl argued, were the homeowners' agents and thus not the cause of Chicago's severe residential segregation. "[W]e are the mirrors," not "the creators," of bigotry, he insisted. The Chicago Real Estate Board—a virtually all-white association of many, but far from all, of Chicago's real estate agents and brokers—was not in the business of solving social problems.[73]

Martin Luther King immediately challenged Mohl's reasoning. He had heard similar arguments from southern restaurant and hotel owners, and in his view they were disingenuous. James Bevel too fixed responsibility for the crisis squarely on the shoulders of the realtors. "The key problem, the core problem," he asserted, "is that realtors refuse to serve Negroes in their offices. And that must change. That is insulting and it is humiliating. And the burden is to change service to Negroes."[74]

In response, Ross Beatty insisted that he and the other real estate representatives lacked "the power" to negotiate for their industry on such a sensitive question. Then Gordon Groebe, an outlying realtor from the Southwest Side, restated the realtors' fundamental position: they were only "agents" who did the bidding of their clients, the sellers. In reply, King rejected the contention that real estate brokers simply reflected community attitudes, and he reminded the conferees that realtors historically had helped mold community prejudice. The CREB's 1917 policy of racial exclusion had shaped national real estate practices. "I must appeal to the decency of the people on the Chicago Real Estate Board," King declared. "You are men confronted with a moral issue."[75]

Groebe knew then that the realtors' position had been breached. "I could say nothing," he recalled. "At that point I was wiped out. My position had been stated and [King] said it was a great moral question. It was no longer law, or reasoning from an agency standpoint." The realtors were rattled. They had expected to be participants in—rather than the focus of—the negotiations. Robert Johnston of the UAW and leading religious leaders—Donald Zimmerman, a Presbyterian official and president of the Church Federation of Greater Chicago, Rabbi Robert Marx, and Bishop Montgomery—affirmed King's demand that the realtors alter their practices. But despite the mounting pressure, the real estate representatives still did not concede the issue.[76]

Frustrated by the realtors' inflexibility, Raby called for an adjournment. But Daley had other ideas. "No, let's not adjourn the meeting," he broke in. "The Chicago Real Estate Board should get on the phone to their members and do something about these demands now." Flustered, the CREB representatives protested that they could not "possibly work out a resolution to these things today." Heineman, however, turned the screws even tighter, telling the realtors that "the monkey, gentlemen, is right on your back." With that, as the lunch hour approached, Heineman called for a recess until 4 P.M.[77]

Stunned by the turn of events, the real estate delegation left for the offices of the Chicago Real Estate Board. There they debated how they could make concessions—which Mayor Daley reportedly urged in a phone call to Ross Beatty—without rejecting all of their principles. Finally, they recognized that they could drop their opposition to a state fair-housing law, which had been regularly introduced to the Illinois state legislature since 1957, as long as it applied to both property owners and brokers. They knew that the Illinois Association of Real Estate Boards would hardly favor such a turnabout, but they also realized that in the second half of the negotiating session they would have to display some flexibility. In so doing, they would produce what Groebe later called "the key to the lock," the first opening from which an accord could eventually be fashioned.[78]

When the conference reconvened, Heineman summoned Ross Beatty, who had been active in Chicago real estate since 1929, to report on the Chicago Real Estate Board's new position. The bespectacled, Princeton-educated, diplomatic Beatty read and then reread a complicated, ambiguous statement that the CREB's chief officers had drafted during the recess. Puzzled by the statement, Raby asked Beatty to explain precisely the realtors' position. "On your demand A, which is to withdraw our support from the suit testing the legality of the Chicago Fair Housing ordinance, No," Beatty replied. "B, to withdraw our opposition to the governor's fair housing executive order, No." But on the last demand the realtors had budged. They would not agree to support an effective state fair-housing law, Beatty said, but they would withdraw their opposition to such a law.[79]

The conference then plunged into heated debate about the significance of the CREB's concession. Bevel reiterated his position clearly. He wanted results. "I want to re-emphasize that we need Negroes to be served in real estate offices. And you people here can see that [that] will happen. That's a conservative, simple, humane request, and let's not confuse the issue with all these A's, B's, C's." Andrew Young and Raby picked up on Bevel's approach and no longer dwelled on the movement's original demands, but now spoke of immediate changes in practices. "I think we must ask: can a Negro walk into a real estate office and be served?" Raby declared.[80]

Bill Berry, who continued to edge the Chicago Urban League as close to direct action as any Urban League chapter in the country, now said that he too regarded the realtors' statement as "totally unacceptable." He then turned the focus back on Daley by asking if the mayor could do anything more to satisfy the movement's demands. Catching Berry off guard, Daley rallied to the real estate board's defense. "I think they've done a lot," he huffed. "It shows a real change that they've come in here indicating that they will no longer oppose open occupancy." Daley's position was not unpopular, and Heineman pressed Berry to agree that the realtors had indeed offered "a concession."[81]

Heineman believed that a settlement was near at hand. The CREB's willingness to drop its opposition to an Illinois open-occupancy law was "a great victory, a major victory," he claimed. This change in the CREB's position "probably insures the passage" of state legislation, he rosily—and mistakenly—predicted. With the civil rights goals virtually met, Heineman thought that the demonstrations could now cease.[82]

Raby, however, remained skeptical about the progress that had been made. He worried as much about the performance of government agencies as about that of the realtors. He wanted to hear whether the Cook County Department of Public Aid would begin placing needy black families in housing outside the ghetto, whether Chicago's urban renewal program would take steps to breach the barriers of segregation, and whether the Chicago Housing Authority would indeed stop building public housing units only in the ghetto. Young demanded, "[W]e need a program. We need to know how much is going to be accomplished in thirty days, and how much in sixty days."[83]

Heineman was unhappy with this new line of argument. "Now, I think we've got to understand what we're talking about here," he said. "We understood that your proposals were on these two pages, and it sounds now like you're changing things." Indeed the movement's proposals did call for specific reforms, while Young, Bevel, and other activists were now insisting upon results. With tensions rising, Raby asked for a fifteen-minute recess. Before the break, Charles Hayes of the Packinghouse Workers reminded the conferees that the movement negotiators could not "tell the guy on the street" that it had forced the real estate board to accept open occupancy "philosophically." "The people," Hayes insisted, "want to hear what we're going to do for them now."[84]

Hayes's warning squared with the sentiments of protest leaders. They had not come prepared to settle after just one session, and now they worried about settling for too little.[85] After the break, Raby presented the movement's new proposal: the conferees should reconvene in a week to survey what reforms had been instituted. In the meantime, to the chagrin of city officials, Raby announced that demonstrations would continue. At that Daley stood up, vowing that the city would honor its commitments if the movement would halt the demonstrations. The hint of a trade infuriated Raby, who well remembered the frustrations of meetings during the summer of 1965 with Daley. In a sharp voice, he retorted that he hoped that someday he could "come before the Mayor of Chicago with what is just and that he will implement it because it is right rather than trading it politically for a moratorium."[86]

Ever the peacemaker, King cooled the rising tensions by praising the session as "a constructive and a creative beginning." Yet he also made it clear that he would not stop marching. That was too much to ask. "We don't have much money," King preached. "We don't really have much education, and we don't have political power. We have only our bodies and you are asking us to give up the one thing that we have when you say, 'Don't march!'" His message was clear: there would be no agreement on this day, but civil rights leaders would work with a smaller group to fashion a satisfactory accord by the following Friday, when all the Summit participants would meet again. Finally, well past 8 P.M., Heineman closed the meeting.[87]

The Summit negotiations changed the complexion of the Chicago campaign, and the next day, August 18, the Agenda Committee—whose role in directing the open-housing thrust had greatly expanded with the onset of negotiations—gathered to reflect on Wednesday's events and to plot strategy. The Summit session revealed the complex networks that linked Chicagoans together, networks far more complicated than those in any southern city in which SCLC had held high-level meetings with the white leadership. Martin Luther King, in fact, uncomfortably found himself chastising another prominent black, Robert Ming, a board member of the Chicago Commission on Human Relations, for insisting that the Chicago Fair Housing Ordinance of 1963 was quite capable of ending housing discrimination in the city. Though Ming now spoke on behalf of the Daley administration, he had been one of King's lawyers when the civil rights leader had been hounded by Alabama tax agents.[88]

For some Chicago protest leaders, too, the Summit session must have seemed extraordinary. Despite scores of protests against Superintendent Willis, the Chicago civil rights movement had never before forced Mayor Daley to negotiate so seriously. Daley, Bill Berry believed, had come to expect "total domination of the black segment of the city," but the Summit conference clearly had been "a total cultural shock for him." Seated at a side table and not at the customary head table, Daley had listened while blacks dared "talk to him about being equal and free."[89]

King, however, warned his colleagues about overly high expectations. Daley, he claimed, "is no bigot," but he "is about my son's age in understanding the race problem." The mayor and other Chicago leaders "fail to understand [the scope] of the evil." "They see it," King added perceptively, "as a matter of individual intent rather than societal sin." Sobered by King's warnings, the Agenda Committee vowed that it would not be swayed by simple promises. Results must be achieved. Nevertheless, as the generally reserved Kale Williams remarked, their task was not an easy one. The Chicago movement had reached a new frontier, for no one knew of a formula certain to promote successful residential desegregation. And yet the movement, Williams stressed, must somehow tell the city how to do just that.[90]

Fervor overwhelmed such worries during a rousing mass meeting that evening. Over fifteen hundred civil rights enthusiasts packed the Greater Mount Hope Baptist Church, and everyone, according to one observer, was "stomping and clapping in time with the music and singing freedom songs." The energized crowd—including another one thousand people outside the church who followed the proceedings through a public address system—listened to short talks by protest leaders while awaiting King's first Chicago speech in nearly two weeks.[91]

King began his address by telling the spirited audience that he hoped to be brief, but immediately conceded that "when you get before an enthusiastic and marvelous crowd like this . . . it's hard for a preacher not to preach." For the next thirty minutes, he surveyed the state of the Chicago movement, warned about the injustice of injunctions, and reiterated his faith in the transforming power of civil rights insurgency. He also countered the mounting criticism of the movement. Many Americans, he noted, wondered why the movement was trying "to legislate this housing matter." King's southern experience, however, had demonstrated that folkways could be changed. White southerners, he reminded his Chicago followers, had once told him that white people "would never sit on buses by Negroes." History, he predicted, would prove his Chicago critics to be equally wrong. King also dismissed charges that civil rights crusaders were provocateurs and disciples of disorder. "[W]e haven't caused the hatred," he declared. "We've just brought to the surface hatred that was already there."[92]

King's speech hit its highest note when he reaffirmed the moral thrust of the Chicago campaign. "We're going to make [Chicago] an open city," he pledged, because "it's practical," "it's sound economics," and, most important, it was right. It was wrong that he couldn't "live somewhere because of the color of my skin," he announced. He would no longer tolerate housing discrimination. "It humiliates me, it does something to my spirit and to my soul, and I'm not going to take it any longer." He finished this thought with a line aimed at restoring any flagging commitment to the open-housing crusade. "I'm going," he stated simply, "to live wherever I want to live."[93]

The next day, while civil rights activists tested over a hundred real estate firms across the city, Mayor Daley did what many observers anticipated he would do: he secured an injunction against the movement. Daley had left Thursday's Summit conference disheartened, but it was not until the next day that the Daley camp's assessment of the meeting became public. "A farce," was how an unnamed official described the negotiating session. "Every time we'd make a concession, they'd switch to another point. They never had any intention of calling off the marches," the disgruntled informant complained. Stymied at the negotiating table, Daley now resorted to a legal stratagem to contain the open-housing marches. The mayor knew that the constitutional right to freedom of assembly barred a sweeping injunction banning all marches, but city lawyers advised that a less comprehensive injunction restricting the size and time of marches might be acceptable, which is exactly what Circuit Court Judge Cornelius J. Harrington granted them on Friday, August 19.[94]

Obtaining the injunction was a provocative move, and that evening Daley, dressed in a blue suit, blue shirt, and a faintly striped tie, interrupted prime-time television programs to explain his action, something he had never done before. He hated injunctions, he told the residents of a city steeped in labor tradition. But faced with the "dilemma of balancing rights"—the right of petition and the right of a person to safety—he felt compelled to seek one. By requiring so much protection, the civil rights marches "adversely affected" the Chicago police's ability to protect the rest of the city.[95]

But Daley did more than issue a straightforward, matter-of-fact explanation for his actions. He deftly used the occasion to criticize civil rights leaders for not taking "the issue out of the streets and onto the conference table." Their obstinacy, he complained, threatened to reduce "the great issue of civil rights . . . to the level of street fighting and the collapse of law and order." The ten-minute speech was a strong performance. Projecting his deep concern for the city's welfare, Daley undercut the Chicago movement's efforts to package perceptions, to present the crisis as an unambiguous case of right against wrong. King and his followers could continue to march if they so desired; the mayor simply insisted that they be reasonable about it. Daley's tough rhetoric and tough actions also helped mend weakened political connections. In the first Summit meeting, he had seemingly consorted with the civil rights forces. Now, with the injunction, he was styling himself the protector of the white neighborhoods. In the course of two days, as one city official put it, Daley telegraphed "two messages" to the diverse city of Chicago.[96]

The great risk of the injunction was that it might torpedo the Summit subcommittee, which was meeting for the first time on Friday afternoon. Chaired by Thomas Ayers, head of Commonwealth Edison and president of the Chicago Association of Commerce and Industry, the subcommittee also included representatives from the civil rights camp, the Daley administration, the Chicago Real Estate Board, and the religious community. The Chicago Freedom Movement sent five representatives, four members of the Agenda Committee, Al Raby, Kale Williams, John McDermott, and Bill Berry, and one from the Action Committee and SCLC's only representative, James Bevel. The civil rights delegation was pained by Daley's decision to seek a court order restricting demonstrations. Obtaining an injunction in the middle of negotiations, complained Berry, "was just a very poor maneuver on [Daley's] part . . . the kind of move that only a powerful despot would try." The injunction so outraged two delegates from the Conference on Religion and Race—Robert Spike, an influential white Protestant clergyman, new to Chicago, who had directed the race relations work of the National Council on Churches from 1963 to 1965, and George Jones, a prominent black businessman—that they were ready to walk out of the negotiations. Only the entreaties of Raby, Bevel, and Berry prevented a hasty exit.[97]

In passing up a perfect excuse to break off negotiations, protest leaders underscored their conviction, as King put it, that demonstrations alone could not "actually solve the problem." A broad-based program backed by Chicago's power elite, they recognized, was essential to race relations progress. They would think long and hard before breaking off talks with city officials, real estate leaders, and business heavyweights. "We are hopeful," Raby said after the first subcommittee meeting, "that in the coming week we will get definite agreements on open housing and get them in writing."[98]

While protest leaders continued to negotiate, the Chicago movement still had to decide how to respond to the injunction. At the Thursday night South Side rally, as word of an impending injunction against the marches spread, civil rights leaders had stressed their defiance. "We will not be enjoined by the courts, social habits, or Mayor Daley," James Bevel had declared. "Get ready. Get your grandmother up from the South so she can keep the kids while we're in jail." Raby had seconded the message. "If the Mayor is going to enjoin me from going to real estate places to look for housing, we're really in trouble," he had asserted. "I don't want him to be surprised if the Negroes fill up the jails of the city of Chicago."[99]

But blustery rhetoric was easier to issue than crafting a wise response to the injunction. Even the aggressive Action Committee, meeting Friday night at Al Pitcher's South Side home, wondered about what to do next. Inspired by Jesse Jackson's argument that the injunction must be broken, the Action Committee—which consisted of a dozen members at this meeting—seemed ready to take that bold step, to engage, as was common in southern campaigns, in civil disobedience. (Despite all the uproar, not once had protest leaders instructed their troops to violate a law that summer.) But King, who had come with Andrew Young to this meeting, urged restraint. Though he believed the injunction was immoral and unconstitutional, he questioned the wisdom of violating it at this time. Were enough people willing to go to jail over the injunction? King wondered. There had been sufficient marchers to carry out the demonstrations plotted thus far, but King and other protest leaders recognized that their nonviolent army was not limitless: it consisted of roughly four thousand committed troops. Would the public side with the movement if its members broke the injunction? King also asked. Further, if they tested the court order, would that shift attention away from the movement's true goal—creating an open city? Rather than violate the injunction, King leaned toward a proposal Pitcher had suggested earlier. The movement should stage in the city, as the injunction allowed, one march of no more than five hundred protesters. Any additional marchers would be sent into suburban communities to demonstrate.[100]

The next morning protest leaders again huddled to plot strategy. This time, as they sometimes did, Bevel, LaFayette, Jackson, and Pitcher joined members of the Agenda Committee—King, Young, Raby, Berry, Williams, McDermott, and the Reverend Clay Evans—in an office at the Chicago Urban League. Jackson once more advocated violating the injunction, but King's position was even firmer than the night before. A new factor, it seems, had crystallized his thinking on the matter. Ever since the city had obtained the court order, movement lawyers had pored over the ambiguously worded document, trying to ascertain the implications if its provisions were flouted. What they concluded was not comforting: it seemed certain that violations would result not in arrests but in fines. Ignoring the injunction, then, would not necessarily lead to the mass jailings that would, as they had in the South, inspire the movement. Moreover, King knew that SCLC, whose financial position had deteriorated since the move to Chicago, could not afford to cover hefty fines.[101]

Despite the commotion over the injunction, the Chicago movement forged onward, following the Pitcher-King line of strategy. On Sunday, August 21, three hundred demonstrators led by Jerry Davis of the AFSC paraded through downtown Chicago Heights, a southern suburb, while James Bevel and Jesse Jackson led another two hundred marchers on a two-mile march through Evergreen Park, a well-to-do, heavily Irish suburb bordering Chicago's Southwest Side. That both civil rights brigades had to brave hostile crowds in these outlying communities dramatized how resistance to integration went beyond the city's borders.[102]

But the day's biggest civil rights protest took place on Chicago's far Southeast Side. King raced from a downtown television studio, where he had appeared on a "Meet the Press" broadcast, to the Liberty Baptist Church on the South Side to head the pilgrimage, his second during the open-housing campaign. Only heavy police protection and a summer downpour—one observer claimed he had "shrunk two feet because of the rain"—prevented widespread violence as the marchers snaked their way for five miles through East Side, a working-class community near Chicago's great steelworks. The march still had its share of drama, as King, dressed in a dark suit and without a raincoat, bantered with the angry crowd. At one point he confronted a group of taunting teenagers, declaring: "You are all good looking and intelligent. Where did all that hate come from?"[103]

Had King been five miles to the northwest, in Marquette Park, he would have found even more hatred that Sunday. Under gray skies and surrounded by a receptive audience, George Lincoln Rockwell, the Nazi party chieftain, delivered a fiery forty-minute address from a makeshift platform draped in front with an oversized swastika. Rockwell urged the cheering crowd to organize a "white guard" to resist integration. White Chicagoans, he declared, must arm themselves to confront the black intruders.[104]

Rockwell was not the only notorious figure in Marquette Park on Sunday. Connie Lynch of the National States Rights Party had traveled from California to hold his own hate rallies. And the Ku Klux Klan had sent an organizer, Evan Lewis of Akron, Ohio, in full regalia to whip up white sentiment against blacks.[105]

Shortly after Rockwell had finished his address, and just as Lynch and Lewis had begun theirs, the Chicago police rushed to arrest the speakers for not having proper permits. Although Rockwell stole away, Lynch and Lewis were rounded up. The intervention enraged the gathered crowd, and two hundred white youths stalked to the local police station, demanding the two men's release.[106]

The Nazi spectacle stunned and angered Chicagoans. Violence against blacks, however terrible, was at least a familiar feature of city life. In a city full of immigrants from southern and eastern Europe, Nazi posturing was not. Yet what was striking about the reaction to the Nazis was the conviction of many whites that the open-housing protests themselves, rather than endemic racial attitudes, had spawned this plague.[107]

This consensus did not emerge spontaneously; it was nurtured. And no one was more influential—and subtly effective—in spreading an alarmist view of the marches than the police superintendent, O. W. Wilson. Throughout August Wilson and his staff had complained that the civil rights forces were not cooperating sufficiently with the police. One of the principal planks in the injunction was the movement's failure to give "adequate notice" to the police department about upcoming protests. Thus when Wilson announced that Chicago's crime rate from mid-July to mid-August had jumped thirty percent over the same period in 1965, Chicagoans paid attention to his explanation for the rise.

To Wilson, the reason was simple. The open-housing protesters, he explained, required so much police protection that criminals ran wild throughout the rest of the city. If anyone remained unconvinced by this argument, Wilson threw in a clincher: in the Chicago Lawn police district, where so many of the protests had taken place and where police deployment had been enormous, crime for July and August 1966 had fallen off significantly from a year earlier. The higher crime rate, Wilson gravely concluded, "can be expected to continue as long as we have these demonstrations."[108]

The Chicago City Council also weighed in with its opinion that the marches were counterproductive. On August 25, the council formally endorsed the injunction by a vote of 45 to 1. "In forty years of public life," declared the powerful alderman Thomas E. Keane, he "could not recall a greater unanimity of expression in favor of an act taken by the Mayor." The black aldermen, in particular, took the opportunity to question the motives of elements of the civil rights movement—but not, significantly, of King himself. William Harvey of the Second Ward called Martin Luther King a "great man," but worried that he was "surrounded by some people who are not right." Ralph Metcalfe sounded a shriller alarm in claiming that some "militants" in the civil rights movement wanted "to see Chicago destroyed." Only Leon Despres denounced the measure. "The obtaining of the injunction was ill-advised," Despres argued. "It was divisive. It placed the full punitive force of the city behind one group of Chicagoans against another."[109]

Despres' reasoning, however, fell on deaf ears both inside and, in many cases, outside of City Hall. "The new marches," wrote Monsignor John M. Kelly, editor and columnist of the *New World*, "have done nothing as far as I can see except to demand the services of a good portion of our police department leaving other areas with less than normal protection." Although a supporter of the goals of the Chicago movement, the University of Chicago Law School professor Philip Kurland backed the city's stand on the civil rights demonstrations. "The city can't, in good faith," Kurland said, "protect only the marchers, with no consideration for the rest of the citizens." Even an outside observer like the *New York Times* now questioned the wisdom of more demonstrations. "[I]t is time for a moratorium on these demonstrations," the paper editorialized. "Their point has already been made; now they have become counterproductive, even destructive."[110]

Though the tide of public opinion was increasingly turning against them, civil rights activists continued to demonstrate. On Tuesday, August 23, as King returned from a brief visit to Atlanta, James Bevel and Jesse Jackson led two hundred marchers on another march through Chicago's East Side. The next day, Jackson and James Orange guided over a hundred more demonstrators through hostile crowds in West Elsdon, thus spotlighting yet another Southwest Side community closed to blacks.[111]

Yet it was the revival of the idea of a Cicero march that truly stirred Chicagoans. Few disputed the Cook County sheriff Richard Ogilvie's prediction that such a march would "make Gage Park look like a tea party." It was big news, then, when on August 20 King announced that the Chicago movement would go to Cicero on Sunday, August 28. This prospect so alarmed Cicero town leaders that they pleaded with Governor Otto Kerner to call out the National Guard to help the town's small police force maintain order. Fearful of increased violence, Kerner consented to their request.[112]

Despite the near state of panic of many public officials and his own doubts about such a venture, King remained publicly committed to a Cicero march. "We're not only going to walk in Cicero, we're going to work and live there," King declared on August 23 at a South Side rally of students, including gang members, at Christ Methodist Church. The prospect of a Cicero trek especially excited some members of the Action Committee. The proposed march on Cicero revived memories of the Selma campaign, which had been punctuated by moments of great drama and capped by the climactic march to Montgomery. A number of members of the Action Committee longed for an equally momentous Chicago finale, a major march with a "national call."[113]

The uproar over the upcoming Cicero excursion completely overshadowed a more important civil rights story, which was taking place not in the streets but in the meeting rooms of the St. James Episcopal Church parish house. After three long days of negotiations on Monday, Wednesday, and Thursday, including a near breakdown, the Summit subcommittee was finally closing in on an agreement. The city negotiators, particularly Marciniak, wanted an accord, though not, as some observers suggested, largely because they trembled at the potential violence of a Cicero march. Cicero, after all, was a separate municipality, not part of Chicago. Marciniak and his colleagues were worried enough about the demonstrations in their own city and wanted movement leaders to endorse a moratorium on marches. Although the civil rights delegation to the subcommittee resisted any blanket moratorium on protests, it was—except, to some extent, for Bevel—ready to settle and thus willing to suspend open-housing demonstrations if progress toward ending housing discrimination was made. Personally drained by the taxing summer, Raby, Berry, McDermott, and Williams suspected that the movement collectively was also tiring. (Serving as a leader in the Chicago movement, McDermott later remarked, was like being a "front-line commander" in the army. "You went to meetings day and night. You were exhausted.") They particularly worried about a decline in the movement's power. They feared the inevitable loss of many "summer soldiers"—especially student and women protesters—who could not be relied on, because of other obligations during the school year, to march once the fall arrived. "[I]t was very difficult for us to think of prolonging [the direct action], intensifying it, and bringing it further, rather than bringing it to a kind of a stopping point," Williams later recalled. Raby especially understood that marches by themselves did not lead to change. The previous summer he had led marches virtually every day with little result. "We didn't agree on anything, we didn't settle on anything, we didn't get any institutionalization of anything," he believed. The civil rights negotiators also worried that more marches would lack the desired educative power. Given the city's injunction, the right to demonstrate, rather than unequal housing opportunities, was likely to become the burning issue. Finally, they knew that generating an atmosphere of creative tension was a means to an end, not an end by itself. "The whole purpose of the movement was . . . to get some sort of meeting," McDermott noted. The goal was not to trigger a race riot or to transform Chicago into a permanently divided city. It was time—and here the Chicago civil rights leaders eventually softened Bevel's resolve to continue demonstrations—to seek institutional solutions to the problems the city faced.[114]

Like good negotiators, the Chicago protest leaders kept their concerns to themselves. They were less silent, however, on another worry. They had come to the painful realization that their original demands did not reach far enough. Hastily drafted, those demands had focused exclusively on housing and called for procedural changes rather than specified results. One participant in the first Summit meeting noted, "So skilled in the techniques of marching and demonstrating, Dr. King's group could never seem to transplant this ability to the conference table, where more concrete proposals could have been anticipated." As they reviewed their position, they recognized that stronger terms were necessary if a Summit agreement was to be an effective instrument for fair housing. Yet even within civil rights circles there was no consensus on whether the movement should seek explicit timetables for integrating Chicago's neighborhoods. Though such targets would naturally give any agreement greater force, some civil rights leaders, including Jesse Jackson, seemed philosophically uncomfortable with fixed goals or quotas.[115]

In some respects these intramovement debates were virtually irrelevant, because it proved nearly impossible to expand the agenda in the middle of negotiations. Ayers, the subcommittee's chairman, slapped down their efforts to incorporate goals and timetables for desegregation into the agreement. In doing so the independently minded Ayers was not acting as a tool of the Daley administration, however. He later insisted that he had "not [been] harassed or talked to by any of the city people." Ayers was a good choice to facilitate an agreement. He was known for his honesty and fairness. As a businessman, he had not been directly involved in the crisis, but he represented a constituency that desired a settlement to the disruptive dispute. Moreover, he was quite acceptable to civil rights forces. A longtime associate of Bill Berry's, Ayers had toiled for many years to strengthen the Chicago Urban League and during the first Summit meeting had exposed his progressive leanings by speaking forcefully on behalf of the Chicago Freedom Movement. Yet despite these sympathies, Ayers—a seasoned negotiator—frowned on adding new demands to ongoing talks.[116]

Ayers did allow one major new proposal to make its way to the bargaining table. He believed that the idea of a supervisory organization charged with monitoring compliance to the agreement and promoting education and action programs to achieve fair housing flowed naturally from the original demands. Backed by Ayers, the proposal encountered no opposition from the other negotiators. Such an organization, the subcommittee delegates all agreed, would be a catalyst—an orderly catalyst—in breaking down residential segregation, not just in Chicago, but in its suburbs as well.[117]

The big day finally arrived. On Friday, August 26, Chicago's power elite reassembled with movement leaders in the Walnut Room of the stately Palmer House hotel for what was widely expected to be the last round of negotiations. The marches, it now seemed, would come to an end, almost a month after the first major open-housing eruption on the Southwest Side. Once again, Ben Heineman chaired the conference. After allowing the press to take pictures, Heineman closed the meeting to outsiders and promptly turned to his friend Ayers, inviting him to read the lengthy report that his subcommittee had with great effort rushed to complete. When he finished reading, Ayers asked for its acceptance by the larger body. Mayor Daley, anxious to reach an agreement and pleased that the report diagnosed the fair-housing question as a wider metropolitan rather than exclusively a city problem, immediately called for a vote.[118]

Raby, however, wanted to slow down the proceedings. Still skeptical of the "personal commitment" of some of the conferees to the goal of open housing and aware that this was the movement's last opportunity to strengthen the terms of the agreement, he wanted hard guarantees of real progress. When, he now asked, would each Chicago community be one percent black? Or even more at the heart of the issue, when would blacks be served by realtors?[119]

No one stepped forward with specific answers to Raby's queries, but one by one Chicago's religious and labor leaders, including Archbishop Cody and William Lee, affirmed their commitment to making Chicago an open city. Pulled by this tide, Ross Beatty felt obliged to speak on the realtors' behalf. He began by reporting progress in his industry, but then betrayed his deep uneasiness with the Summit proceedings by returning to the old theme that the conferees had placed a "tremendous" and unfair "burden" on realtors. At this point a distressed King interrupted Beatty, questioning him about a statement he had made recently on the radio suggesting that open housing would ruin the real estate business. Beatty's uninspiring reply instantly darkened the mood of the session. It seemed as if the civil rights negotiators might now bear down on the realtors and deliver an ultimatum: serve every client regardless of race. But they passed over this chance, and soon Bishop Montgomery, fearful that the agreement was slipping away, spoke up, promising Beatty that the Chicago Real Estate Board could count on support from others in its efforts to educate real estate brokers. Robert Johnston also added his voice to the chorus for conciliation, noting that he had spoken to Walter Reuther in the morning and that the UAW president had promised full cooperation in "the implementation of this agreement."[120]

The crisis seemed to have passed, but Raby, ever wary, requested a recess so that the civil rights leaders could once more evaluate their position. While Raby's request disappointed Heineman and Daley, they had little choice but to accede to the movement's wishes, and the civil rights delegation headed for the fifteenth floor to caucus. What precisely happened at this meeting remains unclear. The final result, however, was plain: despite a lack of unanimity, especially from Bevel, the protest leaders decided to settle.[121]

This decision reflected the will of Martin Luther King, for he commanded so much authority that he could have, had he so chosen, taken the movement down a different path. He could have, as most Action Committee members wished, continued marching. Spirits among his lieutenants were still high. But the inspirational leader now turned pragmatic. There were a host of reasons encouraging a settlement. The Chicago movement could refuse to settle at this late juncture only with grave repercussions. After so many hours of negotiations and so much speculation that an agreement was at hand, the negative fallout of a civil rights rejection would be enormous. Ever alert to the transience of movement power, especially if a campaign came under more fire from liberals and moderates, King—like the civil rights delegation to the Ayers subcommittee—recognized the limits of the size of the Chicago nonviolent army. He also desired a concrete achievement to compensate for the sacrifices made by his followers. Finally, it was not King's nature to reject good-faith negotiations. Local activists themselves had helped to fashion the Ayers accord. The Summit agreement, though not everything that King had hoped for, was certainly far stronger than the settlements that had brought SCLC's Birmingham and St. Augustine campaigns to a close. The pact promised to be a tangible victory—not simply a public relations victory to mask a retreat from an unfriendly Chicago, as some critics suggested—that would boost the stock of the larger, national nonviolent movement. It was an agreement that King could embrace.[122]

When the full conference reconvened, King explained that he still had two more issues—the injunction and the implementation of the impending agreement—that had to be addressed before he could agree to an accord. Bishop Montgomery at once tried to calm King's concerns about implementation by stating that he hoped to have the supervisory body set up within three days. Then Donald Zimmerman rose to deliver a speech on the injunction that stunned the civil rights camp. The injunction, Zimmerman proposed, should not be debated today. It deserved to be tested in the Supreme Court "so that we can know finally what rights people have to assembly and petition." Coming from a religious leader, Zimmerman's remarks—apparently spontaneous, but in fact prearranged to prevent the injunction issue from bogging down a settlement—badly undercut the movement's position on the court order.[123]

Zimmerman's stance angered civil rights activists. Did he not realize that such a course of action would cost tens of thousands of dollars? Did he not recognize that the Chicago Freedom Movement's power—its ability to compel compliance to the agreement—flowed largely from its capacity to stage protests? Moreover, they were dismayed that a religious leader had acted to aid the city's—not the movement's—position. "It was that kind of insipid moral neutrality that characterizes white Protestantism," Andrew Young groaned. Raby issued a blistering rebuttal to Zimmerman, curtly explaining that another legal opinion would not be of much help to blacks.[124]

Afraid that a settlement which had seemed so close was now slipping away, Daley tried to quiet the storm against the injunction with a surprisingly personal confession. He had no love for injunctions, he told the conferees. He had been "raised in a workingman's community in a workingman's home," where the "injustice of injunctions" was clear to all. But the marches had so imperiled the welfare of the city, its civic order, that he had felt compelled to seek an injunction. "There was," he claimed, "no other course for me."[125]

The mood of compromise had been restored. The movement, King now stated, would settle as long as the conferees agreed to separate negotiations about the injunction. Then Heineman called for a vote on the Ayers accord. It was unanimous. The open-housing protests had come to an end. The march on Cicero would be suspended. King rose to deliver a short benediction. He offered his warm appreciation for all the work that had been accomplished in the past week, yet he also reminded everyone that this fine agreement was not an end, but a beginning. The hopes of black Americans had "been shattered too many times" in the past by false promises. "[W]e must," King insisted, "make this agreement work."[126]

Chicago, Congress, the President, and the Nation

5

"I have just been watching the sickening spectacle of the 'superior white race' rioting in response to your march on 'the news' on television," a young housewife from a Chicago suburb wrote to Martin Luther King, only hours after he had been stoned in Marquette Park. She was shocked by the "venom and sadism, not just in the 'backward south,' which we have been feeling superior to, but everywhere in our 'fair city.'" She was not alone in her outrage. "I felt sick at heart when I heard the insults and jeers of the white hecklers on the radio program last night. I just want to let you know that there are many white people who are praying and working for you and your people," another woman wrote. The "horrible and sickening spectacle of the white mob" overwhelmed yet another radio listener, driving her to the point of tears. "I was so ashamed of my race," she said. At the same time a Presbyterian minister from Michigan felt impelled to join the Chicago crusade. "My Christian conscience cannot allow me to stand aside any longer," he confessed. And one woman spoke for many Americans when at the height of the Chicago protests she asked King to "please pray for those of us who do not do enough—that we too may have the courage to do whatever we can and should."[1]

The white belligerence also shocked many in positions of power across the nation. "The marchers were simply attempting to raise and expose to the nation the truth about discriminatory housing practices so that the public—churches, government, and individuals—would demand change in law and practice," an American Friends Service Committee officer told a congressional subcommittee in Washington. "The counter-reaction—whites stoning Negroes—that's going on in Chicago is good in one way," the Urban League's Whitney Young declared. "The real hate there is now coming into the open. Their real attitudes are being revealed."[2]

The reverberations of the open-housing protests were felt far beyond Chicago's borders, a result expected by civil rights strategists. "Selma, Alabama, was our pilot city for the Voting Rights Bill of 1965," King had announced at the outset of the Chicago Freedom Movement, "and I have faith that Chicago . . . could become the metropolis where a meaningful nonviolent movement could arouse the conscience of this nation to deal realistically with the northern ghetto." King's vision percolated down through SCLC's ranks as well. The Birmingham and Selma campaigns had become the standard against which SCLC initiatives were judged. SCLC was trying, Mary Lou Finley told her brother in November 1965, "to create a non-violent movement in Chicago which will force the whole nation . . . to come to terms with the question of getting rid of slums." It was always SCLC's goal, Jimmy Collier insisted, to reach the "largest audience possible."[3]

By early August 1966, it seemed that King and SCLC had once again been prophetic. At the very moment the Chicago open-housing demonstrations heated up, Congress was debating a civil rights bill that included a fair-housing section. In the end, however, a northern Selma remained unattainable. In part King and SCLC, pressed to act quickly and disrupted by the unfamiliar northern setting, did not—and could not, in some cases—follow the lessons that the southern campaigns had taught them. In part, there were stark limits to the extent to which they could influence national response—by the President, the Congress, and the American public—to their Chicago initiatives. Although many Americans seized upon the white reaction to the Chicago marches as evidence of the immediate need for federal legislation against housing discrimination, ultimately most did not. By 1966 civil rights protests—as the national response to the Chicago crusade attested—had lost much of their power to galvanize the nation.

In late April 1966 President Lyndon Johnson played out what had become a White House ritual. After meeting with black leaders, Johnson asked Congress for the third time in three years to pass a civil rights bill. Like its predecessors, this bill was sweeping. It sought to protect civil rights workers from violence and intimidation and to prevent discrimination in the selection of juries. Unlike its predecessors, its most important feature was not directed primarily at the South. Title IV of the bill outlawed discrimination in the sale and rental of housing—a national, not regional, problem. "The time has come," Johnson declared, "to combat unreasoning restrictions on any family's freedom to live in the home and the neighborhood of its choice."[4]

The presence of a fair-housing section in the 1966 Civil Rights Bill resulted directly from Johnson's desire to lead, and not be led by, the crusade for racial justice. Johnson viewed himself, with justification, as America's greatest civil rights President, and he had no intention of resting on his laurels after the passage of the Voting Rights Act in 1965. He wanted to do more. He also wanted to make sure that he would not be outflanked on the civil rights front. Even though black leaders had only fitfully agitated for a federal fair-housing measure, Johnson in the summer of 1965 instructed his staff to prepare a federal law to combat housing discrimination.[5]

Most civil rights leaders desired an expanded fair-housing executive order, which they thought was certain to bring relief to blacks. But White House officials questioned the constitutionality of an expansive executive decree, and they noted its political drawbacks—as its sole architect Johnson not only would bear the brunt of any fallout over the measure but could also be criticized for imperial behavior. Although Johnson no doubt heeded these concerns, he was also, after so many years of working in Congress, himself inclined to seek a legislative remedy. The Johnson administration knew that passage of a comprehensive civil rights bill with a fair-housing plank would be difficult. "The discrimination in housing business is extremely dangerous to pursue this year because of the political repercussions it is likely to have on a number of Congressmen. There is really not much public support for this kind of action," one White House aide remarked in early 1966, as drafting of the bill inched toward completion. Even the principal drafter of the legislation, Attorney General Nicholas Katzenbach, admitted that the bill might not be passed, especially with the fair-housing clause. But Katzenbach argued that the administration should still seek the legislation. He could imagine "worse fates than saddling the Republicans with our failure—if it is failure—to secure enactment."[6]

Congress received the new measure apprehensively. The bill was first directed to the House Judiciary Committee, where liberals and moderates narrowed the coverage of Title IV by exempting privately owned dwellings with less than five units, nearly sixty percent of the nation's housing stock. Even with this surgery, passage of a compromise bill still seemed doubtful. If a compromise bill survived the House, it faced a tougher battle in the Senate, where key senators like Everett Dirksen had proclaimed their opposition. Worse, there was no outcry for the bill's enactment. On the contrary, the loudest voice denounced the new legislation. The National Association of Real Estate Boards (NAREB) mobilized over one thousand local real estate boards to attack the housing clause, and it oversaw a lavishly funded campaign to influence Congress. Congressional mail, according to one report, was running 100 to 1 against the fair-housing clause by June. In addition to white hostility, the militant wing of the black protest movement dismissed the 1966 bill as unimportant. Stokely Carmichael went so far as to call it "a sham." Commenting on the dim prospects for the bill, one congressional aide declared: "There's no national consensus, no outrage, no grassroots."[7]

There was some hope, however, that the national climate for civil rights might improve. At the same time that the 1966 Civil Rights Bill emerged from the House Judiciary Committee, the Chicago Freedom Movement launched its open-housing campaign. Martin Luther King had favored the fair-housing focus in part because, as he told Chicago activists at a high-level strategy meeting in late June, "Congress is debating [the] issue of open housing this session." When King dramatically posted the movement's demands on the door of City Hall in mid-July, one of the document's items called for swift passage of federal fair-housing legislation. The CCCO newsletter for the summer of 1966 declared, "We march in order to mobilize the conscience of a nation."[8]

King and SCLC leaders clearly recognized a link between their demonstrations in Chicago and a federal fair-housing bill. In his early August keynote address at the tenth annual SCLC convention, the Reverend Walter Fauntroy, SCLC's liaison with the federal government, exclaimed, "[w]e need to keep marching in Chicago." The Chicago protests, Fauntroy explained, needed to "raise the issue of our misery and distress to the level where not only will Chicago have to deal with it" but "the conscience of this nation will cry out to Congress." At the same convention the SCLC board of directors issued a resolution stating that the "tragic events of Gage Park in Chicago last week sharply exposed the viciousness of those who patrol and protect the ghetto walls. Our marches into lily-white Chicago neighborhoods provided dramatic witness to the fact that legislation like Title IV is urgently needed to combat destructive confinement of Negroes in overcrowded, ill-equipped ghetto schools—in substandard, rat-infested homes—in crime breeding, filthy streets." Later, on a mid-August "Meet the Press" program, King echoed Fauntroy's and the SCLC board's emphasis on the national dimension of the Chicago campaign. King admitted that "there are many people who are against open housing and who are against having Negroes as their neighbor." Civil rights forces, he added, should nevertheless "go all out to end housing discrimination." Here the civil rights movement in the South was instructive. Southern whites did not want blacks to eat at lunch counters or to have access to other public accommodations, but "this did not stop the nation from having its conscience so aroused" by heroic protests that it demanded corrective federal legislation. "Now I think," King concluded, "the same thing must happen in housing."[9]

Many Americans outside the civil rights movement also saw the connection between the Chicago protests and the Civil Rights Bill of 1966. The Chicago campaign, the *Christian Science Monitor* declared in early August, "is especially timely as Congress wrestles with the 1966 civil-rights law. Open housing has been the issue that bogs down that passage." And yet the early Chicago demonstrations failed to boost the bill. Shortly after the July 31 violence in Marquette Park, the House further narrowed the coverage of Title IV, exempting real estate brokers who sold single-family homes from the antidiscrimination proscription.[10]

The Chicago protests, however, seemed to give Congress yet another opportunity to tackle a national injustice when news of more white violence spread across the country on August 5. "[T]here was little chance the housing section would pass without compromise," the Cleveland *Call and Post*, a black newspaper, asserted, "until Dr. King was stoned during a housing march in Chicago." Many of the leading national newspapers expressed outrage as well. "The ugly events in Chicago serve to remind us that the hour is late and that it is imperative that this country begin to eliminate racial discrimination in the sale and rental of housing," the *Louisville Courier-Journal* wrote. "A few more pictures of white youngsters and their elders hurling rocks and burning cars in such neighborhoods," the *Denver Post* declared, "*should* convince even the dullest of the basic fact about human rights and housing:

all-white neighborhoods not only have 'the problem': they are the problem." In the end, the drama in Chicago had little influence. When the House finally passed the civil rights bill on August 9, the fair-housing section was much weaker than the one that Johnson had proposed.[11]

King and the Chicago Freedom Movement bore some responsibility for the limited national impact of the Chicago open-housing demonstrations. The Chicago movement did not make use of several tested techniques that had helped transform earlier local protests into protests capturing a national audience. In the past, dramatic moves by Martin Luther King himself—such as going to jail or leading a major march—almost guaranteed headlines. But King, preoccupied with SCLC's annual convention in Jackson, Mississippi, for much of August, participated in only two open-housing marches, both of which drew front-page coverage from the *Los Angeles Times*, the *Washington Post*, and the *New York Times*. And King—like most of his fellow marchers that summer—never went to jail in Chicago.[12]

The Chicago movement also ignored tactics successfully employed during the Selma campaign. In 1965 Randolph Blackwell, then SCLC's executive director, oversaw an effort to encourage Americans from across the country to participate in the march from Selma to Montgomery. Telegrams urged northerners, especially clergy, to come to Selma. Food and shelter was found for the thousands of Americans who descended upon the Alabama city. National figures ranging from UAW President Walter Reuther to Nobel laureate Ralph Bunche joined the throng. "I felt that this was the moment when it had to be. And that every force that could be rallied should be rallied at this point," Blackwell later recalled.[13]

In contrast, the Chicago protests were self-contained. The Chicago movement neither called on celebrities to bear witness in its struggle nor sought marchers from outside the Chicago area. Nor did it elicit assistance from national religious networks such as the National Council of Churches or the National Catholic Conference for Interracial Justice as it had during the Albany, Georgia, drive and even more impressively during the Selma campaign. Unlike in the South, there was no pressing need to import white marchers to the already interracial Chicago demonstrations, but the absence of marchers from across the country inevitably blunted the penetration of the Chicago campaign into Americans' daily lives.[14]

The national press never covered the Chicago marches to the extent that it covered the Birmingham and Selma protests.[15] During six weeks of major protests in the spring of 1963, the Birmingham campaign made the front page of the *New York Times* sixteen times. The Selma protests attracted even more attention. Selma stories (or directly related articles) were page one features thirty-five times in a fifty-four-day period in 1965. By comparison, the *New York Times* featured the Chicago protests on the front page only seven times during the twenty-seven-day span of full-scale demonstrations. No wonder that many Americans viewed the Chicago protests, in the words of someone who had also marched at Selma, "as more of a local battle for civil rights."[16]

King and his followers would have largely agreed with that conclusion. In Chicago they were far more absorbed with forcing local officials to promote social change than protest leaders had been in Selma. Particularly local Chicago activists like Raby, Berry, McDermott, and Williams but also other movement leaders recognized that reform in the midwest city would directly affect the lives of hundreds of thousands of blacks. The Selma campaign, in contrast, had involved a small city with only fifteen thousand blacks. In Chicago, pursuing a formidable mission and carrying out the unending responsibilities that accompanied guiding a direct action campaign consumed virtually every waking hour of the freedom movement leadership. McDermott recalled that they "didn't really have a lot of time or energy to think globally."[17]

As August rolled on, however, more and more Chicago activists began discussing "going national." With the city of Chicago's injunction, the press even speculated that the Windy City might soon become the site of an immense civil rights initiative. On August 20, for instance, *Chicago's American* ventured that a "national march on Chicago" was in the offing. It remembered, though not entirely accurately, that twice before—in Birmingham in 1963 and in Selma in 1965—King and SCLC had defied injunctions and accepted mass arrests, which along with white violence were "the necessary ingredients" to national outcry. "Chicago," the *Chicago's American* suggested, "appears to be drawing close to at least the first element—jail." Some Chicago activists also thought that this was their moment. "In my opinion," Robert Lucas of CORE argued, "had King broke that injunction [then] he would have rallied thousands of black people in this city and perhaps across the country to this movement."[18]

Yet King and the Chicago movement never embraced civil disobedience in the summer of 1966. In early July, King had warned Chicagoans that his followers might block traffic on Chicago's expressways. With the injunction, King again hinted that civil rights forces might have to resort to civil disobedience. "We have violated injunctions in the South and we may have to here," he stated. But in the end he and his colleagues chose not to confront Judge Harrington's ambiguous decree, which most likely would have led to heavy fines rather than mass jailings if it had been violated. Electing not to jeopardize ongoing negotiations, they operated within the constraints of the Chicago injunction.[19]

Yet even if the Chicago campaign had sought to broaden its reach, whether it would have focused on the Civil Rights Bill of 1966 is uncertain. King had wired Johnson applauding his announcement in his 1966 State of the Union address of plans to tackle housing discrimination, and he had exhorted a group of United Church of Christ ministers in May to "go all out over America to bring" the President's new civil rights measure "into being and to insist that it will be vigorously enforced, once it is passed," but he never displayed the same enthusiasm for federal fair-housing legislation that he had for national acts against discrimination in public accommodations and for voting rights. From the outset of the Birmingham and Selma initiatives, SCLC leaders had decided what specific injustice they would spotlight. They had embarked on the Chicago project, however, knowing only that their enemy was a more generalized condition—the despair, poverty, and exploitation of slum ghettoes. Neither King nor his SCLC colleagues had come to Chicago with the conviction that a federal prohibition against housing discrimination was a preeminent goal. For the first half of 1966, King had repeatedly expressed his belief that "our basic problem—after all the others—is an economic problem." Only as summer approached were King and his lieutenants persuaded of the desirability of an open-housing campaign, as much for tactical as for strategic reasons. King thus stumped only sporadically for national fair-housing legislation during the Chicago campaign, and when Congress softened Title IV, he became quite dissatisfied with the bill. "The housing section is virtually meaningless," King stated. "It is so watered down that it will hardly do anything to undo the long-standing evil of housing discrimination in this country." And even cagey members of the Action Committee, including James Bevel, the foremost strategist of the Selma campaign, said little to connect events in Chicago with congressional action. Against this backdrop, that the *Washington Post* could run adjacent front-page stories on the Chicago marches and the debate on the 1966 Civil Rights Bill without any cross-reference is no surprise.[20]

King and SCLC were not the only ones who veered from a replay of the Selma script in 1966. A year earlier, during the Selma crisis, Lyndon Johnson had turned the presidency into a civil rights pulpit. "As I watched reruns of the Selma confrontation on television, I felt a deep outrage," Johnson wrote in his memoirs. "I believed that my feelings were shared by millions of Americans throughout the country, North and South, but I knew that it would probably not take long for these aroused emotions to melt away." With dispatch Johnson sent a federal voting rights bill to Congress to correct an intolerable injustice. The Chicago protests, in contrast, did not spur Johnson to act, even though the White House staff kept him informed about the Chicago civil rights crisis (a top aide sent the President a report from Ramsey Clark on August 5 noting that the "situation in Chicago is extremely bad") and many Americans pointed to the Chicago protests as eloquent testimony for the necessity of federal fair-housing legislation. The legislative master ignored this opportunity to assist his fading 1966 civil rights measure.[21]

Johnson's only public comments about the Chicago demonstrations were enigmatic. Asked if he was worried about a backlash in light of "problems in places like Chicago," Johnson replied in an August 24 press conference: "I think there are going to be a lot of problems that exist in Chicago which will be reflected in the elections, without question. I think that the administration at the federal, state, and city level has to be constantly on the alert to do everything they can to face up to the modern-day problems and try to find solutions to them."[22]

In part Johnson's inaction on the Chicago crisis reflected the fact that there was little legal basis for federal intervention. During the Selma campaign, federal judges had presented the Johnson White House with legal grounds to federalize the National Guard when they ruled that the state of Alabama had failed to protect the right of American citizens to vote. In Chicago, by contrast, local authorities were protecting civil rights activists from unruly onlookers. The federal presence in Chicago was restricted to the mediation efforts of the Community Relations Service.[23]

Johnson, moreover, did not itch for a larger federal role. For one thing, he now had little desire to help Martin Luther King. Until the summer of 1965 Johnson and King had fashioned a working relationship, but the Vietnam War soon drove a wedge between the two leaders. Morally repulsed by war and certain that the Vietnam conflict was draining precious resources away from Great Society programs, King delivered in the fall of 1965 a series of speeches denouncing the escalation of the American war effort in Indochina. King's remarks drew a barrage of criticism, including salvos from Senator Thomas Dodd of Connecticut, a Johnson supporter. King had no doubt about the impetus for Dodd's attacks. "Johnson pushed Dodd to do it," he confided to his advisers.[24]

During the Chicago campaign, King kept his views on the Vietnam War largely private, only occasionally speaking against escalation of the conflict. His relative silence stemmed not from respect for Johnson but from his desire to prevent the outcry that further criticism of the war would inevitably unleash from hobbling the Chicago crusade. King's muted criticism of the administration's Southeast Asia policies did not, however, dramatically improve his relations with Johnson. He had never developed as close a rapport with the Texan as he had with John F. Kennedy. Johnson was too much unlike King. King was self-effacing and humble; Johnson tended to be larger than life and dominating. King viewed societal inequities as moral problems; Johnson instinctively sought legislative solutions to gripping injustices. King's relationship with Johnson never became, according to Clifford Alexander, the only black on Johnson's top staff, more than "formal." By 1966 the SCLC chief still praised Johnson publicly on appropriate occasions, but he no longer sought face-to-face meetings with the President. Johnson most likely did not miss meeting with King, for he was much more at home with civil rights leaders like Clarence Mitchell and Roy Wilkins of the NAACP and Whitney Young of the Urban League, men whom Harry McPherson described as "accustomed to dealing with the political machinery of going and lobbying Congress, working with like-minded or reasonably friendly members to fashion a legislative result." That the Johnson administration had cooled toward King was strikingly clear when the SCLC leader was relegated to an absurdly small role during the highly publicized White House Conference on Civil Rights in June 1966. The period was one of heightening distrust between King and Johnson, and the protest leader had no contact with the President during the Chicago open-housing marches.[25]

Yet more than a growing dislike for Martin Luther King and the knowledge that Chicago police were protecting the civil rights demonstrators explain Johnson's silence on the Chicago protests. Two critical political considerations guided the President's behavior as well. First, Johnson recognized that it would be politically insane for a Democratic President with aspirations for another term to meddle in a crisis in a city governed by the most powerful Democratic mayor in the country. Richard Daley never warmed to Johnson as he had to Kennedy, but Johnson cultivated friendly ties with the Chicago political boss while he was President. He praised Daley often. He made sure that Daley was a frequent visitor to the White House. At times he went to great lengths to ingratiate himself. Johnson sent Daley so many photo albums that on one occasion a White House secretary had to remind him that the mayor had already received most of the photographs in the latest proposed gift.[26]

Most important, Johnson had already felt the sting of Daley's wrath. In the fall of 1965, acting on a detailed school segregation complaint filed by the Coordinating Council of Community Organizations, the U.S. Commissioner of Education Francis Keppel suspended more than thirty million dollars of federal aid targeted for Chicago schools. Daley was enraged at the suspension. Chicago members of Congress, especially Roman Pucinski, denounced Keppel. Daley then traveled to New York to attend a ceremony at which the President was presiding. He met with Johnson and condemned the federal action. Upset that his administration had committed an egregious political error, Johnson arranged a meeting with Keppel and other White House advisers. Less than a week after the suspension of federal aid, the money was restored. Almost a year later, Johnson's only recorded phone call about the 1966 civil rights crisis in Chicago was with Mayor Daley, not King.[27]

A broader, even more decisive political concern also influenced Johnson. The White House had come to believe that the era of demonstrations had outlived its usefulness. Johnson was under no illusion that the signing of the Voting Rights Act solved America's racial problems. At his famous commencement address at Howard University in June 1965, he had proclaimed that equality of opportunity for all Americans was not enough. Equality of result was the desired goal. When Johnson presented the 1966 Civil Rights Bill to Congress, he again called upon Americans to expand the traditional definitions of civil rights. "The ghettoes of our major cities—North and South, from coast to coast—

represent," he insisted, "fully as severe a denial of freedom and the fruits of American citizenship as more obvious injustices." But unlike many civil rights activists, Johnson believed more than ever that legislation, not demonstrations, would realize this goal. Never fond of protests, he had tried privately to persuade protest leaders to suspend demonstrations in the months before the 1964 election. And the Johnson administration seemed almost annoyed by the Meredith march, which despite its turbulence, was in part aimed at persuading Americans that civil rights workers needed the federal protection that its 1966 civil rights measure promised. Johnson remained convinced that progress was possible through existing American institutions and political arrangements. And equally important, he sensed that most Americans agreed with his conclusion.[28]

Illinois seemed to offer a dramatic example of the national mood. From its political antennae, the Johnson White House quickly determined that the Chicago open-housing marches would seriously damage the reelection prospects of Senator Paul Douglas, a loyal supporter of Great Society programs. Johnson's attorney general, Nicholas Katzenbach, called Martin Luther King to express concern about the political fallout of the protests for Douglas. On a two-day speaking tour of the Northeast in late August, Johnson stressed the importance of change through established channels and—seeking to respond to mounting white anxiety about race relations developments—criticized those who took the law into their own hands. "Men have the right to use the law, but they also have the responsibility to obey it," he declared. Though Johnson never directly assailed the Chicago protests, his remarks brought no comfort to the Chicago activists.[29]

It was left to Hubert Humphrey, a veteran civil rights advocate, to articulate the administration's position on the Chicago protests. Shortly after Archbishop Cody called for an end to the open-housing marches, the Vice President told a nationwide audience, "the Archbishop's call not only merits support, but it is of urgent necessity that it be respected and responded to effectively." Demonstrators had "gone so far" that they had created a backlash against civil rights, Humphrey asserted. "People are sick and tired of violence and disorder." Humphrey's criticism of the Chicago Freedom Movement exemplified a fundamental difference in opinion between King and the Johnson White House about the efficacy of protests. His remarks also reflected a recognition that the powerful civil rights consensus—the commitment to root out racial injustice that a wide array of Americans and their institutions had expressed in supporting civil rights initiatives from 1963 to 1965—was collapsing.[30]

The phrase "backlash" seemed to be on everyone's lips in 1966. "White Backlash Whips Up," declared *Life* magazine at the height of the Chicago open-housing marches. In September *U.S. News & World Report* headlined "Voter Backlash, Over Race Issue." The next month *Time* detected a "turning point" in American race relations in the rise of "white backlash." A darker, less tolerant side of America, opinion makers warned, was rising.[31]

Such alarmist fears no doubt exaggerated the strength of America's meaner impulses. White America did not succumb to a fierce, sharp reversal in racial attitudes. Public opinion surveys over the course of the 1960s revealed increasing white support for black demands, especially those grounded in the principle of equal opportunity in the public arena. Moreover, governmental initiatives against segregated schools, job discrimination, and voting restrictions moved forward.[32] Nevertheless, though their fears sometimes outran reality, observers of the American scene diagnosed a pronounced trend. The national mood on race shifted after the Selma campaign in early 1965. By 1966 optimistic outlooks had faded as Americans argued over the meaning of urban violence, the stance of black militants, and the national obligation toward black Americans. Racial issues threatened to divide Americans across the country with a force unmatched since Reconstruction. Surveying the scene in early 1967, the historian C. Vann Woodward judged that "1966—call it watershed or turning point—was a critical year in our history." "Reaction," Woodward noted, "had set in, of course, call it backlash or frontlash."[33]

Underlying this turbulence was a dramatic recasting of the popular view of blacks among white Americans. In late 1965 and 1966 images of angry black militants excoriating America and of undisciplined blacks on riotous rampages to destroy their own communities overwhelmed the recently minted images of blacks as courageous, proud fighters on a noble mission to secure their rights against brutish white southerners ready to resort to violence to keep blacks down. To many whites, this New Negro seemed ungrateful, defiant, and dangerous, and with this perception white empathy for the black predicament shrank.[34]

The lack of a unifying target for civil rights forces intensified the racial discord. During the great days of the civil rights movement, from the Birmingham to the Selma campaigns, relatively few northern whites had rejected the black drive for basic civil and political rights. The southern system of racial subjugation clearly contradicted the American image of equality and liberty. But as the Jim Crow South fell, so too did the sense of urgency fueling the crusade to purge the country of unpalatable injustice.[35]

As early as February 1965, Bayard Rustin had concluded that the "classical" phase of the civil rights movement—the destruction of the "legal foundations of racism in America"—had come to an end. The passing of one era inaugurated a troubling time of transition, inflamed by the Watts riot, the Black Power movement, and other explosions and made all the more difficult by the taxing task of identifying new targets and devising new remedies. In this turbulent milieu, the emerging new goals of the civil rights movement were destined to intensify passions and give rise to doubts. Civil rights partisans insisted that equal results, not equal treatment, become the standard of public policy. Even though King and his colleagues, with their Chicago campaign, had elected to spotlight the bias of the housing market, the program of the Chicago Freedom Movement vividly reflected the new emphasis. "To bring about equality of opportunity and of results" was one of its overarching goals.[36]

At the same time, federal policy was edging its way to the same line of reasoning. Despite his insistence in his Howard speech that "it is not enough just to open the gates of opportunity," Lyndon Johnson was not the principal force behind this realignment. Not only did Johnson continue to focus his attacks on individual discrimination—as evidenced by his persistent pursuit of fair-housing legislation until 1968—he also retained his faith in the capacity of an expanding economy, coupled with a panoply of social programs, to better the lot of all Americans. Other federal forces were in the vanguard of employing group measurements to boost black advancement. The Equal Employment Opportunities Commission and the Office of Federal Contract Compliance Programs, for instance, took steps to require proportional worker representation in industries that fell under their jurisdiction. Federal judges meanwhile moved toward race-conscious policies that promoted compensatory justice, the underlying theory behind affirmative action and racial busing.[37]

So gradual was the influence of the change in the goals of the civil rights movement on public policy that the shift did not trigger, but only accelerated, the collapse of the civil rights consensus. More damaging to this consensus was a less revolutionary, more evolutionary, swing in civil rights endeavor: to focus on the North as fully as on the South and to penetrate even more deeply into the lives of Americans. Discriminatory and segregative practices in guarded and fundamental arenas such as the housing market now became full-fledged targets. This dual expansion of civil rights concerns upset many white Americans who applauded the demise of the Jim Crow South, but who found the new demands irksome and threatening. One national survey in 1966 reported that seventy percent of the whites polled believed blacks were pushing too hard for racial change.[38]

Public support for civil rights demonstrations—which had never been overwhelming, even in the first half of the 1960s—was one of the first casualties of the new national mood. With riots erupting on city streets, with angry black rhetoric filling airwaves and headlines, and with the new civil rights agenda less popular, any agitation on racial questions, to many whites, was suspect. More and more whites now seemed unable to distinguish nonviolent direct action from black rioting and the Black Power advocates' denunciations of America. The media perpetuated the confusion. In the summer of 1966, newspapers often lumped together stories about rioting with accounts of peaceful civil rights demonstrations. White approval of civil rights protests, according to an October 1966 poll, dropped below 1963 levels.[39]

SCLC and Chicago activists thus launched their open-housing marches during a deteriorating climate for organized protest—made even worse by the growing national preoccupation with the Vietnam War, which supplanted race issues as the top public concern.[40] Those in the Chicago movement could take comfort in the impressive résumé that accompanied their weapon—nonviolent direct action—and they also knew that nonviolent thrusts, though often criticized, still held high moral ground. They had decided, however, to extend the principle of equal opportunity to one of the most racially exclusive—and zealously defended—institutions in American life: the neighborhood.[41]

Few civil rights demands surpassed the call for fair housing in stirring controversy. No doubt much of the uproar stemmed from the irresponsible campaign by the real estate industry nationwide to whip up opposition to fair-housing laws. But in raising the red flag of "forced housing," a bald distortion of laws intended to extend housing opportunities to every American citizen, realtors played upon basic American convictions. To most whites, a home was a castle, protected by the Constitution. Certainly the federal government did not have the power to tell homeowners to whom they could sell or rent their property.[42]

Closely related to this conviction was the belief that neighborhoods resulted from a series of personal, private choices that were beyond the purview of a meddling government. To seek a close-knit community with control over schools, clubs, and other culture-transmitting institutions was a natural impulse for Americans. It seemed natural to many Americans, in addition, that the upper middle class wanted to live with the upper middle class, that the Irish wanted to live with the Irish, and that whites wanted to live with whites. No citizen, most whites thought, should be excluded from lunch counters, theaters, or other public places, but, for many, exclusion from residential areas was a different matter. Where one lived and with whom one lived was a private affair well outside governmental jurisdiction, especially when undesirable neighbors could depress property values. A Georgia lawyer, who claimed to have voted for Lyndon Johnson in 1964, nicely captured this line of thought when he wrote in August 1966: "The home is the bulwark of our democratic society; it is private and personal, as distinguished from public facilities like restaurants and motels. The cherished right to own one's home implies an inherent right of freedom to sell as one may choose." Like many other Americans, he did not regard fair-housing legislation as a means to secure rights for minorities. Rather, he viewed it as an assault on the rights of the average American. Politicians, he complained, were "presently catering to the whims of minority groups to such an extent that there is little regard for the rights of the majority of Americans."[43]

Beneath this impassioned protection of the homeowner's rights was, of course, a fundamental white antipathy toward having black neighbors. In *An American Dilemma*, Gunnar Myrdal perceptively noted that white southerners had a "rank order of discrimination." Myrdal did not specifically identify exclusion of blacks from white neighborhoods as a top white priority, but his list was clearly constructed on a public/private scale. Southern whites, Myrdal argued, would be much more willing to accept integration of "public facilities" than intermarriage. The 1950s and 1960s demonstrated that Myrdal's "rank order" could also be applied to northern whites. Numerous public opinion polls revealed that most whites—while sympathetic to black access to public accommodations—did not want black families as neighbors.[44]

The fate of fair-housing referenda attested to the strength of such sentiments. Although by 1966 more than fifty states and cities had adopted fair-housing measures, no such law had been approved by a public referendum. Voters in cities as varied as Berkeley, Akron, and Tacoma had defeated fair-housing laws. So too had the citizens of California, a state noted for its progressivism. On the issue of open housing, most whites were not racial liberals. Their outlook resembled that of Chicago's Southwest Siders.[45]

With such strong sentiments against fair housing, the hope held by the Chicago Freedom Movement and its supporters in 1966 that whites would "be stirred into action" if they saw "enough of the sort of hatred displayed" in Gage Park and Marquette Park proved too optimistic. Many Americans—though far from all—sympathized with Chicago whites and interpreted their assaults on civil rights marchers as sincere, even commendable, efforts to protect the hearth and home. "These white people wish to be left alone and should be allowed to live with their own kind of people, or is the white man not supposed to have any freedom?" declared a white woman from Michigan who wondered if there was anyone "in our entire country who will ask or demand that Martin Luther King stop his marches and demonstrations." "The City of Chicago," she insisted, "is being torn asunder by this man who professes to be peaceful and non-violent." Outraged by the Chicago marches into white neighborhoods, a Dolton, Illinois, resident complained to Senator Everett Dirksen: "Most of these people [whites] have worked hard for years to buy their homes in these areas so they can raise their families in a decent community. They must have the right to keep it that way." It is their right, he added, "to have the marchers removed if they aren't wanted."[46]

Unlike the Selma marches, the Chicago demonstrations were readily subject to more than one interpretation. In the eyes of most northerners, even those hostile to demonstrations, the Selma protesters, menaced by heavyset, thuggish law officers, were clearly on the side of the angels. In 1966 the image blurred. With the Chicago police often aggressively protecting civil rights activists from angry whites who claimed to be defending their own turf, many Americans were less certain about who were the heroes and who were the villains. A New Yorker, for instance, assailed "'peaceful demonstration marches' into our predominantly caucasian communities during which these same proponents of violence are protected by these brutal police."[47]

The structure of Chicago protests ensured ambiguity. The consequences of housing discrimination—black relegation to slums and higher rents for inferior shelter—were difficult to convey by marching with a police escort through a white neighborhood. Pictures of southern white officials at a county courthouse, refusing to allow black men and women the right to register to vote, needed no further explanation. Even the *New York Times,* generally sympathetic to the black drive for equality, described the Chicago marches as protesting "alleged" housing discrimination. Senator Paul Douglas detected fundamental differences between southern and northern civil rights campaigns. When later asked by a constituent curious why his wife, who had traveled to Selma, did not march in Chicago, Douglas wrote: "My wife did not march in Chicago this summer, because she felt that the circumstances were totally different, in so far as the law enforcement officers in Chicago and Cook County were trying to maintain the peace and were giving protection to the marchers. This was not the case in Selma." In addition, Douglas continued, "local government officials were trying to work out a solution in Chicago, whereas this was not the case in Selma."[48]

Although the Chicago demonstrations by no means stirred the widely unsympathetic and hostile response that black urban riots evoked, the Chicago campaign clearly did not unfold as perfect civil rights theater. One Marylander told Martin Luther King: "You have done much to develop a weapon of non-violence which has not only been effective, but it has put your opponents to shame and has been effective not only locally, but in the seats of Congress and the public conscience." "But in my opinion," he continued, "this weapon was badly used in Chicago. There were repeated marches into neighborhoods of unsophisticated first and second generation immigrant whites. The results were predictable." This correspondent concluded that "in the eyes of much of America, the Negroes emerged as provocateurs. Hatred has been built up which it will take a generation to overcome." A reporter cut to the heart of the matter when he concluded: "Dr. Martin Luther King's Chicago campaign . . . failed to produce the moral response of earlier campaigns in Montgomery, Birmingham and Selma."[49]

The Chicago protests reinforced the growing doubts about the wisdom of civil rights demonstrations in general. One Ohio woman, who had supported civil rights causes in the past, was now certain that "something is going wrong." "Dr. King please go to the Conference tables and Churches instead of the streets," she urged. At the same time a Connecticut woman scolded King for "not moving beyond the area of street demonstrations." "Surely," she stated, "it is obvious to you that your reception in Chicago stems from the deep insecurity of the people in whose neighborhoods you are demonstrating."[50]

An observer from Shelby, North Carolina, grasped the difficulty of staging successful protests in the post-Selma era. "I believe in the way you are going about righting wrongs," he wrote to King in late August 1966. "But I urge you to reexamine what is happening in Chicago." Southern-style demonstrations would not succeed in Chicago. They had "worked" because they dealt in "the public domain and in legal rights." Open-housing protest only "hardens opposition. It arouses fear against the unfamiliar. It gives excuses to the rabble rousers of both sides."[51]

Even many blacks doubted the wisdom of the Chicago protests. "It is useless for us to tramp around white men's neighborhoods," declared Elijah Muhammad, with typical Black Muslim disdain for Martin Luther King's strategy. From conservative circles came criticism as well. "Demonstrations . . . at times have their positive effects," commented the conservative *Atlanta Daily World* on August 21. "At other times they can almost defeat their intended purpose. Tactics that may be detrimental to the open-occupancy struggle in Chicago must give way to methods that may further the cause." Well-known black civil rights leaders also questioned the Chicago marches. "Any Chicagoan could have advised Dr. King that the Selma technique was not suited to the Chicago Gage Park district," Roy Wilkins, the executive secretary of the NAACP, told a Philadelphia audience in mid-August 1966. Wilkins, who advocated a less confrontational approach to black advancement and whose relationship to King had cooled over the years, may have taken some pleasure from his criticism of the strategy of his rival, but even A. Philip Randolph, the dean of civil rights leaders, argued that the time for marching had passed. After expressing his sadness over the display of whites in Chicago, whose faces were "ugly with rage and resentment," Randolph declared that "the time has come when the street marches and demonstrations have about run their course. I believe that the strategy now in order is to shift from the streets to the conference room."[52]

* * *

Facing reelection battles in the fall and alert to public opposition to open housing and further demonstrations, members of Congress handled the 1966 Civil Rights Bill with circumspection. In a reversal from recent congressional bouts with civil rights legislation, racial conservatives took the offensive. They reminded their colleagues that they had been prophetic about the dangers of passing civil rights legislation. "The history is that violence in the streets has been increased in the same proportion as civil rights legislation has increased. The more laws passed in Washington the greater has been the wanton violence in cities across the nation," an Alabama congressman declared. Conservative southerners especially delighted in the alarm the bill raised among many northern representatives. "For the first time, many of my colleagues from north of the Mason Dixon line have expressed concern that they feel this bill goes too far. I well understand what they mean. It goes too far North," a Mississippi congressman crowed. Finally, racial conservatives said with relief, civil rights fervor was waning. In twelve days of debate, the House gutted a section of the bill that gave the attorney general power to speed the desegregation of public schools, passed an antiriot amendment, and almost dropped Title IV, the fair-housing clause.[53]

The civil rights passion that had suffused the House in the spring of 1965 during the Selma crisis had vanished by August 1966. Mainstream civil rights groups, including the NAACP, the Urban League, and the Leadership Conference for Civil Rights, sought to rally support for the new bill, but they were unable to spark a fire on Capitol Hill. No member of Congress journeyed to Chicago to investigate the open-housing dispute, and in the week of debate on the 1966 bill by the House, which followed the first well-publicized Chicago march, only six congressmen referred directly to the Chicago demonstrations, and all of these references were hostile.[54] William Dickinson, a representative from Alabama, cried for antiriot measures to "give the overworked and overcriticized Chicago police force a well-deserved rest after weeks of attempting to keep crowds under control after they have been inflamed by out-of-state leaders interfering in Chicago's affairs." Congressman Horace Kornegay of North Carolina asked, "Are not many of those on the scene of the current Chicago outbursts of violence the same ones responsible for the gleeful cries of 'burn, baby, burn in Watts'?" An Illinois Democrat, who in the past had always supported civil rights causes, denounced the needless turmoil in Chicago as well. "We are having some very troublesome and dismal days in Chicago," Roman Pucinski complained. "On both sides of this issue, there are powerful forces at play appealing to race hate and prejudice."[55]

In the end the House passed the 1966 Civil Rights Bill. But the fair-housing clause had exacted a great toll. The margin of victory in 1966 (259–157) fell far short of the landslide triumph (333–85) of the Voting Rights Act of 1965. Liberal representatives stood their ground, though far less enthusiastically than in the past. A large number of moderates, however, critical of Title IV, voted against the bill. Congressman Arch Moore of West Virginia, for instance, had voted for the civil rights acts of 1957, 1960, 1964, and 1965, but he could not endorse this bill. "The average American," he noted, "tends to look upon his right to sell realty, as being absolute, and I believe that attitude is steeped deep in the traditions of this nation . . . Legal measures taken to assure equality of housing opportunity necessarily, I believe, constitute an interference with individual property rights." With such sentiments pervasive, the bill's future in the Senate, where the votes of moderates had more impact, looked bleak.[56]

When the Senate began to debate the bill on September 6, all eyes were fixed upon Senator Everett Dirksen of Illinois. In Dirksen's hand, everyone agreed, lay the fate of the measure. The eloquent Senate minority leader had rallied reluctant Republicans to vote for the Civil Rights Act of 1964 and the Voting Rights Act of 1965. But there now was little chance that Dirksen would drop his opposition to the 1966 bill.[57] This measure was bad legislation for the country, he maintained, and he refused to bend to what he considered terrorist tactics by the civil rights movement. Dirksen denounced not only Stokely Carmichael's militant behavior and activities but also "the other leaders who've gone into white areas of Chicago, for instance; that is, after all, calculated harassment. It's a species of intimidation. It's like saying they're either gonna do this or else." On September 14, shortly before the first test of Senate support for the bill, Dirksen, hobbled by a recent hip injury and braced by two crutches, rose in the Senate and delivered a final salvo against the proposed legislation. The open-housing provision, he thundered, was "a package of mischief for the country."[58]

With no signs of an eleventh-hour switch by Dirksen, the Senate fight over the bill was anticlimactic.[59] Sensing victory, southern senators began to filibuster, delivering impassioned harangues against the bill. A few liberal senators countered the southerners' denunciations. Edward

Kennedy, for instance, assailed those who equated a vote for civil rights legislation with an implicit endorsement of rioting. "What about the sickening conduct of those white adults who beat and bloodied Negro schoolchildren in Grenada, Mississippi, for trying to attend a desegregated school?" Kennedy asked. "What about the mobs of whites who screamed obscenities and hurled rocks and bottles at peaceful demonstrators in Chicago?" This filibuster, however, lacked the drama that had marked the previous battles over civil rights legislation. On a number of occasions the Senate was forced to adjourn early because of a lack of a quorum. So many senators busied themselves with other matters that Mike Mansfield, the Senate majority leader, threatened to order the Senate sergeant-at-arms to "arrest" the absent senators and force them to return to the Senate. Finally the Senate leadership decided to call for a cloture vote. If successful, cloture would have broken the southern filibuster by limiting debate. Yet in two separate votes, the cloture motion fell far short of the two-thirds majority needed. Most northern Democrats voted for cloture, but Republican senators followed Dirksen's lead and voted against it. Thus on September 19, the Civil Rights Bill of 1966 was snuffed out.[60]

Many civil rights advocates fumed at the scuttling of the bill. Blame was spread widely. Some racial progressives scored Dirksen for not fulfilling his responsibility to black Americans in a troubled time. They attacked the Senate leadership for mishandling the bill and accused President Johnson of not battling vigorously for it. Certainly Johnson, now more absorbed with fighting the Vietnam War and anxious about white America's hardening attitudes toward racial issues, did not cajole and pressure senators for their civil rights vote as he had on earlier occasions. "I don't think the President has done battle for the bill or given enough leadership to get it through. I haven't seen from the President the kind of crusading spirit as he showed last year in the voting rights bill," Martin Luther King concluded. But there was a more fundamental reason for the defeat of the 1966 bill. Too many white moderates—who opposed critical portions of the bill and who saw no compelling argument for new legislation to help blacks when some black leaders were denouncing America and urban blacks were rioting—had deserted the civil rights camp. Nor were these members of Congress impressed by the Chicago protests. "The most significant and best publicized opposition to the Bill was said to be based on the opposition to 'conduct,' i.e., the marches of the Chicago Freedom Movement through white neighborhoods in Chicago," Roger Wilkins asserted during the fall of 1966. The moderates' defection emboldened the hardliners and sapped the strength of civil rights crusaders, who depended on a coalition of racial moderates and liberals for legislative success. In this election year, moderate senators wanted their votes on fair housing to conform to their constituents' wishes. Consequently, a top Johnson aide concluded, "it would have been hard to pass the Emancipation Proclamation in the atmosphere prevailing now. White people are scared and sore and the consensus is running out—has run out."[61]

King, upon learning of the defeat of the bill, warned: "I want somebody in Washington to know that when that bill died a lot of faith died in America." During the Senate debate on the bill, King had reaffirmed his commitment to a federal fair-housing measure. He had told a large audience in Memphis that he would stage more open-housing protests "in order to dramatize the urgency of the housing problem" so that Congress "will not be able to avoid it, so that the very crisis will cause the nation to act." Yet King must now have more fully understood what his friend and adviser Stanley Levison had told him at the pinnacle of his Selma success. The great civil rights consensus of the mid-1960s was fragile, Levison had written to King in April 1965. "The coalition of Selma and Montgomery, with its supporting multi-millions, is not a coalition with an unrestricted program," Levison warned. "It is a coalition around a fairly narrow objective. It is broad because it unites all classes, except the extreme right, against terror, violence, deprivation of voting rights and elementary human rights." He continued: "It basically is a coalition for moderate change for gradual improvements which are to be attained without excessive upheavals as it gently alters old patterns." And then with emphasis, Levison concluded: "*It is militant only against shocking violence and gross injustice.* It is not for deep radical change." The Chicago campaign had verified the acuity of Levison's analysis. King now worried that blacks understood this truth all too well and doubted the will of America to pursue racial equality. His fears were perhaps best captured in a question an Alabaman posed to him: "Does this shelving of the Civil Rights Bill mean that all the marching and demonstrations were in vain?"[62]

Stalemate in Chicago

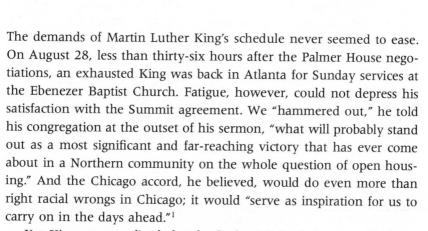

6

The demands of Martin Luther King's schedule never seemed to ease. On August 28, less than thirty-six hours after the Palmer House negotiations, an exhausted King was back in Atlanta for Sunday services at the Ebenezer Baptist Church. Fatigue, however, could not depress his satisfaction with the Summit agreement. We "hammered out," he told his congregation at the outset of his sermon, "what will probably stand out as a most significant and far-reaching victory that has ever come about in a Northern community on the whole question of open housing." And the Chicago accord, he believed, would do even more than right racial wrongs in Chicago; it would "serve as inspiration for us to carry on in the days ahead."[1]

Yet King soon realized that he had misjudged the impact of the summer of 1966. The Summit agreement did not prove to be a springboard for a new Chicago. The task of transforming the midwestern city, he confessed in early 1967, was "greater than even we imagined." Nor did the Palmer House accord revitalize the quest for racial justice. The subsequent months were a time of decline, not renewal, for both the Chicago movement and, more generally, the national civil rights movement.[2]

Not all Chicago activists were as pleased with the Summit agreement as King was. Even as Ben Heineman, Mayor Daley, and King extolled the accord to eager reporters outside the Palmer House, the head of Chicago CORE expressed his disgust at the decision to settle. "[N]othing but another promise on a piece of paper," Robert Lucas asserted. CORE, he predicted, might even resurrect the Cicero march. Later that day, Chester Robinson, director of the West Side Organization, further fueled the unrest. Stunned that King and his fellow leaders had settled for what he regarded as so little, Robinson announced that WSO would march into Cicero on Sunday as originally scheduled, "come hell or high water." "[T]he poor Negro," Robinson raged, "has been sold out by this agreement."[3]

The proposed Cicero march jolted the King camp. A march threatened not only to upend implementation of the Summit pact but to obscure a civil rights victory by highlighting challenges to King's authority. Yet at the moment King's lieutenants began to mobilize to defuse this threat, a break came their way. So many other groups wanted to march—generally small organizations from the militant fringe of the Chicago civil rights movement—that the dissidents, who were united less by a common ideological orientation than by their general disgust with the framing of the Summit agreement, decided to postpone the Cicero demonstration one week, to Sunday, September 4. More time was needed to organize the protest properly, Robinson explained.[4]

A postponement gave King and his colleagues another week to block the Cicero excursion. It also gave them more time to resolve their own differences. Virtually every member of the Action Committee still fumed that the open-housing marches had been suspended prematurely. "[W]e settled too early," Bernard LaFayette said regretfully. "The issue should have been projected until it had national dimensions, but we never even got into the suburbs," Al Pitcher lamented. The Summit agreement came "right when I thought the campaign was about to take off on a more national level," Bill Moyer later recalled. Action Committee members found the terms of the Summit accord especially disturbing. "I was not happy with the agreement," Don Rose remembered. "I knew that it did not contain the things that were uppermost in our agenda, i.e., timetables and programs for desegregation."[5]

From Action Committee circles emerged a critique of the Summit sessions that reflected fissures within the Chicago Freedom Movement. Representatives of the Action Committee complained that the Summit negotiations had been too exclusive. They had been left largely in the hands of four members of the Agenda Committee: Al Raby, Bill Berry, Kale Williams, and John McDermott. Only James Bevel represented the more aggressive wing of the movement. And even experts on Chicago's housing problems like Bill Moyer had had little opportunity to shape the negotiations. Some activists thought that the essentially moderate forces in the movement had dictated the peace. They did not accept Berry's claim that it was the nature of negotiations that "you don't get everything, because if you get everything there would not be any point in negotiating." According to the critics' argument, Berry, Williams, and McDermott, as heads of established human relations organizations, and Raby, as the leader of a broad-based coalition, were more closely linked to Chicago institutions and traditions and thus less inclined to take Chicago to the brink of tumult, the point that many on the Action Committee thought necessary to spur the Daley administration and other centers of power in the city to embrace change and innovation. It seemed to many activists that the civil rights negotiators, constrained by their ties to the city, had flinched at taking the bold steps required to force Chicago to address racial inequities. Such critical analyses circulated, but like good soldiers, the Action Committee members kept their complaints private. No one wanted to embarrass King.[6]

It was a mark of both King's style of leadership and his character that he did not censure his doubting subordinates. Rather, their criticisms prompted him to review his steps and, upon reflection, to admit mistakes. "We should have done just what a labor union does," King later told his followers. "We should have gone back to the members and voted" on whether to accept the Ayers accord.[7]

No amount of self-criticism, however, could impress those who viewed the entire Summit proceedings as irredeemably flawed. At a South Side rally on August 31 at Liberty Baptist Church, Monroe Sharp, head of the militant but diminutive Chicago SNCC, and other disgruntled blacks challenged the SCLC leader. They handed out caustic leaflets alleging that "Daley blew the whistle and King stopped the marches," booed when King was introduced, and chanted "Black Power" as King talked. Ever diplomatic, King stopped speaking and invited Sharp to address the crowd. Sharp accepted the offer, made his way to the front of the church, and began trumpeting the virtues of Black Power and railing against King and the Summit agreement. When Sharp finished, King took the high road, even though he had rarely been so stridently denounced at a civil rights rally. Refraining from recriminations, he launched into a powerful extemporaneous sermon on the vicissitudes of civil rights progress. His words stirred most of his listeners to stand, join hands, and sing "We Shall Overcome."[8]

With this timely performance King seemed to be regaining control of Chicago insurgency. But to be fully successful, he still needed to halt the Cicero march. Fortunately for King, Chester Robinson and other members of his grass-roots, lower-class organization were now having second thoughts about going to Cicero. Despite their tough talk, they really had no desire to undercut King, with whom they had worked amiably in the past. Robinson and his followers, some of whom had joined the open-housing marches, simply did not think that the Summit accord would lead to immediate, concrete improvements in their lives. "I don't think anybody here has seen a thing in those agreements that will benefit you," Robinson told his followers. "So evidently somebody down there didn't know what their people needed." In blunt words, although he specifically exonerated King, he attacked the looseness of the agreement and the very issue that had been under discussion: fair housing. "The people have to speak," he insisted. Robinson's complaint was more a demand for community power and gain than a Black Power assault against the nonviolent movement, however. When on Wednesday, September 1, Robinson met with King, Andrew Young, and Jesse Jackson, the WSO leader was willing to negotiate. The WSO would bow out of the march, Robinson proposed, if King and SCLC would battle for the public housing and welfare reforms that it desired. "We not only want to be free to buy or rent homes in all areas of the city, we also want the homes and apartments in our own area to be decent," Robinson stated. King promptly consented to this arrangement. The Cicero trek had lost one of its sponsors.[9]

Yet the march was still on, for CORE's Robert Lucas, despite numerous entreaties from King and his lieutenants—and scathing criticism from James Bevel, who was offended by a demonstration for which Lucas had not done "any work, study, investigation, or discussion before the action starts"—refused to reconsider his sponsorship. A native of West Virginia, a World War II veteran, and now a United States postal service employee, Lucas was a seasoned Chicago civil rights activist who in 1965 had taken command of Chicago CORE, which like the rest of CORE nationwide had since become a largely black organization. Lucas was known for his willingness to march at a moment's notice. During the anti-Willis protests in the summer of 1965, he had been arrested many times for civil disobedience. A year later he dodged flying objects on open-housing marches. Convinced that the movement had Daley and his cohorts on the run, he was dumbfounded by the original suspension of the Cicero march. He believed that civil rights forces had inexplicably fumbled on the goal line; now someone had to lead blacks into Cicero, if only to prove that they were not afraid.[10]

On Sunday afternoon, September 4, Lucas and two hundred followers, mostly black, paraded into Cicero, Al Capone's old lair. While not the "bloodbath" some observers had predicted, the four-mile, two-and-a-half-hour march was filled with action. Despite the intimidating presence of thousands of police and members of the National Guard, hundreds of angry whites lined Cicero's streets to taunt the protesters. They, unlike other contingents of demonstrators earlier in the summer, did not remain stoic; instead they swapped insults with white hecklers and even fired back debris tossed at them. "Dr. King's marches in Chicago were usually made up of movement people. This march was community people," Linda Bryant Hall, one of the Cicero demonstrators, later recalled. "These people had not attended any workshops on nonviolence," she added perceptively, though with some exaggeration. "They had not listened to any lectures on your fellow man and all." Deep inside Cicero, the protesters stopped for a prayer vigil at the site where Jerome Huey, a black teenager, had recently been killed by white youths while he was looking for work. The emotional scene overwhelmed the deceased's parents, and Mrs. Huey collapsed, crying out, "Oh, Lord, Oh, Lord, this is where my son died!"[11]

The most spectacular moment, however, took place in the final minutes of the march as the demonstrators approached the Chicago city line. Somehow—there is conflicting evidence on how it started—the marchers and their hecklers found themselves fighting each other. The Chicago police and National Guard, bayonets flashing, rushed to stop the melee. Within fifteen minutes the struggle was over and the demonstrators returned to the safety of Chicago.[12]

Widely reported and the subject of much commentary, the Cicero trek ultimately did little to advance the cause of civil rights. The imagery of the Cicero march was even more blurred than that of the open-housing marches earlier in the summer. With newspapers from Atlanta to Los Angeles running headlines such as "Guards Bayonet Hecklers in Cicero's Rights March" and featuring pictures of National Guardsmen in combat fatigues with bayonets fixed chasing white onlookers, it was not at all clear to many white Americans that the Ciceronians were the heavies. To these observers, the Cicero march seemed just one more example of a disturbing larger pattern of irresponsible militants, inexcusably assisted by agents of the state, wreaking havoc.[13]

Impervious to what others thought, Lucas pronounced the Cicero excursion "a great grass-roots march." "[I]t made everyone feel good," he added. Lucas himself "felt really good about the blacks catching the missiles and throwing them back, because it sorely indicated to the whole world that nonviolence had worked in the South but it wasn't about to really work in the North." The CORE leader even threatened to lead more marches. But the city of Chicago did not give him the opportunity. Shortly after his new threat, Lucas was jailed for failing to pay hefty fines for his acts of civil disobedience a year earlier.[14]

Chicago Freedom Movement leaders were happy to get the Cicero uproar behind them. They could now focus on developing new programs for social change, because they knew that the Summit agreement alone would not fulfill their desire for an integrated, tolerant Chicago. Their sweeping "Open City" manifesto of July had pointed out that housing discrimination was just one among many problems that plagued black Chicagoans. Activists, though longing to recuperate after an arduous campaign, turned to this broader agenda.

While the open-housing protests had captured all the headlines, they did not crowd out all other Chicago Freedom Movement projects during the summer. In July and August Operation Breadbasket continued to register victories, even though its director Jesse Jackson moonlighted as a leader of open-housing marches. In late July Breadbasket switched its target from dairy firms to soft drink bottlers. By the end of the month it had fashioned agreements with the industry's two giants, Coca-Cola and Pepsi-Cola, requiring each to hire thirty new black employees. In the fall, with the open-housing protests over, Breadbasket enlarged its staff and broadened its aims. Instead of confronting distributors, it now challenged supermarkets patronized by blacks, demanding that the stores stock black-made products and channel some of their assets into black-owned banks. One by one the big chains—High Low Foods, the National Tea Company, Jewel Foods, and A & P—submitted to Breadbasket demands. So swift was Breadbasket progress that in late 1966 King promoted the young Jackson to an executive position in SCLC.[15]

The unions to end slums also survived the summer, even though a good portion of their staff was redeployed to the open-housing thrust. When those exertions ended, the unions stepped up their pursuit of tenant-landlord agreements. The East Garfield Park union quickly negotiated an accord with an owner of three buildings, but found its next target, Balin Realty, more stubborn. In no time this contest evolved into a battle royal, with disgruntled East Garfield Park residents picketing Gilbert Balin's home in a northwest Chicago suburb and Balin's lawyers threatening the agitators with legal action.[16]

The Lawndale union, meanwhile, had to fight hard for its first victory. After a lengthy rent strike, frequent tenant meetings, and seemingly endless negotiations, the union in April 1967 finally compelled one local landlord, Eva Atlas, to sell her eleven Lawndale apartment buildings to the Kate Maremount Foundation. Shortly afterward the union joined the foundation in a project to rehabilitate six of the buildings.[17]

By early 1967, the tenant union movement seemed on the verge of becoming an important force in Chicago life. The individual unions, which had sprung up across the city, now augmented their power by combining into a federation. This alliance was a remarkable development, in many ways a realization of Bevel's original vision of a vast network of tenant unions empowering propertyless Chicagoans. The federation also fired the spirits of integrationists, for besides the two West Side unions, it consisted of a tenant union from a huge, integrated apartment complex on Chicago's North Side, and JOIN, an SDS-inspired organization for poor whites, largely from Appalachia.[18]

To some, tenant power seemed unlimited. "[I]t is not too unreasonable to predict that the chain of events [the tenant unions] are setting in motion may do to the slums what the trade unions did to the sweatshops," one admirer wrote. Yet the tenant unions never lived up to these high expectations. Organizing tenants—a highly mobile group—proved exceedingly difficult. Moreover, often those slum dwellers with the most resources and initiative were precisely those who most wanted to leave a depressed community, and they did so as soon as they had a chance. In East Garfield Park, where Bevel's West Side contingent had focused its attention, only one of the eleven locals was ever firmly organized. The tenant union movement also foundered on the realities of the marketplace. By the late 1960s city inspection programs had chased away many of the big slumlords who had milked their ghetto properties mercilessly. Left behind in the declining communities were mostly small landlords who rarely reaped great profits and who often abandoned their properties when confronted by angry tenants calling for better services. The Chicago Freedom Movement itself demonstrated that rapacious slumlords were not the sole cause of ghetto housing woes. Less than a year after the Maremount Foundation had taken control of a number of the Atlas buildings, its tenants, angered by insufficient upkeep, resorted to a rent strike despite the foundation's claims that high costs required cutbacks.[19]

While Operation Breadbasket and the unions to end slums carried on, protest leaders searched for new projects now that the city and private institutions had pledged to combat housing discrimination. One venerable target—public school segregation—was no longer available. On August 31, 1966, Benjamin Willis spent his last day as school superintendent, an event that passed almost unnoticed amid the open-housing tumult. His successor, James Redmond, who was known as a progressive, had just arrived from Long Island to take his new post. CCCO would make sure that Redmond did not ignore racial issues (and there would soon be friction between the two), but there would be little purpose in staging protests until the new superintendent had been given a chance to initiate reforms.[20]

With old issues temporarily off limits, protest leaders turned to other targets. For a time, each new day seemed to bring a new key issue. In mid-September Andrew Young told a South Side crowd of the imperative need for the unionization of underpaid workers and urged them to join the workers' fight against Saks Fifth Avenue for union recognition. Jesse Jackson and other activists picketed the exclusive store, but unionization never became a civil rights preoccupation. Later that month at a rally in the Englewood area, Martin Luther King targeted another pressing issue. Outraged by plans to raze local housing to make room for a parking lot servicing the 63rd and Halsted Street shopping region, King promised to spearhead the fight against callous urban renewal projects. Soon Englewood residents, assisted by SCLC staffers, began picketing, boycotting, and marching. Yet though they kept up these protests throughout the fall, the Englewood battle never became a rallying point for activists across the city.[21]

The lack of a new unifying project was not the only problem that the Chicago Freedom Movement faced in the fall of 1966. Although many national publications heralded the Summit pact as capping another civil rights success—"Victory in the North," proclaimed *Newsweek*, "Still King," concluded the *Christian Century*—many others closer to the scene saw the disarray following the agreement as symptomatic of a flawed campaign. "[T]hat agreement," Alderman Despres asserted, "was a treaty to cover Martin Luther King's retreat from Chicago." And resentment over the Summit agreement still festered among insurgents. Timuel Black, a longtime civil rights crusader, went so far as issuing a public letter that detailed a long train of alleged duplicity on the part of Bill Berry, who because of his Urban League work had extensive contacts among Chicago's white leaders. "Bill, do you remember the story of how Jesus Christ was betrayed by one of his own for a few pieces of silver?" Black inquired. In a city where insurgents believed that much of the black leadership—particularly, but not exclusively, black politicians—had been co-opted by the mayor's office, charges of betrayal were serious. Moreover, many CCCO delegates were irked that they had not met as a body to plot policy in over a month. Armed with a host of complaints, disgruntled CCCO representatives sought in early October to oust Al Raby as CCCO's leader, and nearly succeeded.[22]

The Black Power movement also spread discord. During the summer, Chicago activists, immersed in the open-housing protests, had sidestepped internecine fights over the merits of Black Power. But with the end of the marching and the bitterness over the Summit agreement, Black Power sentiments grew in the insurgent ranks. Right after the Palmer House meeting, for example, the *West Side Torch*, the West Side Organization's newspaper, denounced "the amount and quality of white advice given and followed" during the open-housing campaign and "the mystical character of the so-called non-violent philosophy (masochism and sadism)."[23]

Chicago Freedom Movement leaders did not unconditionally reject Black Power. Al Raby, like Martin Luther King, tried to put a positive spin on the concept. "I am for Black Power if it means the political and economic control of a community by its people," Raby declared in the fall of 1966. Yet Raby would not embrace the anti-white, anti-nonviolence thrust that many blacks attached to the phrase. "I believe [Black Power] is self-deceiving if it is used as a symbol to instill fear without having any meaning."[24]

The outlook of King and Raby still appealed to many Chicago activists, but a sense of exasperation had overtaken civil rights forces, particularly SCLC's Chicago staff. "I got very frustrated myself," remembered Jimmy Collier. "In the final analysis," he continued, "when the agreements were made after the demonstrations we didn't really feel that we had anything that we could point to as successful, or a goal that we had accomplished." The Chicago staff members never fully recovered from their disappointment over the glacial progress of ghetto organizing and the outcome of the summer protests, and their ranks thinned rapidly in the fall of 1966 as some returned to school or departed for elsewhere. In these depressing days, SCLC staffers were not immune to the new ideological currents, though King's vision remained alive with much of SCLC's Chicago contingent. As the issue of the "distinction between blacks and whites in the movement" was raised, one white SCLC civil rights worker came to "believe that it was time for white people to leave." Surveying the Chicago civil rights scene that October, Al Pitcher confessed that "[t]he Black Power people have made everyone conscious of the white people in the movement; there is a real question, how long can a white person continue to function in the Movement?"[25]

Like the two blades of a pair of shears, the spread of the Black Power position and the disillusionment over the Summit agreement severed ties uniting Chicago activists and thus imperiled their movement. The Chicago crusade could not afford too many defections. It had never truly mobilized black Chicago. It lacked, for one thing, the full backing of the local black church. With the Reverend J. H. Jackson publicly lambasting the crusade and with many ministers fearful of reprisals by the Daley regime, activists struggled to find pastors who would even host civil rights rallies in their churches. Like their ministers, black Chicagoans on the whole had not stampeded into the movement. There was no sign of active grass-roots support on the scale of the 1963 school boycott. To be sure, the 1966 campaign lacked a mass single-shot protest like a school boycott, which did not require black parents and children to take concrete action but only to refrain from a daily activity. But even during the Chicago Freedom Movement's high point—the open-housing crisis—not more than three percent of the black community participated in a march or a rally.[26]

The cumulative effect of uncertain purpose, inner disharmony, and sagging popular support devastated the Chicago movement's voter registration campaign, the most important initiative in the winter of 1966. The new venture began, however, with high hopes. In early December King flew back to Chicago to announce the launching of "an intensive voter registration and voter motivation drive." Although the effort would not be an overtly partisan attack on the Daley machine, it was designed to spur independent black political power. "We are confident," King declared, that the drive "will have a great impact on Chicago."[27]

To direct this latest operation, King summoned one more SCLC stalwart. Burly, brash, and dynamic, Hosea Williams had become a driving force in SCLC since joining the organization in 1963. Recently he had overseen an extensive voter registration campaign in the South. Having received the call to come north to mount a similar effort, Williams brought more than a dozen of his own experienced staffers with him.[28]

An early January 1967 rally, featuring Ralph Abernathy, Congressman John Conyers of Michigan, and Robert Henry, the black mayor of Springfield, Ohio, kicked off the voter registration drive. Yet though Williams's staff sought to stir up enthusiasm, the campaign never really ignited. Only a few people turned out at City Hall to register to vote on a trial "Freedom Day." Not long afterward Oscar Brown, Jr., entertained over five hundred teenagers at a "Vote-A-Baloo" show. The teenagers enjoyed the entertainment, but few stayed to hear Williams's appeal for volunteers to help register voters. To make matters worse, a Chicago-size blizzard buried the drive's much needed homestretch run. In the end, Williams claimed to have added thirty-two thousand people to the voting rolls. The city more accurately pegged the number at less than five hundred.[29]

Williams had no difficulty explaining the project's failure. It had received little help from Bevel's staff, who, according to Williams, "looked upon the drive as a big joke." Bevel's staff, which was "doing little more than laying around their rooms all day, playing cards, drinking and smoking pot," had even sapped the vitality of his own staff, Williams complained. He could not get his "staff to stay out in the wards and give a full [day's] work." While Williams was not an impartial observer—he had long feuded with Bevel—other observers confirmed the inefficacy of SCLC's Chicago team, especially after the Summit agreement. Stoney Cooks, who became the director of SCLC's Chicago project after Bevel's decision to plunge into the peace movement in early 1967, argued that a new terrain required a new type of field worker. "We have had," Cooks noted, "great march leaders or door-knockers of the 'turner-outers' but not people who could make the transition to tenant organizing or hospital organizing or steward training."[30]

Hosea Williams was too perceptive to put the blame for the debacle solely on his fellow activists. Whatever its shortcomings, his squad had tried to educate black Chicagoans about the consequences of their voting choices. Chicago's blacks, in his view, did not seem to desire libera-

tion. "I have never seen such hopelessness," Williams said. "The Negroes of Chicago have a greater feeling of powerlessness than any I ever
saw." [31]

Even while searching for new projects, protest leaders never forgot that
the final verdict on their movement hung on what happened to the
Summit agreement. Six weeks after the Palmer House meeting, that
judgment was unfavorable. A Summit follow-up committee had quickly
selected James (Joe) W. Cook to chair the "separate, continuing body"
designated by the accord to devise "action programs necessary to
achieve fair housing." But Cook's appointment disappointed Chicago
activists. Though Cook, the president of Illinois Bell, one of Chicago's
largest corporations, would give the new organization prestige and access to the centers of Chicago power, he was an unknown. He had come
to the Midwest from New York only a few months earlier and had no
history of civil rights involvement. Even worse, until November Cook
still lacked a staff for the new fair-housing group. As one civil rights
leader complained, "There's a chairman, but he doesn't have any organization." [32]

Cook was as skeptical about his new post as the movement was
about him. When offered the position by a blue-ribbon delegation of
Chicago's most important religious leaders including Archbishop Cody,
Cook had immediately thought that "the temperature of that potato was
such" that he ought to decline the offer. Not only were some blacks
disenchanted with the Summit agreement, but many whites denounced
it and some even went to City Hall to display their anger. "The races
spoke, religion spoke, but who spoke for the taxpayers of Chicago," was
how one white neighborhood association greeted the Palmer House
accord. "We demand an equal voice and equal rights for the people who
pay for these promises." But for Cook the pull of civic obligation was
too great (especially when strengthened by the proddings of renowned
clerics), and he agreed to take charge of the new organization. [33]

After recruiting a wide array of Chicago-area leaders to become
members of the new organization, Cook set out to raise funds. To begin
with, he obtained $25,000 from foundation grants as seed money. Then
Leonard Spacek, chairman of Arthur Andersen, assumed the fund-rais-
ing chores. Spacek handled this task superbly and raised over $100,000
for the fair-housing body. No doubt many business executives found it

difficult to keep a straight face and tell the nation's leading accountant that their corporations were hard-pressed financially. Spacek had less success in securing the cooperation of labor unions. The United Packinghouse Workers backed the new group, and the UAW contributed $2,000 and also urged its membership and local industries to combat housing bias. Yet despite William Lee's endorsement of the Summit agreement, the Chicago Federation of Labor remained aloof. In the follow-up to the Summit agreement, labor, traditionally regarded as a more steadfast ally of progressive causes than business, was outperformed by management.[34]

In late November 1966, much to the delight of the Chicago Freedom Movement, Cook announced the appointment of Edward Holmgren as the executive director of the recently christened Leadership Council for Metropolitan Open Communities. The long name was chosen after lengthy consideration; in the end it reflected the Daley administration's contention that the housing issue was not just the central city's problem. A native of Chicago and a bomber commander during World War II, Holmgren had worked for the Chicago Housing Authority during its progressive days in the early 1950s under the reformer Elizabeth Wood. He then had gone on to Baltimore, where he had developed a successful neighborhood assistance program. Once back in Chicago, Holmgren moved swiftly to fulfill the Leadership Council's mandate. He knew that many blacks had placed their hopes on the success of the council. "For 17 years I've been looking for a home," wrote one black woman. "[F]ive attempts (with one costly loss) convinced me that even with 9 to 5 equality, my family was doomed to live within the walls of the ghetto. I hope you can open the door for the next generation." Alert to the often conflicting interests of the Leadership Council's diverse constituency—which included realtors, city officials, religious leaders, businesspeople, and civil rights activists—Holmgren recognized that he had to rely on education and persuasion rather than on aggressive action to bring about change. In the council's first months, Holmgren and his small staff arranged three suburban housing conferences, delivered public presentations on equal housing opportunities, and later manned a service to find suitable housing for blacks throughout metropolitan Chicago.[35]

The Leadership Council did not work alone in the quest for open housing. Chicago's religious forces lent material and spiritual support to the cause. The Chicago Conference on Religion and Race ran housing centers to assist minority homeseekers. More important, each religious denomination dedicated itself to spreading racial tolerance and marshaling support for fair housing among its followers. The Catholic Church, for example, developed a full-scale initiative, "A Parish Program for Community Life," to fulfill these goals. Archbishop Cody hoped that a blend of sermons on racial justice and parish-sponsored discussion groups on open housing would break down "barriers between peoples in our community."[36]

Not everyone greeted the religious efforts warmly. Nearly a year after instituting a fair-housing program for the Episcopal Diocese, Bishop James Montgomery and Canon Paul Kyger noted that only half of the Episcopal parishes had faithfully carried it out. There were many dissenters within Catholic ranks, too. Shortly after Archbishop Cody's announcement of the Community Life program, Monsignor Edward M. Burke, the former chancellor of the archdiocese, challenged it, to the cheers of many Southwest Side and Northwest Side whites. "When we fight for the rights of the Negro we cannot overlook the rights of the white person," Burke argued. Whites had made many sacrifices to buy homes for their families, he continued, and they had every right to reject integration if it meant the decline of their property values and their neighborhood. The problem, as Burke saw it, was that blacks too often neglected their "obligations," even while asserting their rights. Catholic leaders quickly condemned Burke's outburst, but to many it was one more depressing piece of evidence "of how the Church can sometimes be more white than Christian."[37]

Civil rights leaders recognized that if the goal of an open city was to be realized, sermons would not suffice. Government officials would have to take positive, affirmative steps to show the way. That William H. Robinson, formerly CCCO's treasurer, had taken over the Cook County Public Aid Department in early 1967 gave the movement hope that this agency would do what it could to break down the walls of residential segregation. If there was to be significant change, however, the Daley administration and its agencies would have to fulfill their Summit obligations.[38]

The city's effort never impressed Chicago activists. The Department of Urban Renewal, for instance, had agreed to "search out the best housing available regardless of location" for all citizens displaced by its projects. Yet a civil rights watchdog committee, directed by Bill Moyer, found no hard evidence that the department followed through on its pledge. When Chicago activists interviewed eight families displaced by the Englewood urban renewal project, they discovered that not one of them had received listings of available apartments outside of South Side black neighborhoods.[39]

The Chicago Housing Authority (CHA) was even more negligent, even though its chairman, Charles Swibel, proudly pointed to improvements in existing CHA housing as evidence of good faith. A new $18,000 lock system had been installed and over a hundred new security guards had been hired, Swibel declared. The CHA, he added, also hoped to sponsor new tenant programs including a week of summer camp for five hundred children.[40]

Swibel, however, was far less effusive about CHA programs "to promote the objectives of fair housing," which the Summit pact called for. Swibel's reticence about progress on this point did not surprise civil rights activists. They knew that since the mid-1950s the CHA had been a prime governmental agent in perpetuating the ghetto by building the Taylor homes and other huge projects in regions of black settlement. Their investigators had detected no evidence of CHA strides toward desegregation. Not one black was placed in two new elderly projects built in all-white neighborhoods a few months after the Summit agreement. In the last half of 1966, not a single black family was placed in a predominantly white family housing project. Similarly, the CHA did not use its leasing program—which subsidized the rent of private sector housing for low-income families—to promote integration. Even the Leadership Council, which was more willing than civil rights forces to tolerate foot-dragging, criticized CHA's performance. The CHA's "basic problem," the council concluded, "was its lack of commitment to its goals of the Summit agreement."[41]

Chicago activists expected greater cooperation from the Chicago Commission on Human Relations (CCHR). More than any other city agency, the CCHR should have been a champion for civil rights. Created in 1943 with the mandate to further interracial understanding, the commission was subsequently entrusted with enforcement of the Chicago Fair Housing Ordinance after its passage in 1963. Yet the CCHR interpreted this duty narrowly. It concentrated on conciliation of complaints rather than on prohibition of bias. As a result, in the first three years of enforcement, despite widespread discrimination by realtors, the CCHR did not recommend the suspension of a single realtor's license.[42]

Civil rights leaders expected the Summit pact to compel the CCHR to enforce the ordinance more aggressively, especially by punishing fair-housing offenders. The state, activists argued, had to become an umpire in the housing market, because it was plain to all that the real estate industry could not reform itself. Though the Chicago Real Estate Board withdrew its opposition to a state fair-housing law that applied equally to brokers and individual owners and CREB president Ross Beatty joined the Leadership Council's executive board, the realtors were hardly moved by the spirit of the Summit agreement. Leading realtors continued to argue that they had been unfairly blamed for housing discrimination. "[P]roperty owners do not want 'fair housing,'" declared Arthur Mohl. "[E]very vote ever taken on the subject among voting citizens, produced a negative result." The CREB continued to contest the legality of the city's fair-housing ordinance in court. As for the realtors' contribution to the Leadership Council, one civil rights leader grumbled that the "Real Estate Board members have done little more than attend meetings, as expected."[43]

The Chicago Commission on Human Relations seemed indifferent to the realtors' obstinacy. It sent, as proscribed in the Summit accord, copies of the ordinance to every licensed realtor in Chicago, but it balked at random testing for discriminatory practices. Such a program constituted entrapment, argued CCHR executive director Edward Marciniak and his board of commissioners. When news circulated that other cities tested for discrimination without legal difficulties, the CCHR dropped this argument; yet it still hesitated on a broad testing program. The commission remained an ineffective watchdog of the housing market, and realtors continued to discriminate against blacks.[44]

Incompetence was not the cause of the CCHR's uninspired performance. Marciniak was an industrious and capable executive director. He had come to the commission in 1960 with liberal credentials, having earned his stripes in the Catholic Worker movement. Moreover, there is no reason to doubt Marciniak's claim that he was an advocate for racial justice. But he believed that neither dramatic protests nor rash city action could resolve highly complex and combustible civil rights issues. "There is no hydrogen bomb which government has, which can wipe out segregation or slums," Marciniak stated. "It has to be accomplished, step by step, big step and small step, steady, pioneering and courageous." He felt that insiders—officials like himself with direct lines to centers of power in the city—could, through persistent and quiet effort, improve race relations. He worried that critics and doomsayers were ultimately obstacles to advancement—that their words and actions could poison the climate for evolutionary reform. Important and numerous signs of racial progress existed, he argued, and they should not be dismissed.[45]

Marciniak's perspective mirrored Richard Daley's. A man of decent instincts, Daley wished for a world free of prejudice. As a hard-nosed realist he had little faith, however, that race could be quickly eliminated as a shaping, fundamental force in American life. He remembered the great Chicago race riot of 1919 that had killed thirty-eight and wounded over five hundred. He recalled the white mobs of the 1940s and 1950s that in seeking to oust blacks who moved into white neighborhoods had defied all official pleas for restraint. And he had just witnessed the open-housing violence of the summer of 1966, indisputable proof that Chicago was still a racial tinderbox. To Daley, Chicago racial problems were so deeply rooted in the city's history—and in the nation's ancient failure to cultivate harmony between the races—that it contradicted common (and political) sense to force integration.[46]

As his subordinates instinctively understood, Daley regarded the Summit agreement as a testament of Chicago's general commitment to an open city and not as a blueprint for grand action. Daley would utter fair-housing pieties and publicly instruct his people to honor the Summit pact. He would even override his powerful political ally, Thomas Keane, when in late November the alderman denied that the Summit accord was a full-fledged agreement between the city and the civil rights movement. He would not, however, put the city in the forefront of the fight against housing segregation and discrimination. He would not order the CHA to move blacks into public housing units in white neighborhoods. Nor would he demand that the CCHR crack down on discriminatory realtors.[47]

Hesitant city leadership was not what Chicago protest leaders had bargained for when they agreed to the Summit accord. And the Chicago civil rights coalition was divided over how to respond. Activists such as Bill Moyer, who believed that fair housing was a critical issue and who would soon leave the AFSC housing program disheartened about the lack of progress, wanted to take a very aggressive stand against foot-dragging city agencies—and even made public private documents criticizing the city's performance. But this tactic was rebuked by Bill Berry and other more moderate leaders, who believed that more subtle, concerted pressure would be most effective. Neither position seemed likely to yield great results, for, as John McDermott later noted, the Chicago Freedom Movement "never had the power afterwards to enforce the agreement." SCLC's Chicago staff had shrunk and its lightning rod, James Bevel, was no longer committed to the Chicago campaign. Moreover, there was no great outcry in the black community that could be tapped to force vigorous compliance. Fair housing by itself had never been an immediate concern of most black Chicagoans. Poor, inner-city blacks, in particular, had never been enamored with the open-housing crusade. "Even though the big problem is how to get open housing extended throughout the city," the Reverend Archie Hargraves, a seasoned activist who worked closely with the West Side Organization, observed, "the low income Negro has other problems to deal with first." Chester Robinson emphasized this point when he told his followers, "Let's fix things right [in the inner city] first." Even the AFSC housing staff, as much the architect of the fair-housing crusade as anyone, paradoxically found itself arguing that the civil rights forces must "organize the Negro community toward open occupancy."[48]

With their movement collapsing, Chicago activists were pleased when Martin Luther King returned to Chicago in late March 1967, his first visit in nearly three months. Briefed by local leaders on the city's disappointing performance, King blasted the Daley administration for neglecting its Summit obligations. The city government, King charged, had "given credence to the apostles of social disorder who proclaimed the housing agreement a sham and a batch of false promises." To stir the Daley forces into action, he would now resume his regular trips to Chicago. "I have about reached the conclusion," he declared, "that it will be necessary to participate in massive demonstrations to dramatize the problems and the failure of the city."[49]

King's warning, however, represented more threat than reality. His thoughts were no longer fixed on Chicago. The year 1966 had been a difficult one for the SCLC chief, arguably his roughest as a national figure. He was still the foremost leader of black America. He still drew large crowds of admirers wherever he spoke. He still had reporters tagging after him as if he were a head of state. But something had changed after the summer of 1966. King's preeminence was no longer assumed. He sensed, as did those around him, that he was no longer riding the crest of social change. The irrepressible columnist Jimmy

Breslin claimed that King "was a flop in Chicago all last summer," while a black militant, Julius Hobson of ACT, criticized King for "marching aimlessly around the Windy City" during the open-housing campaign. "[King] has been outstripped by his times," one observer proclaimed.[50]

King was not a beaten man, however. He would neither return to the South to bask in adulation for his past great deeds nor retreat to a college campus to lead a comfortable life as a famous professor. Instead, he became bolder in adversity. Despite his eroding influence he expanded, rather than compressed, the scope of his work—and as a result Chicago no longer loomed at the center of his plans.

More and more the Vietnam War absorbed King's attention. During the summer of 1966 he had refrained from criticizing the escalating American military involvement in Southeast Asia. But while on a month-long escape to Jamaica for rest and reflection in early 1967, he resolved to jettison caution and make peace with his conscience. Encouraged by Bevel, who was already devoting his energies to ending the Vietnam conflict, King jumped into the antiwar crusade. His principal reason for returning to Chicago in late March 1967 was to participate in a peace march, not to issue threats of more fair-housing demonstrations.[51]

Nothing King had ever done before had provoked so much criticism—from opinion makers, politicians, and fellow civil rights leaders. The carping was so intense, so protracted, that it virtually masked King's simultaneous leftward drift on domestic issues as well. "For years," King told a reporter in the spring of 1967, "I labored with the idea of reforming the existing institutions of the society, a little change here, a little change there. Now I feel quite differently." There must be, he often now declared, a "radical redistribution of economic and political power." No single impulse propelled King leftward. The general trend among important segments of American progressives was toward a tougher questioning of basic American institutions and programs. But there is no question that his work in Chicago hardened his attitude toward a society that distributed its plentiful bounty so unequally. He had been shaken by his firsthand exposure to the casualties of American capitalism as well as of American racism. People on the "outside," he confided to a friend after his Chicago stay, cannot understand "what [ghetto dwellers] are going through."[52]

King was now more committed than ever to ending slums. The longer he dwelled on the question of how to accomplish this goal, the more convinced he became that poverty itself—the fundamental cause of slums—must be tackled first. During the Chicago campaign, King had adopted the view of the ghetto as a domestic colony, a particular arrangement by which the larger society ruthlessly exploited black people. This concept helped spur King and his followers to stage marches protesting a dual housing market that exploited the ghetto. They were, of course, also drawn to an open-housing focus because housing discrimination represented a more traditional civil rights target, the type of target that had been most vulnerable to nonviolent direct action assaults in the South. But by 1967 King downplayed the colonial theme and emphasized more than ever before the basic structural inequities of the American economy and the need for adequate incomes for all Americans. While he continued to stress the social danger of "the constant growth of predominantly Negro central cities ringed by white suburbs," he frankly acknowledged the limitations of the previous summer's open-housing campaign. "We can talk about integrated housing," King told a Senate subcommittee in December 1966, "but if a man doesn't earn enough money to buy a decent house in a neighborhood that is integrated, it won't mean anything." To Stanley Levison, King was even more blunt: "[We] need to make the ghetto more liveable, because no matter how much open housing you have, you'll not get all the poor people out of the ghetto immediately. You have to make life liveable for those who will be in the ghetto."[53]

King's turn to basic economic issues, or "human rights," as he often called them, reflected more than just his evolving diagnosis of America's most critical ills. His focus also demonstrated his realization that further protests for civil rights were unlikely to yield great gains. King launched the Chicago enterprise as a "pilot project," a model for other cities to emulate. Just as the bold protests in 1960 of four black college students in Greensboro, North Carolina, had sparked lunch counter sit-ins in more than fifty cities in nine states and just as SCLC's Birmingham campaign had triggered hundreds of public accommodations protests throughout the country, King had hoped that the Chicago movement would inspire activists in other cities. And yet the Chicago crusade prompted few spin-offs.[54]

In only two cities—Louisville and Milwaukee—were there local movements for which SCLC could claim any credit. For most of the 1960s Louisville, a city with a southern flavor, seemed out of step with the times as it earned a reputation as "the city that integrated without strife." But in late 1966 and 1967 that reputation seemed a cruel jest. At the very moment when the Chicago open-housing protests were attracting national attention, Louisville civil rights crusaders began to agitate for a stronger local fair-housing law. They soon realized that the Board of Aldermen had no intention of passing a more effective measure, even though the city's own human relations commission had endorsed such a proposal. Frustrated over the city's inaction, civil rights activists, now combined into the Committee on Open Housing, took to the streets in early March 1967.[55]

They did so, city officials claimed, under the influence of outsiders. In late February and early March Hosea Williams and over a dozen of his staffers, who had just left Chicago after their unsuccessful voter registration drive, descended on the Kentucky city. For the next few weeks SCLC organizers teamed with Louisville demonstrators, including the Reverend A. D. Williams King, the president of SCLC's Kentucky affiliate and the brother of Martin Luther King, to stage protests at the city hall and the homes of local politicians.[56]

It was not until mid-April, however, when Louisville aldermen voted down a new fair-housing measure, that the open-housing struggle really took off. Louisville crusaders, assisted by SCLC staffers, stepped up their evening marches into the South End, an all-white, lower middle-class section of the city. Hundreds of whites lined the streets, heckling the protesters and throwing firecrackers, eggs, and rocks. The crisis enraged the city's political leaders. Mayor Kenneth A. Schmied, in a misleading warning, told Louisville residents "that these incidents grow in proportion, and in Chicago last year they grew until 27 people were killed." "We must not," he urged, "let that happen here." Like the Daley administration, Louisville city officials obtained an injunction restricting the size and timing of the protests. But unlike Chicago activists, Louisville open-housing crusaders refused to comply with the court order and were arrested for civil disobedience.[57]

In early May Martin Luther King took on the Louisville open-housing cause as his own. Yet when he arrived in the Kentucky city, he found himself in a tight spot. Almost everyone was upset at the Committee on Open Housing's threat to disrupt the Kentucky Derby, Louisville's annual showcase event, if the city council did not enact a stronger open-housing law. A group of black Louisville ministers condemned the planned protests, blaming outside civil rights "technicians" for all the unrest. Even the progressive *Louisville Courier-Journal* wrote, "Open housing has nothing to gain and a great deal to lose by demonstrations at Churchill Downs on Derby Day." King thought so too, and he used his influence to fashion a compromise satisfactory to both the militants and the moderates within the civil rights camp. They would indeed march for open housing—but they would parade through Louisville's downtown so that the Kentucky Derby could run uninterrupted.[58]

Unimpressed, Louisville aldermen again rejected a stronger open-occupancy measure, and one week later King returned to Louisville to apply more pressure. King not only delivered the expected speeches but also followed a demonstration into the South End by car. At the end of the march he tried to talk to some of the hecklers, who, in turn, surrounded his vehicle and began yelling and shouting. Suddenly a rock whizzed into the car, nicking King's neck and lower face. Like the Chicago stoning, this episode stirred King's Louisville followers, but their subsequent, almost daily marches changed nothing. In mid-summer they turned to a voter education drive, convinced that only political power would yield results.[59]

The ties linking SCLC and the Chicago open-housing campaign to the Milwaukee civil rights movement were not as palpable as those to the Louisville movement. No SCLC technicians helped coordinate Milwaukee protests and no Milwaukee civil rights activists credited Chicago developments with inspiring them. Nevertheless, the Chicago crusade did influence the path of Milwaukee protest. James Bevel, for one, had hoped that the Chicago demonstrations would spur "preachers and priests" in other communities to "get together, upon seeing the problem and addressing it to their own situations." Yet "the only guy," Bevel later explained, "who really understood, who went on it, was Father Groppi up in Milwaukee."[60]

By 1967 Father James Groppi had emerged as one of the country's most remarkable social activists. In 1963 the gaunt, curly-haired Catholic priest, not long out of the seminary, was assigned to St. Boniface's Church in the heart of black Milwaukee. Groppi quickly established an extraordinary rapport with black residents, soon becoming the adviser to the NAACP Youth Council, known as the "Young Commandos." In 1965 Groppi spearheaded protests against school segregation; the following year he guided picketers at the home of a local judge who refused to relinquish his membership in an all-white men's club.[61]

But it was the open-housing protests that transformed Groppi into a national figure. Starting in August 1967 Groppi led daily forays into all-white neighborhoods to dramatize the need for a municipal fair-housing law. Angry Milwaukee whites, like their Chicago and Louisville counterparts, assaulted the intruders, triggering dramatic confrontations. Groppi and his followers were not intimidated. They kept on marching. On one occasion, John McDermott and a hundred other Chicagoans traveled to join a Groppi-led demonstration. McDermott and other Chicagoans noted that the Milwaukee campaign differed in many fundamental ways from the Chicago Freedom Movement. The Milwaukee movement was led by a white, and it did not have the same spiritual aura. It was, nonetheless, a dedicated volunteer corps. After sustaining daily protests for weeks, the Milwaukee Common Council finally passed an open-occupancy ordinance.[62]

The Milwaukee movement was largely a response to local conditions, but the Chicago crusade had, at least indirectly, inspired it. Groppi did not participate in the Chicago open-housing marches, but he followed their development, and in the spring of 1967 he joined SCLC activists on a fair-housing trek in Louisville. "Freedom of movement is a God-given right," he told his fellow marchers that day. A few months later he spread the same message throughout Milwaukee.[63]

Whatever the extent of their local importance, the Louisville and Milwaukee movements did not constitute a "revolution"—which was how Martin Luther King had characterized the great eruption of protest following SCLC's Birmingham crusade in 1963. Indeed, the response to the Chicago campaign proved that daring maneuvers by King and SCLC could no longer ignite a civil rights explosion. Blacks were no longer poised for nonviolent protest as they had been in 1963. In the South, black assertiveness had already spent much of its force in the great wave of demonstrations from 1960 to 1965. In the North, where protests had been only modestly successful, the appeal of peaceful picketing and marching was waning; frustration and desperation seemed more likely to be expressed in violence. All over the country, black activists were divided about what to strive for and how to obtain their goals.[64]

Against this troubled, turbulent backdrop, a big fair-housing crusade had little appeal. Many conservative blacks frowned upon agitation over an issue so likely to provoke white hostility. To separatists, open housing reflected the pathetic urge of some blacks to live among whites. Though nearly all blacks believed in the principle of equal housing opportunity, far fewer were eager to extend themselves to obtain fair housing in reality. Unlike the indignity of second-class service at a restaurant or a movie theater, housing discrimination seemed distant to the daily concerns of most blacks. How often did they seek the services of a real estate broker? And what, after all, would be gained by being able to move into white communities that did not want black residents?[65]

King himself seemed anxious to find common ground between the races. During the summer of 1966 he had glimpsed a deeper theme in the white reaction to the open-housing protests. He noted how tragic it was that less wealthy whites would not unite with blacks. "[T]hey are also derivative victims of slavery, of the system of slavery," he stated. "The poor whites too often side with the oppressors, when they should be out there marching with us. Too often, it's the poor white man throwing the brick." If the economic anxieties of blacks and whites could be addressed, other points of racial tension might soften as the races came together for mutual benefit, King believed.[66]

Aware that the Chicago movement had bogged down, sensitive to fair housing's limited appeal even among blacks, and increasingly concerned about fundamental economic issues, King had no desire to captain another Chicago open-housing crusade. Even before disengaging from Chicago, King and SCLC were already plotting a Cleveland campaign. For the summer of 1967 most of SCLC's remaining Chicago staff would be sent to the Ohio city to work with a local civil rights coalition, where they would not press the fair-housing issue. Only one-quarter the size of Chicago and lacking a powerful political boss like Richard Daley, Cleveland, King expected, would not present the tangle of obstacles that Chicago had.[67]

Now even hints of new civil rights initiatives in Chicago triggered apprehension among those who could not be considered enemies of racial justice. When in late March King threatened to resume demonstrations for open housing, Joe Cook of the Leadership Council swiftly labeled such talk as counterproductive. "Certainly anyone who is calling for marches and demonstrations, with their possibility of violence and bloodshed, could 'uncork the bottle'" of racial disturbances, Cook asserted. The *Chicago Defender* discouraged any new dramatic ventures as well. Instead, it argued, King and his forces should work with Chicagoans of good will in the not very "glamorous but constant, daily, unceasing effort to eliminate the grievances of the Negro people." Otherwise, the *Defender* warned, King's course was "almost certain—as he must recognize—to produce strife, and little else." The sounding of such alarms before King and SCLC had undertaken dramatic action underscored the hazards of embarking on new efforts in Chicago.[68]

King was aware of the city's mood, but he knew that a hasty retreat would bring bad feelings.[69] He waited for an opportune moment to disclose his plans. In late May 1967 that occasion arrived when the Leadership Council for Metropolitan Open Communities unveiled "Project: Good Neighbor," a massive fair-housing educational campaign that would blanket the Chicago area with advertisements, newspaper and magazine articles, and television and radio programming about the disturbing consequences of housing discrimination. King interpreted the Leadership Council's initiative generously. "If this progress continues," he said, "I see no need for further demonstrations here." The Chicago Freedom Movement was over.[70]

Epilogue

More than a quarter of a century has passed since Martin Luther King and the Southern Christian Leadership Conference left the South to stage their first northern nonviolent campaign. Since then, the conventional assessment of that effort has remained consistently unfavorable. In the late 1960s most observers considered King's Chicago program a "failure." Two decades later historians and journalists still employed dark adjectives to describe the Chicago venture.[1]

It is easy to explain the popularity of this critical evaluation. The Chicago crusade was clearly not the great triumph that the Selma and Birmingham campaigns had been. It failed to rouse the national conscience, to spark the passage of sweeping legislation, or to electrify the nonviolent civil rights movement. On the local level, too, the Chicago Freedom Movement did not accomplish its professed goals. Despite numerous achievements, it failed to "end the slums" or to make Chicago an "open city."

In the 1990s the South Side and West Side ghettoes are far more troubled and impoverished than they were in the 1960s. Today ghetto dwellers speak wistfully about how much better their neighborhoods were three decades ago. Then, at least, industry, businesses, and representatives of the black middle class could be found in places like North Lawndale, East Garfield Park, and Kenwood-Oakland. Now these communities are largely the preserve of people mired in poverty, hostage to a poor school system and besieged by rampant crime and drugs.[2]

Housing discrimination still plagues black Chicagoans. Although overt white hostility toward blacks has diminished since the 1960s as the pace of neighborhood transition from black to white has slowed, blacks are still not welcomed in all regions of the city, especially those white communities targeted in the summer of 1966 by civil rights forces. Fire bombings and ugly threats occasionally greet the black pioneer. Many realtors continue to employ discriminatory practices—not the old blatant refusal to serve blacks, but subtler, equally effective tactics such as "steering" minority clients to minority neighborhoods. The persistence of a dual housing market, coupled with the legacy of decades of undisguised housing discrimination, has ensured Chicago's standing as one of the most segregated—"hypersegregated," according to one sociologist—big cities in America.[3]

Yet to dismiss the Chicago Freedom Movement as a failure or, in the words of one historian, as a "long fizzle" is unfair. Such assessments overlook the lasting, though not always self-evident, achievements of the Chicago campaign. Many accounts also mistakenly suggest that the Chicago crusade had little impact, whether for good or bad. In addition, these appraisals wrongly imply that King and his troops tripped up when they went north, that they stumbled because they never learned how to operate successfully in a big northern city.[4]

In the short run, there is no question that the open-housing marches inflamed racial "bitterness," especially on Chicago's Southwest and Northwest sides. Local racial progressives tried—with only modest success—to use the open-housing crisis to foster a more sensible dialogue about blacks and their communities, but they received little help from civil rights forces. Despite some efforts to promote interracial understanding—such as SOUL, an AFSC-sponsored group of black and white high school students—Chicago civil rights activists later admitted that during the summer they had not done "a good enough job of communicating our real concern to the people who came to see themselves as the adversaries—the people in these white communities."[5] Even so, the possibilities for a constructive exchange were quite constricted. By the summer of 1966, most Southwest and Northwest Siders did not recognize the legitimacy of the civil rights perspective. Although few white Chicagoans jumped on the bandwagon of the white hate groups and even fewer joined a brazen Nazi-sponsored march in mid-September through the South Side ghetto, many listened to local firebrands denounce the Summit agreement and condemn the leaders, including Archbishop Cody, who they believed had betrayed white interests. The

Southwest Side, in particular, was so stirred up that local moderates issued warnings about the dangers of "too much emotionalism."[6]

More than anyone else, politicians felt the impact of the bungalow belt unrest. In the fall of 1966, on Chicago's Northwest Side, Congressman Roman Pucinski, who had voted for the Civil Rights Bill of 1966, fought for his political life. His Republican challenger John Hoellen, trumpeting his commitment to law and order, ran not so much against Pucinski as against open housing and civil rights demonstrations. Pucinski, not to be outflanked, stressed his outrage at the summer demonstrations and his opposition to forced integration. In the end he eked out a victory. Paul Douglas, a venerable liberal senator who had championed federal fair-housing legislation, was less fortunate. Voters on Chicago's Northwest and Southwest sides turned out in overwhelming numbers for the Republican Charles Percy and thus helped ensure Douglas's defeat. The civil rights explosion, although not the only force at work, accelerated a major political realignment. As the 1966 elections and then the strong local showing of the populist George Wallace in the presidential contest of 1968 revealed, many Northwest and Southwest Side white voters were disengaging themselves from the long-reigning political order of the New Deal. Their stands on would-be national leaders had a distinctly conservative slant.[7]

While the political stars of some fell amid the uproar over the 1966 marches, those of others rose. Father Francis X. Lawlor, for one, had been a relatively obscure biology teacher on Chicago's Southwest Side until the open-housing protests stirred him to plead for community solidarity in the face of the encroaching ghetto. Lawlor was soon widely regarded as an important spokesman for Southwest Side interests, and in early 1968 he became even more than that. After he defied Archbishop Cody's attempt to banish him to Kansas because of his outspokenness on white rights, Lawlor was transformed into a local folk hero. In 1971 he turned his great popularity into electoral success, becoming the first priest ever to serve as a Chicago alderman.[8]

Some political pundits predicted that the turbulence in white middle-class neighborhoods might also upset Mayor Daley's reelection hopes. But when election day came in early April 1967, Daley roared to his biggest victory ever. Political commentators then quarreled over whether the much ballyhooed "backlash" even existed. Daley had run better in Southwest and Northwest Side wards than Percy had in his victorious Senate race against Douglas a few months earlier. Doubtless the uninspired campaign of Daley's colorless opponent, the businessman John Waner, contributed greatly to the landslide. Yet a larger force was also at work. Though the open-housing protests had generated a strong anti-Daley impulse, the mayor smothered it in subsequent months. With civil rights activists clamoring that the Summit agreement had done nothing to promote integration, for whites to remain angry over the accord was difficult. A few days before the April election, Daley won more favor with apprehensive whites by lashing out at Martin Luther King and his lieutenants. When King and Andrew Young announced that there would be more protests next summer, Daley sputtered: "We've been listening to statements from outsiders for a long time, and I think the people of Chicago are about filled up with these kind of statements."[9]

Almost unnoticed at the time was a shift in Daley's political base. Before 1966 Daley had rolled up his biggest pluralities in low-income white and black wards. After 1966 Daley courted middle-income whites more intently. In the fall of 1967 he questioned Superintendent James Redmond's modest plan to bus black students to white schools. In the aftermath of King's assassination in 1968 he denounced black rioters. In 1969 he resisted a court order to build family public housing projects in white communities. In time, then, he became the defender of the white middle class.[10]

As whites rallied to civic organizations and new leaders to protect their interests, black activism faded. In late June 1967 Al Raby and other CCCO leaders tried to mount a protest against federal funding for an atomic accelerator in Weston, Illinois, a hamlet thirty miles west of Chicago. Because the all-white community lacked a fair-housing ordinance, blacks, Raby claimed, would be unable to find convenient housing to benefit from the many new jobs certain to be created by the federal facility. But CCCO could drum up little enthusiasm for a "tent-in" near the proposed accelerator site. Only a handful of activists camped out. Worse still, their sacrifices went unrequited. The Illinois state legislature refused to pass a state fair-housing law, and Congress funded the Weston project.[11]

The unsuccessful Weston protests underscored CCCO's decline. Raby, suffering from "battle fatigue," resigned as CCCO's convenor three months later. He hoped that graduate study would restore his flagging energies and enhance his perspective on the black struggle. Although John McDermott and Bill Berry tried to head off rumors of CCCO's impending death by claiming that this was "a time of healthy pause, a time of stocktaking and re-evaluation of the movement," CCCO ceased functioning within a few weeks.[12]

CCCO's troubles seemed to affirm the old SNCC complaint that SCLC would target a town or city, launch a big media-oriented campaign, bring little real change to the local community, and then jet off to someplace else, leaving the indigenous movement exhausted and frustrated. In a sense, CCCO was a casualty of SCLC's exertions. The arrival of King and SCLC had raised the expectations of many blacks beyond what was attainable. When the harvest of the campaign fell short of expectations, disillusionment and recrimination followed—and CCCO and the local civil rights crusade suffered.[13]

Even those who had been instrumental in cultivating a West Side movement before SCLC's arrival regretted that more had not been done to develop a stronger foundation for future insurgency. A great deal of energy had been expended in the open-housing marches, but they were only part of a longer-range plan in the minds of many West Side activists. Their goal was, Bernard LaFayette stated, to develop local leaders, to cultivate enough individuals "aware of the different forces operating to create unjust circumstances for individuals and groups" and able "to overcome the paralyzing inner fear that thwarts creative action" so that the end product could be a "community of people" who could "organize to restructure the institutions in the community in such a way as to put the control of the community in the hands of the largest number of people." Yet with the rapid dispersal of SCLC's staff in the wake of the Summit accord, the decline of other West Side organizations, James Bevel's turn to the peace movement, and Bernard LaFayette's decision later in 1967 to leave the AFSC's urban affairs program to work in Boston, that effort never received the necessary resources or attention. ("We started a marathon," LaFayette later remarked, "but it ended up being a sprint.")[14]

It is also true that by the middle of 1967 King and SCLC had focused their energies elsewhere. Yet even as SCLC organizers toiled in Cleveland, King began contemplating a more massive undertaking that went beyond the single-city focus so characteristic of SCLC's previous campaigns. He would heed neither Bayard Rustin, who continued to argue for a shift away from protest and toward building a powerful progressive political coalition, nor those who extolled the virtues of intensified community organizing. He worried that change through traditional political channels and community empowerment would be too slow and too uncertain. Undeterred by the deteriorating prospects for reform—the urban riots of the summer of 1967, the ever more strident rhetoric of black militants, the sharp retorts of white critics, all of which also sent SCLC's finances into a tailspin—King decided to launch his most ambitious project yet: a poor people's crusade. In a militant though nonviolent fashion, King and SCLC would descend on Washington with thousands of poor people and stay until Congress and the federal government granted America's disadvantaged relief. The protest by those whose misfortune King sensed even more vividly after the Chicago campaign would be less an appeal to the country's conscience than a demand that the nation do what was right. Perhaps this evolution constituted an abandonment of Chicago and CCCO, but as Raby later argued: "Martin had been criticized in some quarters for not staying in one place. Well, if I looked at him simply as a product and I was trying to market this product, I wonder if the critics would have left him in the first place that he got bogged down until he had accomplished what he had set out to accomplish."[15]

Even on its own terms, it would be a mistake to carry the SNCC critique too far. Throughout the Chicago campaign, King was sensitive to charges that SCLC abandoned local movements after it had basked in the national spotlight. Partly in response to these accusations, SCLC devoted more time—twenty months—to the Chicago crusade than it had to any of its previous initiatives. Well after the open-housing marches, King and SCLC sponsored new projects to reflect their enduring commitment to improve life for Chicago's deprived. In December 1966, SCLC received a four-million-dollar HUD grant to rehabilitate housing in conjunction with the Community Renewal Foundation, a branch of the Chicago City Missionary Society. In the summer of 1967, King and SCLC proudly announced the Chicago Adult Education Program, funded by a $100,000 grant from the U.S. Office of Education and directed by Professor Robert Green of Michigan State University, to boost the skills of Lawndale residents. Moreover, though most of SCLC's West Side staff had left the city by that summer, some, like Billy Hollins, stayed on. In 1968 Hollins became the Chicago director for the Poor People's Campaign. When the full extent of the Chicago civil rights movement is surveyed, SCLC is more properly regarded as the resuscitator of a dying movement in 1965 rather than as the hidden assassin of 1967.[16]

The alliance with SCLC had temporarily revitalized CCCO, but the mounting centrifugal forces of late 1966 and 1967 were too powerful to overcome. Suspicions about the Summit agreement persisted. Controversy about the role of whites in the coalition stirred confusion and indignation. CCCO's treasury, which had reached new heights in 1966, shrank to a deficit in 1967. And as CCCO lost its top leader and the concept of a dynamic, diverse, interracial federation was called into question, many of CCCO's affiliates struggled as well. One of CCCO's most important constituent groups, the Catholic Interracial Council, for instance, was tired, isolated from Archbishop Cody and the archdiocese, and unsure about its role in the troubled days of 1967. Other players in the Chicago Freedom Movement also struggled. By 1967 the West Side Christian Parish, which had expanded its program during 1966, found itself cut off from traditional funding sources, especially suburban churches and the Chicago City Missionary Society. So dismal were its financial prospects that the parish—James Bevel's original command post—drastically reduced its staff less than eight months after the Summit agreement. And the much heralded labor–civil rights alliance never reaped rich benefits. Civil rights forces never fully connected with labor activists on the precise mission of the Lawndale Community Union. Nor could the civil rights activists, with their energies first focused on the open-housing campaign and then exhausted, ever ardently back the inner-city experiment themselves. The Industrial Union Department of the AFL-CIO and a few unions continued to sponsor the Lawndale Community Union, but they failed to define a galvanizing purpose for it.[17]

On top of all of this, there were growing doubts—even increasing despair—about the efficacy of CCCO's approach to social problems. "It is tragic," Raby noted on his retirement, "that after so many young people have marched, and some have died, to see that little has changed." Raby had already signaled a shift in his orientation away from dramatic protests when in the summer of 1967 he founded with Rennie Davis of SDS and other activists a school for community organizers located in Englewood. "Our work last summer—the marches, the Summit Agreement—will help the middle class," Raby said. "But it'll be a long time before the inner city feels the effects." Training talented local organizers, Raby and his colleagues believed, would empower deprived communities. "We want ghetto changes in this generation," Raby insisted.[18]

As an expansive federation of independent local groups, CCCO was something unusual, something special in Chicago public life. Its death did not, however, signal the end of Chicago insurgency. Other organizations, many of which were direct outgrowths of the Chicago Freedom Movement, continued to fight for racial justice.

The Chicago Freedom Movement bequeathed a substantial legacy of community organizations. The East Garfield Park Union to End Slums, though no longer an active entity, lived on in another East Garfield Park group, Fifth City, which counted Minnie Dunlap as one of its leaders. In 1968 the Lawndale Union to End Slums merged with the West Side Federation and Lawndale Peoples Planning Conference to form the Lawndale Peoples' Planning and Action Conference, with Shelvin Hall as a leading spirit. In the late 1960s, Robert Lucas, after plunging into the divisive politics of a dwindling national CORE, began to work for the Kenwood-Oakland Community Organization. A few years later, he became KOCO's executive director as it sought to rehabilitate the depressed Kenwood-Oakland community.[19]

Chicago Freedom Movement veterans devotedly watched over the product of the Summit negotiations, the Leadership Council for Metropolitan Open Communities, after its inception in 1966. Bill Berry served as an officer for the council well into the 1980s, and Kale Williams guided the organization as its executive director from 1972 to 1992. As they toiled for equal housing opportunities, their initial expectations of rapid success dimmed. The housing market—the product of the actions of thousands of men, women, and institutions—is decentralized, immensely complex, and highly resistant to reform. "With voting rights and public accommodations," Kale Williams noted, "there was a federal law that could have substantial impact fairly quickly." In combating employment discrimination, as well, potentially effective approaches existed. Particularly with larger employers, "a decision at the executive level could result in a change in practice in that company at least in a fairly short period of time." But, Williams continued, "the same conditions did not obtain in most of the real estate industry."[20]

The difficulty of the Leadership Council's mission was magnified by the failure of city agencies to live up to their Summit commitments. In part, however, this void was offset by the continued commitment of Chicago's business community. Without the "education" about fair housing that business leaders received from the Summit meetings and ensuing developments, the Leadership Council, Berry once asserted, could easily have taken the path to extinction followed by many 1960s organizations designed to tackle social problems. Yet fortified by substantial financial support, the Leadership Council over the years gained recognition as one of the nation's most effective and innovative fair-housing organizations, especially because of its pioneering legal techniques to fight housing bias. In the mid-1970s, the council took over the Gautreaux program, the outcome of the 1966 suit filed by the Urban League, the West Side Federation, and the American Civil Liberties Union against the Chicago Housing Authority for piling up public housing projects in overcrowded black communities in violation of the 1964 Civil Rights Act. After a long, tortuous legal fight that reached the Supreme Court, the CHA and the Department of Housing and Urban Development were ordered to devise a program to help repair the legacy of discrimination by placing needy Chicagoans in subsidized private housing throughout metropolitan Chicago. Since 1976, as part of the *Gautreaux* decree, over four thousand black families have been relocated, more than half in Chicago suburbs and the rest in Chicago city neighborhoods outside the ghetto, under the Leadership Council's direction. Such programs are not a panacea. They have not reversed traditional resistance to black neighbors among many white Chicagoans (although, in general, there has been a softening of old attitudes since the 1960s) or the fact that many of the most racially exclusive communities in metropolitan Chicago are the wealthiest suburbs along the North Shore and to the northwest of Chicago. Class continues to be a formidable barrier to residential integration. Nevertheless, the Leadership Council, with its vigorous program, is one reason why Chicago blacks, despite persistent housing discrimination, today have a wider range of housing choices than ever before.[21]

More than any other organization, Operation Breadbasket carried the spirit of Chicago insurgency after CCCO declined. Operation Breadbasket took over as the coordinating center for black protest, and its weekly Saturday morning meetings, to which blacks (and some whites) flocked to hear the sparkling oratory of Jesse Jackson, served as the new spiritual engine of Chicago activism. Over the years it was not uncommon for former CCCO representatives like Al Pitcher and Ed Riddick to assist in the running of Operation Breadbasket, which simultaneously developed close ties with the city's black business community and maintained a reputation for militancy. Operation Breadbasket never pursued a truly radical agenda; it retained its focus on the bread-and-butter issue of expanding black opportunity and success within the existing capitalist economy. As the operation grew it provided a secure organizational base for the ascent of Jesse Jackson, who by the end of 1967 was the preeminent protest leader in Chicago. In the wake of Martin Luther King's assassination in 1968, Jackson became so well known nationally that he grew restless under the command of Ralph Abernathy, King's successor as head of SCLC, and broke with SCLC a few years later. Once Operation Breadbasket became independent, Jackson renamed it Operation PUSH and guided the expansion of its programs and the reach of its influence.[22]

Jackson also helped lead the last great collective black protest in Chicago of the 1960s. Angered by the exclusion of minorities from the building trades, the Coalition of United Community Action (CUCA), a federation of sixty organizations, shut down scores of construction sites throughout Chicago in 1969. In many ways these protests seemed a replay of the 1966 demonstrations, as Chicagoans took to the streets to agitate against an undeniable injustice. The CUCA's leadership deepened the parallels. In addition to Jackson, Meredith Gilbert, the first director of the Lawndale Union to End Slums, was a Chicago Freedom Movement veteran. And a third CUCA leader, C. T. Vivian, had been one of King's top lieutenants during SCLC's glory years. The broad mobilization of 1969 was surely hastened by the protest surge of 1966.[23]

The 1969 demonstrations were not, however, the natural descendants of 1966 direct action. The later protests—far more starkly economic in orientation than the open-housing marches—were neither markedly interracial nor grounded in nonviolent principles. Instead they were carried out by blacks and relied heavily on intimidation and the underlying threat of violence. When gang members marched in 1969, they brandished walking sticks. When a CUCA leader confronted a foreman at a construction site, he warned of potential bloodshed if the white laborers did not stop working. The nonviolent protest ethos of the first half of the 1960s had been replaced by defiant anger, bred ultimately by frustration over the slow pace of progress. No longer did protesters carry placards with the "End Slums" emblem, which resembled a peace sign; instead they held signs with messages such as "You own the trades—We own the match—build or burn."[24]

Such strident rhetoric was matched by another rising black organization in the late 1960s, the Black Panthers. Founded in 1966 in Oakland, the Black Panther Party soon represented the most dynamic black radical force in the country. In late 1968 Fred Hampton and Bobby Rush established an Illinois chapter of the party, which quickly attracted much attention from both Chicago's blacks and law enforcement agencies. Energized by the charismatic Hampton, the Panthers mixed a rather traditional social service program with the fiery rhetoric of a coming armed revolution along Marxist-Leninist lines. The Panthers' prominence in Chicago was short-lived, however; in early December 1969 the twenty-one-year-old Hampton and a follower were ambushed in a police raid engineered by the State's Attorney office. The Coalition of United Community Action protests and the Black Panthers' rise in Chicago, coming on the heels of the calamitous West Side riot following King's assassination in 1968, graphically demonstrated the extent to which the protest universe of King and the Chicago Freedom Movement—with its emphasis on nonviolence, brotherhood, and redemption—had passed away.[25]

In addition to new styles of black assertiveness, changing times brought a gradual, though fundamental, change in the political orientation of black Chicago. This shift first became evident in the 1966 fall elections, when two black independents were elected to the state senate. Then in early 1967 two more black independents bested Daley machine-backed candidates for seats on Chicago's City Council. These political pioneers, the founders of the modern black independent political movement in Chicago, won because of hard work in their own precincts, but they also profited from a general backdrop of black dissatisfaction, shaped in large part by black dismay at the white anger and violence of the summer of 1966. "[T]he civil rights movement and the inspiring presence of Dr. Martin Luther King in our midst over the past year," claimed a civil rights enthusiast in 1967, "have changed forever the machine's stranglehold on Chicago's Negro population." Al Raby, though his assessment was more modest, similarly believed that the results of the fall 1966 and spring 1967 elections signaled "a development of increasing political strength and independence for the Negro community."[26]

The machine's ascendancy over black Chicago did not suddenly vanish, but these early black independent victories did presage a seismic shift in Chicago voting patterns. Just as middle-class whites began after 1966 to identify more closely with the Daley machine, Chicago blacks moved in the opposite direction. By the early 1970s Mayor Daley could no longer count on the heavy black support that had propelled him to victory in the 1950s and early 1960s. In the aftermath of the Chicago civil rights movement, race, accompanied by polarizing rhetoric and deep despair, was a more dominant issue in the public life of this traditionally race-conscious city than it had been in the earlier part of the postwar era. A large chunk of Chicago's black electorate gradually became disconnected from the Daley Democratic machine, ready to pledge its loyalty to a new leader.[27]

The new leader proved to be Harold Washington. In 1983 Washington, a former state representative and later a U.S. congressman, rode a remarkable wave of black support to become Chicago's first black mayor. That Washington presided more over a movement than over a campaign reflected his own genius at inspiring the masses and the deep yearning of black Chicagoans for a sympathetic voice at City Hall. A modern phenomenon, the Washington campaign nevertheless had ties to Chicago's protest past. As a state legislator in the 1960s Washington himself had not identified closely with the Chicago Freedom Movement, but he had been sympathetic to its aspirations; now in the 1980s he drew on civil rights veterans to boost his cause. Al Raby, who had left Chicago during the late 1970s, returned to become his campaign manager. Bill Berry served as a senior adviser. Jesse Jackson delivered speeches in the black community on the candidate's behalf, even though his relationship with Washington was prickly. And hundreds of others who had marched, sung freedom songs, or attended rallies twenty years earlier gave to the Washington campaign in countless ways. Old activists now fueled black, reformist political success.[28]

The first years of Harold Washington's mayoralty were trying and tumultuous as he faced bitter opposition from a bloc of defiant white aldermen. By the time of his reelection in 1987, however, Washington had won the "Council Wars" and seemed on the verge of enacting his reform program. But that Thanksgiving he died from a massive heart attack. Out of the subsequent political chaos, Eugene Sawyer, a moderate black alderman who had been closely associated with the Daley administration, was tapped to be the new mayor. Washington's reform coalition was in total disarray. In 1989 Richard M. Daley, the son of the legendary mayor and himself a centrist politician, captured City Hall.[29]

By the early 1990s, most of the key figures of the Chicago Freedom Movement were no longer on the scene. Jesse Jackson left for Washington, D.C., in 1989, and Operation PUSH declined as a result. In the late 1980s, both Bill Berry and Al Raby died. The most visible holdover was Dorothy Wright Tillman, a former SCLC field staffer serving as alderwoman for a tough South Side ward. The Chicago Freedom Movement thus exerted most of its influence on contemporary Chicago public life indirectly. Much of its legacy derived from its role in reorienting Chicago politics in the late 1960s, from the inspiring memory of an era of citizens' activism, and from the enduring strength of the conviction, most eloquently articulated by Martin Luther King, that Chicago need not be a divided city.

The impact of the Chicago Freedom Movement on fundamental social patterns proved to be limited; the campaign did not revitalize North Lawndale or any other ghetto neighborhood. Yet this result cannot be fully understood without referring to the many powerful forces that spun these communities into a downward spiral. Housing discrimination, inadequate public schools, and employment barriers disabled inner-city communities and made them vulnerable to catastrophe. But the ghetto's striking deterioration was also part of a massive shift in the city's economy. As smokestack industries shut down or left the inner city for the suburbs, the sunny South, or overseas, ghetto dwellers lost their traditional jobs. Fewer jobs and less income destabilized the already weak social structure of the ghetto. As the black middle class fled these declining regions, the impoverished became packed together, isolated from the mainstream. This process, replicated throughout America's northern cities, has remained impregnable to city-level reform. Even Harold Washington, despite good intentions and the considerable clout he possessed as Chicago's mayor for nearly five years, failed to reverse these trends in his city. Ironically, perhaps the most fundamental contribution of the Chicago Freedom Movement to this broader process has been to accelerate the opening of more communities to blacks, which ultimately hastened the flight of the black middle class from inner-city neighborhoods. This exodus, in turn, has helped create, in William Julius Wilson's words, "hyperghettoes," regions with a "truncated black class structure" and little organizational strength.[30]

The rise of Jesse Jackson, the election of Harold Washington—these are important developments, rooted in Chicago, but with national repercussions. Yet when Martin Luther King and his followers launched the Chicago Freedom Movement, they yearned for a more immediate impact on American race relations. They hoped to spur a full-scale assault on enduring and pervasive racial injustice, now less the product of the law than of custom and institutional arrangements.

Their hopes remained unrealized, but not, as too many commentators have argued, because of the fundamental incapacity of southern activists, armed with nonviolence—a strategy shaped in the South—to operate in a northern big city. To be sure, King and his followers found Chicago unforgiving. Unfamiliar with the city's dynamics, they stumbled in applying nonviolent direct action to their new theater of action.[31]

As the Chicago project became a memory, King himself privately second-guessed some strategic decisions. He wondered whether the Chicago movement should have selected a more practical goal than ending slums. "[W]e don't want to make the mistakes we made in Chicago by promising to solve all their problems in one summer," King told one of his advisers as SCLC plotted its Cleveland campaign in the summer of 1967. King also, on occasion, expressed regrets for not having gone to Cicero. These were thoughtful criticisms—as was the argument that SCLC should have first gone to a smaller northern city instead of Chicago—but they were also based on the luxury of hindsight and downplayed the powerful imperatives that drove SCLC to select Chicago as its target, to focus on ending slums, and to endorse the Summit accord.[32]

In the end, debate over the mistakes of civil rights leaders should not overshadow what King and SCLC accomplished in Chicago. Ultimately they hit upon a strategy that, in the words of one activist, "worked." Bernard LaFayette, no Pollyanna, was correct when he told his AFSC staff in December 1966 that the Chicago Freedom Movement had proved that "large numbers of people in a northern city can be mobilized for nonviolent direct action in the face of mass violence" and had exposed the myths "that a Negro can live where he wants to in the North" and "that the opposition in the North is always too subtle to dramatize the issues." Though hobbled by the foreign terrain and by a pattern King described as "fits and starts," King and SCLC, with the help of Chicago insurgents, managed, as they had in Birmingham and Selma, to spotlight an injustice for Chicagoans and the nation to behold.[33]

By 1966, however, the temper of the times and the targets of the movement had changed and, in turn, the potential positive resonance of civil rights protest had declined. After Selma, black America was more divided over questions of leadership, goals, and tactics than at any time in the previous few years. It seemed incapable of rallying behind a compelling cause as it had in Birmingham in 1963 and Selma in 1965. Nationally, meanwhile, white sympathy toward civil rights protest—never great, even in America's most generous moments—had rapidly eroded. Alarmed by the fiery rhetoric of some black leaders, repelled by the ghetto rioting, and reluctant to come to grips with their own resentment that blacks still demanded "more" after the advances of the first half of the 1960s, many whites lost their appetite for black insurgency. They became especially disturbed when civil rights crusaders guided the traditional quest for equality of opportunity into more private realms of American life.

Whites across a broad spectrum had applauded the southern black drive for basic political and civil rights. But when activists turned to combat housing discrimination, they attracted far fewer supporters. Even though fair housing was a plea for equal treatment (just as the cry for access to public accommodations and for the right to vote had been), whites everywhere dismissed it as an illegitimate demand that threatened their right to basic, private decisions about the disposal of their property and, even more menacingly, threatened the quality of their neighborhoods. If challenged on fair housing, as in Chicago in 1966 and in Louisville and Milwaukee a year later, whites angrily expressed their deeply felt convictions.

By no means, of course, were progressive impulses entirely stifled. As the cries of dismay over white hostility to Chicago open-housing crusaders demonstrated, many Americans condemned all forms of discrimination against blacks. To an extent, the passage of the Civil Rights Act of 1968, with its prohibition against housing discrimination, reaffirmed a national commitment to equal opportunity. The 1968 legislation lacked the aura of the landmark 1964 and 1965 rights laws, however. The passage of the 1968 act came almost as a surprise, and many viewed it as more a commemoration of King in the wake of his assassination than a response to a national call for reform. Moreover, the inclusion of an antiriot proviso in the act was a stark concession to white dismay over racial trends.[34]

By 1968, the civil rights consensus was a shadow of its former self. With its erosion, the potency of the nonviolent civil rights movement diminished. Historians have rightly judged the late 1960s to mark the decline of the civil rights crusade. They have also argued that a key to understanding the decline was the movement's turn away from equal treatment to more collective, results-oriented demands and the simultaneous unwillingness of the American public to accept the new agenda without hesitation. "The Civil Rights Movement," J. Mills Thornton has written, "died, like a fire deprived of oxygen, when it burned beyond American ideals."[35]

Thornton and others point out a fundamental source of conflict over black demands since the late 1960s. Yet while this interpretive line is compelling as a general framework, it also simplifies and flattens the historical path taken from civil rights success to civil rights stalemate. The crusade for freedom did not initially falter because of resistance to calls for results-driven affirmative action policies in education and employment or even because of demands for restructuring capitalism. Rather, the crusade first staggered over open housing, a more traditional civil rights goal, albeit one with vast social implications. In the civil rights movement, the Chicago Freedom Movement was a decisive, transitional episode. It marked a shift of insurgency from the South to the North, it accelerated Martin Luther King's turn to a more universalistic economic agenda, and, finally, it signaled SCLC's last effort at arousing a national response to the denial of equality of opportunity.

In March 1966, Martin Luther King declared that the civil rights movement, which had accomplished so much in the South, had now begun "the last steep ascent" to an America where "social and economic justice" prevailed. Six months later, however, the crusade for racial justice had reached an impasse. In Chicago, the old formulas applied to new problems did not work. Carefully staged nonviolent protests were now as likely to stir the forces of reaction as to trigger groundswells for reform. In an ironic, tragic twist, the Chicago Freedom Movement contributed to the broader flow of events that was shifting the center of gravity of American public life to the right. Signs of this shift abounded everywhere. In Chicago, Southwest and Northwest Side whites defiantly declared their firm opposition to fair housing. In Washington, President Lyndon Johnson and liberal members of Congress watched helplessly and apprehensively as conservatives, joined by moderates, defeated a civil rights bill for the first time in the 1960s. A new national mood was emerging; the last ascent would prove steeper than either King or his followers ever imagined.[36]

Abbreviations

AFSC	American Friends Service Committee
CA	*Chicago's American*
CCCO	Coordinating Council of Community Organizations
CCHR	Chicago Commission on Human Relations
CCMS	Chicago City Missionary Society
CCRR	Chicago Conference on Religion and Race
CD	*Chicago Defender* (weekly ed.)
CDD	*Chicago Daily Defender*
CDN	*Chicago Daily News*
CHA	Chicago Housing Authority
CHS	Chicago Historical Society
CIC	Catholic Interracial Council
CORE	Congress of Racial Equality
CREB	Chicago Real Estate Board
CSM	*Christian Science Monitor*
CST	*Chicago Sun-Times*
CT	*Chicago Tribune*
CTS	Chicago Theological Seminary
CUL	Chicago Urban League
ESCRU	Episcopal Society for Cultural and Racial Unity
FBI	Federal Bureau of Investigation
HMBC	Horace Mann Bond Center
HOP	Housing Opportunities Program, AFSC
ISHL	Illinois State Historical Library
LAT	*Los Angeles Times*
LBJ	Lyndon Baines Johnson
LC	Library of Congress
LCJ	*Louisville Courier-Journal*
LCMOC	Leadership Council for Metropolitan Open Communities

MLK   Martin Luther King, Jr.
MRL   Municipal Reference Library
MSRC   Moorland Spingarn Research Center
NAREB   National Association of Real Estate Boards
NCCIJ   National Catholic Conference for Interracial Justice
NCR   *National Catholic Reporter*
NR   Not Recorded
NYT   *New York Times*
SCLC   Southern Christian Leadership Conference
SDS   Students for a Democratic Society
SE   *Southtown Economist*
SHSW   State Historical Society of Wisconsin
SNCC   Student Nonviolent Coordinating Committee
SWNH   *Southwest News-Herald*
UAP   Urban Affairs Program, AFSC
UIC   University of Illinois at Chicago
WCMC   Welfare Council of Metropolitan Chicago
WHCF   White House Central Files
WMC   Women Mobilized for Change
WP   *Washington Post*
WSCP   West Side Christian Parish

Notes

Introduction

1. Tape of Northwestern civil rights rally, 4 April 1965, Northwestern University Archives, Evanston, Ill.; *Daily Northwestern*, 2 April 1965, p. 1, and 6 April 1965, p. 1.

2. Adam Fairclough, "State of the Art: Historians and the Civil Rights Movement," *Journal of American Studies*, 24 (Dec. 3, 1990): 387–398; David J. Garrow, *Bearing the Cross: Martin Luther King, Jr., and the Southern Christian Leadership Conference* (New York: William Morrow, 1986); Alan B. Anderson and George W. Pickering, *Confronting the Color Line: The Broken Promise of the Chicago Civil Rights Movement* (Athens: University of Georgia Press, 1987).

3. Allan H. Spear, *Black Chicago: The Making of a Negro Ghetto, 1890–1920* (Chicago: University of Chicago Press, 1967); William M. Tuttle, Jr., *Race Riot: Chicago in the Red Summer of 1919* (New York: Atheneum, 1970); James R. Grossman, *Land of Hope: Chicago, Black Southerners, and the Great Migration* (Chicago: University of Chicago Press, 1989); St. Clair Drake and Horace R. Cayton, *Black Metropolis: A Study of Negro Life in a Northern City,* enl. and rev. ed. (New York: Harcourt, Brace & World, 1970); Arnold R. Hirsch, *Making the Second Ghetto: Race and Housing in Chicago, 1940–1960* (New York: Cambridge University Press, 1983); Nicholas Lemann, *The Promised Land: The Great Black Migration and How It Changed America* (New York: Alfred A. Knopf, 1991). William Julius Wilson's work has done much to illuminate the ghetto poor's plight in Chicago during the 1970s and 1980s. See especially *The Truly Disadvantaged: The Inner City, the Underclass, and Public Policy* (Chicago: University of Chicago Press, 1987). For decades, most scholars have stressed the rise of the ghetto and its implications for blacks, but more recently observers have been developing a new approach to understanding the black experience in the urban North. Joe William Trotter, Jr., among others, has advocated an alternative emphasis. Spurning the "ghetto framework," he has argued for a proletarianization approach, which focuses on the "process of Afro-American, urban-industrial, working-class formation."

Trotter, *Black Milwaukee: The Making of an Industrial Proletariat, 1915–1945* (Urbana: University of Illinois Press, 1985), pp. 264–282.

4. Fairclough, "State of the Art," p. 393.

1. Coming to Chicago

1. Stanley Levison and MLK, FBI 100-111180-9-677, 25 Aug. 1965, and "Executive Staff Meeting," 26–28 Aug. 1965, MLK papers, box 32-9, MLK Library, Atlanta. I have at times omitted names and given more general, rather than specific, addresses of the correspondents I have cited.

2. Al Raby conversation with Kale Williams, ca. 1971, Chicago, Kale Williams files, Chicago; Franklin I. Gamwell interview, 8 Aug. 1988, Chicago; Clayborne Carson et al., eds., *The Eyes on the Prize Civil Rights Reader* (New York: Penguin Books, 1991), p. 311.

3. Anderson and Pickering, *Confronting the Color Line*, p. 157; *New World*, 18 June 1965, p. 21; Raby conversation with Williams. For a detailed, almost day-by-day account of the summer of 1965, see Alan B. Anderson's and George W. Pickering's jointly written appendix, "The Issue of the Color Line: A View from Chicago," pp. 648–789, to their respective dissertations—Anderson, "The Issue of the Color Line: Some Methodological Considerations" (University of Chicago, 1975), and Pickering, "The Issue of the Color Line: Some Interpretative Considerations" (University of Chicago, 1975).

4. Al Raby interview, 12 Sept. 1986, Chicago. On Raby's background, see Robert McClory, "The Activist," *Chicago Tribune Magazine*, 17 April 1983, pp. 27–28, 30, 32–35, 39; *CDN*, 14 June 1965, p. 8; *CD*, 18–24 Jan. 1964, pp. 1, 3.

5. McClory, "The Activist," pp. 28, 30; Raby interview.

6. *CD*, 18–24 Jan. 1964, pp. 1, 3; Raby interview; Meyer Weinberg interview, 30 Dec. 1986, Amherst, Mass.; McClory, "The Activist," pp. 27–28, 30, 32–35.

7. James Q. Wilson, *Negro Politics: The Search for Leadership* (Glencoe, Ill.: Free Press, 1960), p. 7.

8. Council Against Discrimination newsletter, June 1953, p. 3, Regenstein Library, University of Chicago; Hirsch, *Making the Second Ghetto*, pp. 44, 176; Steven M. Gelber, *Black Men and Businessmen: The Growing Awareness of a Social Responsibility* (Port Washington, N.Y.: Kennikat Press, 1974), pp. 47–50, 97–98; Rick Halpern to author, 10 Dec. 1987; Philip S. Foner, *Organized Labor and the Black Worker, 1619–1973* (New York: Praeger, 1974), pp. 304–305. James Q. Wilson discusses the importance of whites in promoting racial change in Chicago during the 1950s. Wilson, *Negro Politics*, p. 90.

9. Wilson, *Negro Politics*, p. 282; *CDD*, 14 Feb. 1957, p. 5. NAACP's national files on the Chicago branch are quite revealing on NAACP activities in the 1950s and 1960s. NAACP papers, group III-C, LC. On the Chicago Urban League, see Arvarh E. Strickland, *History of the Chicago Urban League* (Urbana: University of Illinois Press, 1966), pp. 185–214.

10. *CDD,* 10 Sept. 1955, p. 1, 17 Sept. 1955, p. 2, 29 Oct. 1955, pp. 1, 3; *The Crisis,* Dec. 1955, pp. 627–628; Dempsey J. Travis, *An Autobiography of Black Politics* (Chicago: Urban Research Press, 1987), pp. 273–285.

11. Hirsch, *Making the Second Ghetto,* pp. 68–258; "Five Year Report, 1947–1951, of the Chicago Commission on Human Relations," Regenstein Library, University of Chicago; Drake and Cayton, *Black Metropolis,* I, pp. 50–51; August Meier and Elliot M. Rudwick, *CORE: A Study in the Civil Rights Movement, 1942–1968* (New York: Oxford University Press, 1973), pp. 3–39; Ely M. Aaron report, *Human Relations News of Chicago,* Dec. supplement 1963, pp. 1, 4, Regenstein Library. The key state law was the Illinois Civil Rights Law of 1885, which guaranteed the right of all persons to equal service in restaurants, hotels, taverns, stores, theaters, and other places of public accommodation and amusement.

12. "Five Year Report, 1947–1951," p. 56; *CDD,* 23 Feb. 1966, p. 18; *Time,* 14 Sept. 1953, p. 25; Gelber, *Black Men and Businessmen,* pp. 83–84; *CDN,* 27 June 1957, p. 21; Drake and Cayton, *Black Metropolis,* I, pp. xliii–l.

13. Hirsch, *Making the Second Ghetto,* p. 17; Manning Marable, *Race, Reform and Rebellion: The Second Reconstruction in Black America, 1945–1982* (Jackson: University Press of Mississippi, 1984), pp. xi, 12–41; August Meier and Elliot M. Rudwick, "The Origins of Nonviolent Direct Action in Afro-American Protest: A Note on Historical Discontinuities," in Meier and Rudwick, eds., *Along the Color Line: Explorations in the Black Experience* (Urbana: University of Illinois Press, 1976), pp. 362–363; Drake and Cayton, *Black Metropolis,* II, p. xxvi; John McDermott interview, 7 July 1988, Chicago.

14. Charles R. Branham, "The Transformation of Black Political Leadership in Chicago, 1864–1942" (Ph.D. diss., University of Chicago, 1981), p. 456; Branham, "Black Chicago," in Melvin G. Holli and Peter d'A. Jones, eds., *Ethnic Chicago,* rev. ed. (Grand Rapids, Mich.: William B. Eerdmans, 1984), pp. 338–379; Wilson, *Negro Politics,* pp. 48–93, 214–254, 295–315; Drake and Cayton, *Black Metropolis,* I, pp. 46–51; Martin Kilson, "Political Change in the Negro Ghetto, 1900–1940s," in Nathan Huggins et al., eds., *Key Issues in the Afro-American Experience* (New York: Harcourt Brace Jovanovich, 1971), II, pp. 167–192; James L. Cooper, "South Side Boss," *Chicago History,* 19 (Fall and Winter 1990–91): 67–81; Travis, *An Autobiography of Black Politics,* pp. 146–189.

15. Wilson, *Negro Politics,* pp. 63–64, 123–127; Travis, *Autobiography of Black Politics,* pp. 260–265; Theodore Jones to Roy Wilkins, 30 Dec. 1959, NAACP papers, group III-C, Chicago, June-Dec. 1959 folder, LC; Coordinating Committee for the NAACP, "The N.A.A.C.P., the Chicago Story, What Can and Must Be Done," Citizens School Committee papers, box 16-3, CHS. That the national NAACP was relieved by the change prefigured the problems that the association would have with more militant civil rights groups throughout the 1960s. Gloster B. Current to Archie Weaver, 27 Dec. 1957, NAACP papers, group III-C, Chicago, Nov.-Dec. 1957 folder, LC; memo, Roy Wilkins to Gloster B. Current, 9 Feb. 1960, ibid., Jan.-June 1960 folder.

16. Lemann, *The Promised Land,* pp. 61–67; Grossman, *Land of Hope,* pp. 98–118, 260; A. L. Foster, "Chicago: City of Progress and Opportunity," 1957, CHS; *CST,* 25 May 1960, p. 35; Drake and Cayton, *Black Metropolis,* I, pp. xli–l, and II, pp. xv–xvii; Gertrude Gorman to Gloster B. Current, 1 Nov. 1956, NAACP papers, group III-C, Chicago, Aug.-Dec. 1956 folder, LC. Later many black Chicagoans questioned the optimistic outlook of the 1950s. The Reverend A. P. Jackson, a prominent black Baptist minister, recalled: "We didn't know we were not free . . . We were sleeping." Jackson interview (telephone), 3 Jan. 1992, Chicago.

17. *The Crisis,* May 1956, p. 297, May 1960, p. 320; "Freedom's Call," Oct. 1956, NAACP papers, group III-C, Chicago, Aug.-Dec. 1956 folder, LC; Otis D. Duncan and Beverly Duncan, *The Negro Population of Chicago: A Study of Residential Succession* (Chicago: University of Chicago Press, 1957), pp. 33–45; Travis, *An Autobiography of Black Politics,* p. 303; Faith Rich to Marvin Rich, 14 March 1960, "Chicago CORE Activities from the 1960 Convention to February 2, 1960" and "Chicago Youth Committee for Civil Rights" flyer, Dec. 1960, CORE papers, V:33 (microfilm); *CDD,* 17 July 1966, pp. 3, 5, and 7 Aug. 1966, p. 4; "Report on Rainbow Beach," Aug. 1961, CIC papers, box 46, CHS. For an overview of the expansion of northern civil rights protest in the early 1960s, see Meier and Rudwick, *CORE,* pp. 109–112, 121–126, 182–210.

18. Strickland, *History of the Chicago Urban League,* pp. 225–228; Meier and Rudwick, *CORE,* p. 185; *Chicago Maroon,* 9 Oct. 1962, p. 1; memo, ca. 1962, CORE papers, box 67, MLK Library; Ruth Ford to Hanover Associates, 25 May 1962, CORE papers, V:337 (microfilm).

19. Faith Rich interview, 5 Aug. 1987, Chicago. On June 6, 1954, the Chicago NAACP held a mass rally to celebrate the Supreme Court decision. See *The Crisis,* May 1954, p. 364.

20. "Overcrowding is what triggered black reaction in the early 1960s," Herbert H. Fisher, a Chicago attorney deeply involved in Chicago public school struggles, has commented. Fisher to author, 6 Sept. 1988; Robert A. Liston, "Pugnacious Planner of America's Future," *True,* May 1965, p. 25; *CDN,* 9 Feb. 1960, p. 20; *Integrated Education,* 3 (Dec. 1965–Jan. 1966): 20. For more background on black Chicagoans' quest for equal educational opportunities, see Michael W. Homel, *Down from Equality: Black Chicagoans and the Public Schools, 1920–1941* (Urbana: University of Illinois Press, 1984).

21. John E. Coons, "Chicago," in United States Commission on Civil Rights, *Civil Rights U.S.A.: Public Schools, Cities in the North and West, 1962* (Washington, D.C.: U.S. Government Printing Office, 1962), pp. 223–224; *CDD,* 14 Feb. 1957, p. 5. Because the yearly figures for students on double shift changed, I have drawn on several accounts to determine the percentage of black students on a shortened schedule circa 1961. See [Faith Rich], "De Facto Segregation in the Chicago Public Schools," *The Crisis,* Feb. 1958, p. 90; Teachers for Integrated

Schools, "Hearts and Minds," ca. 1962, CORE papers (addendum), E:IV (microfilm). Anderson and Pickering, *Confronting the Color Line*, pp. 44–102, and Anderson and Pickering, "The Issue of the Color Line," pp. 1–312, offer further discussion of the genesis of black unrest. In recent years sociologists have offered many explanations for the origins of the civil rights movement, but most have focused on southern, not northern, protest. For sociological perspectives on the civil rights movement, see Aldon Morris, *The Origins of the Civil Rights Movement: Black Communities Organizing for Change* (New York: Free Press, 1984), and Doug McAdam, *Political Process and the Development of Black Insurgency, 1930–1970* (Chicago: University of Chicago Press, 1982).

22. Hirsch, *Making the Second Ghetto*, pp. 3–9; *CDN*, 21 Oct. 1959, p. 32.

23. Benjamin Duster interview (telephone), 22 Jan. 1992, Chicago. In early 1961, seven Chatham-area elementary schools had a student-teacher ratio of 38.5, with three schools on double shift. Eight of the nearby white schools had a student-teacher ratio of 29.2, with none on double shift. Herbert H. Fisher, Statement before Subcommittee of House Education and Labor Committee, 17 July 1965, SCLC papers, box 149-10, MLK Library. Fisher, then a Chatham resident, has remarked that "Chatham in the early [1960s] was the recipient of black middle-class families who with two working heads of household were most adversely affected by the overcrowded double-shift school conditions and were also in a better position (if not in public employment of some type) to voice their anger and frustrations." Fisher to author, 6 Sept. 1988; Mae Gregory, *Chatham, 1856–1987: A Community of Excellence* (Chicago: Friends of the Chicago Public Library, 1989), pp. 17–43, 57–62; Wilson, *Negro Politics*, pp. 230–246.

24. Rich interview. In the spring of 1961, the *Chicago Defender* excoriated the NAACP for its failure to act. "We've all talked enough and words vanish on the wind," the *Defender* declared. "The powers that be in this city will react only to political pressure and court orders. We could have the one if we woke up to our strength; and could get the other if the NAACP lawyers get cracking." See *CDD*, 13 March 1961, p. 12.

25. *CDD*, 7 Sept. 1961, p. 2, 18 Sept. 1961, p. 3, 19 Sept. 1961, p. 3; *CD*, 2–8 Sept. 1961, p. 4; *CST*, 7 Sept. 1961, p. 3; *The Crisis*, Oct. 1961, pp. 509–513; Duster interview; Anderson and Pickering, *Confronting the Color Line*, pp. 84–85. According to the *Chicago Defender*, 160 parents sought to enroll 225 students in white, single-shift schools. The parents, the *Defender* reported, came from fourteen local organizations representing one West Side and six South Side communities. A review of the plaintiffs in the *Webb* suit reveals that as a group they were well established. James Webb was a minister, at least one of the other parents was a lawyer (James Montgomery), and two were doctors (C. A. Tompkins and Louis Coggs). Most of the *Webb* plaintiffs did not live in Chatham proper (roughly 75th to 87th Streets between State Street and Cottage Grove Avenue), but rather a few blocks to the south and to the north.

26. *The Bulletin,* 19 Oct. 1961, Saul Alinsky papers, folder 350, UIC; Alma P. Coggs and others to Benjamin C. Willis, 30 Dec. 1961, and Coggs and others to Richard Daley, 1 Jan. 1962, CUL papers (76-116), box 179-5, UIC; Alma P. Coggs interview (telephone), 14 Oct. 1988, Washington, D.C.; *CDD,* 4 Jan. 1962, p. 2, 8 Jan. 1962, p. 3, 18 Jan. 1962, p. 2. The protesters would begin their sit-in during the morning and then would leave at the close of school. This routine was repeated daily for the duration of the sit-in. Eleven out of the seventeen demonstrators arrested on Tuesday, January 16, came from a confined area bounded by South Parkway, 95th Street, and Burnside Avenue. Most of the ten demonstrators arrested the following day came from farther afield. These figures point to the cohesive community networks that nurtured the original sit-in participants.

27. *CDD,* 17 Jan. 1962, p. 3, 18 Jan. 1962, p. 2; *Southeast Economist,* 18 Jan. 1962, pp. 1, 3; *The Bulletin,* 19 Oct. 1961, Alinsky papers, box 350, UIC; *CST,* 9 Feb. 1962, p. 3; William H. Chafe, *Civilities and Civil Rights: Greensboro, North Carolina, and the Black Struggle for Freedom* (New York: Oxford University Press, 1981), p. 99. For more on the Burnside saga, see folders 345–350, 366 in the Alinsky papers, UIC. Coons, "Chicago," in *Civil Rights U.S.A.,* pp. 212–215, is also useful. Among the Burnside protesters arrested, Alma Coggs, Bonita Woods, and James Webb were involved in the *Webb* suit. The Chicago NAACP was not on the sidelines in this incident; Carl Fuqua was also arrested. The Burnside mothers soon launched their own suit against the Board of Education. Later in the year it was dismissed by a federal judge because the plaintiffs had not exhausted administrative remedies. Anderson and Pickering, *Confronting the Color Line,* p. 89; *CDD,* 22 Jan. 1962, p. 2. Alma Coggs, the Reverend James Webb, William Williams, and others closely involved in the fight against school overcrowding joined to form the Chicago Committee for Equal Education. For an early 1962 review of Chicago school problems, including those on the West Side, see this group's pamphlet, "Equal Education for All!," Church Federation of Greater Chicago papers, Chicago Public Schools folder, CHS.

28. *New Guidepost,* June 1962, Faith Rich papers, box 1-4, SHSW, Madison, Wis. The Gregory School on the West Side was, for example, more crowded than most South Side schools, yet West Side protests were not as vigorous. Here the importance of indigenous leadership cannot be overstressed. The Greater Lawndale Conservation Commission, perhaps the West Side's strongest citizen association, was dominated by conservative leadership. Lawndale organizations "were not as strong as those on the Southside and leadership to spearhead an intelligent protest was not in abundance." *CDD,* 13 Feb. 1962, p. 2. Faith Rich, though a white woman, lived in Lawndale and played a leading role in cultivating opposition to school policies on the West Side.

Some of the differences among communities can be seen in a comparison of their socioeconomic characteristics:

	Vernon Park	Woodlawn	North Lawndale
Family income			
% under $3,000	10.5	27.0	24.8
% over $10,000	24.1	7.8	8.7
% Male unemployed	7.4	11.5	10.0
% Male white collar	43.3	23.3	16.1
% Owner-occupied bldgs.	71.0	8.8	17.9
% Substandard bldgs.	2.9	30.0	14.0
Median yrs. of schooling	11.9	9.9	8.7

(The Vernon Park data are based on census tract 695, nearly 80 percent black in 1960. In that year Woodlawn was nearly 90 percent black, and North Lawndale was more than 90 percent black. Evelyn M. Kitagawa and Karl E. Taeuber, eds., *Local Community Fact Book: Chicago Metropolitan Area, 1960* [Chicago: Chicago Community Inventory, 1963], pp. 2–3, 113.)

29. John Hall Fish, *Black Power/White Control: The Struggle of the Woodlawn Organization in Chicago* (Princeton: Princeton University Press, 1973), pp. 12–65; Arthur M. Brazier, *Self-Determination: The Story of the Woodlawn Organization,* ed. Roberta G. and Robert F. DeHaan (Grand Rapids, Mich.: William B. Eerdmans, 1969); Sanford D. Horwitt, *Let Them Call Me Rebel: Saul Alinsky, His Life and Legacy* (New York: Alfred A. Knopf, 1989), pp. 405–407; Elinor Richey, "The Slum That Saved Itself," *Progressive,* Oct. 1963, pp. 26–29; *CDD,* 25 Sept. 1961, p. 6, 28 Nov. 1962, p. 9; *Chicago Courier,* 18 Nov. 1961, p. 4; Anderson and Pickering, "The Issue of the Color Line," p. 302.

30. *CST,* 19 Feb. 1962, p. 25; *New Crusader,* 31 March 1962, p. 13. See Anderson and Pickering, "The Issue of the Color Line," pp. 295–297, on the origins of CCCO.

31. *Dollars and Sense,* Jan. 1986, p. 14; "Bill Berry—and 'The Challenge of Chicago,'" *St. Joseph Magazine,* Feb. 1956, p. 4; Lerone Bennett, Jr., "North's Hottest Fight for Integration," *Ebony,* March 1962, pp. 34–38; Strickland, *History of the Chicago Urban League,* pp. 185–259; Harold Baron interview, 3 July 1991, Chicago.

32. Meier and Rudwick, *CORE,* pp. 225–258; *CDN,* 29 July 1963, p. 1; *CDD,* 23 July 1963, p. 2, 7 Aug. 1963, p. 3; Tim Black, "Chicago Negro Labor and Civil Rights," *Freedomways,* Fall 1966, pp. 313–314; Timuel D. Black to Edwin C. Berry, 7 Sept. 1966, Illinois, Chicago, ESS Other Material, 1967 folder, HMBC, University of Massachusetts at Amherst; CIC Board of Directors minutes, 17 July 1963, CIC papers, box 61, CHS; Anderson and Pickering, *Confronting the Color Line,* pp. 111, 115–116; Don Rose interview, 19 Aug. 1986, Chicago.

33. Chicago Urban League memo, "NAACP Freedom March, July 4, 1963 and the Hooting of Daley," 8 July 1963, CUL papers (76-116), box 179-38, UIC; *CST,* 5 July 1963, pp. 1, 4; *CDN,* 5 July 1963, pp. 1, 4; Baron interview.

34. *CDD,* 15 July 1963, p. 4, 16 July 1963, p. 3, 29 July 1963, p. 5, 6 Aug. 1963, p. 3, 13 Aug. 1963, p. 3, 14 Aug. 1963, p. 4, 15 Aug. 1963, p. 6; *Southeast*

Economist, 4 Aug. 1963, p. 4; Robert Lucas interview, Aug. 1986, Chicago; Robert Lucas interview in Dempsey J. Travis, *An Autobiography of Black Chicago* (Chicago: Urban Research Institute, 1981), pp. 248–249; Anderson and Pickering, *Confronting the Color Line*, pp. 112–113; Frank Ichishita, "A Neighborhood Demonstrates," *Integrated Education*, 1 (Dec. 1963): 35–39; *CDD*, 3 Sept. 1963, p. 2, 4 Sept. 1963, pp. 2–3, 5 Sept. 1963, p. 2, 23 Sept. 1963, p. 4.

35. Kay Kamin, "A History of the Hunt Administration of the Chicago Public Schools, 1947–1953" (Ph.D. diss., University of Chicago, 1970); "Ben Willis: Man in a Hurry," Faith Rich papers, box 1-1, SHSW; Liston, "Pugnacious Planner of America's Future," pp. 15–16, 18–19, 25–28, 30, 32; Stephen London, "Business and the Chicago Public School System, 1890–1966" (Ph.D. diss., University of Chicago, 1968), p. 146; Faith Rich to Marvin Rich, 14 Sept. 1960, CORE papers (addendum), E:IV (microfilm); *CST*, 6 Feb. 1962, p. 5; *CD*, 12–18 Oct. 1963, p. 2. To this day, opinions of Willis vary. Weinberg interview; William Caples interview, 6 Aug. 1987, Chicago. While a vice-president with Inland Steel, Caples served as the president of the Chicago Board of Education in the early 1960s. It should also be noted that although Willis became a divisive force in Chicago, even some of his detractors agreed that a lack of funding was a principal cause of the shortcomings of a Chicago public education. See Robert J. Havighurst, *The Public Schools of Chicago: A Survey for the Board of Education of the City of Chicago* (Chicago: Board of Education of the City of Chicago, 1964), pp. 402–410.

36. Naomi Brodkey, "Public Schools Crisis: Chicago-Style," *New City*, 15 Dec. 1963, pp. 4–8; Anderson and Pickering, *Confronting the Color Line*, pp. 85–86, 96–97, 100, 117–118; Joseph Pois, *The School Board Crisis: A Case Study* (Chicago: Educational Methods, 1964).

37. *SWNH*, 12 Sept. 1963, p. 1, 19 Sept. 1963, p. 1, 26 Sept. 1963, p. 1, 3 Oct. 1963, p. 1, 10 Oct. 1963, p. 1, 17 Oct. 1963, p. 1.

38. *CDN*, 22 Oct. 1963, pp. 1, 6; Anderson and Pickering, *Confronting the Color Line*, pp. 116–120; Anne Brown and David Gordon (pseud.), "School Boycotts: Only the Beginning," *Focus/Midwest*, 2 (no. 11): 19; Weinberg interview; Rose interview; Lawrence Landry, *Standpoint* editorial, WBBM-TV, 6 Nov. 1963, Chicago CORE papers, box 1-8, CHS.

39. Meier and Rudwick, "The Origins of Nonviolent Direct Action," pp. 312–313; Homel, *Down from Equality*, pp. 165, 169, 172; *CDD*, 22 Oct. 1963, p. 3; Rose interview; Landry, *Standpoint* editorial, WBBM-TV, 6 Nov. 1963, Chicago CORE papers, box 1-8, CHS; Minutes, "Exploratory Conference of Persons Interested in National School Boycott, February 3, 1964," New York City, and "Summary: Temporary National Freedom Day Committee," 25 Jan. 1964, Chicago, SNCC papers, A:IX:69 (microfilm).

40. Anderson and Pickering, *Confronting the Color Line*, pp. 120–124, 127–130.

41. *CST*, 26 Feb. 1964, pp. 3, 26, 1 March 1964, pp. 3, 18; Brown and Gordon, "School Boycotts," pp. 18–20, 29; Ramon J. Rivera, Gerald A. McWorter, and Ernest Lillienstein, "Freedom Day II in Chicago," *Integrated Edu-*

cation, 2 (May-June 1964): 34–39; Anderson and Pickering, *Confronting the Color Line,* pp. 130–133.

42. *Chicago Courier,* 3 Feb. 1962, p. 2; memo, June Shagaloff to Gloster B. Current, 14 Dec. 1961, NAACP papers, group III-C, Chicago, June-Dec. 1961 folder, LC; Meyer Weinberg, "De Facto Segregation: Fact or Artifact," *Integrated Education,* 1 (April 1963): 30–33; Anderson and Pickering, *Confronting the Color Line,* pp. 84–85, 116–117.

43. Anderson and Pickering, *Confronting the Color Line,* p. 473.

44. Ibid., p. 129; *CD,* 21–27 March 1964, p. 1; Tom Kahn and August Meier, "Recent Trends in the Civil Rights Movement," *New Politics,* 3 (Spring 1964): 34–53; Raby interview.

45. Anderson and Pickering, *Confronting the Color Line,* pp. 453–457; Raby interview; Rose interview; Anderson and Pickering, "The Issue of the Color Line," pp. 566–571; Bennett, "North's Hottest Fight," p. 35.

46. Anderson and Pickering, *Confronting the Color Line,* pp. 136–137, 141–146.

47. Hal Baron to Ruby Barrett, 30 Nov. 1964, CUL papers (76-116), box 179-37, UIC; Anderson and Pickering, *Confronting the Color Line,* pp. 127–153; *CD,* 1–7 Feb. 1966, p. 1; Citizens Housing Committee, "Housing, Schools and Segregation," Chicago CORE papers, box 3-20, CHS; "CORE Northern Project: Chicago, Ill.," ca. 1964, CORE papers, box 92, MLK Library.

48. *CDD,* 6 July 1964, p. 2, 7 July 1964, pp. 3, 18; Meier and Rudwick, *CORE,* pp. 309–310; Jo Adler memo, 21 Aug. 1964, CORE papers, V:33 (microfilm); Casey Hayden, "Chicago Situation," 17 April 1964, SNCC papers, A:IX:69 (microfilm).

49. Meier and Rudwick, *CORE,* p. 258; *CDN,* 20 Feb. 1965, p. 11. For a rebuttal, see the letter by Albert Raby, Father William E. Hogan, and the Reverend James W. Mack, *CDN,* 2 March 1965, p. 14.

50. Anderson and Pickering, *Confronting the Color Line,* pp. 154–167. Gloster B. Current to Roy Wilkins and others, 15 June 1965, and Syd Finley to Chicago NAACP Branch Executive Committee Members, 15 June 1965, NAACP papers, group III-C, Chicago, Jan.-Aug. 1965 folder, LC, present the NAACP's perspective on these events. Support for Willis shrank in many quarters in 1965. Adams to Gaylord Donnelley, 18 May 1965, Cyrus Hall Adams papers, box 11-3, CHS.

51. Anderson and Pickering, *Confronting the Color Line,* pp. 156–157; *CT,* 11 June 1965, pp. 1–2, 12 June 1965, pp. 1, 4; *CST,* 11 June 1965, pp. 1, 4, 12 June 1965, pp. 1, 10.

52. "A Statement from Al Raby to All Participants in Today's March," 28 June 1965, CCCO papers, box 2-14, MLK Library; "Why We March" flyer, ca. summer 1965, ibid., box 4-8; "Keynote Speech by Albert A. Raby—C.C.C.O. Conference—August 28, 1965," HMBC.

53. Caples interview; Warren Bacon interview, 13 Aug. 1986, Chicago; audio tape, Adams papers, box 38, CHS.

54. Anderson and Pickering, *Confronting the Color Line,* pp. 158–160; *CA,* 18 July 1965, p. 14; Meier and Rudwick, *CORE,* pp. 349–350, 397–401; memo,

James Wagner to Billy Stafford, 9 July 1965, CUL papers (76-116), box 158-22, UIC. Civil rights activists did not seek a cataclysmic shift in Chicago's school population. Raby, for instance, did not favor large-scale busing to promote racial balance.

55. "Keynote Speech by Albert A. Raby," 28 August 1965, HMBC. This figure excludes the thousands who mobilized during Martin Luther King's late July visit to Chicago. For a profile of the Willis marchers, see *CDN*, 24 July 1965, p. 23.

56. *CST*, 13 July 1965, pp. 1, 3.

57. *CDN*, 14 June 1965, p. 8; Anderson and Pickering, *Confronting the Color Line*, pp. 159–160; *CDD*, 1 July 1965, p. 3; *NYT*, 3 July 1965, p. 7.

58. Anderson and Pickering, "The Issue of the Color Line," pp. 741, 751.

59. Gary Orfield, *The Reconstruction of Southern Education: The Schools and the 1964 Civil Rights Act* (New York: John Wiley & Sons, 1969), pp. 164–167. For evidence of the desire of Chicago activists for King to come to Chicago, see Dr. Quentin Young to MLK, 9 June 1965, and Bill Berry to MLK, 9 June 1965, MLK papers, box 5-24, MLK Library. I have stressed CCCO's relative powerlessness as a prime reason that it sought outside help. It is true, however, that before the 1965 marches, CCCO had planned to recruit outside allies. Nevertheless, by late June and early July CCCO's inability to force constructive change directly fueled its recruiting efforts. For a view emphasizing the preplanned character of outside recruitment, see Anderson and Pickering, *Confronting the Color Line*, pp. 159–161.

60. MLK remarks, 7 July 1965, MLK speech file, MLK Library; Leon Despres to MLK, 14 July 1965, and Charles Chew to MLK, 16 July 1965, MLK papers, box 5-25, MLK Library. In early June King announced his intention to join the Chicago struggle before the end of July. *CDN*, 5 June 1965, pp. 3, 14.

61. Meier and Rudwick, *CORE*, pp. 182–212, 329–408; Bayard Rustin, "From Protest to Politics: The Future of the Civil Rights Movement," *Commentary*, Feb. 1965, pp. 25–31; "CORE Northern Project: Chicago, Ill.," ca. 1964, CORE papers, box 92, MLK Library; Clayborne Carson, *In Struggle: SNCC and the Black Awakening of the 1960s* (Cambridge, Mass.: Harvard University Press, 1981), pp. 168–169. CORE originated in the North and developed active northern chapters. It only began to cultivate strong southern chapters after the Freedom Rides, but from 1961 to 1965 its national office concentrated on southern programs.

62. See, for example, John W. Blassingame, *The Slave Community: Plantation Life in the Antebellum South* (New York: Oxford University Press, 1972), pp. 104–107, and Grossman, *Land of Hope*, pp. 98–119.

63. MLK speech, 17 May 1956, MLK speech file, MLK Library. On King's early life, see Taylor Branch, *Parting the Waters: America in the King Years, 1954–1963* (New York: Simon and Schuster, 1988), pp. 39–49, 56–104; Garrow, *Bearing the Cross*, pp. 32–51; Stephen Oates, *Let the Trumpet Sound: The Life of Martin Luther King, Jr.* (New York: Harper & Row, 1982), pp. 10–50; and David Lewis, *King: A Biography*, 2nd ed. (Urbana: University of Illinois Press, 1978), pp. 3–46. During a 1965 speech in Boston King recalled landlords' refusal to rent to him

because he was black. *Boston Globe,* 23 April 1965, p. 1. Moreover, during his rise to prominence after the Montgomery bus boycott of 1955 and 1956, King received regular reminders of the northern blacks' plight from scores of northern admirers. See, for example, letter to MLK, 29 Nov. 1961, Chicago Heights, Ill., MLK papers, box 49, VI-170, Mugar Library, Boston University.

64. For discussions of the origins of SCLC, see Adam Fairclough, *To Redeem the Soul of America: The Southern Christian Leadership Conference and Martin Luther King, Jr.* (Athens: University of Georgia Press, 1987), pp. 11–35, and Fairclough, "The Preachers and the People: The Origins and Early Years of the Southern Christian Leadership Conference, 1955–1959," *Journal of Southern History,* 52 (Aug. 1986): 403–440. SCLC relied on northerners for advice and for financial support. Garrow, *Bearing the Cross,* pp. 66–69, 83–85, 219–220, 451, and Fairclough, *To Redeem the Soul,* pp. 29–32, 47, 96, 255–256. On SCLC's efforts to stir the conscience of the federal government and the North in the late 1950s, see Fairclough, *To Redeem the Soul,* pp. 39–43.

65. Meier and Rudwick, "Origins of Nonviolent Direct Action," pp. 354–357, 362–363. Overall, the 1950s witnessed a drop-off in direct action compared with the 1930s. The career of C. T. Vivian, a future SCLC leader, exemplified the course of nonviolent direct action after World War II. On Vivian, see Morris, *The Origins of the Civil Rights Movement,* pp. 176–177.

66. Charles E. Silberman, *Crisis in Black and White* (New York: Random House, 1964), pp. 9–10; Whitney M. Young, *To Be Equal* (New York: McGraw-Hill, 1964), pp. 10–11; James Farmer, *Freedom—When?* (New York: Random House, 1965), pp. 169–170. Silberman developed some of these themes in his earlier article, "The City and the Negro," *Fortune,* March 1962, pp. 88–91, 139–140, 144, 146, 151–152, 154. Meier and Rudwick argue that CORE members—and implicitly, other civil rights activists—knew in the early 1960s "that beyond constitutional rights lay racism's bitter legacy of inadequate schools, poverty, and rat-infested, overcrowded tenements, but they sought to attack racism's most overt symbol—segregation." Meier and Rudwick, *CORE,* p. 184. Accounts of the barriers to black advancement in the North can be found in important studies such as the Chicago Commission on Race Relations' *The Negro in Chicago: A Study of Race Relations and a Race Riot* (1922), Gunnar Myrdal's *An American Dilemma* (1944), and St. Clair Drake and Horace Cayton's *Black Metropolis* (1945). Yet however illuminating, none of these studies amounted to the sweeping indictment of America as a racist society that became popular in the second half of the 1960s. "Institutional racism" was what Stokely Carmichael and Charles Hamilton, in their popular book *Black Power* (1967), called the force that kept "black people locked in dilapidated slum tenements, subject to the daily prey of exploitative slumlords, merchants, loan sharks and discriminatory real estate agents." As the 1960s passed, fewer and fewer civil rights sympathizers accepted the Americanization theory, popular in the 1950s, which stated that blacks were simply the most recent of the immigrant groups who, like the other groups, after years of seasoning in urban America would assimilate into the American mainstream. For a notable elaboration of this view, see Irving Kristol, "The Negro

Today Is Like the Immigrant Yesterday," *New York Times Magazine,* 11 Sept. 1966, pp. 50–51.

67. Garrow, *Bearing the Cross,* pp. 56–58, 84–85, 164–165, 218–219, 288–289; Branch, *Parting the Waters,* p. 162; Fairclough, *To Redeem the Soul,* p. 32; Lewis V. Baldwin, *There Is a Balm in Gilead: The Cultural Roots of Martin Luther King, Jr.* (Minneapolis: Fortress Press, 1991), pp. 4–6, 15–90.

68. To my knowledge, until 1965 King never made northern racial inequities the major theme of one of his speeches. Often he would refer to northern problems in a sentence or two before moving on to other subjects. For examples of King's reflections on northern race problems, see King speeches, 11 May 1959 and 6 Sept. 1960, MLK speech file, MLK Library. That King often relied on the same formulation—that Americans must confront segregation in the North in "its hidden and subtle form"—in speeches over a six-year span suggests that during the first years of the southern struggle he did not expend much energy analyzing northern racial problems. See King speeches, 1 Dec. 1956, 13 Jan. 1958, 8 Sept. 1962, MLK speech file, MLK Library.

69. MLK, *Where Do We Go from Here: Chaos or Community?* (New York: Harper & Row, 1967), p. 19; Fairclough, *To Redeem the Soul,* p. 197; *Los Angeles Sentinel,* 30 May 1963, p. 1. See also MLK remarks, 23 June 1963, MLK speech file, MLK Library; *St. Louis Post-Dispatch,* 29 May 1963, p. 1; *LCJ,* 30 May 1963, p. 1.

70. *NYT,* 6 Feb. 1964, p. 20, 15 March 1964, p. 46; MLK remarks, 31 May 1964, MLK speech file, MLK Library.

71. *SCLC Newsletter,* July–Aug. 1964, MLK speech file, MLK Library. The SCLC Rochester team included Young, Bevel, James Orange, Richard Boone, Willie Bolden, Lester Hankerson, and Bernard LaFayette; "Activity Report by Bernard LaFayette," AFSC papers, Chicago Regional Office (R.O.) 1964, UAP folder, AFSC Archives, Philadelphia. Later in August part of this contingent rushed to Philadelphia when blacks began rioting there. Fairclough argues that SCLC learned very little from its work in the North in 1964. Fairclough, *To Redeem the Soul,* p. 197.

72. Garrow, *Bearing the Cross,* pp. 342–343; Fairclough, *To Redeem the Soul,* pp. 196–198; *Amsterdam News,* 1 Aug. 1964, pp. 1, 47, 8 Aug. 1964, p. 4, 15 Aug. 1964, pp. 1, 12. The last chapter in King's *Why We Can't Wait* (New York: Harper & Row, 1964) suggests his growing concern about problems of class.

73. Garrow, *Bearing the Cross,* pp. 352–354, 364–367; "Minutes," Savannah Meeting, 30 Sept. 1964, MLK papers, box 29-4, MLK Library; Lewis, *King,* pp. 260–263; "The Quest for Peace and Justice," in Frederick W. Haberman, ed., *Peace: Nobel Lectures, 1951–1970,* III (Amsterdam: Elsevier, 1972), pp. 333–346; Coretta Scott King, *My Life with Martin Luther King* (New York: Holt, Rinehart, and Winston, 1969), p. 17.

74. Harvard Sitkoff, *The Struggle for Black Equality, 1954–1980* (New York: McGraw-Hill, 1981), pp. 188–202.

75. SCLC Board Meeting, Baltimore, 1 and 2 April 1965, MLK papers, box 29-5, MLK Library; Garrow, *Bearing the Cross,* pp. 414–415; *Baltimore Sun,* 2 April 1965, p. 44, 3 April 1965, p. 20; *WP,* 2 April 1965, p. 4.

76. FBI 100-106670-NR (Not Recorded), 14 June 1965; Bayard Rustin interview with T. H. Baker, 30 June 1969, Lyndon Baines Johnson Library, Austin, Tex.; Howell Raines, *My Soul Is Rested: The Story of the Civil Rights Movement in the Deep South* (New York: G. P. Putnam's Sons, 1977), p. 52; Norman Hill interview (telephone), 12 March 1992, Washington, D.C.; MLK remarks, ca. summer 1965, MLK speech file, MLK Library.

77. Garrow, *Bearing the Cross*, p. 429; Fairclough, *To Redeem the Soul*, pp. 47–48, 255–256.

78. Garrow, *Bearing the Cross*, p. 433.

79. Ibid.; Anderson and Pickering, "The Issue of the Color Line," p. 754; *NYT*, 25 July 1965, p. 39; Rose interview. For profiles of the neighborhood rallies, see "Observation" sheets, 24 July 1965, CUL papers (76-116), box 158-22, CHS.

80. *CST*, 26 July 1965, p. 3; *CDN*, 26 July 1965, pp. 1, 5; Garrow, *Bearing the Cross*, pp. 433–434; Anderson and Pickering, "The Issue of the Color Line," p. 755; for a profile of the neighborhood rallies, see "Observation" sheets, 25 July 1965, CUL papers (76-116), box 158-22, UIC; *Winnetka Talk*, 29 July 1965, pp. 1, 4.

81. *CDN*, 26 July 1965, p. 1; *CDD*, 27 July 1965, pp. 3, 15; Garrow, *Bearing the Cross*, p. 434; *New Crusader*, 31 July 1965, p. 3; Conrad Kent Rivers, "The Day King Marched in Chicago," *Negro Digest*, March 1966, pp. 54–58. For a profile of the Monday marchers, see "Observation" sheets, 26 July 1965, CUL papers (76-116), box 158-22, UIC.

82. *Call and Post*, 31 July 1965, p. 1, 7 Aug. 1965, p. 2; Garrow, *Bearing the Cross*, pp. 434–435; *Cleveland Press*, 28 July 1965, p. 4, 29 July 1965, p. D7.

83. *CDN*, 28 July 1965, p. 9; *NYT*, 1 Aug. 1965, p. 59; *Amsterdam News*, 15 Aug. 1964, p. 1; Garrow, *Bearing the Cross*, p. 435.

84. *NYT*, 1 Aug. 1965, p. 59; *Philadelphia Tribune*, 31 July 1965, p. 1; *Philadelphia Sunday Bulletin*, 1 Aug. 1965, p. 1; Garrow, *Bearing the Cross*, pp. 435–436; James O. Williams to Robert Lucas, Chicago CORE papers, box 4-29, CHS. On Moore, see Paul Lermack, "Cecil Moore and the Philadelphia Branch of the National Association for the Advancement of Colored People: The Politics of Negro Pressure Group Organization," in Miriam Ershkowitz and Joseph Zikmund II, eds., *Black Politics in Philadelphia* (New York: Basic Books, 1973), pp. 145–160.

85. *WP*, 3 Aug. 1965, p. 2; *Philadelphia Evening Bulletin*, 2 Aug. 1965, pp. 1–2, 3 Aug. 1965, pp. 1, 3; Garrow, *Bearing the Cross*, pp. 435–436.

86. *WP*, 5 Aug. 1965, p. C1, 6 Aug. 1965, p. 4; *NYT*, 5 Aug. 1965, p. 12; Garrow, *Bearing the Cross*, p. 436.

87. Anderson and Pickering, "The Issue of the Color Line," pp. 760, 762; "Observation" sheet, Sue Bateman, 26 July 1965, CUL papers (76-116), box 158-22, UIC; Philip Hauser to Raby, 30 July 1965, CCCO papers, box 4-14, MLK Library; "Keynote Speech by Albert A. Raby," 28 Aug. 1965, HMBC.

88. Anderson and Pickering, "The Issue of the Color Line," pp. 757–758; Anderson and Pickering, *Confronting the Color Line*, pp. 161–162; *CDN*, 2 Aug.

1965, p. 10, 3 Aug. 1965, pp. 1, 7, 4 Aug. 1965, pp. 1, 10, 5 Aug. 1965, p. 3, 9 Aug. 1965, pp. 1, 6, 10 Aug. 1965, p. 7; *CA,* 3 Aug. 1965, pp. 1, 4; tape of "At Random," 7 Aug. 1965, Adams papers, box 38, CHS. For a profile of one of the Bridgeport marches, see "Observation" sheet, 6 Aug. 1965, CUL papers (76-116), box 158-22, UIC.

89. Tape of "At Random," 7 Aug. 1965, Adams papers, box 38, CHS; Joseph L. Block to Edwin C. Berry, 12 Aug. 1965, Ely Aaron papers, box 2-2, UIC; *CA,* 4 Aug. 1965, pp. 1, 4; *CDN,* 13 Aug. 1965, p. 1; Anderson and Pickering, "The Issue of the Color Line," pp. 784–785; Raby conversation with Kale Williams. On CCCO's expectations, see Anderson and Pickering, "The Issue of the Color Line," pp. 776–777. Chicago CORE wired a request for King and SCLC to return as soon as possible. Robert Lucas to MLK, 11 Aug. 1965, MLK papers, box 5-26, MLK Library.

90. Anderson and Pickering, *Confronting the Color Line,* p. 162; Anderson and Pickering, "The Issue of the Color Line," p. 768; "Southern Christian Leadership Conference, Board Meeting," 9 Aug. 1965, MLK papers, box 29-5, MLK Library.

91. Garrow, *Bearing the Cross,* pp. 439–440; MLK and Stanley Levison, FBI 100-111180-9-677, 25 Aug. 1965.

92. "Executive Staff Meeting," 26–28 Aug. 1965, MLK papers, box 32-9, MLK Library; Garrow, *Bearing the Cross,* pp. 441–443. Al Raby remembered that there was opposition from some SCLC leaders to the Chicago venture. Raby also believed that "the move was inevitable." King could not "remain the national leader of the civil rights movement without dealing with northern problems." Raby interview.

93. At the Atlanta strategy session, there was some discussion about SCLC's working simultaneously in several cities. It was finally decided that it would use Chicago as a "pilot project." "Executive Staff Meeting," 26–28 Aug. 1965, MLK papers, box 32-9, MLK Library.

94. Rose interview; MLK to Edgar Chandler and others, 10 July 1964, MLK papers, box 5-22, MLK Library; Raby interview; Studs Terkel, *Talking to Myself: A Memoir of My Times* (New York: Pantheon Books, 1979), pp. 258–267; *CST,* 2 Sept. 1965, pp. 1, 30; Anderson and Pickering, *Confronting the Color Line,* pp. 162, 176; Garrow, *Bearing the Cross,* pp. 180–181, 225–227, 316–318, 323–326. Local Selma blacks welcomed SCLC to their city in 1965, but I have found no evidence of a formal invitation or call.

95. James Bevel interview, 11 Aug. 1988, Chicago. On Bevel's background and relationship with King, see *CDD,* 25 May 1965, p. 11; Fairclough, *To Redeem the Soul,* pp. 91, 167, 334–335; and Branch, *Parting the Waters,* pp. 263–264, 482–484, 559, 753–754.

96. Bevel interview. Don Benedict's *Born Again Radical* (New York: Pilgrim Press, 1982), pp. 102–119, discusses the Cleveland Inner City Protestant Parish.

97. David Jehnsen interview (telephone), 20 Aug. 1991, Galena, Ohio; Robert Mueller interview (telephone), 7 Feb. 1989, Orangedale, Nova Scotia; CCMS, "Albany Report," 6 Sept. 1962, CIC papers, box 54, CHS. Bevel had been

to Chicago on speaking tours for the AFSC and to serve on the faculty of their Midwest Institutes. "Why a Non-Violent Movement?," WSCP papers, box 1-1, UIC.

98. For more on the WSCP and the appointment of Bevel, see Franklin I. Gamwell, "The West Side Christian Parish: A History of Its Decline," unpublished paper in author's possession, pp. 1–14, 18–24; Mueller and Jehnsen interviews, CCMS papers, vol. 6, WSCP—Program folder, CTS Library, Chicago.

99. Bernard LaFayette interview, 19 Sept. 1987, Chicago; Kale Williams interview with Gary Orfield, 25 Jan. 1986, Chicago; Jehnsen interview; James Farmer, *Lay Bare the Heart: An Autobiography of the Civil Rights Movement* (New York: New American Library, 1985), pp. 9–10, 17–18, 23–24, 27–28; Bevel interview; Chafe, *Civilities and Civil Rights*, pp. 30, 34–37, 74–75. Though now working on different sides of the Mason-Dixon line, Bevel and LaFayette remained close.

100. "Executive Staff Meeting," 26-28 Aug. 1965, MLK papers, box 32-9, MLK Library; Bevel interview; Fairclough, *To Redeem the Soul*, pp. 4–6, 168–172.

101. *CST,* 2 Sept. 1965, pp. 1, 30; MLK, "Why Chicago Is the Target," *Amsterdam News,* 11 Sept. 1965, p. 16.

2. Mobilizing the City

1. *LAT,* 21 Jan. 1966, p. 16; Garrow, *Bearing the Cross,* pp. 456–459.

2. "A Proposal by the Southern Christian Leadership Conference for the Development of a Nonviolent Action Movement for the Greater Chicago Area," MLK papers, box 5-27, MLK Library, Atlanta; "Plan of Action," SCLC papers, box 47-4, MLK Library. King's proposal was dubbed the "Chicago Plan" by the press. See *CDD,* 10 Jan. 1966, p. 10. For reaction to the "Chicago Plan," see *CT,* 13 Jan. 1966, p. 20; memo [Robert F. Squires], 6 Jan. 1966, Msgr. John Egan papers, box 19, University of Notre Dame Archives, Notre Dame, Ind.

3. "A Proposal," MLK papers, box 5-27, MLK Library; *CA,* 6 Jan. 1966, p. 3.

4. "A Proposal," MLK papers, box 5-27, MLK Library; Garrow, *Bearing the Cross,* pp. 456–458; *CST,* 27 Jan. 1966, p. 32.

5. Commentators have offered varying estimates of the size of the Chicago vanguard. The September SCLC–Chicago Project financial work sheet suggests that nine SCLC staffers joined Bevel. The SCLC advance team enlarged during the fall. Most of the SCLC staff lived on near-subsistence salaries. SCLC papers, box 111-4, MLK Library. Originally Bevel had begun to work out of the First Congregational Church, not too far from the edge of the Loop. But the imminent civil rights commotion was too much for the church's small congregation to bear. Even though it had served as the headquarters for the West Side Christian Parish, which actually consisted of a number of churches, First Congregational requested that Bevel and WSCP move their operations elsewhere. William Briggs, a young United Church of Christ minister, offered his large church (which also had a small congregation) to WSCP. Located in the heart of

the West Side ghetto, the new headquarters was much better situated for the movement than First Congregational Church had been. Jehnsen interview; William Briggs interview (telephone), 8 Dec. 1991, Syracuse; Robert Mueller, "Proposal for a Program of Community Development for Social Change to be Conducted by the West Side Christian Parish in Conjunction with the Southern Christian Leadership Conference," p. 3, David C. Jehnsen materials, 86-2-120, MLK Library.

6. Jehnsen interview; Parish Staff to Parish Board, ca. Fall 1965, CCMS papers, vol. 3, WSCP–Budget and Staff Meetings folder, CTS. The AFSC staff did, however, maintain its independence. The AFSC believed that SCLC lacked a strong "organization tradition," which AFSC possessed, and that because "SCLC/WSCP is primarily concerned with raising dramatic issues to have an effect on national conscience" its "interest in [East Garfield Park] is necessarily a short-range one." See "Future of the Urban Affairs Program," 19 Jan. 1966, AFSC papers, Chicago R.O. 1966, UAP–General folder, AFSC Archives, Philadelphia, and memo, Jane Weston to Participants in Staff-Committee Seminar, "Summary of First Session Held November 4," 8 Nov. 1965, AFSC papers, 46-11, UIC.

7. FBI 100-438794-1191, 25 Feb. 1966; *CDN*, 12 Feb. 1966, p. 4; Jimmy Collier interview (telephone), 31 Jan. 1992, Mariposa, Calif.; Jehnsen interview. SCLC Chicago Office financial reports reveal that the following persons received tiny stipends (seventy-five dollars every other week) from SCLC in September and October 1965: Lynn Adler, Luis Andrades, Charles Billups, Julian Brown, Jimmy Collier, Mary Lou Finley, Ann Gillie, Suzi Hill, William Hollins, Eric Kindberg, Sherri Land, Charles Love, Bennie Luchion, LaMar McCoy, James Orange, Felix Valluena, Jimmy Wilson, Maurice Woodard, Dorothy Wright. The SCLC-Chicago project did not have a large budget. Expenses in September totaled $1,554; in October, $1,843; in November, $2,016. SCLC papers, box 111-4, MLK Library. Gillie, Hill, Kindberg, Land, and Orange were part of the Chicago advance team for the King visit in late July 1965. *CDD*, 22 July 1965, p. 3. Out of the originally proposed advance team of eleven, only Adler, Collier, Gillie, Kindberg, Love, Orange, and Wilson came to Chicago. "Executive Staff Meeting," 26–28 Aug. 1965, MLK papers, box 32-9, MLK Library. Many of these field staffers were familiar with big cities. Kindberg and Gillie were from the Midwest. Andrades came from East Harlem. Hollins, Land, and McCoy had Chicago ties and had been involved in the Chicago civil rights movement. Their involvement in the southern movement led to their official association with SCLC. Thomas B. Morgan, "Requiem or Revival?," *Look*, 14 June 1966, p. 71; "Chicago People in Selma—Montgomery, March 7 through April 6," AFSC papers, 23-17, UIC; William Hollins interview (telephone), 4 and 6 Oct. 1991, Atlanta.

8. Chicago *Reader*, 22 Feb. 1985, p. 22; *CT*, 19 November 1981, section IV, p. 1, 28 May 1984, section IV, pp. 1, 3, 20 Jan. 1986, pp. 1, 11; Henry Hampton and Steve Fayer, eds., *Voices of Freedom: An Oral History of the Civil Rights Movement*

from the 1950s through the 1980s (New York: Bantam Books, 1990), pp. 300–301; "James Orange: With the People," *Southern Exposure,* Spring 1981, pp. 110–115. Before coming to Chicago, Orange worked briefly in Philadelphia and Rochester in 1964 as part of SCLC's riot prevention squad.

9. Harold M. Mayer and Richard C. Wade, *Chicago: Growth of a Metropolis* (Chicago: University of Chicago Press, 1969), pp. 375–474; *NYT,* 17 Jan. 1966, p. 94, 9 Jan. 1967, p. 88. For a host of essays on Chicago's ethnics, see Holli and Jones, eds., *Ethnic Chicago.* Gregory D. Squires et al., *Chicago: Race, Class, and the Response to Urban Decline* (Philadelphia: Temple University Press, 1987), pp. 39–40, is helpful on the standard of living of Chicagoans.

10. Hirsch, *Making the Second Ghetto,* pp. 1–39. For a detailed account of the Great Migration, see Grossman, *Land of Hope.* For an evocative account of the post-1940 black migration to Chicago, see Lemann, *The Promised Land,* pp. 3–107.

11. Dempsey J. Travis, *An Autobiography of Black Jazz* (Chicago: Urban Research Press, 1983); Spear, *Black Chicago;* Drake and Cayton, *Black Metropolis,* I, pp. xli–lxx, and II, pp. xv–xxviii; Travis, *An Autobiography of Black Chicago,* pp. 19–135; CCHR, "The Growing Negro Middle Class in Chicago," 1 Sept. 1962.

12. Grossman, *Land of Hope,* pp. 162–167, 259; George M. Fredrickson, *White Supremacy: A Comparative Study in American and South African History* (New York: Oxford University Press, 1981), pp. 221–227, 234–238; Tuttle, *Race Riot;* Thomas L. Philpott, *The Slum and the Ghetto: Neighborhood Deterioration and Middle-Class Reform, 1880–1930* (New York: Oxford University Press, 1978); Drake and Cayton, *Black Metropolis,* I, pp. xliii–xlviii; Harold Baron and Bennett Hymer, "The Negro Worker in the Chicago Labor Market: A Case Study of De Facto Segregation," in Julius Jacobson, ed., *The Negro and the American Labor Market* (Garden City, N.Y.: Anchor Books, 1968), pp. 232–285; Hirsch, *Making the Second Ghetto,* pp. 1–67; Strickland, *History of the Chicago Urban League,* pp. 216–217. Though the black middle class was expanding, blacks on average earned far less than whites. The median family income for whites in 1960 was $7,200; for nonwhites, $4,700. CCHR, "The Growing Negro Middle Class," p. 2.

13. Pierre de Vise, "Chicago's Widening Color Gap," Interuniversity Social Research Committee, Report no. 2 (Chicago: Community and Family Study Center, 1967), pp. 58–82, 145–146; Harold Baron, "Black Powerlessness in Chicago," *Trans-action,* Nov. 1968, pp. 27–33; "James Orange: With the People," p. 113; Hampton and Fayer, eds., *Voices of Freedom,* p. 300; Collier interview.

14. Farmer, *Lay Bare the Heart,* pp. 9–30; Carson, *In Struggle,* p. 157; James Forman, *The Making of Black Revolutionaries,* rev. ed. (Washington, D.C.: Open Hand, 1985), pp. 316–326. Bernard LaFayette was called the "John the Baptist" of the civil rights crusade by more than one activist. Father Daniel Mallette interview, 28 July 1986, Chicago.

15. LaFayette interview; Herman Jenkins interview, 16 Sept. 1991, New York; Jehnsen interview; Hollins interview. For more on AFSC's Urban Affairs Program, see memo, "PPC Funds for Chicago Urban Affairs Program," Kale

Williams to Barbara Moffett and Charlotte Meacham, 11 April 1966, AFSC papers, 1966 CRD Housing Program, box 4, AFSC Archives. For an example of LaFayette's activities, see LaFayette, Monthly Report for August 1965, AFSC papers, 1965 CRD Housing Program, box 3, AFSC Archives.

16. Hirsch, *Making the Second Ghetto,* pp. 192–193; Squires et al., *Chicago,* pp. 25–32; *CDN,* 6 June 1966, pp. 1, 54; Nancy Jefferson interview with Robert Jordan, July 1986, Chicago; *CDN,* 10 June 1966, p. 35. William Briggs, Samuel Smithe, and Meredith Gilbert offer a description of the region in "Testimony Given before Robert Mann Commission Investigating Slum Housing," Gilbert Cornfield files, Chicago. Alphine Jefferson's "Housing Discrimination and Community Response in North Lawndale (Chicago), Illinois, 1948–1978" (Ph.D. diss., Duke University, 1979) is also helpful.

17. *CT,* 13 March 1966, p. 6; Lew Kreinberg interview, 11 Aug. 1986, Chicago; Mallette interview; Jehnsen interview; Briggs interview.

18. Hampton and Fayer, eds., *Voices of Freedom,* p. 299; Bevel interview; Collier interview.

19. "Executive Staff Meeting," 26–28 Aug. 1965, MLK papers, box 32-9, MLK Library; James Bevel, "Direct Action Report, Chicago, Illinois," 12–13 April 1966, SCLC papers, box 131-10, MLK Library; *CD,* 4–10 Sept. 1965, p. 1; Anderson and Pickering, "The Issue of the Color Line," pp. 770–772. Other civil rights groups had spoken of the need to relate more fully to the black poor. See Meier and Rudwick, *CORE,* pp. 313–318.

20. *CST,* 12 Sept. 1965, p. 38; *CA,* 17 Oct. 1965, p. 2.

21. Bevel, "SCLC–Chicago Project," 26 Oct. 1965, MLK papers, box 5-26, MLK Library; Collier interview. Many of Bevel's reports were actually written by his assistant, Mary Lou Finley. She also wrote about the Chicago campaign as a graduate student in sociology at the University of Chicago. Finley interview (telephone), 11 March and 5 May 1989, Seattle.

22. "JOIN Progress Report, December 16, 1965," SDS papers, series 2.B-54 (microfilm); Bevel interview; Bevel, "SCLC–Chicago Project," 8 Nov. 1965, SCLC papers, box 150-22, MLK Library; "Activities of HOP/Chicago's New Assistant Director, or Footsteps of Neophyte Jerry Davis," 20 Sept.–3 Oct. 1965, AFSC papers, 1965 CRD Housing Program, box 3, AFSC Archives. In large part because of these workshops, Jimmy Collier of SCLC thought the Chicago project was "a well-planned campaign compared to others we had been involved in." Collier interview.

23. Bevel interview; Finley interview; Fairclough, *To Redeem the Soul,* p. 167; Mueller interview; Richard Murray interview, 31 Aug. 1988, Chicago; Collier interview; Patti Miller Stone interview (telephone), 2 Sept. and 2 Nov. 1988, Fairfield, Iowa; Gamwell interview; "Report by Susannah Gross, October 11–25, 1965," AFSC papers, 1965 CRD Housing Program, box 3, AFSC Archives; Bevel, "SCLC–Chicago Project," 26 Oct. 1965, MLK papers, box 5-26, MLK Library. Bevel wore a yarmulke because he identified with many Judaic concepts. *CST,* 12 Sept. 1965, p. 36. On Bevel's philosophy, see "James Bevel," 2 April 1965

and 3 April 1965, Bevel file, folder 1, UIC. Not one to set his thoughts in writing, Bevel seemed to exemplify the "organic intellectual." For a discussion of this type of intellectual, see George Lipsitz, *A Life in the Struggle: Ivory Perry and the Culture of Opposition* (Philadelphia: Temple University Press, 1988), pp. 9–11. Bevel's outlook, unlike Perry's, was shaped by the Christian tradition.

24. Alvin Pitcher, "The Chicago Freedom Movement: What Is It?," Nov. 1966, in David J. Garrow, ed., *Chicago 1966: Open Housing Marches, Summit Negotiations, and Operation Breadbasket* (New York: Carlson, 1989), p. 175; Fairclough, *To Redeem the Soul*, pp. 4, 168; Finley interview; Carson, *In Struggle*, pp. 20, 24, 30, 137–141; James Miller, *"Democracy Is in the Streets": From Port Huron to the Siege of Chicago* (New York: Simon and Schuster, 1987), pp. 141–154, 196–198, 204–208, 214–217, 225–226.

25. "Report by Susannah Gross," AFSC papers, 1965 CRD Housing Program, box 3, AFSC Archives; Jenkins interview; Hollins interview; Mary Lou Finley, "The Open Housing Marches: Chicago, Summer '66," Spring 1967, in Garrow, ed., *Chicago 1966*, p. 3.

26. Miller Stone interview; Briggs interview; Moyer, "Housing Opportunities Program: Chicago Metropolitan Area, October 1965–October 1966," AFSC papers, 1966 CRD Housing Program, box 4, AFSC Archives; Mueller interview. Sara Evans's and Harry Boyte's concept of "free space" is useful in uncovering the deeper meaning of the Wider Community Staff and other movement-related meetings. Difficult to define, free spaces are usually settings in which "ordinary citizens can act with dignity, independence, and vision." See Sara M. Evans and Harry C. Boyte, *Free Spaces: The Sources of Democratic Change in America* (New York: Harper & Row, 1986), pp. 17–25, 182–202.

27. *CST*, 12 Sept. 1965, p. 36; Jehnsen interview; Jenkins interview; Anderson and Pickering, "The Issue of the Color Line," p. 777; Anderson and Pickering, *Confronting the Color Line*, pp. 176–178, 184. There were plans drawn in the summer of 1965 for a school campaign "until Willis is dropped." See especially the proposal from Walter Fauntroy's office, "Programatic [*sic*] Action Proposal for Chicago," MLK papers, box 5-26, MLK Library.

28. Bevel interview; Finley interview; Hollins interview; Collier interview; memo, "Speech by Reverend James Bevels [*sic*]," Sergeant John P. O'Malley and Patrolman Elliot A. Mathews to Deputy Superintendent, 9 Feb. 1966, Msgr. Daniel Cantwell papers, box 35-7, CHS; "Nonviolence and the Chicago Movement," CCMS papers, vol. 3, WSCP–Budgets and Staff Meetings folder, CTS; "Why a Non-Violent Movement?," WSCP papers, box 1-1, UIC; *CDN*, 16 July 1966, p. 15; Anderson and Pickering, *Confronting the Color Line*, p. 183.

29. Bevel, "SCLC–Chicago Project," 26 Oct. 1965, MLK papers, box 5-26, MLK Library; Garrow, *Bearing the Cross*, p. 452; *West Side Torch*, 14 Oct. 1965, p. 1, and 11 Nov. 1965, p. 1, UIC; Bernard LaFayette, Monthly Report, Oct. 1965, AFSC papers, 1965 CRD Housing Program, box 3, AFSC Archives.

30. Bevel, "SCLC–Chicago Project," 26 Oct. 1965, MLK papers, box 5-26, MLK Library; Bevel, "SCLC—Chicago Project," 8 Nov. 1965, SCLC papers, box

150-22, MLK Library; *CDD*, 30 Nov. 1965, p. 11; Mueller, "Proposal for a Program of Community Development for Social Change," p. 8, Jehnsen materials, 86-2-120, MLK Library.

31. Pitcher, "The Chicago Freedom Movement," pp. 174–175; Abernathy, *And the Walls Came Tumbling Down*, p. 372; Anderson and Pickering, *Confronting the Color Line*, p. 177; Raby interview; Raby conversation with Williams; Jehnsen interview; Miller Stone interview. Frustrated by Bevel, Bill Berry of the Urban League once said that he "just did not want to have any more to do with him." Berry conversation with Kale Williams, 1972, Chicago.

32. Finley, "The Open Housing Marches," p. 2; Garrow, *Bearing the Cross*, pp. 448–451; Fairclough, *To Redeem the Soul*, pp. 165–167; Kreinberg interview; McDermott interview; Miller Stone interview. Bill Berry believed Young was "pretty fundamental," someone who "understood how the world moved." Berry conversation with Williams. Some West Side organizers, in contrast, thought Young was a restraining force on the movement. Jenkins and Hollins interviews.

33. Garrow, *Bearing the Cross*, pp. 448–449; Anderson and Pickering, *Confronting the Color Line*, p. 183; *NYT*, 11 Oct. 1965, p. 44; *New World*, 15 Oct. 1965, p. 22.

34. Anderson and Pickering, *Confronting the Color Line*, p. 185; Lucas interview; CIC Board of Directors Meeting minutes, 14 Oct. 1965, CIC papers, box 110, CHS.

35. Mary Lou Finley to Doug Finley, 27 November 1965, copy in author's possession; Finley interview; Collier interview; Jehnsen interview.

36. Résumé of ESCRU Board discussion, 13 Nov. 1965, ESCRU papers, box 62-3, MLK Library; *CDD*, 10 Jan. 1966, p. 10; Bruce Cook, "King in Chicago," *Commonweal*, 29 April 1966, p. 176; Peggy Way to Don Benedict, 15 Nov. 1965, CCMS papers, vol. 3, WSCP–Budget and Staff Meetings folder, CTS; Anderson and Pickering, *Confronting the Color Line*, pp. 185–186.

37. Bernard LaFayette, Monthly Report for September 1965, AFSC papers, CRD 1965 Housing Program, box 3, AFSC Archives; Anderson and Pickering, *Confronting the Color Line*, p. 188; Peggy [Way] to Don Benedict, 1 Dec. 1965, CCMS papers, vol. 7, WSCP–Federation folder, CTS; West Chatham Community Improvement Association, SCLC papers, box 47-4, MLK Library; memo [Robert F. Squires], 6 Jan. 1966, Egan papers, box 19, University of Notre Dame Archives; Way to Benedict, 15 Nov. 1965, CCMS papers, vol. 3, WSCP–Budget and Staff Meetings folder, CTS.

38. One veteran Chicago activist, Gus Savage, recalls urging King not to focus on the West Side because its residents lacked the resources to underpin the Chicago Freedom Movement. Travis, *An Autobiography of Black Politics*, pp. 255–256.

39. *CDD*, 24 Jan. 1966, p. 3, 27 Jan. 1966, p. 3; Coretta Scott King, *My Life with Martin Luther King, Jr.*, pp. 278–279; *CT*, 26 Jan. 1966, p. 8. No one, however, fixed up Ralph Abernathy's West Side apartment. Abernathy, *And the Walls*

Came Tumbling Down (New York: Harper & Row, 1989), p. 371. By residing on the West Side, King, according to Al Raby, was stating that he "was not going to ignore this community." Raby interview.

40. Stanley Levison to unidentified, FBI 100-111180-9-NR, 14 March 1966; *CD*, 29 Jan.–4 Feb. 1966, p. 1; letter to MLK, 7 Feb. 1966, MLK papers, box 96-13; letter to MLK, from 300 block of West 18th Street, n.d., ibid., box 95-7; MLK to Bayard Rustin and Stanley Levison, 1 Feb. 1966, FBI 100-111180-9-837; *LAT*, 21 Jan. 1966, p. 16; *NYT*, 27 Jan. 1966, p. 37; *CSM*, 31 Jan. 1966, p. 3.

41. *CD*, 19–25 Feb. 1966, p. 1; Rose interview. One black Chicagoan minister, A. P. Jackson, knew that this episode was not simply trivial. "There was a picture in *Jet* magazine of Dr. King shooting pool," Jackson remembered. "I guess that would shock a lot of conservative religious folks. There was a preacher shooting pool." Jackson interview. Gary Marx's 1964 surveys are especially illuminating on the question of King's popularity. Unlike most pollsters, Marx sought information on the climate of black opinion in a number of specific cities. In Marx's surveys, an overwhelming number of black Chicagoans (92 percent) selected Martin Luther King as the single man who had "done the most to help Negroes." King also received a very low disapproval rating. Gary T. Marx, *Protest and Prejudice: A Study of Belief in the Black Community* (New York: Harper & Row, 1967), pp. 26–27. In a 1967 survey of Chicago black opinion Martin Luther King once again achieved very high approval ratings. Donald J. Bogue and Richard McKinlay, "Militancy for and against Civil Rights and Integration in Chicago: Summer 1967," Interuniversity Social Research Committee, Report no. 1 (Chicago: Community and Family Study Center, 1967), pp. 51–53.

42. Mallette interview; *NYT*, 24 Feb. 1966, p. 75; Garrow, *Bearing the Cross*, pp. 461–462. King had already visited 1321 South Homan and had met with the Towneses, the family in need in the building. *CDN*, 11 Feb. 1966, p. 10.

43. *CDD*, 24 Feb. 1966, p. 3 and 28 Feb. 1966, p. 3; *NYT*, 24 Feb. 1966, p. 75, 5 March 1966, p. 10; *CDN*, 24 Feb. 1966, p. 3. That Bender owned the 1321 South Homan building was particularly unfortunate. In the press, Bender was described as a good, honest man, plagued by emphysema, who was losing sleep over the takeover. He died a few months later.

44. For a profile of the Townes family, see Betty Washington's series in *CDD*, 14–17 March 1966, p. 4.

45. *NYT*, 24 Feb. 1966, p. 75, 25 Feb. 1966, p. 18; Kreinberg interview; Mallette interview; letter to MLK, from 900 block of West Cullerton, 7 March 1966, box 95-19, and letter to MLK, 9 March 1966, box 96-1, in MLK papers, MLK Library. Kreinberg, like many West Side activists, sought to make sure that King's presence would not simply aid the national movement but improve the quality of life of local residents. King's advisers were also aware that King's time in Chicago should be carefully planned. "Dr. King's chief role will be the detailed selling of ideas," one memo read. "In mass meetings, his role should be one of teaching, not preaching." "Phase 1: Orientation and Indoctrination," Ralph Helstein papers, box 8, SHSW, Madison, Wis. My understanding of Chicago activ-

ists' mobilizing efforts has been enriched by Lawrence Goodwyn's commentary on movement building in *The Populist Moment: A Short History of the Agrarian Revolt in America* (New York: Oxford University Press, 1978). See especially pages vii–xxiv, 20–94.

46. Bevel interview; Murray interview; "Minutes—East Garfield Park Leadership Conference," 8 Jan. 1966, and "Planning Committee Meeting," 11 Jan. 1966, AFSC papers, Chicago R.O. 1966, UAP–East Garfield Park Community Development folder, AFSC Archives; Charles Livermore, "Resume of a Speech Made by Rev. James Bevel," 14 Sept. 1965, Cantwell papers, box 14-1, CHS; Joel Schwartz, "Tenant Power in the Liberal City, 1943–1971," in Ronald Lawson, ed., *The Tenant Movement in New York City, 1904–1984* (New Brunswick, N.J.: Rutgers University Press, 1986), pp. 172–179; Meier and Rudwick, *CORE,* pp. 244–246; Miller, *"Democracy Is in the Streets,"* pp. 184–217; Collier interview. Mary Lou Finley credited Bevel with the "inspiration about how we might go about organizing the ghetto"—the tenant union. Finley to Doug Finley, 27 Nov. 1965, copy in author's possession.

47. Silberman, *Crisis in Black and White,* pp. 331, 334–335; Fish, *Black Power/White Control,* pp. 3–65; Horwitt, *Let Them Call Me Rebel,* pp. 363–449.

48. *CDD,* 4 Feb. 1965, pp. 3, 12; Gamwell, "The West Side Christian Parish," pp. 18–20; minutes, 13 Sept. 1965, CCMS papers, vol. 6, WSCP–Programs folder, CTS; "Statement of Objectives and Programs: October, 1965," ibid.; *CA,* 6 June 1966, pp. 1, 6; Robert Mueller, "History of the West Side Christian Parish," CCMS papers, vol. 6, WSCP–Programs folder, CTS. I disagree with David Satter's analysis that "[w]hat SCLC plans to do on the West Side, is very similar to what Saul Alinsky and the IAF did in Woodlawn." Satter, "The West Side and the Plight of the Urban Poor," *Chicago Maroon Magazine,* 4 March 1966, p. 1.

49. Bevel interview. Harry C. Boyte has discerned a hardening of Alinsky's philosophy from the 1940s to the 1960s. See Boyte, *CommonWealth: A Return to Citizen Politics* (New York: Free Press, 1989), pp. 47–62, 67–68, 75–76, 184.

50. William Moyer interview (telephone), 6 Aug. 1988 and 8 Oct. 1966, San Francisco; Jehnsen interview; Collier interview; Mueller, "Proposal for a Program of Community Development for Social Change," Jehnsen materials, 86-2-120, MLK Library; "Community Relations Roundup," 9–14 Dec. 1965, Barbara Moffett files, Philadelphia. Evidently not all SCLC leaders were averse to Alinsky methods. C. T. Vivian interview with Vincent Browne, 20 Feb. 1968, Chicago, MSRC, Howard University, Washington, D.C. Some SCLC field staffers did not think much of these strategic debates. Hollins interview. Alinsky retained sympathizers even among those who aided the freedom movement. Kreinberg interview and Kris Ronnow interview, 24 Aug. 1987, Chicago.

51. FBI 100-106670-2267, 2 Feb. 1966; "Report on Southern Christian Leadership Conference Mass Meeting in Garfield Park," Charles O. Ross to John H. Ballard, 2 Feb. 1966, WCMC papers, box 91-7, CHS; *CD,* 29 Jan.–4 Feb. 1966, p. 1. For a report on civil rights organizing, see *NYT,* 27 Jan. 1966, p. 37.

52. *CD,* 5–11 Feb. 1966, p. 1; *The New Guidepost,* June 1962, Faith Rich

papers, box 1-4, SHSW; Mueller, "Executive Director's Report," 10 Feb. 1966, WSCP papers, box 1-1, UIC; FBI 100-106670-2288, 8 Feb. 1966.

53. Mueller, "Executive Director's Report," 10 Feb. 1966, WSCP papers, box 1-1, UIC. For more information on the evolution of the East Garfield Park Union to End Slums, see memo, "Proposal for a Union to End Slums," Housing Committee–East Garfield Park Conference to End Slums to Steering Committee–East Garfield Park, 3 March 1966, Jehnsen materials, 86-2-63, MLK Library; "Agreement between Condor-Costalis Real Estate Company and East Garfield Park Union to End Slums," 13 July 1966, Gilbert Cornfield files. The EGPUES was intended to be a federation; it did not wish to supplant existing organizations. Not all East Garfield Park organizations affiliated with the EGPUES. The Midwest Community Council was an important holdout. Urban Affairs Weekly Report, 2 April 1967, AFSC papers, 1967 CRD Housing Program, box 4, AFSC Archives.

54. Jehnsen interview; *CDD*, 16 May 1966, p. 3; *CDN*, 9 June 1966, pp. 3–4.

55. By design the EGPUES closely resembled a labor union. See Mueller, "Proposal for a Program of Community Development for Social Change," p. 8, Jehnsen materials, 86-2-120, MLK Library; Bevel, "Direct Action Report," 12–13 April 1966, SCLC papers, box 131-10, MLK Library; memo, "Proposal for a Union to End Slums," 3 March 1966, Jehnsen materials, 86-2-63, MLK Library; Jehnsen interview.

56. Briggs interview; *Quaker Services*, Spring 1968, AFSC papers, 1968 CRD Housing and Urban Affairs, box 3, AFSC Archives; Minnie Dunlap and Lela Mosley interviews, 29 Aug. 1988, Chicago; Henry Santiestevan, "Fresh Wind in the Ghetto," *Agenda*, Feb. 1967, pp. 9–10; *CDN*, 9 June 1966, p. 4.

57. "We Are Being Robbed" flyer, Jehnsen material, 86-2-66, MLK Library; "Who Makes and What Is a Slum" flyer, ibid., 86-2-67; "Together: An Introduction to the Union to End Slums" brochure, ibid., 86-2-71; Mueller, "Proposal for a Program of Community Development for Social Change," pp. 3–4, ibid., 86-2-120. Some residents were disturbed by the militant, inflammatory rhetoric employed by some organizers. Kenneth Young to MLK, 23 March 1966, MLK papers, box 38-9, MLK Library.

58. Jenkins interview; Jehnsen interview; memo, Samuel Smithe and Meredith Gilbert to Southern Christian Leadership Conference, 20 Feb. 1967, SCLC papers, box 46-17, MLK Library; memo, Gilbert Feldman to Charles Chiakulas, "Tenants Union to End Slums," 15 July 1966, Charles Chiakulas papers, box 33, Tenants Action Committee folder, Walter Reuther Library, Detroit.

59. Hollins interview. A review of SCLC financial records suggests that there were at least nineteen workers on subsistence status in Chicago by the spring of 1966. The following were listed as subsistence workers at some point between January 1966 and May 1966: Lynn Adler, Luis Andrades, Charles Billups, Carolyn Black, Julian Brown, Jimmy Collier, Mary Lou Finley, Suzi Hill, Billy Hollins, Claudia King, Sherrie Land, Charles Love, Bennie Luchion, Earless Ross, Brenda Travis, Monroe Walker, Jimmy Wilson, Maurice Woodard, Dorothy

Wright. SCLC papers, boxes 90-2, 90-7, 91-9, 92-4, 92-8, 93-3, 93-11, 94-5, MLK Library.

60. Jenkins interview; Collier interview; Finley, "The Open Housing Marches," p. 6; Finley interview; *CD,* 12–18 March 1966, p. 1; Hollins interview. A note to SCLC headquarters captured the problems faced by the Chicago staff. "In the Urban Movement," the memo stated, "we have found that it takes a very creative worker with a large degree of self-discipline and individual autonomy to survive. There is apparently a great transition from the rural black belt to the Robert Taylor homes of Chicago." SCLC leaders, it continued, had "failed to provide the necessary orientation and creative guidelines whereby one might easily make that transition." Memo, SCLC Field Staff to SCLC Executive Staff, SCLC papers, box 145-16, MLK Library.

61. *CD,* 19–25 Feb. 1966, p. 1; Briggs interview; Santiestevan, "Fresh Wind in the Ghetto," pp. 9–12; CCCO newsletter, March 1966, p. 3, CCCO papers, box 2-10, MLK Library; "Agreement between Condor-Costalis Real Estate Company and the East Garfield Park Union to End Slums," 13 July 1966, Cornfield files; FBI 100-106670-2424, 29 March 1966; Morgan, "Requiem or Revival?," pp. 70–75; Jehnsen interview.

62. Urban Affairs Weekly Report, 19 June 1966, 10 July 1966, 17 July 1966, and Urban Affairs Report, 26 June and 3 July 1966, AFSC papers, 1966 CRD Housing Program, box 4, AFSC Archives; "CORE Northern Project: Chicago, Ill.," ca. 1964, CORE papers, box 92, MLK Library; Fish, *Black Power/White Control,* pp. 60–61; Meier and Rudwick, *CORE,* p. 245; Gilbert Cornfield, "A Review of Tenant Organizations in Chicago," Cornfield files; Gilbert Cornfield interview, 21 July 1988, Chicago. William Briggs and Bruce D. Christie, "The Anatomy of a Struggle for Tenants' Rights," in *Renewal,* March 1967, pp. 21–22, chronicles the conflict between East Garfield Park residents and Condor and Costalis. Bernadine Dohrn, a University of Chicago law student and a future member of the Weatherman underground organization, was among students helping tenants.

63. Only a month before JOIN (Jobs or Income Now), an outgrowth of SDS organizing in a lower-class, largely white Chicago neighborhood, had forged a tenant-landlord pact with a local landlord, perhaps the first of its kind. The Condor and Costalis agreement was even more revolutionary than the JOIN accord. *CST,* 26 May 1966, pp. 4, 36. "Agreement," 20 May 1966, SDS papers, series 2.B-46 (microfilm); "Agreement between Condor-Costalis," 13 July 1966, Cornfield files. The introduction of the agreement noted that "Unique among its features is its recognition of the tenants' right to withhold their rent if the landlord violates the contract. There have been other written agreements between landlords and tenants in which the landlord agreed to make certain repairs in his building; but these agreements did not provide for direct and immediate tenant recourse through rent strikes if the agreement were violated." The agreement also provided the tenants with the right to sue in the event of landlord noncompliance. See also Gilbert Feldman testimony in Sol Tax, ed., *The*

People vs. The System: A Dialogue in Urban Conflict (Chicago: Acme Press, 1968), p. 278. It is difficult to measure precisely how revolutionary this agreement was because of the highly localized nature of rent strikes across the country. Schwartz, "Tenant Power," in Lawson, ed., *The Tenant Movement in New York City*, pp. 134–208, offers a useful comparison.

64. Jenkins interview; Gilbert Cornfield, untitled paper on tenant unions, Cornfield files.

65. Livermore, "Resume of a Speech Made by Rev. James Bevel," 14 Sept. 1965, Cantwell papers, box 14-1, CHS; MLK, "Why Chicago Is the Target," *Amsterdam News*, 11 Sept. 1965, p. 16; *Illinois State Register*, 7 Oct. 1965, p. 2.

66. Al Raby to CCCO Delegates, "Proposals for Coordinating and Servicing Member Organizations and the Chicago Freedom Movement," ca. early 1966, CCCO papers, box 1-17, MLK Library; Anderson and Pickering, *Confronting the Color Line*, p. 188.

67. *CDD*, 4 Jan. 1966, p. 3; Orfield, *The Reconstruction of Southern Education*, p. 198; *CDD*, 1 Dec. 1965, p. 1, 13 Dec. 1965, p. 3, 17 Jan. 1966, p. 3, 19 Jan. 1966, p. 3, 27 Jan. 1966, p. 3, 21 Feb. 1966, p. 3, 24 Feb. 1966, p. 3, 17 March 1966, p. 3; *CDN*, 24 Feb. 1966, p. 3; "Mobilization Plans," March 1966, SCLC papers, box 46-17, MLK Library. Some observers believed that Chuchut was unfairly singled out by "a small hard core of fanatics." Cyrus Adams to Carl A. Fuqua, 22 March 1966, Adams papers, box 18-3, CHS.

68. *CDN*, 27 May 1966, p. 4; Bernard Brown, *Ideology and Community Action: The West Side Organization of Chicago, 1964–1967* (Chicago: Center for the Scientific Study of Religion, 1978), pp. 61–63.

69. Chafe, *Civilities and Civil Rights*, pp. 119–152; Barbara Reynolds, *Jesse Jackson: The Man, the Movement, the Myth* (Chicago: Nelson-Hall, 1975), pp. 18–46.

70. FBI 100-106670-2288, 8 Feb. 1966; "Kenwood-Oakland Community Organization History," CUL papers (76-116), box 159-16, UIC; CCCO newsletter, Jan. 1966 and Feb. 1966, CCCO papers, box 2-10, MLK Library; "K.O.C.O. Progress Report," 13 Oct. 1966, CUL papers (76-116), box 159-16, UIC; Raby conversation with Williams; *CD*, 5–11 Feb. 1966, p. 2.

71. Gary Massoni, "Perspectives on Operation Breadbasket," in Garrow, ed., *Chicago 1966*, pp. 193–194; David Wallace, "From the Fullness of the Earth: The Story of Chicago's Operation Breadbasket," *Chicago Theological Seminary Register*, Nov. 1966, p. 16; Drake and Cayton, *Black Metropolis*, II, pp. 412–429; C. Eric Lincoln and Lawrence H. Mamiya, *The Black Church in the African American Experience* (Durham, N.C.: Duke University Press, 1990), pp. 207–212. Franklin H. Littell of the Chicago Theological Seminary was also involved in the early discussions. Evans came to Chicago from Brownsville, Tennessee, in 1945. Only after meeting Jesse Jackson, his biographer writes, did "Evans' eyes" begin "to open" to the extent of racial inequality in Chicago. Dorothy June Rose, *From Plough Handle to Pulpit: The Life Story of Rev. Clay Evans* (Ivyland, Penn.: Neibauer Press, 1981), pp. 44–45.

72. Fairclough, *To Redeem the Soul*, p. 177; Drake and Cayton, *Black Metropo-*

lis, II, pp. 743–744; Meier and Rudwick, *CORE,* pp. 188–190, 234–235; *CDD,* 28 March 1966, p. 4, 11 July 1963, p. 3, 15 July 1963, p. 3, 3 Sept. 1963, p. 4, 5 Sept. 1963, pp. 3, 6, 23 Sept. 1963, p. 2, 1 Oct. 1963, p. 3, 1 July 1964, p. 13; Moyer interview; *The Crisis,* Feb. 1964, pp. 116–121.

73. FBI 100-106670-NR, 22 Nov. 1965; Garrow, *Bearing the Cross,* p. 462; *CD,* 5–11 Feb. 1966, pp. 1–2; Massoni, "Perspectives on Operation Breadbasket," pp. 194–195. The Reverend John Porter and the Reverend George Edgar Riddick of the Church Federation of Greater Chicago and Chicago SNCC believed that one of the great weaknesses of the Chicago movement until the ascendancy of Operation Breadbasket in 1967 was the lack of pastors in positions of leadership. Porter interview, 12 Aug. 1986, Chicago; and Riddick, "The Movement: Quo Vadis, Watchman?," *SNCC: Notes and Comments,* April 1966, Chicago CORE papers, box 4-29, CHS. The Reverend A. P. Jackson disputes this assessment; he believes that though neither Raby nor Berry had religious backgrounds, they, like other CCCO leaders, recognized the importance of the black churches. Jackson interview. In 1965, leading black ministers had formed "Clergy for Quality and Equality in Education" to protest school segregation. Although it collaborated with CCCO's anti-Willis efforts, the group remained distinct—as the ministers desired. Anderson and Pickering, *Confronting the Color Line,* p. 152. The African Methodist Episcopal Church offered its support to the Chicago crusade in September. *CST,* 10 Sept. 1965, p. 32.

74. FBI 100-106670-2303, 14 Feb. 1966; FBI 100-106670-2325, 21 Feb. 1965; Massoni, "Perspectives on Operation Breadbasket," pp. 198–199.

75. Massoni, "Perspectives on Operation Breadbasket," pp. 198–203; Wallace, "From the Fullness of the Earth," pp. 16–20.

76. Memo to J. H. Johnson and Hale Nelson, 20 Jan. 1966, LCMOC papers, box 154, CHS. On Chicagoans' contribution to the Albany campaign, see Stephen Rose, "Albany, Georgia: A Report," *New City,* Oct. 1, 1962, pp. 7–9. The *New World,* 12 March 1965, p. 2, and 2 April 1965, p. 2, chronicles the reactions of Chicagoans who traveled to Selma. The Chicago Freedom Movement also sought the backing of Chicago's growing Latin-American community. See *CDD,* 16 June 1966, p. 4.

77. *Chicago Maroon,* 22 Oct. 1965, p. 6, 1 Feb. 1966, pp. 1–2, 1 July 1966, p. 8; *CDD,* 15 March 1966, p. 9; FBI 100-438794-1181, 17 Feb. 1966; *Chicago Illini,* 11 April 1966, p. 1; Haynes Johnson, "Martin Luther King Goes North," *Washington Evening Star,* 17 April 1966, pp. 1, 12; *CDN,* 31 May 1966, p. 3, 22 June 1966, p. 19; *Chicago Maroon,* 24 June 1966, p. 1; Miller Stone interview.

78. FBI 100-106670-2362, 1 March 1966; FBI 100-438794-NR, 8 March 1966; FBI 100-106670-2303, 14 Feb. 1966.

79. MLK speeches, 17 Sept. 1965, before District 65, UAW, and 7 Oct. 1965, before Illinois AFL-CIO, MLK speech file, MLK Library; *Illinois State Register,* 7 Oct. 1965, pp. 1–2; Foner, *Organized Labor and the Black Worker,* pp. 332–354. For criticism of organized labor's race record, see Herbert Hill, "The Racial Practices of Organized Labor: The Contemporary Record," in Jacobson, ed., *The Negro and*

the American Labor Movement, pp. 286–357. Convinced that the labor and civil rights movements had much in common, Bevel had addressed a group of labor leaders and encouraged their participation in planned protest activities. FBI 100-438794-844, 1 Nov. 1965.

80. Barbara Warne Newell, *Chicago and the Labor Movement: Metropolitan Unionism in the 1930s* (Urbana: University of Illinois Press, 1961), pp. 221–224; Milton Derber, *Labor in Illinois: The Affluent Years, 1945–1980* (Urbana: University of Illinois Press, 1989), pp. 230–251; J. David Greenstone, *Labor in American Politics,* 3rd ed. (Chicago: University of Chicago Press, 1977), pp. 81–106.

81. *CST,* 26 July 1950, p. 43; Sidney Lens, "Radical without a Cause," *Chicago,* May 1980, pp. 179–181, 217; *Federation News,* 4 Feb. 1950, p. 1; Tuttle, *Race Riot,* pp. 108–156; Drake and Cayton, *Black Metropolis,* I, pp. 312–342; Newell, *Chicago and the Labor Movement,* pp. 236–242; Chicago Area Chapter of Negro American Labor Council, "What Is the Council?," Timuel Black papers, box 3, CHS; Derber, *Labor in Illinois,* pp. 74–76, 395–396. For evidence of the CFL's support for the national civil rights movement, see *Federation News,* 20 June 1964, p. 1, 20 March 1965, pp. 1, 4, 3 April 1965, p. 7. Before the Illinois Rally for Civil Rights in 1964, the CFL "urged all affiliates to support the rally and to send representatives to the rally."

82. Anderson and Pickering, *Confronting the Color Line,* p. 174; Charles Hayes interview with Rick Halpern and Roger Horowitz, 27 May 1986, tape 152, side 2, UPWA Oral History Project, SHSW; Charles Hayes to Charles Chiakulas, 4 Feb. 1966, Chiakulas papers, box 31, Reuther Library; William Lee to Charles Hayes, 4 Feb. and 8 Feb. 1966, William Lee papers, box 12-7, CHS; *Packinghouse Worker,* March 1966, p. 3, April 1966, p. 7; Foner, *Organized Labor and the Black Worker,* p. 363; *CT,* 17 Feb. 1966, p. 20; *CST,* 17 Feb. 1966, p. 28.

83. Hayes to Lee, 18 Feb. 1966, and Lee to Hayes, 25 Feb. 1966, William Lee papers, box 12-7, CHS; *Federation News,* Jan.-Sept. 1966; Hill interview; handwritten minutes on back of "Proposal: Establishment of Five Trade Union Centers," Chiakulas papers, boxes 30 and 33, Reuther Library; Chiakulas to Jack Conway, box 31, and "Conference on Working Poor and Union Centers," 31 March 1966, box 31, ibid. The CFL-owned radio station, WCFL, did provide solid coverage of the Chicago Freedom Movement, according to Don Rose and Junius Griffin. *Federation News,* 5 Sept. 1966, p. 50.

84. Melody Heaps conversation (telephone), 23 July 1992, Chicago; "Proposal: Establishment of Five Trade Union Centers," box 33; Chiakulas to Jack Conway, 27 April 1966, box 31; SCLC, CCCO, and Chicago Project to Jack Conway, box 33, SCLC folder; "Conference on Working Poor and Union Centers," 31 March 1966, box 32; untitled overview of Community Unions, box 30; "Program for Organizing Unemployed and Underemployed in Chicago," box 33. All of these documents are in the Chiakulas papers, Reuther Library. See also *CDD,* 4 Aug. 1966, p. 6.

85. Heather Tobis Booth interview (telephone), 22 Sept. 1991, Washington, D.C.; Cornfield interview; Bevel, "Direct Action Report," 12–13 April 1966,

SCLC papers, box 131-10, MLK Library; Derber, *Labor in Illinois*, pp. 142–146; Jerry Wurf to MLK, 8 Feb. 1967, MLK papers, box 5-31, MLK Library; Garrow, *Bearing the Cross*, p. 536; Joan Turner Beifuss, *At the River I Stand: Memphis, the 1968 Strike, and Martin Luther King* (New York: Carlson, reprint, 1989). Throughout the late winter and spring of 1966 there were occasional reports on the organizing initiative. It was never a major Chicago Freedom Movement focus, however.

86. Stephen C. Rowe, "Some Notes on the History and Present Moment of the Chicago Conference on Religion and Race," and anonymous, "The Chicago Conference on Religion and Race," CCRR papers, CHS; Mathew Ahmann, ed., *Race: Challenge to Religion* (Chicago: Henry Regnery, 1963), p. 167; memo to J. H. Johnson and Hale Nelson, 20 Jan. 1966, LCMOC papers, box 154, CHS. Many members of the CCRR were influential laypeople. In the fall, Bevel met with the CCRR to brief it on SCLC's plans for a Chicago movement. Executive Board Meeting, 21 Oct. 1965, CCRR papers, box 3, CHS.

87. *Chicago Reporter*, Nov. 1984, pp. 6–7; *NCR*, 23 June 1965, p. 1; Charles Dahm, *Power and Authority in the Catholic Church: Cardinal Cody in Chicago* (Notre Dame: University of Notre Dame Press, 1981), pp. 2, 16–17.

88. Mallette interview; McDermott interview; Horwitt, *Let Them Call Me Rebel*, pp. 372–373, 388–389; "A Report on Our Program and Our Progress in the Negro Convert-Apostolate," in "The Catholic Church and the Negro," 1960, p. 4, CUL papers (76-116), box 158-34, UIC. Boxes 2386, 2396, 2397, 2789, 3394 in the Cardinal Albert Meyer papers, Archives, Archdiocese of Chicago, are also helpful in understanding the Catholic Church's relationship to racial change.

89. Although in 1958 the Roman Catholic Bishops of the United States issued a landmark statement denouncing racial discrimination and segregation, it was not until the Selma campaign that the Catholic Church became deeply involved in the national crusade for racial justice. In large measure Catholic inactivity stemmed from a demographic fact: most Catholics lived in northern cities; comparatively few resided in the South. William A. Osborne, *The Segregated Covenant: Race Relations and American Catholics* (New York: Herder and Herder, 1967), pp. 203–225.

90. *CDD*, 23 July 1963, p. 9; "Why We Picketed," *Community*, September 1963, pp. 4–7; Peter F. Steinfels, "The Students and Mrs. Lewis," *New City*, 15 June 1963, pp. 7–10; McDermott interview; Tim Murnane, "Interracial Fireman," *Today*, June 1963, pp. 3–5; Jack Star, "Editor for the Public Conscience," *Chicago*, Aug. 1980, pp. 118–122. The papers of the Catholic Interracial Council of Chicago at the Chicago Historical Society throw much light on the Catholic effort to improve race relations.

91. McDermott interview; CCMS, "Albany Report," 6 Sept. 1962, CIC papers, box 54, CHS; *New World*, 19 March 1966, p. 12; MLK speech, 29 Oct. 1964, CIC papers, box 95, CHS; *CD*, 31 July–6 Aug. 1965, p. 13.

92. *CST*, 4 Feb. 1966, p. 3.

93. Garrow, *Bearing the Cross*, p. 466; Anderson and Pickering, *Confronting the Color Line*, p. 190; *CDD*, 14 Feb. 1966, p. 11, 28 Feb. 1966, p. 4; Foner, *Organized Labor and the Black Worker*, p. 363.

94. *CDD*, 14 March 1966, p. 3; MLK speech, 12 March 1966, CUL papers (76-116), box 169-28, UIC.

95. Stanley Levison to unidentified, FBI 100-111180-880a, 16 March 1966. Robert Kennedy was also interested in King's Chicago work. See Kennedy to MLK, MLK papers, box 24-50, MLK Library.

96. In 1963, for instance, local elites—including the black newspaper and most black ministers—were initially very cool to SCLC's plan to stage a civil rights campaign in Birmingham. Branch, *Parting the Waters*, pp. 703, 725–726, 759–760; Fairclough, *To Redeem the Soul*, p. 119; Garrow, *Bearing the Cross*, p. 240.

97. Garrow, *Bearing the Cross*, pp. 465–466; *New Crusader*, 5 March 1966, pp. 1–2; *CDN*, 18 Aug. 1962, pp. 1, 14; Drake and Cayton, *Black Metropolis*, II, pp. xxi–xxii; Marx, *Protest and Prejudice*, pp. 106–112. See also C. Eric Lincoln, *The Black Muslims* (Boston: Beacon Press, 1961).

98. *NYT*, 25 Feb. 1966, p. 18; *SNCC: Notes and Comment*, April 1966, Chicago CORE papers, box 4-27, CHS; *CA*, 8 June 1966, p. 12; FBI 100-438794-NR, 24 May 1966. Bevel's team did meet with ACT members. Bevel, "SCLC–Chicago Project," 8 Nov. 1965, SCLC papers, box 150-22, MLK Library.

99. *CDD*, 13 April 1966, p. 13; *New Crusader*, 5 Feb. 1966, p. 2, 19 Feb. 1966, p. 2, 21 May 1966, p. 4. "Da Brien" regularly warned that SCLC "preachers" were out to line their own pockets.

100. *CT*, 20 Jan. 1986, p. 11; *CSM*, 15 March 1967, p. 15; letter to MLK, 9 March 1966, MLK papers, box 94-10, MLK Library; letter to MLK, ca. Feb. 1966, ibid., box 94-23; *CD*, 23–29 Oct. 1965, p. 12; letter to MLK, 28 June 1966, SCLC papers, box 22-17, MLK Library; *New Crusader*, 5 March 1966, p. 4. James Q. Wilson's categorization of 1950s black leaders into the 1960s is useful here. A "moderate style" was very much in evidence. Wilson, *Negro Politics*, pp. 169–280. Chauncey Eskridge, King's own associate, was reprimanded by the State Commission on Substandard Housing because of building code violations in a West Side apartment building he owned. Ironically, Eskridge served as legal counsel for the Chicago Freedom Movement in the takeover of the 1321 South Homan building. "Report from Bob Johnson . . . ," MLK papers, box 10-3, MLK Library. Some prominent black Chicagoans felt that civil rights leaders failed to seek out their assistance. John Sengstacke, publisher of the *Chicago Defender*, remembered that he had little contact with Martin Luther King during the Chicago campaign. "I told Martin I knew why he hadn't talked to me," Sengstacke later reported. "Because people had told him I was part of the establishment. But maybe I could have showed him how to get Daley's goat." Lawrence Muhammad, "John Sengstacke: A Feisty Spirit Rules a Declining Empire," *Chicago Reporter*, June 1982, pp. 4–5; *CDD*, 18 July 1966, p. 3.

101. *CT*, 25 Feb. 1966, p. 4, 22 July 1966, p. 5; *CDD*, 9 March 1966, p. 3.

102. *NYT*, 30 June 1967, p. 15; *CDD*, 15 Dec. 1966, p. 4.

103. "About Dr. J. H. Jackson," Claude Barnett papers, box 385-8, CHS; Hosea L. Martin, "The Rev. Joseph Jackson: Chicago's Paradoxical Pastor," *Chicago Tribune Magazine*, 18 June 1967, pp. 24–25, 53–54. Consult also Peter J. Paris, *Black Leaders in Conflict: Joseph H. Jackson, Martin Luther King, Jr., Malcolm X, Adam Clayton Powell, Jr.* (New York: Pilgrim Press, 1978), pp. 44–69.

104. J. H. Jackson, *Unholy Shadows and Freedom's Holy Light* (Nashville, Tenn.: Townsend Press, 1967), pp. 76–77; J. H. Jackson, *A Story of Christian Activism: The History of the National Baptist Convention, U.S.A., Inc.* (Nashville, Tenn.: Townsend Press, 1980), pp. 281–286; Charles H. King, "The Untold Story of the Power Struggle between King and Jackson," *Negro Digest*, May 1967, p. 71; Baldwin, *There Is a Balm in Gilead*, pp. 207–210.

105. "Statement by Dr. J. H. Jackson," 10 Sept. 1961, Barnett papers, box 385-6, CHS; "About Dr. J. H. Jackson," ibid., box 385-8; Martin, "The Rev. Joseph Jackson," *Chicago Tribune Magazine*, pp. 24–25, 53–54.

106. Jackson, *A Story of Christian Activism*, pp. 413–495; King, "The Untold Story," pp. 6–8, 71–79; Branch, *Parting the Waters*, pp. 55–56, 335–339, 500–502, 505–507; Garrow, *Bearing the Cross*, pp. 165–166; Baldwin, *There Is a Balm in Gilead*, pp. 210–222. The decisive episode in the King-Jackson break took place at the NBC's annual convention in Kansas City in 1961, when King backed the Reverend Gardner Taylor's bid to replace Jackson as president. After a melee in the large auditorium, one of Jackson's supporters tumbled off the speakers' platform and died shortly thereafter. In the convention's aftermath, Jackson, who retained his post, indicted King as the mastermind of "the invasion of the convention floor . . . which resulted in the death of a delegate." There would never be a King-Jackson reconciliation.

107. Jackson, *Unholy Shadows*, pp. 149–150; *New Crusader*, 2 April 1966, pp. 1–2.

108. Fred C. Bennette, Jr., "Report on Operation Breadbasket," SCLC papers, box 131-9, MLK Library. Jackson's opposition posed problems for the Chicago Freedom Movement, but they were not crippling. Baldwin, *There Is a Balm in Gilead*, p. 223.

109. Travis, *An Autobiography of Black Politics*, pp. 242–244; *CST*, 8 Sept. 1965, p. 32; *NYT*, 8 Sept. 1965, p. 24; "By-Laws of Chicago Conference to Fulfill These Rights," pamphlet file, MRL, City Hall, Chicago. Ralph Abernathy was not surprised by the attacks from established black politicians. "What was going on here," Abernathy later wrote, "was no different in kind from what had gone on in Montgomery and Birmingham." Abernathy, *And the Walls Came Tumbling Down*, pp. 366–367.

110. Ben Joravsky and Eduardo Camacho, *Race and Politics in Chicago* (Chicago: Community Renewal Society, 1987), p. 36; Larry O'Brien to LBJ, 11 Aug. 1965, Name file, Richard Daley, WHCF, box 10, LBJ Library, Austin, Tex. I have quoted O'Brien's report of his conversation with Rostenkowski.

111. Charles Swibel interview with Bruce Thomas and Robert Nathan, July

1986, Chicago; *Time,* 15 March 1963, p. 24; Lemann, *The Promised Land,* pp. 166–167.

112. *CDN,* 11 July 1966, p. 22. My portrait of Daley is drawn from Mike Royko, *Boss: Richard J. Daley of Chicago* (New York: E. P. Dutton, 1971); Len O'Connor, *Clout: Mayor Daley and His City* (Chicago: Henry Regnery, 1975); David Halberstam, "Daley of Chicago," *Harper's,* Aug. 1968, pp. 25–36; Jane Byrne, *My Chicago* (New York: W. W. Norton, 1992), pp. 165–250; Frank Sullivan, *Legend: The Only Inside Story about Mayor Richard J. Daley* (Chicago: Bonus Books, 1989), pp. 64–73, 155–168; Ralph Whitehead, Jr., "The Organization Man," *American Scholar,* 44 (Spring 1975): 351–357; Milton Rakove, *Don't Make No Waves, Don't Back No Losers: An Insider's Analysis of the Daley Machine* (Bloomington: Indiana University Press, 1975); and William Braden's warm remembrance of Daley in the *Chicago Sun-Times* during December 1986, which was based on many interviews, including members of Daley's family and normally reticent associates.

113. Clifford Alexander to John Marcin, 12 May 1966, Gen LE/HU2, WHCF, box 71, LBJ Library; Hampton and Fayer, eds., *Voices of Freedom,* p. 302; *CDN,* 28 May 1963, p. 14; *CSM,* 1 Feb. 1966, p. 9; *CDD,* 21 Feb. 1966, p. 30. For evidence of Daley's liberal side, see Daley speech, "Urban Opportunity," 17 Feb. 1965, Daley speech collection, UIC. On Chicago's antipoverty efforts, see Seymour Z. Mann, *Chicago's War on Poverty,* Center for Research in Urban Government, Report no. 5 (Chicago: Loyola University, 1966); J. David Greenstone and Paul E. Peterson, *Race and Authority in Urban Politics: Community Participation and the War on Poverty* (New York: Russell Sage Foundation, 1973), pp. 19–24; Lemann, *The Promised Land,* pp. 244–245; *CT,* 2 Jan. 1966, pp. 1–2, 5 Jan. 1966, p. 15. Until the late 1960s, Joseph Epstein has argued, "the general view of Chicago's longtime mayor, Richard J. Daley, was of a New Dealish liberal, a man of fairly decent instincts, and in matters having to do with city government a figure of towering competence." *Commentary,* Sept. 1971, p. 86.

114. Whitehead, "The Organization Man," p. 355. The Daley regime had control of at least thirty thousand patronage jobs. See Hal Higdon, "Daley Is Chicago," *New York Times Magazine,* 11 Sept. 1966, pp. 182, 184. Chicago blacks were very underrepresented in all Chicago leadership positions. See Baron, "Black Powerlessness," pp. 27–33. On Daley's acquiescence to the perpetuation of the second ghetto, see Hirsch, *Making the Second Ghetto,* pp. 256–257.

115. Braden, "How Daley Handled Racial Issues," *CST,* 11 Dec. 1986, pp. 77–78; Edward Marciniak conversation (telephone), 27 Jan. 1992; Charles Livermore interview (telephone) 15 Feb. 1992, South Wales, New York. There is considerable disagreement about Daley's position on race. On the one hand, John Allswang has written that "Daley was provincial, insensitive, and unsympathetic to the plight of urban blacks." Nicholas Lemann notes that Daley on occasion spoke disparagingly about blacks. See Allswang, "Richard J. Daley: America's Last Boss," in Paul M. Green and Melvin G. Holli, eds., *The Mayors: The Chicago Political Tradition* (Carbondale and Edwardsville, Ill.: Southern Illinois

University Press, 1987), p. 157, and Lemann, *The Promised Land,* p. 272. On the other hand, one of Daley's colleagues, Edward Marciniak, recalled an incident when Daley, while listening to a black man's testimony of his struggle to scratch out a life for his family, became choked up. Marciniak had otherwise only seen Daley, who was not highly emotional, so aggrieved in public by remembrances of President John F. Kennedy.

116. McDermott interview; *CST,* 11 Dec. 1986, pp. 77–78; Lemann, *The Promised Land,* pp. 90–91. Daley would not endorse noticeably special efforts for blacks such as strict hiring goals for minorities. He advocated efforts to end discrimination but not to equalize results. *Human Relations News of Chicago,* Summer 1965, pp. 1–2.

117. Arnold Hirsch, "The Cook County Democratic Organization and the Dilemma of Race, 1931–1987," in Richard M. Bernard, ed., *Snowbelt Cities: Metropolitan Politics in the Northeast and Midwest since World War II* (Bloomington: Indiana University Press, 1990), pp. 63–90, presents a useful overview of this subject. Whitehead, "The Organization Man," pp. 351–357, is also helpful.

118. Chicago *Reader,* 25 July 1980, p. 30; *CT,* 29 April, 1983, p. 21; Porter interview; Jackson interview; Jenkins interview. Jenkins did not think the black church a consistent ally of the Chicago movement. Indeed, he later noted, black ministers "were the enemy in many cases."

119. Len O'Connor, 7 Jan. 1966, MLK papers, box 5-28, MLK Library; Travis, *An Autobiography of Black Politics,* pp. 313–320; *CDD,* 23 Oct. 1963, p. 2; *CST,* 26 Feb. 1964, pp. 3, 24. Claude Holman of the Fourth Ward delighted in assailing Leon Despres, a white alderman who was known as the only "black" alderman because of his racial stances, whenever Despres introduced pro-black legislation or castigated the City Council for gross neglect of human issues. Leon Despres interview, 10 Sept. 1986, Chicago.

120. Joravsky and Camacho, *Race and Politics,* p. 36.

121. *CDD,* 12 Oct. 1976, p. 9; Reynolds, *Jesse Jackson: The Man, the Movement, the Myth,* pp. 56–57; Raby interview; Rose, *From Plough Handle to Pulpit,* pp. 45–46.

122. *CDN,* 24 July 1965, pp. 1, 4; Edward Marciniak interview, 5 July 1991, Chicago. Daley even invited King to meet with him on his July 1965 visit. Daley to King, 16 July 1965, MLK papers, box 5-27, MLK Library.

123. *CT,* 3 March 1966, p. 1 and 30 March 1966, p. 7; *CST,* 10 July 1966, pp. 5, 66; *NYT,* 24 March 1966, p. 33. Saul Alinsky commented on Daley's cooptative power. "[King] moves into a slum, and Daley has the place fixed up on him," Alinsky noted. "Every time Daley has taken the issue away from him." *WP,* 17 July 1966, p. 8. Civil rights forces did not think the city's focus on the West Side was a "coincidence." Bevel, "Direct Action Report," 12–13 April 1966, SCLC papers, box 131-10, MLK Library. The city of Chicago was developing its own assault on slum conditions before the intensification of the SCLC-CCCO campaign in January 1966. See [Ray Hilliard], "Proposal for a Massive Attack

by the City of Chicago to Eradicate Slums from the Chicago Community," 20 Oct. 1965, Metropolitan Housing and Planning Council papers, box 8-5, UIC.

124. *CST,* 10 July 1966, pp. 5, 66.

125. "People in Progress, Chicago: 1966," *Annual Report of the Committee on Urban Opportunity,* MRL; Jehnsen interview.

126. *CST,* 28 Jan. 1966, p. 3; *CDD,* 22 Feb. 1966, p. 46, 16 June 1966, p. 21. The only biography of Wilson is William J. Bopp, *"O.W.": O. W. Wilson and the Search for a Police Profession* (Port Washington, N.Y.: Kennikat Press, 1977). On the FBI's surveillance of the Chicago movement, see David J. Garrow, *The FBI and Martin Luther King, Jr.* (New York: W. W. Norton, 1981), pp. 176–179. For evidence of Chicago police surveillance see memo, "Speech by Reverend James Bevels [*sic*]," Sergeant O'Malley and Patrolman Mathews to Deputy Superintendent, 9 Feb. 1966, Cantwell papers, box 35-7, CHS, and chapter 4 in Frank Donner, *Protectors of Privilege: Red Squads and Police Repression in Urban America* (Berkeley: University of California Press, 1990). The Chicago police followed King's movements closely in part because they were fearful of violence against him. Edward McClellan interview, 17 Aug. 1987, Chicago. Praise of the race relations efforts of the Chicago police waned in the late 1960s. Travis, *An Autobiography of Black Politics,* pp. 285–286.

127. *CDD,* 28 March 1966, pp. 3–4; *CT,* 25 March 1966, p. 6; *NYT,* 25 March 1966, p. 37; Daley to MLK, 25 March 1966, MLK papers, box 5-29, MLK Library.

128. Collier interview; *NYT,* 24 March 1966, p. 33; Bevel, "Direct Action Report," 12–13 April 1966, SCLC papers, box 131-10, MLK Library.

129. MLK speech, 27 Jan. 1966, MLK speech file, MLK Library; MLK speech, 12 March 1966, CUL papers (76-116), box 169-28, UIC. See also "A Proposal," MLK papers, box 5-27, MLK Library. Bevel was not the first theorist to compare the ghetto to an internal colony. By 1965 the colonial analogy had already crept into scholarly and social activist discourse. Harold Cruse had referred to American race relations as "domestic colonialism" in the early 1960s, but the concept received wider dissemination with Kenneth Clark's widely read 1965 book, *Dark Ghetto.* Malcolm X referred to the colonial analogy with great regularity in 1964 and 1965; see George Breitman, ed., *Malcolm X Speaks: Selected Speeches and Statements* (New York: Grove Press, 1965). Frantz Fanon stressed the colonial condition of nonwhite peoples in *The Wretched of the Earth.* Fanon's book was first published in Paris in 1961; an English edition came out in 1965. Charles Hamilton and Stokely Carmichael relied on a similar formulation in *Black Power,* published in 1967. For a brief overview of the rise of the concept of internal colonialism, see Robert Blauner, "Internal Colonialism and Ghetto Revolt," pp. 52–53, in Gary T. Marx, ed., *Racial Conflict: Tension and Change in American Society* (Boston: Little, Brown, 1971). Not everyone found the "internal colony" theme persuasive. David Satter blasted the Chicago Freedom Movement's analysis of urban problems. To Satter, the notion that exploitative out-

siders had created slum ghettoes was simplistic and naive. It was virtually impossible, Satter argued, for landlords to make a profit from their slum holdings. Moreover, most characteristics of slums, such as the rampant dirt and garbage, resulted from tenant negligence and a misdirected welfare program. Only if the ghetto dwellers built "their own institutions" and organized "to become a part of the power structure"—to help themselves, in other words—could slums be ended. Satter adds to our understanding of the perpetuation of the slums, but he misinterprets the SCLC's Chicago campaign. It is true that King and Chicago activists spotlighted the daily exploitation that helped make ghettoes slums. But they also hoped to draw ghetto dwellers into the Chicago movement and thus restore their faith in a better future and revitalize their sense of self-reliance and responsibility to their fellow citizens. See David Satter, "The West Side," *Chicago Maroon Magazine,* 4 March 1966, pp. 1, 10–11, and *Journal of Housing,* 23 (Dec. 1966): 642–646.

130. Higdon, "Daley Is Chicago," p. 184.

131. MLK speech, 12 March 1966, CUL papers (76-116), box 169-12, UIC; memo, "Speech by Reverend James Bevels [*sic*]," Sergeant O'Malley and Patrolman Mathews to Deputy Superintendent, 9 Feb. 1966, Cantwell papers, box 35-7, CHS. On the role of the civil rights movement and consciousness-raising, see Richard H. King, "Citizenship and Self-Respect: The Experience of Politics in the Civil Rights Movement," *Journal of American Studies,* 22 (April 1988): 7–24. For more on King's emphasis on self-reliance, see *CDN,* 9 June 1966, pp. 3–4.

132. *CT,* 20 Jan. 1986, p. 9; Bevel interview; Mary Lou Finley to Harold and Helen Finley, 24 Oct. 1965, copy in author's possession; *Chicago Maroon,* 1 July 1966, p. 8; David Satter, "West Side Story: Home Is Where the Welfare Check Comes," *New Republic,* 2 July 1966, p. 16; Robert Mueller, "Statement of Objectives and Programs: October, 1965," CCMS papers, vol. 6, WSCP–Programs folder, CTS.

133. Miller Stone interview; Collier interview; Hollins interview; Satter, "The West Side," p. 11. On the ghetto poor, see especially William Julius Wilson, *The Truly Disadvantaged,* pp. 6–8, and Wilson, "Studying Inner-City Social Dislocations: The Challenge of Public Agenda Research," *American Sociological Review,* 56 (Feb. 1991): 1–14.

134. As this book stresses, black Chicago was not a monolith. Like the rest of Chicago, it consisted of the well-off and the poor, activists and conservatives, the strivers and the disheartened. Consequently the Chicago Freedom Movement met with a range of responses, and each type of response merits its own analysis. In addition, black ghetto institutions, culture, and behavior changed over time. On the black poor in the 1960s, see especially Ulf Hannerz, *Soulside: Inquiries into Ghetto Culture and Community* (New York: Columbia University Press, 1969), a study of Washington inner-city blacks which discusses the ghetto dweller's tendency not to join organized protest efforts. See also Lee Rainwater, ed., *Soul* (Chicago: Aldine Publishing, 1970); Lee Rainwater, "Crucible of Identity: The Negro Lower-Class Family," *Daedalus* 95 (Winter 1966): 176–216; Elliot

Liebow, *Talley's Corner: A Study of Negro Streetcorner Men* (Boston: Little, Brown, 1967); Elijah Anderson, *A Place on the Corner* (Chicago: University of Chicago Press, 1978).

135. FBI 100-106670-2461, 22 April 1966; Bevel, "Direct Action Report," 12–13 April 1966, SCLC papers, box 131-10, MLK Library; *NYT,* 24 March 1966, p. 3.

136. Garrow, *Bearing the Cross,* p. 468; *NYT,* 24 March 1966, p. 33; *CDN,* 9 June 1966, pp. 3–4; *CST,* 27 January 1966, p. 32. The Chicago project was consuming more and more of SCLC's funds. In March, expenses for the Chicago campaign ran $5,805. The next month they jumped to $10,369. In May they reached $11,208. "Financial Report of the Southern Christian Leadership Conference," SCLC papers, box 63-30, MLK Library.

3. The Open-Housing Marches

1. *Newsweek,* 15 Aug. 1966, p. 29; *Baltimore Sun,* 6 Aug. 1966, p. 5.

2. *WP,* 17 July 1966, p. 8, 25 July 1966, p. 1; *CT,* 24 July 1966, p. 3.

3. *SWNH,* 25 Aug. 1966, p. 12; letter to Albert Dreisbach, ESCRU papers, box 62-15, MLK Library, Atlanta; Frank H. Prugh, "Selma in Chicago?," *Wall Street Journal,* 24 Aug. 1966, p. 10; McDermott interview. In early August, Stanley Levison commented, "[that] the whites should riot is very good for us." Levison to unidentified caller, FBI 100-111180-9-1021, 4 Aug. 1966. Many Southwest Side whites intuitively grasped that the white violence played into the hands of the Chicago Freedom Movement. At the Bogan area march on August 12, a woman remarked: "This is terrible. If [the demonstrators] stayed away we wouldn't have this mess. We are encouraging them." *SWNH,* 18 Aug. 1966, pp. 3, 12.

4. *CA,* 11 Sept. 1966, p. 8; Edward Marciniak to Chicago Commission on Human Relations, "Estimate of Potential Racial Tension for the Summer," 26 April 1966, Adams papers, box 18-4, CHS; *CST,* 5 June 1966, pp. 4, 68; *CDN,* 31 May 1966, p. 3, 22 June 1966, p. 19; Miller Stone interview; Robert Mueller, Executive Director's Report, 20 June 1966, CCMS papers, vol. 6, WSCP–Programs folder, CTS.

5. "Notes of Meeting of Representatives of Voluntary Group Service Agencies with Dr. Martin Luther King," 16 Feb. 1966, CUL papers (76-116), box 169-9, UIC; *CA,* 18 July 1966, pp. 1, 11; Bevel, "Direct Action Report, Chicago, Illinois," 12–13 April 1966, SCLC papers, box 131-10, MLK Library; "James Orange: With the People," pp. 113–114.

6. *CST,* 5 June 1966, p. 4; Useni Eugene Perkins, *Explosion of Chicago's Black Street Gangs, 1900 to the Present* (Chicago: Third World Press, 1987), pp. 15–42; Minutes of Task Force of City-Wide Agencies, 10 Oct. 1966, WCMC papers, box 66-7, CHS.

7. *Cleveland Press,* 8 June 1967, p. B5; Gary Stallings, "On the Way to See the Man," *Focus/Midwest,* 4 (nos. 11–12): 14–17.

8. *CDD*, 11 May 1966, p. 3, 12 May 1966, p. 3; Stallings, "On the Way to See the Man," pp. 14–17; James Bevel speech, 9 May 1966, CUL papers (76-116), box 169-9, UIC.

9. FBI 100-106670-2531, 17 May 1966; FBI 100-106670-2541, 23 May 1966; "Notes on Woodlawn from Daily Reports of Field Staff, Chicago Commission on Youth Welfare and Police District 9, Chicago Police Department for Period April 4 to July 7, 1966," WCMC papers, box 677-5, CHS; *CST*, 5 June 1966, pp. 4, 68; *CA*, 18 July 1966, pp. 1, 11; Livermore interview. The *Chicago Defender* expressed reservations about SCLC's work with gangs. *CDD*, 15 June 1966, p. 15.

10. CIC Board of Directors Meeting minutes, 20 Jan. 1966, CIC papers, box 109, CHS; Anderson and Pickering, *Confronting the Color Line*, pp. 192–194; Fish, *Black Power/White Control*, pp. 112–114.

11. Garrow, *Bearing the Cross*, p. 457; "Outline for Discussion of Proposed Freedom March," MLK papers, box 5-30, MLK Library; Edwin C. Berry to MLK and Al Raby, 23 May 1966, CUL papers (76-116), box 169-9, UIC.

12. Garrow, *Bearing the Cross*, pp. 475–476; Fairclough, *To Redeem the Soul*, pp. 309–310.

13. Garrow, *Bearing the Cross*, pp. 476–478; Fairclough, *To Redeem the Soul*, pp. 314–315; Carson, *In Struggle*, pp. 133–228.

14. Carson, *In Struggle*, p. 223; Fairclough, *To Redeem the Soul*, pp. 320–321; Garrow, *Bearing the Cross*, pp. 485–488; MLK, *Where Do We Go from Here*, p. 33.

15. *CDN*, 20 June 1966, p. 5; FBI 100-106670-2593, 14 June 1966; Urban Affairs Weekly Report, 19 June 1966 and Urban Affairs Report, 26 June and 3 July 1966, AFSC papers, 1966 CRD Housing Program, box 4, AFSC Archives, Philadelphia; Raby interview. Bevel was in Africa during this period. Bevel interview.

16. *Newsweek*, 11 July 1966, pp. 26, 31–32.

17. "Program of the Chicago Freedom Movement," 10 July 1966, in Garrow, ed., *Chicago 1966*, pp. 102–103. This document is the most complete statement of the Chicago movement's analysis of urban problems. The principal drafters were Al Pitcher, Harold Baron of the Chicago Urban League, and George Edgar Riddick of the Church Federation of Greater Chicago. Interesting too are the many rough drafts of the program. See, for instance, "Goals and Demands of the Chicago Freedom Movement," WCMC papers, box 501-5, CHS. According to Hal Baron, the program was more "window dressing" than a concrete program of action. Baron interview.

18. "Program of the Chicago Freedom Movement," pp. 97–104.

19. Moyer interview; *CDN*, 25 Feb. 1966, p. 12. SCLC was unable to recover the money it expended on 1321 South Homan. It did, however, spur the Chicago Dwellings Association, the nonprofit arm of the Chicago Housing Authority, to assume control of the property and rehabilitate it. Chauncey Eskridge to MLK, 29 June 1966, MLK papers, box 10-3, MLK Library.

20. Collier interview; *La Vida*, 18 Dec. 1965, p. 6; Finley, "The Open Housing Marches," pp. 6–8; *CDD*, 21 Feb. 1966, p. 30; Raby interview.

21. Raby interview; Anderson and Pickering, *Confronting the Color Line,* pp. 193–194.

22. Len O'Connor, 7 Jan. 1966, MLK papers, box 5-28, MLK Library; Despres interview; *CT,* 26 March 1966, p. 6.

23. *The Crisis,* Aug.-Sept. 1963, pp. 431–432; Meier and Rudwick, *CORE,* pp. 125–126, 183–186, 241–243; Allen J. Matusow, *The Unraveling of America: A History of Liberalism in the 1960s* (New York: Harper & Row, 1984), pp. 68–69; tape of Northwestern Civil Rights Rally, 4 April 1965, Northwestern University Archives, Evanston, Ill.; MLK statement, FBI 100-106670-2206, 7 Jan. 1966; *CDN,* 19 Feb. 1966, p. 16. Bevel often spoke of the importance of the limited housing choices available to blacks. He did not, however, couch these remarks in the larger context of an impending strike against housing discrimination as much as in the context of a strike to end slums. *CST,* 12 Sept. 1965, p. 36.

24. Moyer interview; Hal Freeman, "Integration in Suburbia," *Panorama (CDN),* 22 Jan. 1966, p. 3. Other Chicago civil rights groups, in particular the Citizens Housing Committee, had worked on the issue of housing. Citizens Housing Committee, Report to CCCO-SCLC Conference, 9 Oct. 1965, CUL papers (76-116), box 159-30, UIC.

25. Moyer interview; Bevel interview; LaFayette interview; Bill Moyer, "An Analysis of the System of Housing of Negroes in Chicago," AFSC papers, 1966 CRD Housing Program, box 4, AFSC Archives.

26. Moyer interview; *CDN,* 11 April 1975, pp. 5–6; *Oak Leaves,* 12 May 1966 to 28 July 1966; Bill Moyer to Charlotte Meacham, 24 June 1966, AFSC papers, Chicago R.O. 1966, HOP Correspondence folder; memo, Elbert Ransom to Charlotte Meacham, 26 May 1966, AFSC papers, 1966 CRD Housing Program, box 4; Moyer, "Project Open Communities," March 1966, AFSC papers, Chicago R.O. 1966, HOP–Open Communities folder. All three documents are in AFSC Archives.

27. Moyer interview; Moyer, "Open Communities: A Prospectus for a Nonviolent Project to Achieve Open Occupancy throughout the Chicago Area," March 1966, AFSC papers, 1966 CRD Housing Program, box 4, AFSC Archives; Rose Helper, *Racial Policies and Practices of Real Estate Brokers* (Minneapolis: University of Minnesota Press, 1969), pp. 224–226, 277–278, 288–290; Anderson and Pickering, *Confronting the Color Line,* pp. 46–47. Moyer pointed to the problems of diffuseness caused by any direct attack on slums. There was not, Moyer noted, "a National Association of Slum Landlords with a license by the federal government, and a state license, and a Chicago chapter of slum landlords that were licensed by the city and the state."

28. Moyer, "Open Communities," March 1966, AFSC papers, 1966 CRD Housing Program, box 4, AFSC Archives; *CA,* 14 July 1966, pp. 1, 3.

29. Williams interview with Orfield; Bevel interview; Raby interview; LaFayette interview; McDermott interview; Jackson, *Unholy Shadows,* pp. 250–253.

30. Bevel interview; LaFayette interview; Finley, "Open Housing Marches," pp. 7–9; Jesse Jackson, "A Strategy to End Slums," SCLC papers, box 149-35, MLK Library; Fairclough, *To Redeem the Soul,* p. 292; Moyer interview.

31. Anderson and Pickering, *Confronting the Color Line*, pp. 200–201; Urban Affairs Report, 26 June and 3 July 1966, AFSC papers, 1966 CRD Housing Program, box 4, AFSC Archives. The editors of *Renewal*, a Chicago-based magazine funded by the City Missionary Society, thought it "a strange juxtaposition to try to include Martin Luther King's original battle cry for Chicago, 'End The Slums[,]' in the category of 'open occupancy.'" *Renewal*, Sept. 1966, p. 2.

32. Richard Murray interview; *WP*, 25 July 1966, p. 8; Berry conversation with Kale Williams; FBI 100-106670-2629, 6 July 1966. "My memory," Williams later recalled, "is that all of us, including Martin and Andy, but particularly Martin and Andy felt that there had to be some large visible activity that summer, that they couldn't afford to be disorganized for another year."

33. McDermott interview.

34. Berry conversation with Williams; Hollins interview; Jehnsen interview; Heaps conversation.

35. CCCO meeting minutes, 24 May 1966, AFSC papers, Chicago R.O. 1966, UAP, Communities and Organizations–CCCO folder, AFSC Archives; Anderson and Pickering, *Confronting the Color Line*, pp. 192–194; Ed Riddick, "The Movement: Quo Vadis, Watchman?," *SNCC: Notes and Comments*, April 1966, Chicago CORE papers, box 4-27, CHS.

36. Collier interview; Jenkins interview; Fish, *Black Power/White Control*, p. 110; *CST*, 10 July 1966, p. 66; Booth interview; Heaps conversation; Finley, "The Open Housing Marches," p. 44; Jehnsen interview; Robert Mueller, "The Summer of the Miscarriage," CCMS papers, vol. 6, WSCP–Programs folder, CTS.

37. Pitcher, "The Chicago Freedom Movement," p. 176; Fairclough, *To Redeem the Soul*, pp. 287–288; LaFayette interview; Robert Mueller, Executive Director's Report, 20 June 1966, CCMS papers, vol. 6, WSCP–Programs folder, CTS. Mueller noted that SCLC and WSCP staff had gone to the troubled Puerto Rican area.

38. *CDN*, 11 July 1966, p. 16; *CA*, 9 June 1966, p. 4; Berry conversation with Williams.

39. *CST*, 11 July 1966, p. 4; *CA*, 11 July 1966, p. 1.

40. The speakers included Dr. Edgar Chandler and the Reverend Sergio Herrero, president of the Spanish-American Federation, and James Meredith, who had recovered from his wounds incurred in Mississippi. *CST*, 12 July 1966, p. 18; *CDD*, 11 July 1966, p. 3.

41. *NYT*, 11 July 1966, pp. 1, 19; *WP*, 11 July 1966, pp. 1, 5; *CST*, 11 July 1966, p. 2; FBI 100-106670-2633, 12 July 1966.

42. MLK speech, 10 July 1966, CUL papers (76-116), box 169-28, UIC; *CDD*, 11 July 1966, pp. 3, 4; *WP*, 11 July 1966, p. 1.

43. *CDN*, 11 July 1966, p. 16; *CA*, 11 July 1966, p. 4; Carson et al., eds., *The Eyes on the Prize Civil Rights Reader*, pp. 300–303.

44. Benedict, *Born Again Radical*, pp. 172–173; *CDN*, 12 July 1966, p. 4.

45. Benedict, *Born Again Radical*, pp. 173–175; *CDN*, 12 July 1966, p. 4; Marciniak interview.

46. Benedict, *Born Again Radical,* pp. 175–176; *CDN,* 12 July 1966, p. 4.

47. *NYT,* 12 July 1966, p. 26; *CA,* 12 July 1966, p. 3; *WP,* 12 July 1966, pp. 1–2; *CA,* 9 July 1966, p. 3.

48. *CDD,* 12 July 1966, p. 3; "At Random" tape, 9 July 1966, Adams papers, box 38, CHS; *CA,* 12 July 1966, p. 3; *NYT,* 12 July 1966, p. 26; *WP,* 12 July 1966, p. 1.

49. Bernard O. Brown, "WSO and the Riot on the Near West Side," WSCP papers, box 4, CHS. See also Brown, *Ideology and Community Action,* pp. 49–59.

50. Brown, "WSO and the Riot," WSCP papers, box 4, CHS; *CST,* 14 July 1966, pp. 3, 20; *CDD,* 14 July 1966, p. 4.

51. Brown, "WSO and the Riot," WSCP papers, box 4, CHS; *CT,* 13 July 1966, pp. 1, 6; *CA,* 13 July 1966, pp. 1, 3.

52. Brown, "WSO and the Riot," WSCP papers, box 4, CHS; *CDD,* 14 July 1966, pp. 3–4; *CDN,* 13 July 1966, p. 4; *CST,* 14 July 1966, pp. 3, 20; FBI 100-106670-NR, 13 July 1966.

53. Brown, "WSO and the Riot," WSCP papers, box 4, CHS; *CT,* 14 July 1966, pp. 1, 4; *CA,* 14 July 1966, pp. 1, 4.

54. *CT,* 15 July 1966, pp. 1, 4; *CA,* 15 July 1966, pp. 1, 3; *CDD,* 18 July 1966, pp. 3–4; *CST,* 16 July 1966, p. 2; Jenkins interview; Chicago Federation of Settlements and Neighborhood Centers Report, 14 July 196[6], CUL papers (76-116), box 15-30, UIC. The rumored transfer of a popular white Catholic priest also fueled tensions in Lawndale. Mallette interview.

55. *CT,* 16 July 1966, pp. 1–2; *CST,* 16 July 1966, p. 3; *CA,* 16 July 1966, p. 3.

56. *CDN,* 15 July 1966, p. 12; *New World,* 22 July 1966, p. 1; "Conference called by Junius Griffin . . . ," July 1966, Edward Marciniak files, Chicago.

57. Don Benedict conversation (telephone), 13 Jan. 1992, Chicago; Berry conversation with Williams; McDermott conversation with Williams, ca. 1971, Chicago; Marciniak interview; *CT,* 16 July 1966, pp. 1–2; *CST,* 16 July 1966, p. 3; Rabbi Robert Marx, "Chicago Summer," *Shema,* Sept. 1966, pp. 3–4. It is difficult to reconstruct the precise sequence of events on Friday, July 15; newspaper accounts and subsequent recollections do not match well. King, civil rights leaders, and members of the clergy, including Archbishop Cody, met Friday morning. After this meeting, a core group of civil rights and religious leaders gathered and resolved, according to Berry, McDermott, and Benedict, to meet with Daley later that day. They had great difficulty contacting him, so they went to City Hall. "We didn't have an appointment with the mayor and . . . in a sense became involved in a sit-in," Berry later recalled. Marciniak remembered arranging the impromptu meeting through Father Edward Egan, one of Archbishop Cody's key aides. Most likely, Egan was with Cody and other leading religious figures at Marillac House on Chicago's West Side issuing an appeal for peace. After delivering their statement, these religious leaders then went to City Hall and joined the other contingent awaiting Mayor Daley.

58. *CST,* 17 July 1966, p. 4; *CA,* 16 July 1966, pp. 1, 3, 20 July 1966, p. 15;

CT, 20 July 1966, p. 6; *CDN,* 15 July 1966, pp. 10, 12; *CDD,* 18 July 1966, pp. 3–4; *Time,* 22 July 1966, pp. 18–19.

59. MLK speech, 12[14] July 1966, MLK speech file, MLK Library; *CDN,* 15 July 1966, p. 10; *LAT,* 24 July 1966, section G, p. 2; *West Side Torch,* 15–19 July 1966, p. 4; *CA,* 19 July 1966, p. 7. For more on 1960s rioting, see Matusow, *The Unraveling of America,* pp. 360–367; Joe R. Feagin and Harlan Hahn, *Ghetto Revolts: The Politics of Violence in American Cities* (New York: Macmillan, 1973); *Report of the National Advisory Commission on Civil Disorders* (New York: Bantam Books, 1968); Sidney Fine, *Violence in the Model City: The Cavanagh Administration, Race Relations, and the Detroit Riot* (Ann Arbor: University of Michigan Press, 1989).

60. *CA,* 16 July 1966, pp. 1, 3, 14 July 1966, p. 1; Brown, "WSO and the Riot," WSCP papers, box 4, CHS; Kale Williams, "The Open Housing Campaign—Chicago 1966," AFSC papers, Chicago R.O. 1966, HOP folder, AFSC Archives; *NYT,* 16 July 1966, pp. 1, 8; "Chicago Debriefing," Maria Pappalardo to Barbara Moffett and others, 29 July 1966, AFSC papers, 1966 CRD Housing Program, box 4, AFSC Archives; *LAT,* 24 July 1966, section G, p. 2.

61. *CDD,* 18 July 1966, p. 13; *CT,* 22 July 1966, p. 5, 16 July 1966, pp. 1–2; *LAT,* 22 July 1966, pp. 1, 12; *WP,* 18 July 1966, p. 5; FBI 100-106670-2642, 19 July 1966; "Conference called by Junius Griffin . . . ," July 1966, Marciniak files; *CA,* 14 July 1966, p. 4, 16 July 1966, p. 3; MLK speech, 12[14] July 1966, MLK speech file, MLK Library.

62. *SE* (southern ed.), 17 July 1966, p. 1; *CA,* 12 August 1966, p. 4; *SWNH,* 14 July 1966, p. 1; Finley, "The Open Housing Marches," pp. 14, 20.

63. Evelyn M. Kitagawa and Karl E. Taeuber, eds., *Local Community Fact Book: Chicago Metropolitan Area, 1960* (Chicago: Chicago Community Inventory, 1963), pp. 2–5, 140–141; Chicago Fact Book Consortium, *Local Community Fact Book: Chicago Metropolitan Area—1970 and 1980 Censuses* (Chicago: Chicago Review Press, 1984), pp. 161–162; LaFayette interview.

64. *SE* (southern ed.), 13 July 1966, p. 1; *CA,* 12 July 1966, pp. 1, 3; *CDN,* 12 July 1966, p. 4; *SE* (central ed.), 17 July 1966, p. 1.

65. There are no legal boundaries demarcating the Southwest Side. I consider it to include the following community areas, as defined by University of Chicago sociologists in the 1920s and 1930s: Chicago Lawn, Gage Park, Ashburn, Auburn-Gresham, Archer Heights, Clearing, Garfield Ridge, West Elsdon, Brighton Park, and West Lawn. In 1960 more than three hundred thousand people lived in this region. As West Englewood underwent racial transition in the early 1960s, the predominantly white western half of West Englewood increasingly identified with the Southwest Side. In addition, from 1960 to 1966 many blacks moved into the eastern part of Auburn-Gresham. In 1960 only a few blacks lived in this community area. By 1966 Auburn-Gresham was nearly thirty-five percent black. *CST,* 13 Jan. 1967, p. 4.

66. *SWNH,* 14 July 1966, pp. 3, 10. The *Southwest News-Herald,* located near 63rd and Kedzie in Chicago Lawn, is a privately published newspaper serving

the Southwest Side of Chicago, particularly the community areas of Chicago Lawn, Gage Park, West Lawn, Clearing, Archer Heights, Garfield Ridge, West Elsdon, and Ashburn. In 1966 its circulation topped twenty-eight thousand. I have relied heavily on the *Southwest News-Herald* for my reconstruction of the Southwest Side's history.

67. Hirsch, *Making the Second Ghetto*, pp. 40–67. In 1960, except for one public housing project in Garfield Ridge, fewer than 150 blacks lived west of Western Avenue. See *Southwest News-Herald* from 1960 to 1962 for evidence of the area's overall insulation from racial issues.

68. Robert Reicher, "The Clergy, the Police, and Visitation Parish," *New City*, Sept. 1963, pp. 7–9; *SWNH*, 12 Sept. 1963, p. 1; *CDN*, 16 Sept. 1963, pp. 1, 6. Starting in the late 1950s both the state of Illinois and the city of Chicago had considered adopting measures prohibiting real estate discrimination. In the spring of 1963 the Illinois legislature deferred action until the following year on fair-housing legislation. To ensure that the state legislators did not forget the sentiment of the Southwest Side, the *Southwest News-Herald* boomed in an editorial headline: "Open Occupancy is Wrong." *SWNH*, 2 May 1963, p. 2, 1 Aug. 1963, p. 2. Open-occupancy ordinances had been regularly and futilely introduced to the Chicago City Council by the Fifth Ward alderman Leon Despres. In 1963 Despres teamed up with the black independent alderman Charles Chew to introduce a strong fair-housing measure. Daley, however, desired a milder ordinance, one for which he could assume credit. So Daley turned to Murray, an ardent supporter in the City Council. "Mayor Daley called me in and said that the city needed a fair-housing ordinance and would I draft it," Murray later recalled. "I said, 'Mr. Mayor, why me? The people in my ward will destroy me.' He said, 'Jim, we've got to have it.' He never told me why; I didn't ask. It might have been political, a move for the black aldermen. My own feeling is that he did it for the good of the city." Despres interview; Joravsky and Camacho, *Race and Politics in Chicago*, p. 33; James Murray interview, 9 Sept. 1986, Chicago.

69. Opposition to open-housing proposals ran deep. A 1967 survey by State Representative Carl Klein revealed that 684 out of 692 residents opposed state fair-housing legislation. In a similar 1965 survey, opposition stood at ninety-two percent. *SWNH*, 16 March 1967, p. 1; John J. Lanigan to Governor Otto Kerner, 16 July 1966, Kerner papers, box 1139-1, ISHL, Springfield, Ill.; Statement, Property Owners Coordinating Committee, Egan papers, box 19, University of Notre Dame Archives, Notre Dame, Ind.

70. Moyer interview; Rose interview; Richard Murray interview; Frank H. Prugh, "Selma in Chicago?," *Wall Street Journal*, 24 Aug. 1966, p. 10; Kitagawa and Taeuber, eds., *Local Community Fact Book*, pp. 2–5, 52–53, 140–141, 146–147, 303–304; Chicago Fact Book Consortium, *Local Community Fact Book*, pp. 48–49, 161–162, 167–168. In 1960, over fifty-four percent of dwellings in Chicago Lawn were owner-occupied, slightly under thirty percent of the families earned more than $10,000 annually, and over fifty percent of the residents were

foreign-born or had at least one foreign-born parent. Lithuanian, Polish, and German backgrounds were most common, though not predominant. In Gage Park over sixty percent of the dwellings were owner-occupied, a quarter of the families earned more than $10,000, and over half were foreign-born or had foreign or mixed parentage. Persons of Czechoslovakian and Polish descent, the most common ethnic backgrounds, each constituted roughly five percent of the total population.

71. *CA*, 12 July 1966, pp. 1, 3; memo, Bernard LaFayette, "'2–5' Proposal for General Strategy," AFSC papers, 1966 CRD Housing Program, box 4, AFSC Archives; Kale Williams, "Notes toward an Analysis of the Chicago Freedom Movement—Summer 1966," AFSC papers, 1967 CRD Housing and Urban Affairs, box 4, AFSC Archives.

72. *SE* (central ed.), 17 July 1966, p. 1; FBI 100-106670-NR, 15 July 1966.

73. *SE* (southern ed.), 17 July 1966, p. 1; *CA*, 15 July 1966, p. 3; *CST*, 14 July 1966, p. 1; Garrow, *Bearing the Cross*, p. 496.

74. *SWNH*, 21 July 1966, p. 1.

75. *SWNH*, 28 July 1966, p. 1; Anderson and Pickering, *Confronting the Color Line*, pp. 216–217. Heretofore a steering committee had served as the command post of the Chicago Freedom Movement.

76. Anderson and Pickering, *Confronting the Color Line*, pp. 215–221; Finley, "The Open Housing Marches," pp. 29–30; Pitcher, "The Chicago Freedom Movement," pp. 155–156, 163. One list of the Agenda Committee, in addition to the names mentioned in the text, included: Archie Hargraves of the Urban Training Center, Arthur Brazier of TWO, William Robinson of CCCO, James Wright of the UAW, Chester Robinson of WSO, and two black ministers, Arthur Griffin and Clay Evans. Agenda Committee, CIC papers, box 92, CHS. Williams and McDermott were the only two whites on the list.

77. Memo, LaFayette to Action Committee, "'2–5' Proposal for General Strategy," AFSC papers, 1966 CRD Housing Program, box 4, AFSC Archives; Maria Pappalardo, "Chicago Logs," 13 Aug. 1966, ibid.; Pitcher, "The Chicago Freedom Movement," pp. 167–168.

78. *CT*, 25 July 1966, p. 6; "Chicago Freedom Movement" flyer, SCLC papers, box 47-6, MLK Library; FBI 100-106670-NR, 26 July 1966; *SWNH*, 28 July 1966, p. 1.

79. *WP*, 25 July 1966, p. 8; Kale Williams, "Notes toward an Analysis of the Chicago Freedom Movement," May 1967, AFSC papers, 1967 CRD Housing and Urban Affairs, AFSC Archives; "Chicago Freedom Movement—South Side Action Center," SCLC papers, box 47-6, MLK Library.

80. Garrow, *Bearing the Cross*, p. 498; Chicago SNCC, *Black Power: Notes and Comment*, Aug. 1966, CUL papers (76-116), box 169-12, UIC; *SWNH*, 28 July 1966, p. 1; *CT*, 30 July 1966, p. 7; "Action—Gage Park," SCLC papers, box 47-5, MLK Library; FBI 100-106670-2648, 29 July 1966.

81. Rose interview; *NYT*, 31 July 1966, p. 56.

82. Kay Holper, "A Sunday Afternoon Walk in Marquette Park," CCCO papers, box 1-27, MLK Library; Karen Koko, "Chicago's Race March—A Walk on the Wild Side," *NCR,* 10 Aug. 1966, p. 1; *NYT,* 1 Aug. 1966, pp. 1, 15; AP to Leon Despres, "Memories of the 1st Gage Park," 31 July 1966, Despres papers, box 63-3, CHS; Rose interview.

83. Gene Marine, "'I've Got Nothing against the Colored, Understand,'" *Ramparts,* Nov. 1966, p. 18; Holper, "A Sunday Afternoon," CCCO papers, box 1-27, MLK Library. Partial arrest records published by the *Chicago Tribune* and other eyewitness accounts indicate that many of the perpetrators of the white violence were from the Southwest Side. Eleven of the seventeen people arrested on July 31 were from the Southwest region. This general pattern persisted throughout the summer. Numerous eyewitness accounts suggest that white crowds were largely composed of local residents and not of outsiders. See [*Southtown Economist*], MRL clipping file and CCCO newsletter, Summer 1966, p. 3, CCCO papers, box 2-11, MLK Library. Professor Horace Lunt of Harvard University kindly reviewed the arrest lists to help me identify the ethnicity of the names of those arrested. Although a survey of surnames has inherent limitations as a method of determining ethnic background, Professor Lunt's findings support my belief that the Southwest Side crowds were composed of many individuals from "new" immigrant groups, those who largely came to America after 1890, including persons of Lithuanian, Polish, and Slavic descent.

84. Holper, "A Sunday Afternoon," CCCO papers, box 1-27, MLK Library; *CT,* 1 Aug. 1966, p. 1; *CA,* 1 Aug. 1966, pp. 1, 5.

85. *CA,* 1 Aug. 1966, pp. 1, 5; Barbara Moffett, "Notes on Talk with Kale Williams," 1 Aug. 1966, AFSC papers, 1966 CRD Housing Program, box 4, AFSC Archives; *CT,* 2 Aug. 1966, p. 3; *NYT,* 2 Aug. 1966, p. 22; *CDD,* 2 Aug. 1966, p. 3.

86. *CA,* 13 July 1966, p. 4.

87. Urban Affairs Weekly Report, 7 Aug. 1966, AFSC papers, 1966 CRD Housing Program, box 4, AFSC Archives; memo, Sanford M. Sherizen to Clotee Best, 2 Aug. 1966, CUL papers (76-116), box 158-22, UIC; memo, Bennett Hymer to Clotee A. Best, 3 Aug. 1966, ibid., box 158-23; memo, Paul Heitmann to Hampton McKinney, 4 Aug. 1966, ibid., box 169-1; *CT,* 3 Aug. 1966, p. 2, 4 Aug. 1966, p. 10; *LAT,* 3 Aug. 1966, p. 9, 4 Aug. 1966, p. 11; *NYT,* 4 Aug. 1966, p. 15; FBI 100-106670-NR, 4 Aug. 1966.

88. Urban Affairs Weekly Report, 7 Aug. 1966, AFSC papers, 1966 CRD Housing Program, box 4, AFSC Archives; MLK speech, "Thrust from the Ghetto," WMAQ (Chicago), 15 Aug. 1966, CUL papers (76-116), box 182, tape 5, UIC.

89. John McDermott lecture, 19 Jan. 1986, Chicago; *CA,* 2 Aug. 1966, p. 11; *CDN,* 2 Aug. 1966, p. 6.

90. Rabbi Robert Marx letter, 5 Aug. 1966, CCCO papers, box 3-14, MLK Library; Marx, "Chicago Summer: Another Analysis," *New City,* Sept. 1966, pp. 8–11; FBI 100-106670-NR, 5 Aug. 1966.

91. *CT,* 6 Aug. 1966, pp. 1–2; *Baltimore Sun,* 6 Aug. 1966, pp. 1, 5; *CA,* 6 Aug. 1966, pp. 1, 3, 7; *CDN,* 6 Aug. 1966, p. 1; *CST,* 9 Aug. 1966, p. 4; Hampton and Fayer, eds., *Voices of Freedom,* pp. 312–313.

92. Marine, "'I've Got Nothing,'" p. 18. In my analysis of the Southwest Side response to the open-housing protests, I have concentrated on the reaction to the July 31 and August 5 marches in the Gage Park–Chicago Lawn area. But almost the entire Southwest Side subsequently experienced upheaval. The Chicago Freedom Movement held one more march in the Gage Park area (August 14), two in the vicinity of Bogan High School (August 12 and 14), and one in West Elsdon (August 24). White extremists held two major rallies in Marquette Park on August 14 and August 21. My research suggests that my explanation of the July 31 and August 5 white reactions also holds for the other marches. Many factors contributed to different levels of violence: the weather, the effectiveness of police deterrence, the premarch initiatives taken by community leaders to prevent mob action, and the perception in each community of its vulnerability to racial transition. For further discussion of the response of the working class and lower middle class to racial change, see J. Anthony Lukas, *Common Ground: A Turbulent Decade in the Lives of Three Boston Families* (New York: Alfred A. Knopf, 1985); Ronald Formisano, *Boston against Busing: Race, Class, and Ethnicity in the 1960s and 1970s* (Chapel Hill: University of North Carolina Press, 1991); and Jonathan Rieder, *Canarsie: The Jews and Italians of Brooklyn against Liberalism* (Cambridge: Harvard University Press, 1985).

93. *NYT,* 6 Aug. 1966, p. 52; *CST,* 6 Aug. 1966, p. 6; *LAT,* 6 Aug. 1966, p. 14. See *LAT,* 13 Aug. 1966, p. 1, for a description of a particularly ugly incident in which a young black man passing near an open-housing march was splashed with acid.

94. *SWNH,* 4 Aug. 1966, pp. 1, 10; Edward Vondrak interview, 14 Aug. 1986, Chicago. On the Southwest Side see especially Lee Rainwater's "Making the Good Life: Working-Class Family and Life-Styles," in Sar A. Levitan, ed., *Blue-Collar Workers: A Symposium on Middle America* (New York: McGraw-Hill, 1971), pp. 204–229.

95. *SWNH,* 4 Aug. 1966, p. 1; *CDN,* 2 Aug. 1965, p. 10, 3 Aug. 1965, pp. 1, 7, 10 Aug. 1965, pp. 1, 7; *SE* (central ed.), 24 July 1966, p. 3.

96. *SWNH,* 4 Aug. 1966, p. 1; Paul Good, "Bossism, Racism, and Dr. King," *The Nation,* 19 Sept. 1966, p. 242.

97. Moyer interview; *CDN,* 10 Aug. 1966, p. 7; *New World,* 19 Aug. 1966, p. 4; *NYT,* 21 Aug. 1966, p. 5.

98. Vondrak interview; *LAT,* 7 Aug. 1966, section G, p. 2; Kitagawa and Taeuber, eds., *Local Community Fact Book,* pp. 303–304. Even for the first third of the twentieth century Chicago should not be thought of as the product of exclusive ethnic enclaves. Philpott, *The Slum and the Ghetto,* pp. 130–145.

99. "Thrust from the Ghetto," 15 Aug. 1966, CUL papers (76-116), box 182, tape 5, UIC. See also Hirsch, *Making the Second Ghetto,* pp. 195–198.

100. *NYT,* 21 Aug. 1966, p. 5; letter to Senator Paul Douglas, from 5700 block of South Kolmar Street, 5 Aug. 1966, Douglas papers, box 722-2, CHS.

101. Moderates condemned lawlessness, but they still opposed open housing. See *SWNH,* 4 Aug. 1966, p. 1. For a critique of the *SWNH*'s moderation, see Howard Packer letter, *SWNH,* 25 Aug. 1966, p. 10.

102. Other than the Cicero and Trumbull Park disturbances in the 1950s, most incidents of white hostility toward Chicago blacks received relatively scant public attention. Much of Arnold Hirsch's searching analysis of the anxieties and worldview of white ethnics in the 1940s and 1950s can be applied to the Southwest Side in the 1960s. Hirsch, *Making of the Second Ghetto,* pp. 40–67, 188–211. Southwest Siders were also reacting against the zeitgeist of the 1960s and thus shared many of the grievances of those opposed to busing in Boston. The Southwest Side response can be seen as a forerunner of the expression of "reactionary populism" that Ronald Formisano detects in his study of the Boston busing crisis. Formisano, *Boston against Busing,* pp. 3, 172–202, 235–238.

103. Letter to Senator Paul Douglas, from 3100 block of West 71st Street, 5 Aug. 1966, Douglas papers, box 722-2, CHS. In the summer of 1966, Southwest Siders expressed their outrage at civil rights legislation. For instance, see letter to Governor Otto Kerner, from 3500 block of West 72nd Place, 6 Aug. 1966, Kerner papers, box 803, ISHL. For letters attacking Governor Kerner's fair housing executive order, see Kerner papers, boxes 1137 and 1138. For evidence of a general dissatisfaction with the drift of society, see *SWNH,* 13 Jan. 1966, p. 10.

104. Letter to Governor Otto Kerner, from 5500 block of South Meade Avenue, 4 Aug. 1966, Kerner papers, box 1139-1, ISHL; letter to Governor Otto Kerner, from 6800 block of South Kenneth Avenue, 12 Aug. 1966, ibid., box 1138-1; *SWNH,* 13 Jan. 1966, p. 10, 11 Aug. 1966, p. 10.

105. *SWNH,* 25 Aug. 1966, p. 6.

106. Chicago Freedom Movement flyer, LCMOC papers, box 153, AFSC folder, CHS; *NCR,* 10 Aug. 1966, p. 1; *New World,* 5 Aug. 1966, pp. 1, 4; *CST,* 7 Aug. 1966, p. 51.

107. *SWNH,* 11 Aug. 1966, pp. 1–3, 10; *Newsweek,* 29 Aug. 1966, p. 64.

108. *SWNH,* 4 Aug. 1966, p. 10, 11 Aug. 1966, pp. 1, 10, 25 Aug. 1966, p. 2. See Gerald D. Suttles, *The Social Construction of Communities* (Chicago: University of Chicago Press, 1972), pp. 21–42, for an extended discussion of the concept of the "defended neighborhood." Formisano argues that the Boston residents opposed to busing were "children of the 1960s" who adopted many of the tactics of the civil rights movement. In a real sense Southwest Siders did too, but they also sustained an older indigenous tradition of white militancy in Chicago. See Formisano, *Boston against Busing,* pp. 138–146, 172–202, and Hirsch, *Making the Second Ghetto,* pp. 40–99.

109. Rakove, *Don't Make No Waves,* pp. 150–151; *SWNH,* 6 Oct. 1966, p. 10. Some residents believed that the police restrained the white crowds too harshly.

After the August 14 Gage Park march, the Chicago Lawn Civic Association announced that it was going to file a complaint against Chicago police for using excessive force. *SWNH,* 18 Aug. 1966, p. 17.

110. *CT,* 3 Aug. 1966, p. 2; *SWNH,* 11 Aug. 1966, p. 1; *SE* (central ed.), 10 Aug. 1966, p. 1.

111. *CDN,* 10 Aug. 1965, pp. 1, 7; *LAT,* 10 Aug. 1966, p. 7.

112. *CA,* 6 Aug. 1966, p. 3.

4. The City in Crisis

1. *NCR,* 17 Aug. 1966, p. 5; *CST,* 10 Aug. 1966, p. 3.

2. *CDN,* 15 Aug. 1966, p. 12.

3. McDermott interview; "At Random" tape, 9 July 1966, Adams papers, box 38, CHS.

4. *CT,* 8 Aug. 1966, p. 1; *NYT,* 8 Aug. 1966, p. 1; *LAT,* 8 Aug. 1966, pp. 1, 11; *CST,* 8 Aug. 1966, p. 1; WGN files, 7 Aug. 1966, FF1719, CHS.

5. *CT,* 8 Aug. 1966, p. 2; Finley interview.

6. Fairclough, *To Redeem the Soul,* pp. 7–8; Kale Williams interview with Orfield; Finley, "The Open Housing Marches," pp. 27–28; Kale Williams, "The Open Housing Campaign—Chicago 1966," AFSC papers, Chicago R.O. 1966, HOP folder, AFSC Archives, Philadelphia, and Williams, "Notes toward an Analysis of the Chicago Freedom Movement," ibid., 1967 CRD Housing and Urban Affairs.

7. *CT,* 7 Aug. 1966, pp. 1–2; *NCR,* 17 Aug. 1966, p. 5.

8. *NCR,* 17 Aug. 1966, p. 5; *National Observer,* 15 Aug. 1966, p. 5. For a socioeconomic profile of Belmont-Cragin, see Kitagawa and Taeuber, eds., *Local Community Fact Book,* pp. 52–53, and Chicago Fact Book Consortium, *Local Community Fact Book,* pp. 48–50. After the July 31 violence, twenty-six Southwest Side Catholic and Protestant clergy issued a statement calling for local residents to respect the demonstrators' constitutional right to march. *SWNH,* 4 Aug. 1966, p. 1. For an example of Northwest Side attitudes, see letter to Len O'Connor, from 5200 block of W. Altgeld, 13 Aug. 1966, O'Connor papers, box 2, CHS.

9. *Washington Evening Star,* 8 Aug. 1966, p. 3; Chris Kelley to Albert Dreisbach, 12 Aug. 1966, ESCRU papers, box 62-15, MLK Library, Atlanta.

10. CCCO newsletter, Fall 1966, CCCO papers, box 2-11, MLK Library; *CDN,* 24 July 1965, p. 23; *CA,* 11 Aug. 1966, pp. 1, 44. Finley, "The Open Housing Marches," pp. 18–19, offers a profile of the marchers. Ivory Perry, a seasoned activist from St. Louis, also traveled to Chicago. Lipsitz, *A Life in Struggle,* pp. 128–129.

11. *SWNH,* 1 Sept. 1966, p. 7; *CA,* 11 Aug. 1966, pp. 1, 44; Leroy Herring interview, 28 Aug. 1991, Chicago; Robert Lucas interview with John Britton, 20 Feb. 1968, MSRC, Howard University, Washington, D.C.; Hollins interview; Al Pitcher testimony in Tax, ed., *The People vs. The System,* p. 83. The composition

of the marches, it appears, did not change dramatically during the season of open-housing protests.

12. Dunlap interview; Jenkins interview; Finley, "The Open Housing Marches," pp. 19, 44; Briggs interview; Williams, "Notes toward an Analysis of the Chicago Freedom Movement—Summer 1966," AFSC papers, 1967 CRD Housing and Urban Affairs, AFSC Archives; Brown, *Ideology and Community Action*, p. 12. One survey in 1964 reinforced the general feeling that during the 1960s the poor tended not to rally toward civil rights demonstrations. Marx, *Protest and Prejudice*, pp. 49–79.

13. McDermott interview. Doug McAdam emphasizes the importance of prior connections to participation in stressful civil rights endeavors. McAdam, *Freedom Summer* (New York: Oxford University Press, 1988), pp. 62–65. Often scholars of the 1960s refer to the special relationship between blacks and Jews. In Chicago, Catholics played a particularly prominent role in the movement. Major Jewish groups did not join CCCO. For more on Jewish participation, however, see Jonathan Kaufman, *Broken Alliance: The Turbulent Times between Blacks and Jews in America* (New York: Charles Scribner's Sons, 1988), pp. 157–170.

14. Anderson and Pickering, *Confronting the Color Line*, p. 220; Joseph W. Kitagawa, "Search for *Koinonia* and Social Justice—A Glimpse of W. Alvin Pitcher: Alumnus, Colleague and Friend," pp. 3–18, in W. Widick Schroeder and Gibson Winter, eds., *Beliefs and Ethics: Essays in Ethics, the Human Sciences, and Ministry in Honor of W. Alvin Pitcher* (Chicago: Center for the Scientific Study of Religion, 1978), pp. 3–18; Williams interview with Orfield.

15. Finley, "The Open Housing Marches," p. 19; McDermott interview; Kale Williams, "The Open Housing Campaign—Chicago 1966," AFSC papers, Chicago R.O. 1966, HOP folder, AFSC Archives.

16. *Philadelphia Tribune*, 2 Aug. 1966, p. 1; *NYT*, 2 Aug. 1966, p. 22; Alice Tregay interview with Michael Benedetto, 18 May 1986, Chicago; "The Essence of a Non-Violent Demonstration," CCCO papers, box 2-8, MLK Library. Billy Hollins also noted that even some on the SCLC staff embraced nonviolence only as a tactic, not as a way of life. Hollins interview. Richard Murray remembers James Bevel confronting one marcher out of step with the nonviolent spirit and insisting on a change in behavior. Murray interview.

17. MLK, *The Trumpet of Conscience* (New York: Harper & Row, 1968), p. 58; "James Orange: With the People," pp. 113–114; LaFayette interview.

18. Jackson interview; Williams interview; Finley, "The Open Housing Marches," pp. 20–23.

19. Jackson interview; Finley, "The Open Housing Marches," pp. 16–17.

20. "Church and Pastor's History" flyer, New Friendship Baptist Church files, Chicago; Herring interview; CCMS, "Albany Report," 6 Sept. 1962, CIC papers, box 54, CHS; *CD*, 27 Aug.–3 Sept. 1966, p. 3; Ewell Reagin, "The Southern Christian Leadership Conference: Strategy and Purpose," Sept. 1966, appendix II, pp. 1–3, WSCP papers, box 4, CHS.

21. *CDD*, 11 July 1963, p. 3; *CD*, 8–14 Feb. 1964, p. 16; CCMS, "Albany Report," 6 Sept. 1962, CIC papers, box 54, CHS; the Reverend Donald Moore conversation (telephone), 24 July 1992, Chicago; *CD*, 5–11 Feb. 1966, pp. 1–2; Jackson interview. According to a study by the Church Federation of Greater Chicago, the Greater Mount Hope Baptist Church had a congregation of roughly five hundred members. The New Friendship Baptist Church, according to one of its deacons in the 1960s, had well over a thousand congregants. List of Churches, 20 Nov. 1964, Church Federation of Greater Chicago papers, Community Renewal Foundation folder, CHS; Herring interview. Freeman, Lambert, Clay Evans, John Porter, and A. P. Jackson were the most important black ministers on the South Side who actively supported the Chicago Freedom Movement. Their churches were staging grounds for rallies and demonstrations. Jackson, the pastor of Liberty Baptist Church, stressed the importance of independence in determining the extent of an individual church's participation in the movement. "The membership of Liberty," Jackson noted, "made sure that I was independent of any politicians, so we never accepted money from any politicians or anyone else. So I could afford to have [King] come to Liberty because we were not afraid of any reprisal from Mayor Daley." Jackson interview.

22. Finley, "The Open Housing Marches," pp. 16–17.

23. *CDN*, 9 Aug. 1966, p. 11; WGN files, 9 Aug. 1966, FF1728, CHS.

24. *CDN*, 9 Aug. 1966, p. 11; WGN files, 9 Aug. 1966, FF1728, CHS.

25. McDermott conversation with Williams; Rose interview; *CDN*, 10 Aug. 1966, pp. 1, 6.

26. Finley, "The Open Housing Marches," p. 26; Maria Pappalardo, "Chicago Logs," 12 and 13 Aug. 1966, AFSC papers, 1966 CRD Housing Program, box 4, AFSC Archives; *CA*, 10 Aug. 1966, p. 10; *CDN*, 10 Aug. 1966, p. 1; Anderson and Pickering, *Confronting the Color Line*, p. 230. Civil rights activists also worried that the Bogan area was too well prepared for a march. *CT*, 11 Aug. 1966, pp. 1–2.

27. Finley, "The Open Housing Marches," p. 26; Anderson and Pickering, *Confronting the Color Line*, pp. 230–231; *CT*, 11 Aug. 1966, pp. 1–2; Pappalardo, "Chicago Logs," 12 Aug. 1966, AFSC papers, 1966 CRD Housing Program, box 4, AFSC Archives.

28. Finley, "The Open Housing Marches," pp. 29–32; Pitcher, "The Chicago Freedom Movement," p. 156. Though Bevel was the dominant figure on the Action Committee, he stressed collective decision making. In her notes on her Chicago experience, Maria Pappalardo states that the Action Committee was upset about the August 10 meeting and its relations with the Agenda Committee. It even drafted a position paper to try to outline the respective roles of the two committees. Pappalardo, "Chicago Logs," 13 Aug., 15 Aug., 18 Aug. 1966, AFSC papers, 1966 CRD Housing Program, box 4, AFSC Archives.

29. McDermott conversation with Williams; Pappalardo, "Chicago Logs," 18 Aug. and 19 Aug. 1966, AFSC papers, 1966 CRD Housing Program, box 4, AFSC

Archives; Finley, "The Open Housing Marches," p. 43. Martin Luther King's frequent absence from Chicago during the open-housing crusade—he was in the South from August 6 to August 17—exacerbated leadership tensions. There were also tensions at other levels within the movement. Bert Ransom, the director of the South Side Action Center, for instance, complained that protest leaders did not always seem to have confidence in the people working under them. On another occasion, Charley Brown, a march marshal, objected that too often march leaders did not adequately convey changes in plans to others in the field. Pappalardo, "Chicago Logs," 14 Aug. and 15 Aug. 1966, AFSC papers, 1966 CRD Housing Program, box 4, AFSC Archives. The internal tensions within the Chicago Freedom Movement were by no means unique. During the Birmingham campaign, for example, Fred Shuttlesworth battled with other SCLC leaders, and during the Selma campaign SNCC-SCLC conflict was intense. Garrow, *Bearing the Cross*, pp. 256–257, 404–406, 409–410.

30. Alice Tregay interview with Benedetto; Leo Holt conversation (telephone), 31 Jan. 1992, Markham, Ill.; Coggs interview; letter to Paul H. Douglas, 22 Aug. 1966, Douglas papers, box 722-2, CHS.

31. *CT,* 30 July 1966, p. 7; *CST,* 30 July 1966, p. 7; Coretta Scott King, *My Life with Martin Luther King, Jr.,* pp. 287–288; Joan P. Brown to Coretta Scott King, 12 Aug. 1966, WMC papers, box 1-1, UIC; memo, Steering Committee to Women Mobilized for Change, 26 Aug. 1966, ibid.

32. Notes, 20 July 1966, and "An Open Letter of Concern," 29 July 1966, WMC papers, box 1-1, UIC. On the flexing of women's muscles, see Sheila Wexler to Joan Brown, ibid. On the special duty of women, see "Fact Sheet," n.d., ibid. Women on SCLC's Chicago staff also began to discuss gender issues during 1965–1966. Finley interview. Women have played important roles in the black quest for full citizenship. For a discussion of women and the southern civil rights movement, see Sara Evans, *Personal Politics: The Roots of Women's Liberation in the Civil Rights Movement and the New Left* (New York: Alfred A. Knopf, 1979).

33. It is difficult to measure precisely the response to the marches. On August 10, 1966, WBBM-TV, Chicago's CBS affiliate, conducted a survey (which admittedly was not scientific) that reported over eighty percent of Chicagoans indicating that they thought Dr. King's actions had backfired. WBBM-TV bulletin, 16 Aug. 1966, Marciniak files, Chicago.

34. *SE* (central ed.), 10 Aug. 1966, p. 1; *CT,* 9 Aug. 1966, p. 3, 10 Aug. 1966, p. 5; *SE* (southern ed.), 28 Aug. 1966, p. 1.

35. *CT,* 9 Aug. 1966, p. 3; *CST,* 10 Aug. 1966, p. 3. John Hoellen conversation (telephone), 15 Jan. 1992, Chicago. Hoellen remembered that the mayor was "very distressed."

36. "People around Daley would say to me that 'Dick has changed.' Something's happened to him. He's very disturbed," one alderman remembered. Leon Despres interview with John Britton, 20 Feb. 1968, Chicago, MSRC.

37. Rose interview; Richard Murray interview; *CDN,* 8 Aug. 1966, p. 1; Kale Williams, "The Open Housing Campaign—Chicago 1966," AFSC papers, Chicago

R.O. 1966, HOP folder, AFSC Archives, and Williams, "Notes toward an Analysis of the Chicago Freedom Movement," ibid., 1967 CRD Housing and Urban Affairs, box 4. David Garrow has argued that by the time of the Birmingham campaign, SCLC had discarded nonviolent persuasion for nonviolent coercion. Garrow, *Protest at Selma: Martin Luther King, Jr., and the Voting Rights Act of 1965* (New Haven: Yale University Press, 1978), pp. 222–236.

38. *CT,* 14 June 1965, p. 2; Roman Pucinski to Lyndon Johnson, 9 Aug. 1966, Gen HU2, WHCF, box 14, LBJ Library, Austin, Tex.; *CA,* 11 Aug. 1966, p. 6, 10 Aug. 1966, p. 9; *LAT,* 5 Aug. 1966, p. 13; *Baltimore Sun,* 10 Aug. 1966, p. 8; *NYT,* 10 Aug. 1966, p. 28; *CST,* 3 Aug. 1966, p. 4, 10 Aug. 1966, p. 5.

39. *CDD,* 10 Aug. 1966, p. 12; *New Crusader,* 6 Aug. 1966, pp. 1, 3; *Woodlawn Booster,* 11 Aug. 1966, Despres papers, clipping file, CHS; *CA,* 10 Aug. 1966, pp. 1, 10. The black politicians also hesitated over a proposed ban on building new public housing projects in largely black areas. Harold Washington, later the mayor of Chicago, attended this meeting.

40. *Woodlawn Booster,* 11 Aug. 1966, Despres papers, clipping file, CHS; *CA,* 10 Aug. 1966, pp. 1, 10; *New Crusader,* 6 Aug. 1966, pp. 1, 3; Despres interview.

41. *CT,* 18 Aug. 1966, p. 22; *CA,* 10 Aug. 1966, p. 32; *CDN,* 9 Aug. 1966, p. 12, 10 Aug. 1966, p. 12. For more on newspaper reaction, see Thomas James Kelly, "White Press/Black Man: An Analysis of the Editorial Opinion of the Four Chicago Daily Newspapers toward the Race Problem" (Ph.D. diss., University of Illinois at Urbana-Champaign, 1971), p. 253.

42. Editorial, "Riots in Chicago #1," Kerner papers, box 1140-2, ISHL, Springfield, Ill.; "Minutes, Radio-Television Meeting," 12 Aug. 1966, and "Minutes of the Meeting," 12 Aug. 1966, Marciniak files. See also "Committee to Study Revision of Broadcast Procedures in Riot Situations to Chicago Area Broadcast News Executives," 5 May 1966, and Dan Overmyer to Neil Regan and Edward Marciniak, 25 Aug. 1966, ibid.

43. *CST,* 7 Aug. 1966, p. 50; *Chicago Maroon,* 12 Aug. 1966, p. 1.

44. *CST,* 11 Aug. 1966, p. 4; *CA,* 11 Aug. 1966, p. 6; *CDN,* 11 Aug. 1966, p. 11. There are conflicting reports on whether the discussions with labor leaders took place on Tuesday, August 9, or Wednesday, August 10.

45. *CA,* 11 Aug. 1966, p. 1, 17 Aug. 1966, pp. 1, 5; *CD,* 12–18 March 1966, p. 1; Carl Shier interview, 9 Sept. 1987, Chicago. On the UAW's ties to the civil rights cause, see MLK to Walter Reuther, 30 June 1966, box 20-18, and MLK to Robert Johnston, 11 May 1966, box 5-30, in MLK papers, MLK Library. John Barnard, *Walter Reuther and the Rise of the Auto Workers* (Boston: Little, Brown, 1973), pp. 173–174, 185–186. The Walter Reuther papers at Wayne State University throw little light on the UAW's relationship to the Chicago Freedom Movement.

46. "Excerpts from remarks of Regional Director Robert Johnston at UAW Illinois Civil Rights Conference," 30 March 1967, LCMOC papers, box 185, CHS; *CST,* 12 Aug. 1966, p. 26; *CA,* 12 Aug. 1966, pp. 1, 5; *CDN,* 12 Aug. 1966, p. 5; *NYT,* 12 Aug. 1966, p. 20; Carl Shier conversation, 13 Aug. 1987, Chicago.

Johnston knew that not all whites among the UAW rank and file endorsed fair-housing demonstrations.

47. Archbishop John P. Cody letter, 7 July 1966, Cantwell papers, box 16-1, CHS; *New World,* 15 July 1966, pp. 1, 10. Cody himself did not attend the rally; he was abroad at the time.

48. *CST,* 21 May 1966, p. 38. Some New Orleans clergy had criticized Cody for not promoting Catholic school integration aggressively enough and for not permitting priests to participate in civil rights demonstrations. Edward R. F. Sheehan, "Not Peace But the Sword," *Saturday Evening Post,* 28 Nov. 1964, p. 34.

49. "Chicago Debriefing," Maria Pappalardo to Barbara Moffett, Charlotte Meachem, and others, 29 July 1966, AFSC papers, 1966 CRD Housing Program, box 4, AFSC Archives; Anderson and Pickering, *Confronting the Color Line,* pp. 220–222; *SWNH,* 28 July 1966, p. 1; LaFayette interview; "Statement Issued by His Excellency, the Most Rev. John P. Cody, D.D.," 10 Aug. 1966, LCMOC papers, box 153, CIC folder, CHS; *New World,* 12 Aug. 1966, p. 26.

50. *CT,* 13 Aug. 1966, p. 10; *CDN,* 12 Aug. 1966, p. 5; *NYT,* 12 Aug. 1966, p. 20; Catholic Interracial Council of Chicago Statement, 11 Aug. 1966, LCMOC papers, box 153, CIC folder, CHS. Father Thomas Heaney also offered a reply to Cody's plea in the *Hyde Park Herald,* 17 Aug. 1966, pp. 1, 3. Bevel's comments about Archbishop Cody angered many Catholics who supported the Chicago Freedom Movement. *New World,* 19 Aug. 1966, p. 4.

51. Dahm, *Power and Authority,* p. 3.

52. Ibid., pp. 3–4. Chicago Catholic social activism did not spring from nowhere. The Chicago Archdiocese had long had an activist bent. In the 1930s and 1940s, Chicago Catholics supported the Catholic Worker movement to foster unity among the working class and organized the Christian Family movement to improve intergroup relations.

53. "Why We Picketed," *Community,* Sept. 1963, pp. 4–7; Peter F. Steinfels, "The Students and Mrs. Lewis," *New City,* 15 June 1963, pp. 7–10. On Chicago Catholic participation in the Selma protests, see *New World,* 12 March 1965, p. 2, 19 March 1965, pp. 1–2, 4, 12, and 2 April 1965, pp. 1–2. On Catholic participation in the 1965 Willis protests, see *NCR,* 23 June 1965, p. 1, and 7 July 1965, p. 1.

54. For an introduction to this fascinating controversy, see Monsignor Daniel Cantwell's "Letter to My Friends," *New City,* 1 Aug. 1965, p. 5, and 15 Sept. 1965, pp. 15–16, and the many replies to Cantwell's criticism of clergy participation in anti-Willis marches. Cantwell wrote: "I went to Selma as a priest desiring to show my deepest moral and religion indignation at what had taken place there. The issue was clear—and as never before in my lifetime Americans shared my indignation."

55. *New World,* 25 June 1965, p. 24, 9 July 1965, p. 20. For more examples of 1966 reaction to the marches, see *New World,* 12 Aug. 1966, p. 26. There is evidence that Cody did not think highly of Martin Luther King. The Chicago FBI agent Marlin W. Johnson visited Cody shortly after King had met with Cody

in early February 1966. Johnson reported that Cody was not impressed with King and "appreciated" the Bureau's information on the civil rights leader. FBI 100-106670-2330, 24 Feb. 1966; U.S. House of Representatives, *Investigation of the Assassination of Martin Luther King, Jr.: Hearings before the Select Committee on Assassinations of the U.S. House of Representatives,* 95th Congress, 2nd session, 1978, VI, 263; and Garrow, *The FBI and Martin Luther King,* p. 176. The issue of Cody's relationship to racial issues is also complicated because of Cody's leadership style, which is best described as authoritarian. He disliked challenges to his authority by members of his flock. My thoughts on the Chicago Catholic Church have been enriched by interviews with the following individuals: McDermott; Mallette; Michael Lawson, 30 Aug. 1988, Chicago; Father Anthony Vader, 14 July 1988, Chicago; Sister Margaret Traxler, 16 Aug. 1988, Chicago; Father Rollins Lambert, 21 Aug. 1987, Chicago; Dr. Edgar Chandler, 12 Oct. 1987, Concord, New Hampshire.

56. *CA,* 12 Aug. 1966, pp. 1, 4, 13 Aug. 1966, p. 3; *SWNH,* 4 Aug. 1966, pp. 1, 10; *CDN,* 12 Sept. 1964, pp. 8–9; *SE* (southern ed.), 10 Aug. 1966, p. 1, 14 Aug. 1966, pp. 1–2, 17 Aug. 1966, p. 1; James Murray interview; *SE* (central ed.), 17 Aug. 1966, p. 1; *CT,* 13 Aug. 1966, p. 1; *NYT,* 13 Aug. 1966, p. 8; *LAT,* 13 Aug. 1966, p. 1. For an account by a marcher, see Pappalardo, "Chicago Logs," 12 Aug. 1966, AFSC papers, 1966 CRD Housing Program, box 4, AFSC Archives. The open-housing violence so shocked some whites in march-targeted neighborhoods that they even found themselves siding with the civil rights protesters. See Anonymous to Len O'Connor, 17 Aug. 1966, Len O'Connor papers, box 2, CHS; *The Garfieldian,* 24 Aug. 1966, p. 8N, Manuscripts Division, Chicago Public Library; *SE* (central ed.), 17 Aug. 1966, p. 5.

57. *SE* (southern ed.), 17 Aug. 1966, p. 1; *SWNH,* 18 Aug. 1966, p. 17; memo, Bennett Hymer to Pat Fitzgerald, 17 Aug. 1966, CUL papers (76-116), box 158-26, UIC; *CA,* 15 Aug. 1966, pp. 1, 6.

58. *CA,* 15 Aug. 1966, p. 1; Fred C. Shapiro, "The Last Word (We Hope) on George Lincoln Rockwell," *Esquire,* Feb. 1967, p. 105.

59. Shapiro, "The Last Word," pp. 101–105, 137–144; *The Stormtrooper,* Feb. 1962, p. 6; *Intra-Party Confidential Newsletter,* 7 June 1963, p. 3; Sanford Sherizen to Pat Fitzgerald, 16 Aug. 1966, CUL papers (76-116), box 158-26, CHS; *CDD,* 8 Aug. 1966, p. 3; *CA,* 15 Aug. 1966, pp. 1, 6; *SWNH,* 18 Aug. 1966, p. 1.

60. Letter to Everett Dirksen, from 6600 block of South Marshfield, Chicago, 6 Aug. 1966, Dirksen papers, Correspondence, 1966 carton no. 21, Everett Dirksen Center, Pekin, Ill.; *New Crusader,* 20 Aug. 1966, p. 3; *NYT,* 16 Aug. 1966, p. 16; Marciniak interview; Hoellen conversation. "I don't think anybody thought in terms of the 1919 race riot," Marciniak said. "[T]his was a powder keg that was traveling down the streets of Chicago and later on the Northwest Side and it could explode or be fired." Hoellen, on the other hand, did worry about a repetition of 1919.

61. *CA,* 13 Aug. 1966, p. 3; *CT,* 13 Aug. 1966, p. 2; CCRR press release, 12 Aug. 1966, Marciniak files.

62. CCHR minutes, 9 Aug. 1966, 13 Oct. 1966, Marciniak files; Anderson and Pickering, *Confronting the Color Line*, pp. 159–160, 230–231; Garrow, *Bearing the Cross*, pp. 501–502.

63. CCHR minutes, 9 Aug. 1966, 13 Oct. 1966, Marciniak files; *CA*, 11 Aug. 1966, p. 1, 12 Aug. 1966, p. 1; Caples interview. Bill Berry noted that he was at work on a meeting with real estate officials at the same time that the CCRR was. Berry conversation with Williams. Beatty tried to arrange a meeting. *CA*, 11 Aug. 1966, p. 6.

64. CCRR Executive Board Meeting minutes, 20 Aug. 1965, CCRR papers, box 3, CHS; CCRR Executive Board Meeting minutes, 19 July 1966, ibid.; *New World*, 22 July 1966, p. 1; Marx, "Chicago Summer," *Shema*, p. 4; *CST*, 16 June 1965, pp. 1, 18. For more on the CCRR's relationship to the Chicago Freedom Movement, see Summary of Program Review Meetings, 29 Nov. 1965, CCRR papers, box 3, CHS. King and Raby met with CCRR members on August 4. See Executive Board Meeting minutes, 4 Aug. 1966, ibid. The CCRR's role disappointed civil rights activists. "I have always," McDermott later noted, "faulted the Conference for not taking the movement into its confidence, for not sitting down with us as much as they could have," and for not "going on . . . to arrange negotiations to help the movement get everything it possibly could get." McDermott conversation with Williams. That Arthur Brazier, a member of the Agenda Committee, also sat on the CCRR's executive board, is further evidence of the peculiar nature of the northern civil rights struggle. On CCRR's fair-housing work, see *CST*, 2 Feb. 1965, p. 17.

65. Marciniak interview.

66. Bishop James Montgomery interview, 8 Sept. 1986, Chicago; *Memphis Commercial Appeal*, 16 Aug. 1966, p. 5.

67. *CA*, 17 Aug. 1966, pp. 1, 4; Pappalardo, "Chicago Logs," 15 Aug. 1966, AFSC papers, 1966 CRD Housing Program, box 4, AFSC Archives.

68. *CA*, 16 Aug. 1966, pp. 1, 4, 17 Aug. 1966, p. 4.

69. Swibel interview with Thomas and Nathan; *CA*, 17 Aug. 1966, pp. 1, 5; Kathleen Connolly, "The Chicago Open-Housing Conference," Jan. 1967, in Garrow, ed., *Chicago 1966*, p. 74; John McKnight, "The Summit Negotiations: Chicago, August 17, 1966–August 26, 1966," in Garrow, ed., *Chicago 1966*, p. 112; CCRR Executive Board Meeting minutes, 16 Aug. 1966, CCRR papers, box 4, CHS; *Chicago's American Magazine*, 15 Jan. 1967, pp. 8–9; "Ben W. Heineman," LCMOC papers, box 98, CHS; Ben W. Heineman interview with Joe B. Frantz, 16 April 1970, Chicago, LBJ Library; *LAT*, 29 Aug. 1966, pp. 1, 7. The selection of Heineman as chairman was not made in consultation with the Chicago movement. McDermott conversation with Williams. Among others attending the conference were Archbishop Cody; Leonard Spacek, chairman of Arthur Andersen Co.; and William D. Caples, an Inland Steel vice president and future president of Kenyon College.

70. McKnight, "Summit Negotiations," pp. 112–114; *CA*, 17 Aug. 1966, p. 1; Marciniak interview; *New World*, 19 Aug. 1966, pp. 1, 9; John McKnight inter-

view, Chicago, 19 Aug. 1986; FBI 100-106670-NR, 26 Aug. 1966. McKnight was the regional officer for the United States Civil Rights Commission. The Ely Aaron papers at the University of Illinois–Chicago throw light on Aaron's career as the president of the Chicago Commission on Human Relations. I have given a truncated discussion of the Summit proceedings. For a fuller account, see McKnight's notes of the meetings.

71. McKnight, "Summit Negotiations," p. 115. Bevel and Bert Ransom of the AFSC were initially the only members of the Action Committee selected to join the Chicago movement's delegation, which was dominated by the Agenda Committee. At Bevel's insistence, Jesse Jackson joined this negotiating team. Pitcher was later included. Finley, "The Open Housing Marches," p. 34, and Pitcher, "The Chicago Freedom Movement," pp. 161–162.

72. *LAT,* 29 Aug. 1966, pp. 1, 7; McKnight, "Summit Negotiations," pp. 115–118; William Mullen, "Portrait of a Power Broker," *CT,* 11 April 1982, section 2, pp. 1–2; Swibel interview with Thomas and Nathan; *CT,* 2 Dec. 1986, pp. 1, 12; Connolly, "The Chicago Open-Housing Conference," pp. 70–73, 79–80; Devereux Bowly, Jr., *The Poorhouse: Subsidized Housing in Chicago, 1895–1976* (Carbondale, Ill.: Southern Illinois University Press, 1978), pp. 111–135; Williams interview with Orfield. Swibel also met with movement leaders after the first Summit session to strike a deal. McDermott believes that because the Daley administration lacked strong contacts with civil rights forces, Swibel, who was a friend of Bill Berry, tried to fill a vacuum. McDermott conversation with Williams. According to Marciniak, Swibel "was trying to work something out and I know he was in and out of the mayor's office." Marciniak interview.

73. Helper, *Racial Policies and Practices of Real Estate Brokers,* pp. 143–151, 187–190, 275–280, 287–290, 293–296; McKnight, "Summit Negotiations," pp. 118–119. For a more extended discussion of Chicago realtors' philosophy, see Ross Beatty, "Statement of the Chicago Real Estate Board before the Meeting called by the Conference on Religion and Race," 17 Aug. 1966, FBI 100-106670-NR, 26 Aug. 1966. My views of the Chicago real estate industry have been informed by the comments of John Baird, a progressive realtor. Baird was a delegate to the Summit conference for the Metropolitan Housing and Planning Council. John Baird interview, 6 Aug. 1987, Chicago.

74. McKnight, "Summit Negotiations," pp. 119–120.

75. Ibid., pp. 120–121; Gordon Groebe interview, 27 Aug. 1991, Chicago; Helper, *Racial Policies and Practices of Real Estate Brokers,* p. 229.

76. Groebe interview; McKnight, "Summit Negotiations," p. 121.

77. McKnight, "Summit Negotiations," p. 122.

78. Groebe interview; Connolly, "The Chicago Open-Housing Conference," p. 77. For more on the Chicago Real Estate Board, see Helper, *Racial Policies and Practices of Real Estate Brokers,* pp. 190–217, 247–262.

79. McKnight, "Summit Negotiations," pp. 123–124; *CDN,* 27 Aug. 1966, pp. 1, 4; Ross Beatty interview in Betsy Pegg, *Dreams, Money, and Ambition: A History of Real Estate in Chicago* (Chicago: Chicago Real Estate Board, 1983),

pp. 153–155. It should be noted that the CREB represented only a portion of Chicago's eight thousand real estate agents and brokers. *CSM*, 26 Aug. 1966, p. 12. Mohl was a leading figure in the NAREB and had recently testified against the fair-housing section of President Johnson's latest civil rights bill.

80. McKnight, "Summit Negotiations," pp. 124–126.

81. Ibid., pp. 126–127.

82. Ibid., p. 127. The CREB only agreed to drop its opposition to a state fair-housing law *if* the law applied to individual property owners as well as to realtors. It would have taken a near miracle for the Illinois legislature to pass such legislation. In 1967 the Illinois Senate, long dominated by downstate Republican lawmakers, rejected a fair-housing law. Thomas M. Landye and James J. Vanecko, "The Politics of Open Housing in Chicago and Illinois," in Lynn W. Eley and Thomas W. Casstevens, eds., *The Politics of Fair-Housing Legislation* (San Francisco: Chandler, 1968), p. 104.

83. McKnight, "Summit Negotiations," pp. 128–130. Mary Lou Finley suggests that the West Side Organization's work on welfare issues stirred the Chicago movement to call for reforms in the Department of Public Aid's housing placement program. Finley, "The Open Housing Marches," pp. 13–14.

84. McKnight, "Summit Negotiations," pp. 129–131.

85. *CA*, 17 Aug. 1966, p. 5; McDermott interview; *Memphis Commercial Appeal*, 16 Aug. 1966, p. 5.

86. McKnight, "Summit Negotiations," pp. 120, 131–133. Early in the negotiations, in an exchange between the realtors and Heineman, the possibility of a subcommittee was raised. In their meeting the day before the Summit session, CCRR representatives had also discussed the possibility of a smaller subcommittee to carry out negotiations. Executive Board Meeting minutes, 16 Aug. 1966, CCRR papers, box 4, CHS.

87. McKnight, "Summit Negotiations," pp. 133–136.

88. Ibid., p. 127; Garrow, *Bearing the Cross*, p. 130.

89. Anderson and Pickering, *Confronting the Color Line*, p. 255; *Dollars and Sense*, Jan. 1986, p. 29; Pappalardo, "Chicago Logs," 18 Aug. 1966, AFSC papers, 1966 CRD Housing Program, box 4, AFSC Archives.

90. Anderson and Pickering, *Confronting the Color Line*, pp. 255–256; Pappalardo, "Chicago Logs," 18 Aug. 1966, AFSC papers, 1966 CRD Housing Program, box 4, AFSC Archives.

91. Pappalardo, "Chicago Logs," 18 Aug. 1966, AFSC papers, 1966 CRD Housing Program, box 4, AFSC Archives; *CA*, 19 Aug. 1966, p. 1.

92. MLK speech, 18 Aug. 1966, MLK speech file, MLK Library; *SE* (central ed.), 21 Aug. 1966, p. 1.

93. MLK speech, 18 Aug. 1966, MLK speech file, MLK Library.

94. *CA*, 18 Aug. 1966, pp. 1, 4; *CT*, 19 Aug. 1966, p. 2; *CST*, 19 Aug. 1966, p. 1. For a copy of the injunction, see Jackson, *Unholy Shadows*, pp. 254–263. Frank Ditto of the Oakland Committee for Community Improvement was listed as one of the defendants. Ditto, known as a radical, was not truly a member of

the Chicago Freedom Movement, but had been leading his own demonstrations in July and August in Mayor Daley's neighborhood, Bridgeport. Ditto's efforts received little publicity, but they are a reminder that the Chicago Freedom Movement did not represent all protest activity in Chicago, even in the summer of 1966.

95. *CDN,* 20 Aug. 1966, p. 1; *CA,* 20 Aug. 1966, pp. 1, 3, 22 Aug. 1966, p. 3; *NYT,* 20 Aug. 1966, pp. 1, 20.

96. *CA,* 20 Aug. 1966, pp. 1, 3; Jackson, *Unholy Shadows,* pp. 157–158; Marciniak interview.

97. *CDN,* 27 Aug. 1966, p. 4; Berry conversation with Williams; *Dollars and Sense,* Jan. 1986, p. 30; *CT,* 20 Aug. 1966, p. 5; *CA,* 20 Aug. 1966, p. 3; *NYT,* 18 Oct. 1966, p. 28. The core members of the Summit subcommittee were Al Raby, James Bevel, Bill Berry, John McDermott, Kale Williams, George Jones, Charles Swibel, Edward Marciniak, and Ross Beatty. Thomas Ayers was the chairman. Neither King nor Daley participated directly in the negotiations. King would have joined the talks only if Daley—the only other figure of roughly comparable stature—had joined also.

98. "'Meet the Press' Television News Interview," 21 Aug. 1966, reprinted in James M. Washington, ed., *A Testament of Hope: The Essential Writings of Martin Luther King, Jr.* (New York: Harper & Row, 1986), p. 387; *CA,* 20 Aug. 1966, p. 3.

99. *CA,* 19 Aug. 1966, p. 4.

100. Pappalardo, "Chicago Logs," 19 Aug. 1966, AFSC papers, 1966 CRD Housing Program, box 4, AFSC Archives; James R. McGraw, "An Interview with Andrew J. Young," *Christianity and Crisis,* 22 Jan. 1968, p. 326; Kale Williams, "Notes toward an Analysis of the Chicago Freedom Movement," May 1967, AFSC papers, 1967 CRD Housing and Urban Affairs, box 4, AFSC Archives. Al Pitcher believed that the comparatively small number of marchers had even dictated the outcome of the open-housing crusade. "King was never able to get more than fifteen hundred people" for a march, Pitcher noted. "And you can't close the city down with only fifteen hundred people." William R. Witherspoon, *Martin Luther King, Jr.: To the Mountaintop* (Garden City, N.Y.: Doubleday, 1985), p. 202.

101. Pappalardo, "Chicago Logs," 20 Aug. 1966, AFSC papers, 1966 CRD Housing Program, box 4, AFSC Archives; *CA,* 17 Aug. 1966, p. 5, 20 Aug. 1966, pp. 1, 3; Holt conversation. Holt, one of the lawyers offering advice to the Chicago Freedom Movement, commented that the Daley administration was not going to allow a repetition of "the experience in the South" of the effect of mass jailings.

102. *CA,* 22 Aug. 1966, pp. 1, 4; *Suburbanite-Economist,* 24 Aug. 1966, pp. 1–2; *CT,* 22 Aug. 1966, pp. 1–2; memo, Hamilton Jenkins to Bill Berry, 22 Aug. 1966, CUL papers (76-116), box 69-1, UIC; memo, Pete Meyer to Bill Berry, 21 Aug. 1966, ibid.

103. *NYT,* 22 Aug. 1966, p. 1; Jackson interview; *CA,* 22 Aug. 1966, p. 4; *Daily Calumet,* 22 Aug. 1966, p. 1; memo, Sanford Sherizen to Pat Fitzgerald, 24

Aug. 1966, CUL papers (76-116), box 69-1, UIC. The Liberty Baptist Church was a familiar spot for King; the church's pastor, A. P. Jackson, was a Morehouse graduate and a backer of the civil rights movement.

104. *SWNH*, 25 Aug. 1966, pp. 10, 19; *SE* (central ed.), 24 Aug. 1966, p. 1; *CT*, 22 Aug. 1966, pp. 1–2; *CDN*, 22 Aug. 1966, p. 7.

105. *SE* (central ed.), 24 Aug. 1966, p. 1. For information on the National States Rights Party, see *The Thunderbolt*, the party's official organ. For more on Connie Lynch, see Trevor Armbrister, "Portrait of an Extremist," *Saturday Evening Post*, 22 Aug. 1964, pp. 80–83.

106. *SWNH*, 25 Aug. 1966, p. 19; *CDD*, 22 Aug. 1966, p. 3; *CD*, 20–26 Aug. 1966, p. 1; *SE* (central ed.), 24 Aug. 1966, p. 1.

107. *CDN*, 22 Aug. 1966, p. 1; *SE* (central ed.), 24 Aug. 1966, pp. 1–2. The city of Chicago's proposals for ending the crisis, delivered by Ely Aaron at the first Summit session, reflected mainstream opinion. Aaron asked for an immediate moratorium on marches into the neighborhoods "to avoid turning these communities into battlegrounds for extremist and racist elements who are now flocking to these neighborhoods to foment more trouble, to prevent injury to innocent citizens and to stop aggravating further the wounds of racial division, thus making it even harder to achieve reconciliation and freedom of residence in these neighborhoods." "Proposals of Ely Aaron . . . ," 17 Aug. 1966, FBI 100-106670-NR, 26 Aug. 1966; *New World*, 19 Aug. 1966, p. 1. Many Southwest Siders found it shocking that the Nazis staged rallies in Marquette Park, which was bordered by a Lithuanian neighborhood. Disgusted by the Nazis, one old Lithuanian said, "My God . . . this is what I ran away from in the old country!" Some Southwest Siders feared that the Nazis meant "a new and more dangerous problem" for the community. *SWNH*, 25 Aug. 1966, p. 10, 18 Aug. 1966, p. 10; *NYT*, 21 Aug. 1966, p. 5.

108. Jackson, *Unholy Shadows*, pp. 258–259; *CDD*, 24 Aug. 1966, p. 3; *CST*, 10 Aug. 1966, p. 5; *CDN*, 16 Aug. 1966, p. 1; *CA*, 24 Aug. 1966, p. 10.

109. Jackson, *Unholy Shadows*, p. 158; *CST*, 26 Aug. 1966, pp. 3, 14; *CA*, 24 Aug. 1966, p. 10; "Remarks of Alderman Leon M. Despres in the Chicago City Council on August 25, 1966," Despres papers, box 63-3, CHS.

110. *New World*, 19 Aug. 1966, p. 4; *CA*, 22 Aug. 1966, p. 4; *NYT*, 25 Aug. 1966, p. 36; Andrew Greeley, "Chicago Summer," *New City*, Aug. 1966, p. 19.

111. *CT*, 24 Aug. 1966, p. 3; *SWNH*, 25 Aug. 1966, p. 1; *SE* (central ed.), 28 Aug. 1966, pp. 1–2; *Baltimore Sun*, 24 Aug. 1966, p. 9; FBI 100-106670-NR, 26 Aug. 1966, describes a quiet Belmont-Cragin march that took place on Thursday, August 25.

112. *NYT*, 23 Aug. 1966, p. 35, 25 Aug. 1966, p. 24. Bill Berry and Kale Williams also met with Governor Kerner to discuss the Chicago marches. *CST*, 23 Aug. 1966, pp. 1, 3.

113. *CA*, 24 Aug. 1966, p. 1; *LAT*, 25 Aug. 1966, p. 1; Moyer interview. "[W]e were building up a campaign over time," Moyer recalled. Bernard La-Fayette and Don Rose also believed that the campaign was intensifying. La-

Fayette interview and Rose interview. SCLC's Albert Sampson raised the issue of a national call at the Action Committee meeting on August 18. Pappalardo, "Chicago Logs," 18 Aug. 1966, AFSC papers, 1966 CRD Housing Program, box 4, AFSC Archives.

114. *CDN*, 27 Aug. 1966, p. 4; Marciniak interview; Berry conversation with Williams; Raby interview; McDermott interview; John McDermott conversation (telephone), 5 August 1992, Chicago; Williams interview with Orfield; Pitcher testimony in Tax, ed., *The People vs. The System*, pp. 83–84; Garrow, *Bearing the Cross*, pp. 516, 518–519. There is not enough documentation for a detailed account of the subcommittee proceedings. For an overview, see *CDN*, 27 Aug. 1966, pp. 1, 4; *CST*, 25 Aug. 1966, pp. 3, 22, 26 Aug. 1966, p. 3; Pappalardo, "Chicago Logs," 22, 23, and 24 Aug. 1966, AFSC papers, 1966 CRD Housing Program, box 4, AFSC Archives; Connolly, "The Chicago Open-Housing Conference," pp. 84–85.

115. McDermott conversation with Williams. On the movement's effort to incorporate timetables and goals into the agreement, see Anderson and Pickering, *Confronting the Color Line*, pp. 260–262, and Garrow, *Bearing the Cross*, pp. 518–519. The notion of specified goals did not delight every activist, some of whom thought it too similar to the discredited concept of quotas. Pappalardo, "Chicago Logs," 23 Aug. 1966, AFSC papers, 1966 CRD Housing Program, box 4, AFSC Archives. Kale Williams called the subcommittee negotiations "the most intensive mutual education and negotiation that I have ever experienced." Williams, "The Open Housing Campaign—Chicago 1966," AFSC papers, Chicago R.O. 1966, HOP folder, AFSC Archives.

116. Thomas Ayers interview with Bruce Thomas, 10 July 1986, Chicago; Alfredo S. Lanier, "Retiring Tom Ayers Put Corporate Power behind Racial Justice," *Chicago Reporter*, Nov. 1979, pp. 4–5; London, "Business and the Chicago Public School System," pp. 126–160; Anderson and Pickering, *Confronting the Color Line*, pp. 260–262. Marciniak later recalled that some of the subcommittee negotiations "were rough because I know I was obnoxious at that point." Marciniak interview.

117. *CDN*, 27 Aug. 1966, p. 4; Anderson and Pickering, *Confronting the Color Line*, pp. 260–262; Williams interview with Orfield; McDermott conversation with Williams; Ayers interview with Thomas. Ayers remembered that Herbert Nexon, a lawyer, helped draft the subcommittee document. Marciniak recalled that he too participated in the drafting and was assisted by one of his assistants, Hal Freeman. Marciniak interview.

118. Connolly, "The Chicago Open-Housing Conference," pp. 49–50; McKnight, "Summit Negotiations," pp. 136–137; Marciniak interview; Edward Marciniak interview with Corinne L. Benedetto, 23 June 1986, Chicago. Heineman had just returned from Washington, where he had attended a White House Cabinet meeting. The expansion of the definition of the problem to include the suburbs was, according to Marciniak, "the city's victory." The city of Chicago

could not, without a commitment by suburban communities, seek to open up its neighborhoods without triggering an explosion of white flight.

119. McKnight, "Summit Negotiations," p. 137.

120. Ibid., pp. 137–140.

121. Ibid., p. 141; Connolly, "The Chicago Open-Housing Conference," pp. 86–87; *CDN,* 27 Aug. 1966, p. 4; Garrow, *Bearing the Cross,* p. 521. McKnight suggests that both Jackson and Bevel opposed acceptance of the Ayers report.

122. MLK speech, 28 Aug. 1966, MLK speech file, MLK Library; Fairclough, *To Redeem the Soul,* pp. 131–133, 188–189. Andrew Young thought along similar lines. SCLC was working on many projects in Chicago, but the city was, Young remembered, "so much bigger than any city that we'd worked in in the South. We knew we couldn't do them all at the same time. And that we couldn't sustain an aggressive movement much longer. So we were trying to find a way to wind it up, maybe institutionalize it." Hampton and Fayer, eds., *Voices of Freedom,* pp. 314–315.

123. McKnight, "Summit Negotiations," pp. 141–142. Connolly, "The Chicago Open-Housing Conference," pp. 86–87, discusses the fears of Eugene Callahan and the CCRR.

124. McKnight, "Summit Negotiations," pp. 142–143; McGraw, "An Interview with Andrew J. Young," p. 326. Overall, many civil rights activists thought organized white religion in Chicago coveted social order more than social change. McDermott interview. Some CCRR members cautioned their associates against becoming a middle force. At the August 16 meeting, Robert Spike declared, "The Conference cannot afford to be neutral." CCRR Executive Board Meeting minutes, Aug. 1966, CCRR papers, box 4, CHS.

125. McKnight, "Summit Negotiations," pp. 142–143.

126. Ibid., pp. 143–145.

5. Chicago, Congress, the President, and the Nation

1. Letter to MLK, 5 Aug. 1966, Arlington Heights, Ill., SCLC papers, box 22-21, MLK Library, Atlanta; letter to MLK, 6 Aug. 1966, Prospect Heights, Ill., ibid.; letter to MLK, 6 Aug. 1966, ibid., box 22-14; letter to MLK, 8 Aug. 1966, Battle Creek, Michigan, MLK papers, box 96-17, MLK Library; letter to MLK, 7 Aug. 1966, SCLC papers, box 22-21, MLK Library. The Chicago protests had an international dimension as well. "Every slogan, every taunt, every epithet of hatred from Chicago is magnified many times in the press of the 'non-committed' nations around the world." Letter to Father James Groppi, 31 Aug. 1966, Pakistan, Father James Groppi papers, box 5-6, University of Wisconsin–Milwaukee.

2. James Harvey testimony, U.S. Congress, Senate, Committee on Judiciary, *Civil Rights, Hearings before the Subcommittee on Constitutional Rights of the Committee*

on the Judiciary, 89th Cong., 2nd sess., 4 Aug. 1966, p. 1520; *Atlanta Constitution*, 12 Aug. 1966, p. 12.

3. *Amsterdam News*, 11 Sept. 1965, p. 16; Mary Lou Finley to Doug Finley, 27 Nov. 1965, copy in author's possession; Collier interview.

4. *Congressional Quarterly Weekly Report*, 6 May 1966, p. 943. A full history of the 1966 Civil Rights Bill remains to be written. For discussions of the context in which the bill was proposed, debated, and defeated, see Matusow, *The Unraveling of America*; James Harvey, *Black Civil Rights during the Johnson Administration* (Jackson: University and College Press of Mississippi, 1973); Paul Conkin, *Big Daddy from the Pedernales: Lyndon Baines Johnson* (Boston: Twayne, 1986); Vaughn Davis Burnet, *The Presidency of Lyndon B. Johnson* (Lawrence: University Press of Kansas, 1983); Steven Lawson, "Civil Rights," in Robert A. Divine, ed., *Exploring the Johnson Years* (Austin: University of Texas Press, 1981). Hugh Davis Graham, *The Civil Rights Era: Origins and Development of National Policy* (New York: Oxford University Press, 1990), pp. 27–254, and Charles and Barbara Whalen, *The Longest Debate: A Legislative History of the 1964 Civil Rights Act* (Cabin John, Md.: Seven Locks Press, 1985) cast light on earlier civil rights measures.

5. Joseph A. Califano, Jr., *A Presidential Nation* (New York: W. W. Norton, 1975), p. 47; Graham, *The Civil Rights Era*, pp. 258–262; Ramsey Clark interview with Harri Baker, 30 Oct. 1968, Washington, D.C., LBJ Library, Austin, Tex. By threatening to request publicly an expanded executive order on housing discrimination, the President's Committee on Equal Opportunity in Housing played an important role in prompting the Johnson administration to pursue fair-housing legislation. See memo, David Lawrence to LBJ, 2 April 1965, Ex HU 2-2, WHCF, box 47, and memo [Lawrence] to LBJ, 3 Dec. 1964, ibid., LBJ Library. I do not share the critical view of Johnson and post-1965 civil rights issues that Matusow offers. Matusow writes that Johnson's 1966 civil rights proposals are best explained as "shirking responsibility while appearing to fulfill it." Matusow, *Unraveling of America*, p. 206. The first volume of Robert Dallek's biography offers insight into Johnson's views of blacks and civil rights. Dallek, *Lone Star Rising: Lyndon Johnson and His Times, 1908–1960* (New York: Oxford University Press, 1991), pp. 367–368, 517–520.

6. Denton Watson, *Lion in the Lobby: Clarence Mitchell, Jr.'s Struggle for the Passage of Civil Rights Laws* (New York: William Morrow, 1990), pp. 662–663; memo, Lee C. White to Louis Martin, 11 Dec. 1965, Lee White files, WHCF, box 3, LBJ Library; memo, Charles D. Roche to Lawrence O'Brien, 11 March 1966, Charles Roche files, WHCF, box 1, ibid.; memo, Nicholas deB. Katzenbach to Henry Wilson, 15 March 1966, SP 2-3/1966/HU2, WHCF, box 76, ibid.

7. *NYT*, 1 May 1966, section IV, p. 2; *CSM*, 28 July 1966, p. 3; Jack D. Watson (President of Dallas Real Estate Board) letter, 15 June 1966, Emanuel Celler papers, box 470, LC; Arnold Aronson memo, "Civil Rights Act of 1966," 7 June 1966, Leadership Conference on Civil Rights papers, box 1-4, SHSW, Madison, Wis.; *New Republic*, 2 July 1966, p. 9; *NYT*, 27 July 1966, pp. 1, 25; *WP*, 25 July 1966, p. 10. At times the Johnson White House and civil rights forces

worked at cross-purposes on the 1966 bill. See memo, Henry Wilson to Bill Moyers, 29 July 1966, Henry Wilson files, WHCF, box 11, LBJ Library. The National Association of Home Builders (NAHB) also joined the NAREB's opposition. Civil rights forces found this distressing, for the NAHB was considered more progressive than the NAREB. *Trends in Housing,* July 1966, pp. 1–2. The Johnson White House was receiving discouraging reports from members of Congress about opposition to the civil rights bill. Rep. Olin Teague of Texas reported that ninety percent of those polled in his district opposed the new civil rights measure. Olin E. Teague to Lyndon Johnson, 23 June 1966, PR16, WHCF, box 354, LBJ Library.

8. Anderson and Pickering, *Confronting the Color Line,* p. 201; Carson et al., eds., *The Eyes on the Prize Civil Rights Reader,* p. 302; CCCO newsletter, Summer 1966, p. 2, CCCO papers, box 2-11, MLK Library. Some Chicago protest leaders saw the connection between the Chicago open-housing protests and the Civil Rights Bill of 1966. Rose interview and Raby interview. Others were less certain. Kale Williams conversation, 22 July 1987, Chicago; Briggs interview.

9. Walter Fauntroy address, 9 Aug. 1966, SCLC papers, box 131-12, MLK Library; "The 1966 Civil Rights Act," Resolution of SCLC Board of Directors, CUL papers (76-116), box 169-7, UIC; "'Meet the Press' Television Interview," 21 Aug. 1966, reprinted in Washington, ed., *A Testament of Hope,* p. 388.

10. *CSM,* 4 Aug. 1966, p. 11; *NYT,* 4 Aug. 1966, p. 1; *CDD,* 18 Aug. 1966, p. 16.

11. *Call and Post,* 13 Aug. 1966, p. 1; *Louisville Defender,* 11 Aug. 1966, p. 3; *LCJ,* 8 Aug. 1966, p. 6; *Denver Post,* 8 Aug. 1966, p. 18; *LAT,* 10 Aug. 1966, pp. 1, 11; *WP,* 14 Aug. 1966, p. 2; Steven F. Lawson, *In Pursuit of Power: Southern Blacks and Electoral Politics, 1965–1982* (New York: Columbia University Press, 1985), p. 75.

12. *NYT,* 6 Aug. 1966, p. 1, 22 Aug. 1966, p. 1; *LAT,* 6 Aug. 1966, p. 1, 22 Aug. 1966, p. 1. King was not a frequent marcher during the Albany, Birmingham, St. Augustine, or Selma campaigns. He did, however, spend time in jail in Albany, Birmingham, and Selma.

13. Raines, *My Soul Is Rested,* p. 449. See Garrow, *Protest at Selma,* pp. 31–132, for a narrative of the Selma campaign.

14. Mathew Ahmann to the author, October 1987. Andrew Young did correspond with officials of the National Council of Churches at the height of the Chicago open-housing campaign. See David Hunter to Andrew Young, 16 Aug. 1966, and Andrew Young to David Hunter, 23 Aug. 1966, in SCLC papers, box 44-25, MLK Library. The national office of ESCRU offered assistance to its Chicago chapter during the open-housing marches. Albert Dreisbach to Sally Church, 11 Aug. 1966, ESCRU papers, box 62-15, MLK Library. The NCC papers are at the Presbyterian Historical Society, Philadelphia, and the NCCIJ papers are at Marquette University, Milwaukee, Wisconsin.

15. Because of the lack of records, it is impossible to determine which stories ABC, NBC, and CBS highlighted on their national news broadcasts,

which by the mid-1960s had become the major source of news for most Americans. Burns W. Roper, *A Ten Year View of Public Attitudes toward Television and Other Mass Media, 1959–1968* (New York: Television Information Office, 1969), pp. 2–4. A number of Chicago activists do recall their satisfaction with network news coverage of the open-housing protests. Moyer and Rose interviews.

16. *New York Times,* April-May 1963, Feb.-March 1965, July-Aug. 1966; Robert Dallek to the author, 4 Jan. 1988. The Albany campaign of 1962 made the front page of the *New York Times* fourteen times in fifty days; the St. Augustine campaign of 1964 did so five times in twenty-nine days. That the Johnson White House received over twenty-two thousand pieces of mail regarding the Selma crisis in one week in March 1965 is further evidence that the Alabama protests attracted national attention. By contrast, the White House never received more than two hundred letters on civil rights in any week during August 1966. See Mail Summaries, 1965–1966, WHCF, LBJ Library. To conclude that the Chicago protests were simply regarded as a local affair, however, would be a mistake. In leading newspapers across the country in August 1966 the Chicago campaign was frequently front-page news. From August 1 (the day after the explosive Chicago Lawn march) to August 27 (the day after the Summit accord), the *San Francisco Examiner,* the *Memphis Commercial Appeal,* and the *Minneapolis Tribune* each featured the Chicago drama four times. The *Milwaukee Journal* printed five front-page stories about Chicago. The *Denver Post* ran six. The *Atlanta Constitution* and the *Washington Post* headlined the Chicago marches seven times; the *Louisville Courier-Journal* did so eight times. The *Birmingham Post-Herald* offered ten front-page stories, and the *Philadelphia Evening Bulletin* presented eleven. A survey of coverage of the Birmingham, Selma, and Chicago campaigns provides a comparative perspective (on front-page stories between April 3 and May 13, 1963, for Birmingham; between February 2 and March 27, 1965, for Selma, and between August 1 and August 27, 1966, for Chicago):

	Birmingham (41 days)	Selma (54 days)	Chicago (27 days)
Charlotte Observer	10	22	2
New Orleans Times-Picayune	8	16	8
Baltimore Sun	13	27	9
Los Angeles Times	14	38	12

17. Kale Williams conversation, 22 July 1987; McDermott interview; Collier interview.

18. *CA,* 20 Aug. 1966, p. 3; Lucas interview with Britton.

19. *CA,* 9 July 1966, p. 3, 20 Aug. 1966, p. 3. The Summit agreement stunned some Chicago activists precisely because it prevented a climactic mo-

ment similar to that provided by the Selma to Montgomery march. These protest leaders continue to believe that had the Chicago Freedom Movement waited longer before reaching an agreement to halt the demonstrations, the Chicago protests would have had far more national resonance. Moyer interview and LaFayette interview.

20. MLK to LBJ, 12 Jan. 1966, MLK papers, box 13-8, MLK Library; MLK, *The Ware Lecture* (Boston: Department of Adult Education, Universalist Unitarian Association, 1966); Garrow, *Bearing the Cross*, pp. 225–230, 358–360; Fairclough, *To Redeem the Soul*, pp. 116, 208–210; *CDN*, 27 May 1966, p. 4; *NYT*, 14 Aug. 1966, section IV, p. 1; *WP*, 6 Aug. 1966, p. 1.

21. Lyndon Baines Johnson, *The Vantage Point: Perspectives on the Presidency, 1963–1969* (New York: Holt, Rinehart and Winston, 1971), pp. 161–162; memo, Harry McPherson to LBJ, 5 Aug. 1966, Harry McPherson files, WHCF, box 22-3, LBJ Library.

22. *Congressional Quarterly Weekly Report*, 26 Aug. 1966, p. 1873.

23. Garrow, *Protest at Selma*, pp. 83–88, 114–115; "Preliminary Program Analysis: Community Relations Service," 8 Feb. 1967, Administrative History of the Department of Justice, LBJ Library; Clifford Alexander to Michael Yarbourgh, 16 Aug. 1966, LG/Government, WHCF, box 13, LBJ Library. John McKnight, Chicago director of the U.S. Civil Rights Commission, kept abreast of the Chicago Freedom Movement, but he acted largely without instructions from Washington. McKnight interview. The FBI, of course, did monitor events in Chicago, but did not play a visible role. Garrow, *The FBI and Martin Luther King, Jr.*, pp. 174–178, and Garrow, *Bearing the Cross*, p. 468.

24. Garrow, *Bearing the Cross*, pp. 429–430, 443–446; Fairclough, *To Redeem the Soul*, pp. 271–274; MLK to Stanley Levison and others, FBI 100-111180-9-695a, 12 Sept. 1965. Though his daily remarks received far less attention, James Bevel often denounced the Vietnam War in quite flamboyant terms.

25. *Chicago Maroon*, 1 Feb. 1966, pp. 1–2; Garrow, *Bearing the Cross*, pp. 469–470, 472–473; *CA*, 28 Aug. 1966, p. 13; Clifford Alexander interview with Joe D. Frantz, 17 Feb. 1972, Washington, D.C., LBJ Library; Hampton and Fayer, eds., *Voices of Freedom*, p. 338. The holdings of the LBJ Library are useful in fleshing out the King-LBJ relationship. See also Andrew Young interview with Thomas A. Baker, 18 June 1970, Atlanta, LBJ Library. King's last White House visit was on April 28, 1966, for the delivery of Johnson's 1966 civil rights message. Diary cards, LBJ Library. After the House amended Title IV of the civil rights bill, SCLC issued a scathing attack on Johnson for a failure of leadership. "The 1966 Civil Rights Act," Resolution of SCLC Board of Directors, CUL papers (76-116), box 169-7, UIC.

26. When in 1962 Johnson was honored by the Chicago Catholic Interracial Council, Daley did not even bother to send an emissary. O'Connor, *Clout: Mayor Daley and His City*, pp. 166–167. Johnson sent Daley pictures six times and photo albums twice before the Chicago open-housing marches. Memo, Mary S. to LBJ, 3 Oct. 1966, Ex LG/Chicago, WHCF, LBJ Library.

27. Francis Keppel interview, 15 Feb. 1988, Cambridge, Mass. Joseph Califano recalls this episode in *Governing America: An Insider's Report from the White House and the Cabinet* (New York: Simon and Schuster, 1981), pp. 221–222; Richard Daley to LBJ and Nicholas deB. Katzenbach, 16 Aug. 1966, Diary cards, LBJ Library. When Daley complained about the suspension of federal funds, Johnson was about to meet with Pope Paul VI. Never before had an American President met with a Roman Catholic Pope in the United States. As he headed to a Waldorf-Astoria suite to see the Pope, Johnson, Califano remembers, "was still talking about Chicago." For a full account of the Chicago federal school aid controversy, see Orfield, *The Reconstruction of Southern Education*, pp. 151–207. See also memo, Harold Baron to Edwin C. Berry, "Title VI of the U.S. Civil Rights Act of 1964, and the Federal Aid Controversy in Chicago," 5 Nov. 1965, United States Community Relations Service files, FOIA. Nearly two years after the federal aid incident, the rift between the Johnson White House and Daley had not completely healed. See memo, Wilbur J. Cohen to Califano, Ex LG/Chicago, WHCF, box 7, LBJ Library. Califano told Johnson that Daley was "all for you" but did not like the Washington bureaucrats "who were trying to 'take over the city of Chicago and run it.'" Memo, Joseph Califano to LBJ, 18 Aug. 1967, Name file, WHCF, box 10, LBJ Library.

28. Conkin, *Big Daddy*, p. 192; Garrow, *Bearing the Cross*, pp. 338–339, 343, 476–478, 486, 489; Fairclough, *To Redeem the Soul*, p. 318; John Doar to Grady Smith, 23 Sept. 1966, LE/HU2, WHCF, box 71, LBJ Library. In 1966, Gallup polls indicated that Americans increasingly felt that Johnson was moving too fast on civil rights. See Hazel Erskine, "The Polls: Speed of Racial Integration," *Public Opinion Quarterly*, 32 (Fall 1968): 514–521.

29. Anderson and Pickering, *Confronting the Color Line*, p. 255; LBJ speech, 20 Aug. 1966 at Kingston, Rhode Island, *Congressional Quarterly Weekly Report*, 2 Sept. 1966, p. 1932.

30. "Thrust from the Ghetto," WMAQ (Chicago), 15 Aug. 1966, CUL papers (76-116), box 182, tapes 5, 6, 7, UIC; *NYT*, 13 Aug. 1966, p. 7.

31. *Life*, 19 Aug. 1966, pp. 30–31; *U.S. News & World Report*, 19 Sept. 1966, pp. 34–36; *Time*, 7 Oct. 1966, pp. 29–30. *Newsweek*, *Fortune*, and *Business Week* all carried articles on white backlash. The term "backlash" had been widely used in 1964, but was largely absent from the American scene in 1965.

32. Graham, *The Civil Rights Era*, pp. 278–392. For an overview of American racial attitudes over the last fifty years, see Howard Schuman, Charlotte Steeh, and Lawrence Bobo, *Racial Attitudes in America: Trends and Interpretations* (Cambridge: Harvard University Press, 1985). In the fall of 1966, some racial reactionaries did claim that the civil rights tide had been reversed. Pleased by the fact that "Northern white people did attack the demonstrators" in the summer of 1966, the editors of *The Citizen* saw this as "more than a white backlash." *The Citizen*, Nov. 1966, p. 5.

33. William Brink and Louis Harris, *Black and White: A Study of U.S. Racial Attitudes Today* (New York: Simon and Schuster, 1967), p. 220; Jonathan Rieder, "The Rise of the 'Silent Majority,'" in Steve Fraser and Gary Gerstle, eds., *The*

Rise and the Fall of the New Deal Order, 1930–1980 (Princeton: Princeton University Press, 1989), p. 254; Gary Orfield, "Race and the Liberal Agenda: The Loss of the Integrationist Dream, 1965–1974," in Margaret Weir, Ann Shola Orloff, and Theda Skocpol, eds., *The Politics of Social Policy in the United States* (Princeton: Princeton University Press, 1988), pp. 324–338; Thomas Byrne Edsall with Mary Edsall, *Chain Reaction: The Impact of Race, Rights, and Taxes on American Politics* (New York: W. W. Norton, 1991), pp. 32–73; C. Vann Woodward, "What Happened to the Civil Rights Movement?," *Harper's*, Jan. 1967, p. 33. The Harris organization conducted the most frequent surveys of public opinion on race relations. In a late 1966 Harris poll, only a tiny percentage of whites believed that Stokely Carmichael was helping the cause of blacks. Most of the public opinion surveys on the impact of urban rioting were conducted in the wake of the 1967 uprisings. As expected, whites denounced rioting. Hazel Erskine, "The Polls: Demonstrations and Race Riots," *Public Opinion Quarterly*, 31 (Winter 1967–68): 663, 668–675.

34. James L. Sundquist, *Politics and Policy: The Eisenhower, Kennedy, and Johnson Years* (Washington, D.C.: Brookings Institution, 1968), p. 281; Brink and Harris, *Black and White*, p. 220; Rieder, "The Rise of the 'Silent Majority,'" p. 256; Graham, *The Civil Rights Era*, p. 234. Bayard Rustin believed that television "contributed to the image of the black man as antiwhite, violence prone, and emburdened with hate." Rustin, *Strategies for Freedom: The Changing Patterns of Black Protest* (New York: Columbia University Press, 1976), p. 45. Crime rates soared in the 1960s. Gerald David Jaynes and Robin M. Williams, Jr., eds., *A Common Destiny: Blacks and American Society* (Washington, D.C.: National Academy Press, 1989), pp. 457–461. The extent of rising crime committed by blacks gathered greater attention after 1965. *U.S. News & World Report*, 12 Sept. 1966, p. 108.

35. Orfield, "Race and the Liberal Agenda," p. 314; McAdam, *Political Process and the Development of Black Insurgency*, pp. 214–216.

36. Rustin, "From Protest to Politics," *Commentary*, Feb. 1965, pp. 25–31; "Program of the Chicago Freedom Movement," July 1966, p. 100. The concept of compensatory policy also underpinned the frequent calls for a domestic Marshall plan or Freedom Budget. See MLK, *Why We Can't Wait*, pp. 134–141, and *NYT*, 1 July 1963, p. 1. Anxiety over the preferential treatment of blacks was a common reaction in the mid-1960s. See, for example, "In Search of the Next Move," *New City*, 1 Oct. 1965, pp. 2–4. In Harris surveys over ninety percent of whites objected to "the idea" of job preference for Negroes. Brink and Harris, *Black and White*, p. 278.

37. Graham, *The Civil Rights Era*, pp. 233–254, 278–290, 372–373, 461; J. Harvie Wilkinson III, *From Brown to Bakke: The Supreme Court and School Integration, 1954–1978* (New York: Oxford University Press, 1979), pp. 102–118.

38. Woodward, "What Happened to the Civil Rights Movement," pp. 33–34; Brink and Harris, *Black and White*, p. 220.

39. Paul Good, *The Trouble I've Seen: White Journalist/Black Movement* (Washington, D.C.: Howard University Press, 1975), pp. 247–272; Brink and Harris,

Black and White, pp. 220–221. By October 1966, eighty-five percent of whites believed that demonstrations hurt the cause of blacks (only forty-nine percent felt this way in June 1963). See Erskine, "Demonstrations and Race Riots," p. 659.

40. By 1966 the Vietnam War had replaced civil rights as the country's most pressing issue in the eyes of most Americans. George Gallup, *The Gallup Poll: Public Opinion, 1935–1971,* III (New York: Random House, 1972), pp. 1934, 2009.

41. *CA,* 31 July 1966, p. 13; Erskine, "The Polls: Negro Housing," *Public Opinion Quarterly,* 31 (Fall 1967): 484–486.

42. In the fall of 1966, more than half of all whites, according to a Harris poll, objected to a national open-housing law. See Erskine, "The Polls: Negro Housing," pp. 483–498. On the zealous protection of private property, see, for instance, the essays in Ellen Frankel Paul and Howard Dickman, eds., *Life, Property, and the Foundations of the American Constitution* (New York: State University of New York Press, 1989).

43. Jaynes and Williams, *A Common Destiny,* pp. 117, 122–124; Lawrence Bobo, Howard Schuman, and Charlotte Steeh, "Changing Racial Attitudes toward Residential Integration," in John M. Goering, ed., *Housing Desegregation and Federal Policy* (Chapel Hill: University of North Carolina Press, 1986), pp. 154, 157, 160, 162; letter to LBJ, 29 Aug. 1966, LE/HU2, WHCF, box 71, LBJ Library. Other Americans echoed the lawyer's sentiments. Letter to Len O'Connor, 10 Aug. 1966, O'Connor papers, box 2, CHS. Bobo and others reveal that traditionally white Americans have embraced the general principle of equal housing opportunities far more than specific measures to realize that principle in day-to-day life. The American tendency to separate private and public matters helps to explain the great uproar over school desegregation in the late 1960s and early 1970s. As the Boston busing crisis of 1974 and 1975 revealed, many whites were willing to turn to violence to protect the integrity of public schools that they considered their own. To many white Bostonians, busing blacks to Charlestown and South Boston public schools represented a direct intrusion into the private life of those communities. See Lukas, *Common Ground.*

44. Gunnar Myrdal, *An American Dilemma: The Negro Problem and Modern Democracy* (New York: Harper & Brothers, 1944), pp. 60–67. A 1963 Harris poll revealed that while most whites did not object to sitting next to a black on a bus, at a lunch counter, or in a theater, they did not want a black family next door. A 1965 Gallup poll found that fifty-two percent of northern whites were disturbed by the prospect of several black families from the South moving into their neighborhood. Erskine, "The Polls: Negro Housing," pp. 483–498. Social distance, sociologists have asserted, is a key factor in white attitudes toward blacks. Whites are much more likely to accept a single black family in the neighborhood than to accept many black families. Bobo, Schuman, and Steeh, "Changing Racial Attitudes," pp. 159–163.

45. For an extensive discussion of fair-housing laws up to 1967, see Eley and Casstevens, eds., *The Politics of Fair-Housing Legislation.* On California's fair-

housing battle, see Raymond Wolfinger and Fred Greenstein, "The Repeal of Fair Housing in California: An Analysis of Referendum Voting," *American Political Science Review*, 62 (Sept. 1968): 753–769. On white resistance to concrete fair-housing policies, see Bobo, Schuman, and Steeh, "Changing Racial Attitudes," pp. 156–159, 163.

46. Letter to MLK, 6 Aug. 1966, SCLC papers, box 22-14, MLK Library; letter to Rep. Gerald R. Ford, 8 Aug. 1966, Allegan, Mich., Ford congressional papers, series B, box 33-54, Ford Presidential Library, Ann Arbor, Mich.; letter to Senator Everett Dirksen, 10 Aug. 1966, Dolton, Ill., Dirksen papers, Correspondence, 1966, carton 18, Dirksen Center, Pekin, Ill. From his examination of the response to Selma, Garrow highlights the great importance of a strong correspondence between an audience's convictions and the goals of protesters. See Garrow, *Protest at Selma*, pp. 133–160.

47. Letter to Senator Everett Dirksen, New York, Dirksen papers, Correspondence, 1966, carton 29, Dirksen Center; letter to Governor Otto Kerner, 7 Aug. 1966, New York, Kerner papers, box 605-3, ISHL, Springfield, Ill.

48. *NYT*, 8 Aug. 1966, p. 1; Senator Paul Douglas to Mrs. Claude Arnold, 23 Oct. 1966, Carterville, Ill. Douglas papers, box 722-2, CHS. David Garrow underscores how a shift in imagery in the television age can have immense consequences for protests. Garrow, *Protest at Selma*, pp. 161–168.

49. Letter to MLK, 13 Nov. 1966, Chevy Chase, Md., MLK papers, box 97-2, MLK Library; *NCR*, 5 Oct. 1966, p. 3.

50. Letter to MLK, 11 Aug. 1966, Tremont, Ohio, SCLC papers, box 22-18, MLK Library; letter to MLK, 6 Aug. 1966, Ridgefield, Conn., ibid., box 22-15.

51. Unsigned letter to MLK, 23 Aug. 1966, Shelby, N.C., MLK papers, box 96-10, MLK Library. One member of Congress stated that "every time Martin Luther King appears on TV the opposition to the civil rights act tightens in the Senate." Robert Donovan, "Land of Confusion, Conflict, Crises," *LAT*, 4 Sept. 1966, section C, p. 2.

52. *Philadelphia Evening Bulletin*, 17 Aug. 1966, p. 39, 29 Aug. 1966, p. 31; *Atlanta Daily World*, 21 Aug. 1966, p. 5; *The American Federationist*, Nov. 1966, p. 2. See also letter to LBJ, 11 Aug. 1966, Los Angeles, Calif., SCLC papers, box 22-17, MLK Library; letter to MLK, 6 Aug. 1966, Philadelphia, Pa., ibid., box 22-18; *CD*, 27 Aug.–2 Sept. 1966, p. 8. That many blacks did not view fair housing as a top priority helps explain criticism of the Chicago protests. See the 1963 National Opinion Research Center (NORC) poll cited in Mildred Schwartz, *Trends in White Attitudes toward Negroes* (Chicago: NORC, 1967), p. 92.

53. Lawson, *In Pursuit of Power*, pp. 75–76; U.S. Congress, House, Congressman Jack Edwards (R-Ala.) remarks, 89th Congress, 2nd sess., 27 July 1966, *Congressional Record* 112:17226; Congressman Prentiss Walker (R-Miss.) remarks, 29 July 1966, ibid., 112:17595.

54. *NYT*, 27 July 1966, pp. 1, 25; Watson, *Lion in the Lobby*, pp. 660–680; Garrow, *Protest at Selma*, pp. 53, 172; U.S. Congress, House, Congressman Thomas G. Abernethy (D-Miss.) remarks, 1 Aug. 1966, *Congressional Record*

112:17740; Congressman Roman Pucinski (D-Ill.) remarks, 8 Aug. 1966, ibid., 112:18467; Congressman William Dickinson (R-Ala.) remarks, 8 Aug. 1966, ibid., 112:18471; Congressman Horace Kornegay (D-N.C.) remarks, 8 Aug. 1966, ibid., 112:18472; Congressman L. H. Fountain (D-N.C.) remarks, 8 Aug. 1966, ibid., 112:18472; Congressman John J. Williams (D-Miss.) remarks, 8 Aug. 1966, ibid., 112:18479. I have sought to distinguish references to Chicago open-housing from the many congressional references to the West Side rioting in Chicago of July 1966.

55. Congressman William Dickinson remarks, 8 Aug. 1966, *Congressional Record* 112:18471; Congressman Horace Kornegay remarks, 8 Aug. 1966, ibid., 112:18472; Congressman Roman Pucinski remarks, 8 Aug. 1966, ibid., 112:18467. It is difficult to determine how tightly Daley controlled the Democratic representatives from the Chicago region. A transcript of a phone conversation between John F. Kennedy and Richard Daley suggests that Daley felt that he controlled these congressmen completely. John F. Kennedy and Richard Daley telephone transcript, 28 Oct. 1963, John F. Kennedy Library, Boston.

56. *NYT,* 7 Aug. 1966, section IV, p. 2. To some extent, the voting patterns of 1965 and 1966 were similar. As in 1965, most southern Democrats rejected the 1966 bill, while most northern Democrats supported it, though with less enthusiasm than a year earlier. Most striking, however, was the crossover by many representatives (especially Republicans, border state Democrats, and California representatives) who had voted for the Voting Rights Act of 1965. Generally known as racial moderates, these members of Congress often pointed to Title IV, the fair-housing section, as the reason for their defections. See *Congressional Record* 112:17759, 18209, 18397, for explanations for opposition to the 1966 bill by the following supporters of the Voting Rights Act: Frank Chelf (D-Ky.), Delbert Latta (R-Ohio), and John Anderson (R-Ill.). It is also clear that many Republicans exploited the fair-housing issue for partisan advantage. Douglas Kiker, "The Washington Report," *Atlantic,* Nov. 1966 pp. 4–12. Comparisons between votes on the 1965 Voting Rights Act and the 1966 Civil Rights Bill are particularly revealing because no elections had altered the composition of Congress. See the votes of July 9, 1965, and August 9, 1966 (*1965 Congressional Quarterly Almanac,* pp. 976–977; *1966 Congressional Quarterly Almanac,* pp. 898–899):

	1965 Voting Rights Act vote of July 9, 1965 (For–Against)	1966 Civil Rights Bill vote of August 9, 1966 (For–Against)
Republicans	112–24	76–62
Democrats	221–61	183–95
Northern Dems.	181–1	169–17
Southern Dems.	33–60	14–78
Total	333–85	259–157

57. *WP,* 9 Sept. 1966, pp. 1, 4. Attorney General Katzenbach tried to persuade Dirksen to change his mind but to no avail. Memo, Nicholas deB. Katzenbach to LBJ, 9 Sept. 1966, Ex LE/HU2, WHCF, box 65, LBJ Library.

58. Dirksen, quoted in "Today Show" transcript, 15 Sept. 1966, Dirksen papers, Remarks and Releases, Dirksen Center; *WP,* 15 Sept. 1966, p. 4. Dirksen was not alone in his criticism of King. See J. B. Pinkas letter, *CD,* 22–28 Oct. 1966, p. 4.

59. Even the White House had given up. Harry McPherson made a reference in a September 14 memo to "[w]hen the civil rights bill goes down the drain." Memo, Harry McPherson to Nicholas deB. Katzenbach, 14 Sept. 1966, Harry McPherson files, WHCF, box 22-2, LBJ Library.

60. U.S. Congress, Senate, Senator Edward M. Kennedy remarks, 16 Sept. 1966, *Congressional Record* 112:23011; *NYT,* 7 Sept. 1966, pp. 1, 38, 8 Sept. 1966, pp. 1, 37, 9 Sept. 1966, pp. 1, 27.

61. *NYT,* 10 Sept. 1966, p. 19; Roger Wilkins speech, 19 Sept. 1966, Washington, D.C., Administrative History of the Department of Justice, LBJ Library; memo, Harry McPherson to Nicholas deB. Katzenbach, 20 Sept. 1966, Harry McPherson files, WHCF, box 22-2, LBJ Library. One of the Johnson administration's liaisons with the black community, Louis Martin, recognized that the drama of the summer of 1966 had set back civil rights progress. Memo, Louis Martin to Harry McPherson, 15 Sept. 1966, Ex HU4, WHCF, box 59, ibid. The Johnson White House also complained of the lack of grass-roots liberal support. In early 1967 McPherson wrote, "One of our problems last year, in my opinion, was the diminished fervor with which many churchmen undertook to support the bill—compared with their efforts in 1964 and 1965." Harry McPherson to Arthur E. Walmsley, 17 Feb. 1967, LE/HU2, WHCF, box 71, ibid. Senate voting patterns on cloture in 1965 versus 1966 reveal the diminished support as well (*1965 Congressional Quarterly Almanac,* p. 1040; *1966 Congressional Quarterly Almanac,* p. 978, for second cloture vote taken September 19, 1966):

	1965 Voting Rights Act cloture vote (For–Against)	1966 Civil Rights Bill cloture vote (For–Against)
Republicans	23–9	10–20
Democrats	47–21	42–21
Northern Dems.	42–4	38–4
Southern Dems.	5–17	4–17
Total	70–30	52–41

62. *WP,* 20 Sept. 1966, p. 1; *NYT,* 10 Sept. 1966, p. 19; Stanley Levison to MLK, 7 April 1965, MLK papers, box 14-40, MLK Library; letter to MLK, 22 Sept. 1966, Alabama, ibid., box 98-10.

6. Stalemate in Chicago

1. MLK speech, 28 Aug. 1966, MLK speech file, MLK Library, Atlanta.

2. *CSM,* 14 March 1967, p. 9.

3. *LAT,* 27 Aug. 1966, pp. 1, 5; *NYT,* 27 Aug. 1966, pp. 1, 17; *CA,* 27 Aug. 1966, p. 3; *West Side Torch,* 26 Aug.–9 Sept. 1966, p. 4; Hampton and Fayer, eds., *Voices of Freedom,* p. 316.

4. Brown, *Ideology and Community Action,* pp. 65–66; Garrow, *Bearing the Cross,* pp. 527–528.

5. LaFayette interview; "Black Power in Chicago: Prospects and Perils, An Interview with Dr. Alvin Pitcher," *Perspectives,* Winter 1967, p. 11, WSCP papers, box 4, CHS; Moyer interview; Rose interview; Pappalardo, "Chicago Logs," 29 Aug. 1966, AFSC papers, 1966 CRD Housing Program, box 4, AFSC Archives, Philadelphia; Hollins interview; Briggs interview. Meyer Weinberg and David Jehnsen were among the rank and file who objected to the Summit agreement. Weinberg interview and Jehnsen interview. Many Chicago Freedom Movement sympathizers applauded the agreement. Jenkins interview and Nancy Jefferson in Hampton and Fayer, eds., *Voices of Freedom,* pp. 316–317. On the sources of opposition, see Pitcher testimony in Tax, ed., *The People vs. The System,* p. 84.

6. Finley, "The Open Housing Marches," pp. 34–35; Moyer interview; Briggs interview; Berry conversation with Williams; Pitcher testimony in Tax, ed., *The People vs. The System,* p. 84.

7. Anderson and Pickering, *Confronting the Color Line,* p. 279; Pappalardo, "Chicago Logs," 29 Aug. 1966, AFSC papers, 1966 CRD Housing Program, box 4, AFSC Archives.

8. Anderson and Pickering, *Confronting the Color Line,* p. 276; Garrow, *Bearing the Cross,* p. 527; *CA,* 1 Sept. 1966, p. 6; *CT,* 1 Sept. 1966, p. 5; "Who Speaks for the Black Man in Chicago?," undated, ESS Other Material, HMBC, University of Massachusetts at Amherst; FBI 100-106670-2679, 7 Sept. 1966.

9. Brown, *Ideology and Community Action,* pp. 68–73; Garrow, *Bearing the Cross,* p. 528; *CA,* 31 Aug. 1966, p. 6; *West Side Torch,* 9–23 Sept. 1966, p. 1. Raby and some other Chicago activists believed that WSO's leaders changed their course because they were worried about the potentially disastrous fallout of a renegade Cicero venture. WSO, after all, received most of its funding from the Chicago City Missionary Society, whose board of directors included Thomas Ayers, author of the Summit agreement. Raby conversation with Williams. Don Benedict, director of the CCMS, did not believe that such institutional constraints would have had an effect on Chester Robinson. WSO had already undertaken militant initiatives that would not have pleased individuals on the CCMS board of trustees. Benedict conversation; Brown, *Ideology and Community Action,* p. 66.

10. *NYT,* 5 Sept. 1966, p. 8; *CDD,* 7 Sept. 1966, p. 6; *CA,* 5 Sept. 1966, p. 4; Lucas interview; Lucas interview in Dempsey Travis, *An Autobiography of Black Chicago,* pp. 248, 251–255; Meier and Rudwick, *CORE,* pp. 383–384; Robert

McClory, "Desolation Row," Chicago *Reader,* 21 March 1986, pp. 22–34; *CT,* 1 Sept. 1966, p. 5.

11. *CA,* 5 Sept. 1966, pp. 1, 4; *CST,* 5 Sept. 1966, pp. 2–3, 10; *CT,* 5 Sept. 1966, pp. 1–2; *Cicero Life,* 7 Sept. 1966, pp. 1, 8, 13; *Atlanta Constitution,* 5 Sept. 1966, p. 17; Hampton and Fayer, eds., *Voices of Freedom,* p. 318.

12. *CA,* 5 Sept. 1966, pp. 1, 4; *CT,* 5 Sept. 1966, pp. 1–2; *NYT,* 5 Sept. 1966, pp. 1, 8; *Birmingham Post-Herald,* 5 Sept. 1966, p. 1; *Atlanta Constitution,* 5 Sept. 1966, p. 17.

13. *LAT,* 5 Sept. 1966, p. 1; *Atlanta Constitution,* 5 Sept. 1966, p. 1; *Philadelphia Evening Bulletin,* 5 Sept. 1966, pp. 1, 3; *LCJ,* 5 Sept. 1966, pp. 1–2. For commentary on "irresponsible demonstrating," see *LCJ,* 2 Sept. 1966, p. 7, and letter to Major General Francis P. Kane, 6 Sept. 1966, Kerner papers, box 1137, ISHL, Springfield, Ill.

14. *Detroit News,* 5 Sept. 1966, p. 12; Lucas interview; Hampton and Fayer, eds., *Voices of Freedom,* p. 319; *CA,* 6 Sept. 1966, pp. 1, 5.

15. Gary Massoni, "Perspectives on Operation Breadbasket," pp. 202–213; Gordon Ewen, "The 'Green Power' of Operation Breadbasket," *Commerce,* April 1968, pp. 24–25, 49–54, 64.

16. FBI 100-106670-NR, 13 Sept. 1966, 19 Sept. 1966, 26 Sept. 1966; Urban Affairs Weekly Report, 30 Oct. 1966, 20 Nov. 1966, 11 December 1966, all in AFSC papers, 1966 CRD Housing Program, box 4, AFSC Archives; Urban Affairs Weekly Report, 8 Jan. 1967, 15 Jan. 1967, 2 April 1967, 7 May 1967, all AFSC papers, 1967 CRD Housing and Urban Affairs, box 4, AFSC Archives; East Garfield Park Organizing Staff to James Bevel and others, 2 Sept. 1966, Chiakulas papers, box 21, Reuther Library, Detroit.

17. Urban Affairs Weekly Report, 9 Oct. 1966 and 30 Oct. 1966 in AFSC papers, 1966 CRD Housing Program, box 4, AFSC Archives; Urban Affairs Weekly Report, 27 Jan. and 23 April 1967, AFSC papers, 1967 CRD Housing and Urban Affairs, box 4, AFSC Archives. See also "Community Union Center, Membership Meeting—Minutes," 19 Jan. 1967, "Atlas Tenants Meeting," 16 Dec. 1966, "Atlas Tenants Meeting," 19 Dec. 1966, "Negotiation Meeting," 19 Dec. 1966, boxes 31 and 32 in the Chiakulas papers, Reuther Library. On the Lawndale union's chronic shortage of funds and manpower, see memo, Samuel Smithe and Meredith Gilbert to SCLC, 20 Feb. 1967 and Meredith Gilbert to Cardinal Cody, 7 Aug. 1967, SCLC papers, box 46-17, MLK Library, Atlanta.

18. Gilbert Cornfield, "A Review of Tenant Organizations in Chicago," Cornfield files, Chicago; *LCJ,* 8 Feb. 1967, p. 9; *CA,* 2 Sept. 1966, p. 6, 3 Sept. 1966, p. 3; Richard Rothstein, "Evolution of the ERAP Organizers," *The New Left: A Collection of Essays* (Boston: Porter Sargent, 1969), pp. 282–284; Gilbert Feldman testimony in Tax, ed., *The People vs. The System,* p. 280.

19. Cornfield, "A Review of Tenant Organizations in Chicago," Cornfield files; *CSM,* 14 March 1967, p. 9; Kale Williams to Barbara Moffett, 9 Dec. 1966, AFSC papers, 1966 CRD Housing Program, box 4, AFSC Archives; Urban Affairs Weekly Report, 11 Dec. 1966, ibid., 1967 Housing and Urban Affairs; Jenkins

interview; Briggs interview; Sally Olds, "Tenant Unions Seek to Put an End to Slums," *Christian Century,* 6 Dec. 1967, p. 1580; Bowly, *The Poorhouse,* pp. 151–154. When Jesse Jackson returned in 1978 to South Hamlin Avenue, where Martin Luther King had rented an apartment, he said, "We used to think that if we took the profits out of the slums that the landlords would lose their power. We didn't understand that the slum landlords could simply walk away from the investment." *CST,* 9 April 1978, pp. 9, 46.

20. Anderson and Pickering, *Confronting the Color Line,* pp. 222, 287–288, 334–335.

21. FBI 100-106670-NR, 12 Sept. 1966; FBI 100-106670-NR, 19 Sept. 1966; MLK speech, 15 Sept. 1966, Lucy Montgomery papers, tape 5, side 2, part 2, SHSW, Madison, Wis.; FBI 100-106670-NR, 28 Nov. 1966; Pitcher, "The Chicago Freedom Movement," pp. 156–157.

22. *Newsweek,* 5 Sept. 1966, pp. 20–21; *Christian Century,* 7 Sept. 1966, p. 1071; Despres interview with Britton; Timuel D. Black to Edwin C. Berry, 7 Sept. 1966, Illinois, Chicago ESS, Other Material, 1967 folder, HMBC; Anderson and Pickering, *Confronting the Color Line,* pp. 284–287. Black's letter suggests that internal tensions had plagued the Chicago civil rights movement for many months. The timing of this open letter—only a few days after the Summit agreement—reflected the extent of disaffection over the decision to settle. See also *CDD,* 7 Sept. 1966, p. 3. National verdicts on the Summit pact were mixed. The National Committee Against Discrimination in Housing journal extolled it; *The New Republic* called it "a very short-term compromise" that was "obviously no major victory for King's Chicago Freedom Movement." *Trends in Housing,* Oct. 1966, p. 5; *New Republic,* 17 Sept. 1966, pp. 9–10.

23. *West Side Torch,* 26 Aug.–9 Sept. 1966, pp. 1, 4; Hampton and Fayer, eds., *Voices of Freedom,* p. 319.

24. *Tempo* (Chicago Teachers College), 19 Oct. 1966, p. 1.

25. Pitcher, "The Chicago Freedom Movement," p. 160; Collier interview; Jehnsen interview; Jenkins interview; Finley interview; Miller Stone interview; McDermott interview; "Black Power in Chicago," p. 13. SCLC payroll files show a sharp reduction in its Chicago staff within weeks after the Summit pact. The size of the staff dropped from a high of twenty-seven subsistence workers in mid-August to fourteen by early October. Many of those who left had been with the Chicago project for months, including Luis Andrades, Jimmy Collier, Suzi Hill, Sherrie Land, Charles Love, Bennie Luchion, and Maurice Woodard. SCLC papers, boxes 96-97, MLK Library.

26. Finley, "The Open Housing Marches," pp. 19–24. The total cumulative participation for all of the rallies, vigils, and marches during the summer of 1966 was roughly seventy thousand. But this figure does not mean that seventy thousand different blacks participated in a civil rights event. Whites were frequent participants, and many individuals took part in multiple events. Moreover, more than half of the cumulative total of seventy thousand was the product of the Soldier Field rally in July. Roughly thirty-five thousand people attended that event. The Bogue-McKinlay study suggests that black participa-

tion in the civil rights movement was broader than I have argued. Their study, conducted in the spring of 1967, involved interviews with over seven hundred black Chicagoans. They found that nearly twelve percent of their informants said that they had taken part in a civil rights demonstration in the summer of 1966. This is a surprisingly high percentage, which if extrapolated over the entire black population suggests that well over a hundred thousand different blacks demonstrated in the summer of 1966. Bogue and McKinlay, "Militancy for and against Civil Rights and Integration in Chicago," p. 51.

27. MLK statement, 2 Dec. 1966, CUL papers (76-116), box 169-9, UIC.

28. Fairclough, *To Redeem the Soul,* pp. 94–95; *CDD,* 26 May 1965, pp. 11, 25; Hosea Williams statement, 2 Dec. 1966, CUL papers (76-116), box 169-9, UIC; Dana Swan conversation, 11 June 1991, Atlanta.

29. *Newsweek,* 13 Feb. 1967, pp. 37–38; Minutes, SCLC papers, box 171-21, MLK Library; FBI 100-106670-NR, 10 Jan. 1967; Anderson and Pickering, *Confronting the Color Line,* pp. 298, 306; Urban Affairs Weekly Report, 15 Jan. 1967, AFSC papers, 1967 CRD Housing and Urban Affairs, box 4, AFSC Archives; "Reports of the Voter Registration and Political Education Campaign of the SCLC/CCCO," 2 March 1967, SCLC papers, box 171-9, MLK Library. Though the totals were incomplete, the SCLC-CCCO report claimed that slightly over three thousand registered voters were added to the rolls. The report also included comments by the organizers that suggest that they considered the voter drive a failure.

30. Hosea Williams to MLK, 8 March 1967, MLK papers, box 35-18, MLK Library; FBI 100-438794-1761, 30 Jan. 1967; Stoney Cooks to MLK, "S.C.L.C. and Its Future Structure and Program," ca. 1967, MLK papers, box 33-8, MLK Library. Furthermore, Bevel was making plans to join the peace movement and therefore was unable to provide much guidance to his staff. Bevel interview. Williams unfairly blamed Bevel for all his troubles. From the start of the voting drive there were problems. Williams's organizers were unhappy with their new setting. They grumbled about inadequate salaries. They griped about the cold weather. They criticized the lack of leadership. They bemoaned the lack of responsiveness on the part of black residents. "Staff meeting," 14 Dec. 1966, SCLC papers, box 171-20, MLK Library; *NYT,* 16 Jan. 1967, p. 22. Stoney Cooks argued that SCLC needed a new "hiring or firing policy" because in the past "S.C.L.C. . . . enlisted too many people who were no more than sympathetic people who get caught up in the heroic Romanticism" of the civil rights movement.

31. *NYT,* 16 Jan. 1967, p. 22; *Newsweek,* 13 Feb. 1967, pp. 37–38. Williams's public comments angered King. See FBI 100-106670-NR, 23 Jan. 1967.

32. Anderson and Pickering, *Confronting the Color Line,* p. 445; Williams interview with Orfield; "Black Power in Chicago," p. 10.

33. James Cook speech, 17 Jan. 1967, LCMOC papers, box 176, CHS; *SE* (central ed.), 31 Aug. 1966, p. 1; *CA,* 29 Aug. 1966, p. 4.

34. "Original Council Membership" files, LCMOC papers, box 176, CHS; Cook speech, 24 April 1967, ibid., box 172; Williams interview with Orfield;

Board Meeting minutes, 24 April 1967 and 24 Oct. 1967, LCMOC papers, box 147, CHS; *New World,* 15 Dec. 1967, p. 8.

35. Williams interview with Orfield; Edward Holmgren interview (telephone), 15 Jan. 1989, Evanston, Ill.; letter to Edward Holmgren, 17 Feb. 1967, LCMOC papers, box 148, CHS; "Twelve Months of Leadership Council Activity: A Staff Report," 27 Nov. 1967, ibid., box 147; newsletter, Jan. 1968, ibid., box 140; Edward Holmgren testimony in Tax, ed., *The People vs. The System,* pp. 256–259. Illinois governor Otto Kerner attended the suburban housing conferences. John McDermott believed that the principal reason for the Leadership Council's moderation was that most of the money came from big business, and "[t]here is no major businessman in Chicago who can ignore City Hall, and so there are none of them able to risk supporting an organization which openly challenges Daley." McDermott interview, 19 March 1968, WSCP papers, box 4, CHS.

36. "Summary of Summit Implementation Programs by Religious Bodies," CCRR papers, box 4, CHS; "Programs Announced by Religious Bodies to Implement the Summit Agreement," LCMOC papers, box 171, CHS; "A Parish Program for Community Life," 1966, NCCIJ papers, series 20, box 5, Marquette University Archives, Milwaukee; Archbishop John C. Cody letter, 19 Dec. 1966, ibid., series 11, box 1; *New World,* 10 Feb. 1967, p. 13, 7 April 1967, p. 13.

37. Community Relations Committee minutes, 29 Nov. 1967, LCMOC papers, box 175, CHS; *NCR,* 1 Feb. 1967, p. 3; Gage Park Civic News, LCMOC papers, box 148, CHS. For vehement support of Burke's position, see Cantwell papers, box 11, CHS. Civil rights activists generally never felt that the religious effort was strong enough. See, for instance, Mathew Ahmann to Andrew Young, 4 Jan. 1967, NCCIJ papers, series 34, box 14, Marquette University Archives.

38. *CD,* 11–17 Feb. 1967, p. 1.

39. Anderson and Pickering, *Confronting the Color Line,* pp. 443–444; Al Raby and others to LCMOC, "Implementation of the Summit Agreement by Public Agencies," LCMOC papers, box 153, CHS. For an extended discussion, see Mary Lou Finley, "After the Summit Agreement for Open Housing: The Government Agencies and Their Commitments: Follow-up," unpublished paper in author's possession, June 1967, pp. 54–59; William Moyer to CCCO Delegates' Retreat, "Report of the Follow-up Committee of Summit Agreement," 23 Oct. 1966, CCCO papers, box 2-4, MLK Library.

40. Finley, "After the Summit," pp. 34–35. For an example of how Swibel glossed over substantive reform, see Swibel statement, 1 Dec. 1966, LCMOC papers, box 151, CHS.

41. *CT,* 2 Dec. 1986, pp. 1, 12; Finley, "After the Summit," pp. 35–51; Raby and others to LCMOC, "Implementation," LCMOC papers, box 153, CHS; Board Meeting minutes, 27 Nov. 1967, ibid., box 147; memo, Dan Walker, 10 Nov. 1967, ibid., box 195.

42. Hirsch, *Making the Second Ghetto,* pp. 42, 44; Finley, "After the Summit," pp. 2–4.

43. "The President's Report," Chicago Real Estate Board, 10 May 1967, LCMOC papers, box 195, CHS; Arthur Mohl to Len O'Connor, 10 Jan. 1967, O'Connor papers, box 3, CHS; Joint Action Board minutes, 5 Jan. 1967, LCMOC papers, box 153, CHS. There were signs that realtors such as Ross Beatty recognized that progress had to be made on the open-housing question. See Ross Beatty to Joe Cook, 2 Feb. 1967, LCMOC papers, box 147, CHS, and "Report by Arthur F. Mohl to the Community Relations Committee of the Leadership Council," April 1967, ibid., box 175.

44. Finley, "After the Summit," pp. 15–19, 30–31; Raby and others to LCMOC, "Implementation," LCMOC papers, box 153, CHS; "Housing Opportunities Program, Chicago Metropolitan Area, October 1965–October 1966," AFSC papers, 1966 CRD Housing Program, box 4, AFSC Archives.

45. Marciniak profile, Cantwell papers, box 24-1, CHS; Marciniak, "'We Are Making Headway,'" *CSM*, 15 March 1967, p. 15; Marciniak to Leon Despres, 12 Sept. 1966, Cantwell papers, box 16-1, CHS; *Human Relations News of Chicago*, Dec. supplement 1965, p. 3; Marciniak interview. Marciniak's letter to Despres was a response to Despres's withering criticism. Despres to Marciniak, 22 Aug. 1966, Despres papers, box 13-3, CHS.

46. William Braden, "Chicagoans Liked the Job He Did," *CST*, 14 Dec. 1986, pp. 61–62; William Braden, "How Daley Handled Racial Issues," *CST*, 11 Dec. 1986, pp. 77–79; Frank Sullivan, *Legend: The Only Inside Story about Mayor Richard J. Daley* (Chicago: Bonus Books, 1989), pp. 123–127.

47. Anderson and Pickering, *Confronting the Color Line*, pp. 297, 299. Daley never repudiated the Summit agreement. But in terms of Daley's ultimate perspective on the agreement, his actions spoke louder than his words. The city resisted a 1969 federal court ruling that the CHA must reform its site selection and tenant assignment procedures, which had been proved discriminatory, and must build most of its new public housing units in white neighborhoods as an ameliorative measure for past practices. Paul Kleppner, *Chicago Divided: The Making of a Black Mayor* (DeKalb, Ill.: Northern Illinois University Press, 1984), pp. 45–47. It should also be noted that the Daley administration lacked decisive, controlling power over Chicago's residential patterns. But progressive change would have been accelerated had the city provided firm leadership on the questions of housing discrimination and segregation.

48. See "Al Memo," CUL papers (76-116), box 162-11, UIC; McDermott lecture; Archie Hargraves speech, 30 Nov. 1967, LCMOC papers, box 173, CHS; Brown, *Ideology and Community Action*, p. 68; Chester Robinson testimony in Tax, ed., *The People vs. The System*, p. 85; "Proposed Operation for Decongesting Negro Ghettoes," Dec. 1966, AFSC papers, Chicago R.O. 1966, AFSC Archives; La-Fayette interview. There is survey evidence indicating that lower-income blacks did not support open housing as fervently as those who were more well-to-do. Bogue and McKinlay, "Militancy for and against Civil Rights and Integration in Chicago," pp. 5, 18; Marx, *Protest and Prejudice*, p. 21.

49. *CT*, 25 March 1967, p. 4.

50. *New York World Journal Tribune,* 17 April 1967, Gen HU4, WHCF, box 61, LBJ Library, Austin, Tex.; *Washington Evening Star,* 22 Aug. 1966, p. 16; Andrew Kopkind, "Soul Power," *New York Review of Books,* 24 Aug. 1967, p. 3.

51. Garrow, *Bearing the Cross,* pp. 543–559; Fairclough, *To Redeem the Soul,* pp. 333–342; *CT,* 26 March 1967, p. 3.

52. David Halberstam, "The Second Coming of Martin Luther King," *Harper's,* Aug. 1967, pp. 47–48; *New World,* 2 June 1967, p. 13; MLK to Stanley Levison, Andrew Young, and Harry Watchel, FBI 100-111180-9-1376a, 25 July 1967; Garrow, *Bearing the Cross,* pp. 527–574.

53. *NYT,* 2 April 1967, p. 76; Garrow, *Bearing the Cross,* pp. 536–538, 569, 581; U.S. Congress, Senate, Committee on Governmental Operations, *Hearings before the Subcommittee on Executive Reorganizations of the Committee on Government Operations,* 89th Cong., 2nd session, 1966, 2991; Fairclough, *To Redeem the Soul,* p. 328.

54. *CSM,* 5 Jan. 1966, p. 12.

55. *Look,* 13 Aug. 1963, pp. 41–44; Hunter Thompson, "A Southern City with Northern Problems," *Reporter,* 19 Dec. 1963, pp. 26–29; George C. Wright, "Desegregation of Public Accommodations in Louisville," in Elizabeth Jacoway and David R. Colburn, eds., *Southern Businessmen and Desegregation* (Baton Rouge: Louisiana State University Press, 1982), pp. 191–210; *LCJ,* 24 Aug. 1966, pp. 1, 28, 27 Aug. 1966, p. B1. Ralph Abernathy visited Louisville on August 24, 1966, and warned that Louisville might get a Chicago-style campaign within the next six months. For an article reviewing the Louisville open-housing crisis, see *LCJ,* 30 April 1967, p. 18.

56. *LCJ,* 21 Feb. 1967, p. B1, 28 Feb. 1967, p. B1, 7 March 1967, p. B1, 11 March 1967, p. B1, 13 March 1967, pp. 1, 18, 30 April 1967, p. 18; *Louisville Defender,* 2 March 1967, p. 1.

57. *LCJ,* 12 April 1967, p. 1, 14 April 1967, p. 1, 15 April 1967, pp. 1, 14, 30 April 1967, p. 18.

58. *LCJ,* 4 May 1967, p. 16, 6 May 1967, pp. 1, 12, 7 May 1967, pp. 1, 28; *NYT,* 7 May 1967, p. 40; Garrow, *Bearing the Cross,* pp. 550, 560. King had also spent a day in Louisville in late March. *LCJ,* 31 March 1967, pp. 1, 20, B1. "We echo the demand made by our fellow ministers and churchmen in the Chicago area that the technicians 'get the hell out of Louisville,'" declared a prominent black clergyman.

59. *LCJ,* 11 May 1967, pp. 1, 32, 12 May 1967, p. 1, 1 June 1967, p. B1, 3 June 1967, p. B1, 10 June 1967, p. B1, 18 June 1967, p. B1; *Louisville Defender,* 18 May 1967, p. 1, 29 June 1967, p. 8; Garrow, *Bearing the Cross,* pp. 561–562.

60. Bevel interview. Father James Groppi papers at the University of Wisconsin–Milwaukee are of little help on the issue of Chicago-Milwaukee connections.

61. *Milwaukee Journal,* 4 Nov. 1985, pp. 1, 11, 30 Aug. 1966, p. 6.

62. *Time,* 15 Sept. 1967, p. 25; *Newsweek,* 2 Oct. 1967, p. 67; *New World,* 22 Sept. 1967, pp. 1, 3; Joint Action Board minutes, 9 Oct. 1967, LCMOC papers, box 153, CHS; *Milwaukee Journal,* 4 Nov. 1985, pp. 1, 11.

63. *NCR,* 15 Aug. 1965, p. 4; *LCJ,* 13 March 1967, pp. 1, 18.

64. *NYT,* 7 Feb. 1967, pp. 1, 26; Carson, *In Struggle,* pp. 215–229; Matusow, *The Unraveling of America,* pp. 345–375.

65. *Louisville Defender,* 11 Aug. 1966, p. 6; *Philadelphia Evening Bulletin,* 17 Aug. 1966, p. 39; Schwartz, *Trends in White Attitudes toward Negroes,* p. 92; Schuman, Steeh, and Bobo, *Racial Attitudes in America,* pp. 144–147, 157–162; Marx, *Protest and Prejudice,* p. 21. By 1966 many blacks were arguing that politics, not protest, was now the best way to attain desired goals. Clearly, however, many blacks nevertheless felt passionately about the need for open housing. See letter to Len O'Connor, 5 June 1967, O'Connor papers, box 3, CHS. Among American intellectuals there were also doubts about the primacy of open housing. Frances Fox Piven and Richard Cloward, "Desegregated Housing: Who Pays for the Reformers' Ideal?," *New Republic,* 17 Dec. 1966, pp. 17–22.

66. *CA,* 28 Aug. 1966, p. 12; Lewis, *King,* pp. 368, 374–375.

67. *Cleveland Press,* 16 May 1967, pp. 1, 4; Halberstam, "Second Coming," p. 41. Throughout 1967 SCLC was hounded by large debts accrued from the Chicago campaign. Stoney Cooks to Andrew Young and James Harrison, SCLC papers, box 149-29, MLK Library.

68. *CT,* 28 March 1967, p. 6; *CD,* 15–21 April 1967, p. 1.

69. For evidence of decline of the Chicago Freedom Movement, see Timuel Black to MLK, 3 April 1967, MLK papers, box 5-32, MLK Library.

70. *CA,* 26 May 1967, p. 5. On the results of Project: Good Neighbor, see "Twelve Months of Leadership Council Activity: A Staff Report," 27 Nov. 1967, LCMOC papers, box 147, CHS.

Epilogue

1. Halberstam, "Second Coming," p. 43; McDermott lecture. Adam Fairclough titled one of his chapters in *To Redeem the Soul of America,* a history of SCLC, "Defeat in Chicago." Godfrey Hodgson has dismissed the Chicago campaign as a "rout" in *America in Our Time: From World War II to Nixon, What Happened and Why* (New York: Random House, 1976), p. 269. Milton Viorst called the campaign "disastrous" in *Fire in the Streets: America in the 1960s* (New York: Simon and Schuster, 1979), p. 379. The Marxist scholar Manning Marable has also labeled it a "failure." Marable, *Black American Politics: From the Washington Marches to Jesse Jackson* (London: Verso, 1985), p. 208. Recently Denton Watson commented on "King's fiasco" in Chicago in *Lion in the Lobby,* p. 677.

2. William Julius Wilson, *The Truly Disadvantaged: The Inner City, the Underclass, and Public Policy* (Chicago: University of Chicago Press, 1987), pp. 20–62; Loic J. D. Wacquant and William Julius Wilson, "The Cost of Racial and Class Exclusion in the Inner City," *Annals of the American Academy of Political and Social Science,* 501 (Jan. 1989): 8–25; Wilson, "The Urban Underclass in Advanced Industrial Society," in Paul E. Peterson, ed., *The New Urban Reality* (Washington, D.C.: Brookings Institution, 1985), pp. 129–160.

3. Michael Selinker, "Reports of Bias Crime Decline in 1989," *Chicago Re-*

porter, March 1990, pp. 6–7; Kale Williams, "The Dual Housing Market in the Chicago Metropolitan Area," in U.S. Commission on Civil Rights, "Housing: Chicago Style—A Consultation Sponsored by the Illinois Advisory Committee to the United States Commission on Civil Rights" (Oct. 1982), pp. 38–42; Squires et al., *Chicago: Race, Class, and the Response to Urban Decline,* pp. 102–106; Gary Orfield, "How to Open the Housing Market," and David Hartmann, "Race Ethnic Composition of the Chicago SMSA: Post Census Estimates Using Annual Birth and Death Data," in Orfield, ed., "Fair Housing in Metropolitan Chicago: Perspectives after Two Decades—A Report to the Chicago Area Fair Housing Alliance" (1987), pp. 1–45, 375–444; Robert McClory, "Segregation City," Chicago *Reader,* 30 Aug. 1991, p. 16; *CT,* 5 June 1992, section 2, p. 9. Some scholars insist that the dual housing market is at the root of America's most fundamental racial and social problems. Orfield, "Ghettoization and Its Alternatives," in Peterson, ed., *The New Urban Reality,* pp. 161–193.

4. Alonzo Hamby, *Liberalism and Its Challengers* (New York: Oxford University Press, 1985), pp. 176–179.

5. Jackson, *Unholy Shadows,* p. 164; Kale Williams, "The Open Housing Campaign—Chicago 1966," AFSC papers, Chicago R.O. 1966, HOP folder, AFSC Archives, Philadelphia; *SWNH,* 25 Aug. 1966, p. 1; Finley, "The Open Housing Marches," pp. 28–29; Pappalardo, "Chicago Logs," 18 Aug. 1966, AFSC papers, 1966 CRD Housing Program, box 4, AFSC Archives. It is important to note that the open-housing violence also spurred progressive forces. The Southwest Community on Peaceful Equality (SCOPE), for instance, attracted larger crowds than ever before in the fall of 1966. John McManus, SCOPE's former chairman, has remarked that "while some blamed us for the marches, the net result was that a number of community leaders got off the fence and stood up for racial justice. As a result our position became respectable." John McManus to author, 20 Nov. 1987. Today far fewer Southwest and Northwest Siders adhere to the militant white position than did twenty-five years ago.

6. *SWNH,* 8 Sept. 1966, p. 1, 15 Sept. 1966, pp. 1, 10, 29 Sept. 1966, p. 1; *WP,* 11 Sept. 1966, p. 2. The *Southwest News-Herald* was particularly disturbed by the rise of the militant Operation Crescent, which committed itself to the preservation of white communities. *SWNH,* 8 Dec. 1967, p. 14. One survey of Chicago whites found that over fifty-five percent thought that race relations had worsened over the past year and that half were less enthusiastic about rapid integration than they had been twelve months earlier. Bogue and McKinlay, "Militancy for and against Civil Rights," pp. 49–50.

7. *NYT,* 21 Sept. 1966, pp. 1, 33; *Jefferson Park Press,* 2 Nov. 1966, p. 1; *CDN,* 9 Nov. 1966, pp. 1, 3–4; Hoellen conversation; Paul Douglas, *In the Fullness of Time: The Memoirs of Paul Douglas* (New York: Harcourt Brace Jovanovich, 1972), pp. 585–587. In 1968 George Wallace garnered more votes from two Southwest Side wards, the thirteenth and the twenty-third, than from anywhere else in the city. There was no more dramatic loser in the wake of the open-housing

protests than the Southwest Side alderman James Murray. Branded as a traitor because of his sponsorship of the 1963 Chicago Fair Housing Ordinance, Murray saw his political career derail in 1966. *SWNH*, 5 Jan. 1967, pp. 1, 10–11; James Murray interview.

8. Father Francis X. Lawlor letter, 14 March 1967, LCMOC papers, box 153, Better Communities Council folder, CHS; *SE* (central ed.), 25 Sept. 1966, pp. 1–2; Brian J. L. Berry, *The Open Housing Question: Race and Housing in Chicago, 1966–1976* (Cambridge, Mass.: Ballinger, 1979), pp. 177–192.

9. *CDN*, 5 April 1967, pp. 3, 8; *CT*, 24 March 1967, p. 3.

10. Kleppner, *Chicago Divided*, pp. 53–54, 83–84.

11. *SE* (central ed.), 21 Aug. 1966, p. 1, 28 Dec. 1966, p. 1; FBI 100-106670-NR, 28 June 1967; Anderson and Pickering, *Confronting the Color Line*, · p. 331.

12. *CT*, 20 Sept. 1967, p. 6; *New World*, 29 Sept. 1967, pp. 1–2.

13. Mary King, *Freedom Song: A Personal Story of the 1960s Civil Rights Movement* (New York: William Morrow, 1987), pp. 426–427. From the start of the Chicago Freedom Movement, some Chicago activists were anxious that the SNCC critique of SCLC might prove accurate. Mallette interview. Despite FBI and local Chicago police surveillance of the Chicago Freedom Movement, there is no evidence to suggest that public authorities engaged in clandestine efforts to destroy CCCO.

14. Memo, Bernard LaFayette to CCCO Delegates, 23 Oct. 1966, CCCO papers, box 1-27, MLK Library, Atlanta; Jehnsen interview; LaFayette interview; Jenkins interview; Urban Affairs Weekly Report, 10–17 Sept. 1967, AFSC papers, 1967 CRD Housing and Urban Affairs, box 4, AFSC Archives.

15. Fairclough, *To Redeem the Soul*, pp. 326–329, 345, 357–363; Garrow, *Bearing the Cross*, pp. 572–585; Raby interview.

16. FBI 100-106670-NR, 23 Dec. 1966; press release, "SCLC Starts Adult-Education Project for 1,000 Jobs in Chicago Ghettoes," SCLC papers, box 122-5, MLK Library; Hollins interview; *CST*, 9 May 1968, p. 3; Raby conversation with Williams.

17. Anderson and Pickering, *Confronting the Color Line*, pp. 192, 318, 329, 336; John McDermott to Lawrence A. O'Shield, 15 Aug. 1967, CIC papers, box 90, CHS; McDermott interview; Gamwell, "The West Side Christian Parish," pp. 29–31; Heaps conversation; *CD*, 23–29 Sept. 1967, p. 1.

18. *CT*, 20 Sept. 1967, p. 6; Ernece B. Kelly, "The Movement Goes Underground," *Focus/Midwest*, 5 (no. 38): 10–11, 40–42; Kale Williams, "Civil Rights—Some Questions and Answers," AFSC papers, 1967 CRD Housing and Urban Affairs, box 4, AFSC Archives.

19. Dunlap interview; *CDD*, 18 Dec. 1968, p. 2; Lucas interview; Travis, *An Autobiography of Black Chicago*, pp. 254–255.

20. Williams interview with Orfield; McClory, "Segregation City," p. 29.

21. Berry conversation with Williams; Williams, "The Dual Housing Mar-

ket," in *Housing: Chicago Style*, pp. 38–47; Berry, *The Open Housing Question*, pp. 19–118; McClory, "Segregation City," pp. 16, 18–19, 22–23, 26, 28; Squires et al., *Chicago: Race, Class, and the Response to Urban Decline*, pp. 106–126.

22. Reynolds, *Jesse Jackson*, pp. 80–421; Thomas R. Peake, *Keeping the Dream Alive: A History of the Southern Christian Leadership Conference from King to the Nineteen-Eighties* (New York: Peter Lang, 1987), pp. 287–289.

23. Alex Poinsett, "Crusade against the Craft Unions," *Ebony*, Dec. 1968, pp. 33–42; *NYT*, 10 Aug. 1969, p. 79, 23 Sept. 1969, p. 56; *CT*, 14 Aug. 1969, p. 3; *CDD*, 23 July 1969, p. 3, 26 Aug. 1969, p. 3. Robert Lucas and Archie Hargraves were among the other protest leaders of 1966 who participated in CUCA initiatives.

24. Poinsett, "Crusade against the Craft Unions," pp. 40–41; *CT*, 13 Aug. 1969, pp. 1, 10, 14 Aug. 1969, p. 3; *NYT*, 9 Sept. 1969, p. 44, 27 Sept. 1969, p. 18; *CDN*, 22 Sept. 1969, pp. 1, 11, 23 Sept. 1969, pp. 3–4; *CDD*, 9 Sept. 1969, pp. 3–4; Derber, *Labor in Illinois*, pp. 70–81.

25. Hampton and Fayer, eds., *Voices of Freedom*, pp. 511–535; Kenneth O'Reilly, *"Racial Matters": The FBI's Secret File on Black America, 1960–1972* (New York: Free Press, 1989), pp. 303–305, 310–315; Carson et al., eds., *The Eyes on the Prize Civil Rights Reader*, pp. 504–538; Travis, *An Autobiography of Black Politics*, pp. 407–458.

26. William Cousins interview, 20 Aug. 1987, Chicago; Ann Prosten, "Chicago's Negroes and the Daley Machine," April 1967, Illinois, Chicago ESS, Other Material, 1967, HMBC, University of Massachusetts at Amherst; Raby letter, ca. Spring 1967, CCCO papers, box 2-6, MLK Library. Though William Cousins received little help from Chicago Freedom Movement organizers, he did feel that by running for alderman as a black independent that he was part of the civil rights movement.

27. William J. Grimshaw, "The Daley Legacy: A Declining Politics of Party, Race, and Public Unions," in Samuel K. Gove and Louis H. Masotti, eds., *After Daley: Chicago Politics in Transition* (Urbana: University of Illinois Press, 1982), pp. 57–87; Kleppner, *Chicago Divided*, pp. 71–90. Grimshaw and Kleppner disagree over the timing of the black voter shift. Grimshaw suggests that it began after 1966. Kleppner singles out 1968. Both scholars agree that by the late 1960s race had replaced class as the critical factor in Chicago politics. Until then, lower-income Chicagoans had been the backbone of the Democratic machine.

28. Gary Rivlin, *Fire on the Prairie: Chicago's Harold Washington and the Politics of Race* (New York: Henry Holt, 1992), pp. 20, 55, 80–82, 126–182; Travis, *An Autobiography of Black Politics*, pp. 461–601; Kleppner, *Chicago Divided*, pp. 135–239; McDermott lecture; Raby interview; Baron interview.

29. Rivlin, *Fire on the Prairie*, pp. 207–383, 409–420.

30. Wacquant and Wilson, "The Cost of Racial and Class Exclusion," pp. 11–18; Wilson, "Public Policy Research and *The Truly Disadvantaged*," in Christopher Jencks and Paul E. Peterson, eds., *The Urban Underclass* (Washington, D.C.: Brookings Institution, 1991), pp. 462–476; Wilson, *The Truly Disadvan-*

taged, p. 143. For an argument stressing the primacy of cultural traits, see Nicholas Lemann, "The Origins of the Underclass," *Atlantic,* June 1986, pp. 31–61. White abandonment of the central city and increased housing opportunities for blacks has eased the shortage of shelter available to blacks. Arnold R. Hirsch, "The Causes of Residential Segregation: A Historical Perspective" in *Issues in Housing Discrimination: A Consultation/Hearing of the United States Commission on Civil Rights, Washington, D.C., November 12–13, 1985,* I, pp. 56–74.

31. Hamby, *Liberalism and Its Challengers,* pp. 176–179; Fairclough, *To Redeem the Soul,* pp. 279–307.

32. MLK to Stanley Levison, FBI 100-111180-9-1345a, 24 June 1967; MLK speech, 29–31 May 1967, MLK speech file, MLK Library. Later Bevel said publicly that the marches should not have been suspended. *CDN,* 2 March 1967, p. 14. For examples of King's defense of the Chicago campaign, see "'Drive to End Slums,'" *CSM,* 14 March 1967, p. 9. The focus of the Cleveland project became the successful election of Carl Stokes as the first black mayor of a major American city.

33. McDermott interview; Bernard LaFayette, Urban Affairs Special Report, 4 Dec. 1966, 1966 CRD Housing Program, AFSC Archives; MLK, "'Drive to End Slums,'" *CSM,* 14 March 1967, p. 9. The significance of their achievement is best illuminated through a comparative approach. In his study of the civil rights movement in Greensboro, North Carolina, William Chafe argues that once the public accommodations and voting rights issues were settled, "black protest leaders found it impossible to mobilize recruits for direct action protests." This was not the case in Chicago. Chafe, *Civilities and Civil Rights,* pp. 156–157.

34. Lawson, *In Pursuit of Power,* pp. 81–88.

35. J. Mills Thornton, "Comment" in Charles Eagles, ed., *The Civil Rights Movement in America* (Jackson: University of Mississippi Press, 1986), p. 151.

36. MLK, "Freedom's Crisis: The Last Steep Ascent," *Nation,* 14 March 1966, pp. 288–292.

A Note on
Primary Sources

Oral Histories

Oral histories were invaluable sources for this study, although they generally proved more valuable and more trustworthy for recapturing the larger spirit or mood of the times than for reconstructing specific episodes or moments. Most important were the nearly sixty interviews, ranging in length from forty-five minutes to several hours, that I conducted with former participants in the Chicago civil rights drama of the 1960s. Their recollections and analysis left me with a much more vivid sense of what those years were like. I interviewed the following individuals: Warren Bacon, John Baird, Harold Baron, James Bevel, Heather Tobis Booth, William Briggs, William Caples, Edgar Chandler, Alma Coggs, Jimmy Collier, Gilbert Cornfield, William Cousins, Leon Despres, Minnie Dunlap, Benjamin Duster, Mary Lou Finley, Franklin I. Gamwell, Gordon Groebe, Archie Hargraves, Leroy Herring, Norman Hill, William Hollins, Edward Holmgren, Harold Howe, A. P. Jackson, David Jehnsen, Herman Jenkins, Myrtle Kemp, Francis Keppel, Lou Kreinberg, Bernard LaFayette, Rollins Lambert, Michael Lawson, Charles Livermore, Robert Lucas, Edward McClellan, John McDermott, John McKnight, Daniel Mallette, Ed Marciniak, Russ Meeks, Patti Miller Stone, James Montgomery, Lela Mosley, William Moyer, Robert Mueller, James Murray, Richard Murray, John Porter, Al Raby, Faith Rich, Kris Ronnow, Don Rose, Florence Scala, Carl Shier, Margaret Ellen Traxler, Anthony Vader, Edward Vondrak, and Meyer Weinberg. I have also profited from conversations about the Chicago Freedom Movement with Paula Baron, Don Benedict, Eula Cobb, Harvey Cox, St. Clair Drake, Richard Hatcher, Melody Heaps, John Hoellen, Leo Holt, Mary Ceil McManus, Barbara Moffett, Maria Pappalardo, and Kale Williams.

This study has also benefited from oral histories collected by other individuals, who have graciously shared their findings with me. Most important were three interviews with Edwin C. Berry, John McDermott, and Al Raby conducted by Kale Williams in the early 1970s. Helpful, too, were Corrine Benedetto's interviews with Ed Marciniak and Eugene Callahan; Michael Benedetto's interview with James and Alice Tregay; Gary Orfield's interview with Kale Williams; Bruce Thomas's and Rob Nathan's interview with Charles Swibel; and Bruce Thomas's interviews with Thomas Ayers and Robert Marx. The oral history collections at the Moorland Spingarn Research Center at Howard University and at the Lyndon Baines Johnson Library in Austin, Texas, were also useful.

Manuscript Collections

In my search for documentation, I examined over fifty manuscript collections. The starting point for a study of the Chicago Freedom Movement are the collections housed at the Martin Luther King, Jr., Library at the King Center for Nonviolent Social Change in Atlanta. Most important are the papers of the Southern Christian Leadership Conference and of King himself. In addition, the King Library's modest collection of Coordinating Council of Community Organizations papers are also of interest. The Martin Luther King, Jr., papers at Boston University are particularly useful in tracing King's growing concern over northern racial problems in the early 1960s.

The Chicago Historical Society and the Special Collections Department of the University of Illinois at Chicago are the places to begin for information on Chicago civil rights activity in the 1960s. Much good information can be found in the Chicago Catholic Interracial Council papers, the Chicago CORE papers, the Chicago Conference on Religion and Race papers, the Cyrus Hall Adams papers, the Welfare Council of Metropolitan Chicago papers, the Monsignor Daniel Cantwell papers, the West Side Christian Parish papers, and the Leadership Council for Metropolitan Open Communities papers, all housed at the Chicago Historical Society. The voluminous Chicago Urban League papers and the Saul Alinsky papers are the essential collections at the University of Illinois at Chicago. Additional papers of various groups and individuals located at these two depositories are useful on specific topics as noted below.

Of other sources outside of Chicago, especially valuable are the records of the Chicago chapter of the American Friends Service Committee at the AFSC Archives in Philadelphia, particularly for understanding how and why housing discrimination became the primary focus of the Chicago Freedom Movement. On Chicago race relations more generally, the Chicago branch files in the NAACP papers at the Library of Congress are helpful. So too are the clipping files and collected documents on the Chicago civil rights movement at the Horace Mann Bond Center of the University of Massachusetts at Amherst. The papers of the Episcopal Society for Cultural and Racial Unity, CORE, and SNCC at the King Library contain information on their respective Chicago affiliates. The CORE and SNCC papers, along with those of Students for a Democratic Society (SDS), are now available on microfilm.

For additional insights into the origins of SCLC's involvement in Chicago, consult the James Bevel file at the University of Illinois at Chicago and the portion of the West Side Christian Parish records housed within the Chicago City Missionary Society papers at the Chicago Theological Seminary. Gilbert Cornfield's own files and the Charles Chiakulas papers at the Walter Reuther Library at Wayne State University in Detroit are revealing on the Chicago movement's relationship to labor and the formation of the tenant unions. The William Lee papers at the Chicago Historical Society shed light on the Chicago Federation of Labor's coolness toward the Chicago Freedom Movement. The United Packinghouse Workers papers at the State Historical Society of Wisconsin in Madison contain some information on the role of one of the most progressive labor unions. The Women Mobilized for Change papers at the University of Illinois at Chicago are helpful on the role of women in the Chicago civil rights movement.

On the white ethnic explosion over the open-housing marches, see constituent letters to public officials in the Paul Douglas papers at the Chicago Historical Society, the Otto Kerner papers at the Illinois State Historical Library in Springfield, Illinois, and the Everett Dirksen papers at the Dirksen Center in Pekin, Illinois. The files of the South Lynne Community Council, which worked for peaceful coexistence between blacks and whites, are deposited at the Chicago Historical Society.

Unfortunately no collection of Mayor Richard Daley's personal papers is available to scholars. At the University of Illinois at Chicago there exists a collection of Daley speeches up to 1966. For insight into the Daley administration's response to the Chicago Freedom Movement, consult the papers of Alderman Leon Despres at the Chicago Historical Society. Ed Marciniak shared with me his files from his tenure as executive director of the Chicago Commission on Human Relations.

On the open-housing crisis, see the Chicago Conference on Religion and Race papers and the Len O'Connor papers at the Chicago Historical Society. Old footage from the Chicago television station, WGN, brings to life many events that can otherwise only be read about. The WGN files are also housed at the Chicago Historical Society. The Cantwell papers and the Catholic Interracial Council papers, along with the National Catholic Conference for Interracial Justice papers at Marquette University, the Cardinal Albert Meyer papers at the archives of the Archdiocese of Chicago, and the Monsignor John Egan papers at the University of Notre Dame, detail the Catholic response to racial issues. The Church Federation of Greater Chicago papers and the Rabbi Robert Marx papers at the Chicago Historical Society contain valuable information about the Protestant and Jewish responses, respectively.

A good approach to the national repercussions of the Chicago Freedom Movement is through an examination of the public mail sent to King, Douglas, Dirksen, Kerner, and Gerald Ford, whose congressional papers are in the Ford Presidential Library in Ann Arbor, Michigan. Unfortunately, constituent letters about civil rights matters in 1966 dispatched to the White House cannot be found in the White House Central Files at the Johnson Library. These letters were directed, when they were received, to the Justice Department. Nevertheless, the LBJ Library is a treasure store of information about civil rights developments in 1966. The White House Central Files under the heading "Human Rights—Equality of the Races" are essential for re-creating the history of the Civil Rights Bill of 1966. A useful guide to the Johnson Library holdings on civil rights is Steven F. Lawson, "Civil Rights," in Robert A. Divine, ed., *Exploring the Johnson Years* (Austin: University of Texas Press, 1981). At the Library of Congress, the papers of Emanuel Celler and of the Leadership Conference for Civil Rights contain important material on civil rights questions in 1966.

Government Documents

The Federal Bureau of Investigation's extensive surveillance of Martin Luther King, Jr., and SCLC has left researchers with an important collection of documents concerning the Chicago Freedom Movement. FBI files consist of an almost day-by-day account of King's and SCLC's activities during their Chicago stay. The FBI-King file (code 100-106670) is fuller and more helpful than the FBI-SCLC file (code 100-438794). Especially important are FBI transcripts of telephone conversations between King and his adviser Stanley Levison. Because King did not keep a diary or write many personal letters, these transcripts offer rare glimpses into his private thoughts. University Publications of America recently released microfilm copies of FBI surveillance files. The Chicago Police Department's "Red Squad" maintained much closer surveillance of the Chicago Freedom Movement than did the FBI; the "Red Squad" files are housed at the Chicago Historical Society.

My reconstruction of the rise and fall of the Civil Rights Bill of 1966 depended on the transcripts of the lengthy House and Senate discussion of the legislation printed in the *Congressional Record* as well as the House and Senate subcommittee hearings on the bill. The special Senate subcommittee investigation into urban problems, chaired by Abraham Ribicoff and Robert F. Kennedy, is illuminating on questions of big city ills.

Students of Chicago's past are fortunate that regular statistical handbooks based on the United States Census are available. See Evelyn M. Kitagawa and Karl E. Taeuber, eds., *Local Community Fact Book: Chicago Metropolitan Area, 1960* (Chicago: Chicago Community Inventory, 1963) and the Chicago Fact Book Consortium, *Local Community Fact Book: Chicago Metropolitan Area—1970 and 1980 Censuses* (Chicago: Chicago Review Press, 1984). The regular publication of the Chicago Commission on Human Relations, *Human Relations News of Chicago,* and other CCHR reports can be found in the Municipal Reference Library located at Chicago City Hall, which also houses scores of departmental publications from the Daley administration.

Memoirs

All of Martin Luther King, Jr.'s published works are invaluable, especially *Where Do We Go from Here: Chaos or Community?* (New York: Harper & Row, 1967). James M. Washington, ed., *A Testament of Hope: The Essential Writings of Martin Luther King, Jr.* (New York: Harper & Row, 1986) is also useful. The recollections of Ralph David Abernathy can be found in *And the Walls Came Tumbling Down* (New York: Harper & Row, 1989). The writings on the Chicago Freedom Movement by Al Pitcher, Mary Lou Finley, and Kathleen Connelly in David J. Garrow, ed., *Chicago 1966: Open Housing Marches, Summit Negotiations, and Operation Breadbasket* (Brooklyn: Carlson, 1989) are essential. Henry Hampton and Steve Fayer, eds., *Voices of Freedom: An Oral History of the Civil Rights Movement from the 1950s through the 1980s* (New York: Bantam Books, 1990) contains a section of reminiscences about the Chicago Freedom Movement. Clayborne Carson et al., eds., *The Eyes on the Prize Civil Rights Reader: Documents, Speeches, and Firsthand Accounts from the Black Freedom Struggle, 1954–1990* (New York: Penguin Books, 1991), is another useful volume. The Reverend Clay Evans's story can be found in Dorothy June Rose, *From Plough Handle to Pulpit: The Life Story of Rev. Clay Evans, "a Man with a Mission"* (Ivyland, Penn.: Neibauer Press, 1981).

Lyndon Baines Johnson offers his perspective on American race relations in the mid-1960s in *The Vantage Point: Perspectives on the Presidency, 1963–1969* (New York: Holt, Rinehart and Winston, 1971). Among the memoirs by Johnson aides, Harry McPherson, *A Political Education* (Boston: Little, Brown, 1972), is informative on civil rights questions.

Newspapers

In the mid-1960s Chicago was fortunate to have four major daily papers: the *Chicago Tribune,* the *Chicago Sun-Times,* the *Chicago Daily News,* and *Chicago's American.* I have drawn heavily on all four papers, but I found the coverage of the open-housing crisis by *Chicago's American* to be more detailed than that of any of the other dailies. In part this level of coverage resulted from the exhaustive reporting of Lu Palmer, one of the few black reporters then working for Chicago's major newspapers.

The *Chicago Defender* (both the daily and weekly editions) is indispensable for black Chicago's perspective on civil rights developments. For a more militant black viewpoint, see the files of the *West Side Torch* at the University of Illinois at Chicago. The *New Crusader,* on the other hand, offered a black conservative critique of the Chicago Freedom Movement.

My understanding of the Southwest Side's reaction to the open-housing marches was based largely on the coverage of two local newspapers, the weekly *Southwest News-Herald* and the bi-weekly *Southtown Economist.* For insight into the response of other white regions, the following community newspapers are helpful: *The Daily Calumet* (Southeast Chicago), the *Suburbanite-Economist* (south suburban Chicago), *Oak Leaves* (Oak Park), *Cicero Life, Belmont Central Leader* (Belmont-Cragin), and the *Jefferson Park Press*.

The Catholic press also devoted extensive coverage to civil rights issues and is instructive on the Catholic Church's stance on race relations. The *New World*, the official weekly newspaper of the Chicago Archdiocese, is the place to begin, but the Kansas City–based *National Catholic Reporter* is also useful. The *Federation News* is revealing on the response of the Chicago Federation of Labor toward civil rights endeavors.

The Chicago Freedom Movement received extensive coverage from many newspapers across the country. Because they had their own reporters in Chicago, the *New York Times* and the *Los Angeles Times* are of considerable value, especially for July and August 1966. The *Washington Post* printed informative, entertaining, and often acerbic commentary on the Chicago scene by Nicholas Von Hoffman. The *Christian Science Monitor* regularly devoted feature articles to Chicago civil rights developments, as did the *National Observer*. For the open-housing crisis I surveyed the coverage of a host of other big city newspapers. Most relied on UPI and AP wire reports for their stories. The *Baltimore Sun* and the *Louisville Courier-Journal* often carried rather full stories.

The black press across America covered Chicago insurgency in varying degrees. Most helpful were the New York *Amsterdam News, Atlanta Daily World, Louisville Defender,* Cleveland *Call and Post,* and *Los Angeles Sentinel.*

Finally, every student of Chicago's recent history will want to consult the vast newspaper clipping files at the Municipal Reference Library.

Periodicals

Much valuable information about Chicago, race relations, and civil rights activity can of course be gleaned from articles in major periodicals of the period, including *Time, Newsweek, Look, New Republic, Harper's, Commentary,* and *Nation*. Often, however, even more informative articles were published in more specialized journals, frequently of religious inspiration, such as *Community, Christian Century, Commonweal, Focus/Midwest, Integrated Education, New City, Ramparts,* and *Renewal*.

Index

130, 131–132, 171, 175, 177, 194, 212; and community organizing, 58, 61, 66; and organized labor, 71; and religious community, 72–75, 127–128, 137–138; critics of, 76–81, 85, 89, 128, 183; competition for, 87; and black gangs, 93, 95; rallies of, 105–107, 137, 138; and riots, 113; Assembly of, 117; Action Committee of, 118, 140, 161, 162, 163, 166, 170, 179, 196, 197, 286n28, 292n71; Agenda Committee of, 118, 140, 145, 158, 159, 161, 163, 196, 280n76, 286n28, 292n71; and Daley administration, 131–132, 141–142, 151; leaders of, 136, 200, 203, 231; women in, 140–141, 167, 287n32; goals of, 185, 220, 233; fissures within, 196; assessment of, 221–235

Chicago Housing Authority (CHA), 10, 153, 154, 157, 207, 209, 211, 228, 313n47

Chicago Mortgage Bankers, 153

Chicago Real Estate Board (CREB), 114, 153, 293n79; 1917 resolution of, 101; march on, 139, 152; negotiations with, 149–150, 155–156, 157, 161, 169, 210; and property owners, 154, 293n82

Chicago's American, 144, 178

Chicago Sun-Times, 144

Chicago Teachers College, 9

Chicago Tribune, 25, 144, 281n83

Christian Century, 202

Chuchut, Mildred, 66

Church, black, 4, 67, 137, 204, 264n73, 270n118

Church Federation of Greater Chicago, 54, 155

CIC. *See* Catholic Interracial Council

Cicero, 9, 104, 166, 171, 196, 198, 233; riots in, 99, 139

Citizens Crusade Against Poverty, 71

Civil disobedience, 27, 78, 79, 80, 87, 108, 113, 147, 162, 178, 179, 198, 200, 215

Civil Rights Act of 1964, 28, 29, 65–66, 70, 127, 192, 228, 234

Civil Rights Act of 1968, 6, 234

Civil Rights Bill of 1966, 5, 179, 182, 183, 191–194, 222, 235, 306n56, 307nn59,61; fair-housing section of,

174, 175, 177, 192; and Chicago protests, 176, 180, 299n8

Civil Rights Commission, U.S., 153, 301n23

Civil rights movement, 3, 29, 243n21; in North, 2, 11; field staffers of, 4, 49, 54; local leaders of, 4, 7, 9, 50, 52, 68; Chicago, 9, 10, 27, 49, 52, 53, 54, 65, 71, 83, 86; in South, 13, 235, 319n33; and urban blacks, 38; and backlash, 184–185, 235, 302nn31,32; classical phase of, 185; change in goals of, 185–186; decline of, 195, 234–235

Clark, Jim, 51, 53, 86, 93

Clark, Ramsey, 180

Class, 3, 4, 127, 228, 318n27

Clements, Father George, 123

Clergy Alliance of Chicago, 18, 68, 138

Clergy, 5, 22, 25, 67, 72, 79–80, 147, 264n73, 286n21, 289n54; and fair housing, 123, 127–128, 147

Cleveland, Ohio, 34, 35, 39, 40, 218, 224, 233, 319n32

Coalition of United Community Action (CUCA), 229, 230

Cody, Archbishop John, 106, 128, 145–147, 169, 206, 208, 221, 222, 226, 277n57, 289nn47,48, 291n69; and MLK, 73, 75, 111, 151, 289n55; and moratorium on marches, 145, 183; leadership style of, 290n55

Coggs, Alma, 16, 244n27

Collier, A. L., 61

Collier, Jimmy, 44, 53, 59, 63, 104, 173, 203, 256n22

Collins, George, 84

Committee on Racial Equality. *See* Congress of Racial Equality

Communism: accusations of, 28, 128, 129

Community organizing, 15–17, 29, 49, 58, 59–64, 67, 87, 93, 104–105, 225, 226, 227

Condor, John, 63, 64, 262n63

Confronting the Color Line (Anderson and Pickering), 3

Congress, U.S., 173–175, 179, 180, 181, 191–194, 223, 225, 235, 299n7, 306n55

Congress of Racial Equality (CORE), 11, 13, 14, 24, 29, 52, 58, 77, 95, 248n61, 249n66; demonstrations of, 16, 19, 25,